Writing the Book of the World

Writing the Book of the World

Theodore Sider

CLARENDON PRESS · OXFORD

OXFORD

UNIVERSITY PRESS

Great Clarendon Street, Oxford OX2 6DP

Oxford University Press is a department of the University of Oxford.
It furthers the University's objective of excellence in research, scholarship,
and education by publishing worldwide in

Oxford New York

Auckland Cape Town Dar es Salaam Hong Kong Karachi
Kuala Lumpur Madrid Melbourne Mexico City Nairobi
New Delhi Shanghai Taipei Toronto

With offices in

Argentina Austria Brazil Chile Czech Republic France Greece
Guatemala Hungary Italy Japan Poland Portugal Singapore
South Korea Switzerland Thailand Turkey Ukraine Vietnam

Oxford is a registered trade mark of Oxford University Press
in the UK and in certain other countries

Published in the United States
by Oxford University Press Inc., New York

British Library Cataloguing in Publication Data

Data available

Library of Congress Cataloging in Publication Data

Data available

Typeset by Ted Sider
Printed in Great Britain
on acid-free paper by
MPG Books Group, Bodmin and King's Lynn

ISBN 978-0-19-969790-8

10 9 8 7 6 5 4 3 2

For Jill

Preface

The central theme of this book is: realism about structure. The world has a distinguished structure, a privileged description. For a representation to be fully successful, truth is not enough; the representation must also use the right concepts, so that its conceptual structure matches reality's structure. There is an objectively correct way to "write the book of the world".

Realism about *predicate* structure is fairly widely accepted. Many—especially those influenced by David Lewis—think that some predicates (like 'green') do a better job than others (like 'grue') at marking objective similarities, carving nature at the joints. But this realism should be extended, beyond predicates, to expressions of other grammatical categories, including logical expressions. Let "there schmexists an *F*" mean that the property of being an *F* is expressed by some predicate in some sentence of this book. 'Schmexists' does not carve at the joints; it is to the quantifier 'there exists' as 'grue' is to 'green'. Likewise, the question of joint-carving can be raised for predicate modifiers, sentential connectives, and expressions of other grammatical categories. (Structure is a generalization and extension of Lewisian naturalness.)

I connect structure to fundamentality. The joint-carving notions are the fundamental notions; a fact is fundamental when it is stated in joint-carving terms. A central task of metaphysics has always been to discern the ultimate or fundamental reality underlying the appearances. I think of this task as the investigation of reality's structure.

Questions about which expressions carve at the joints are questions about how much structure reality contains. Whether reality contains causal, or ontological, or modal structure is a matter of whether causal predicates, quantifiers (or names), and modal operators carve at the joints. Such questions lie at the center of metametaphysics. Those who say that questions of ontology are "merely verbal", for example, are best regarded as holding that reality lacks ontological structure. Such deflationary metametaphysical stances are thus themselves metaphysical stances. There is no ametaphysical Archimedean point from which to advance deflationary metametaphysics, since any such metametaphysics is committed to at least this much substantive metaphysics: reality *lacks* a certain sort of structure.

A subsidiary theme is: ideology matters. There is an unfortunate tendency, perhaps encouraged by bad terminology, to psychologize Quine's notion of ideology: to regard a theory's choice of primitive notions—its ideology—as a merely psychological or linguistic or conventional matter (in contrast to the entities it postulates—its ontology—which is part of its objective content). Philosophers reject their opponents' ideology in psychological/semantic terms: "I don't understand what you mean by that." And when introducing their own ideology, the hurdle to be passed is again psychological/semantic: primitive notions must be "intelligible". But there is a squarely metaphysical issue concerning any proposed piece of ideology (including logical and quasi-logical ideology such as modal operators or second-order quantifiers): does reality contain the requisite structure? If it does, then "intelligibility" in previously "understood" terms is not required for successful reference to and theorizing about that structure, no more in metaphysics than in physics.

A shift of focus from psychological/semantic to metaphysical constraints on ideology is at times liberating for metaphysics, but it also keeps our feet on the ground, by restraining the tendency to evade ontological commitments by adding to ideology. A fundamental theory's ideology is as much a part of its representational content as its ontology, for it represents the world as having structure corresponding to its primitive expressions. And the world according to an ideologically bloated theory has a vastly more complex structure than the world according to an ideologically leaner theory; such complexity is not to be posited lightly.

Fixating on ontology while ignoring ideology is both too narrow and incautious.[1] It is too narrow because the goal of metaphysics is to give a fundamental description of the world, and doing so requires more than merely saying what there is. It is incautious because it uncritically assumes that quantificational structure is fundamental. If quantificational structure is indeed fundamental (as I think it is), ontology deserves its place in fundamental metaphysics. But if quantificational structure is not fundamental, then ontological inquiry deserves little more attention within fundamental metaphysics than inquiry into the nature of catcher's mitts.

A final theme is a "pure" conception of metaphysics, free of certain encumbrances. One encumbrance is doing metaphysics primarily in modal terms. Against this, there is a growing consensus that modal notions are too coarse for metaphysics, and that notions in the vicinity of "fundamentality", "in virtue of", and the like, should not be understood in modal terms. A second encumbrance is linguistic entanglements. Here too, there is a growing consensus: that it is not so important for metaphysical and linguistic theory to neatly mesh. The fundamental metaphysics underlying a discourse might have a structure quite unlike that suggested by the discourse. Whereas a good linguistic theory must fit the suggested structure, good metaphysics must fit the underlying structure.[2]

This book presented an organizational challenge. Theory-then-applications would have been neatest, but the concept of structure is unfamiliar enough that readability demanded early applications. My compromise was to intermingle. Chapter 1 introduces the concept of structure and describes in a preliminary

---

[1] Dorr (2004, section 1) and Schaffer (2009a) make related complaints.

[2] Kit Fine's (1994a; 2001) recent work has been especially influential in forging both consensuses.

way how it will be applied. Chapter 2 begins to present the theory, arguing that structure is primitive and objective, and defending an epistemology of structure. Chapters 3–5 turn to applications, showing how structure illuminates explanation and laws, reference, epistemology, physical geometry, substantivity, and metametaphysics. Chapters 6–8 return to theory, arguing that expressions of any grammatical category (not just predicates) can be evaluated for structure, addressing various abstract questions about how structure behaves, and criticizing certain rival concepts (such as truthmaking and ground). Chapters 9–12 return to applications, showing how the metaphysics of four domains—ontology, logic, time, and modality—looks when conceptualized in terms of structure. Chapter 13 concludes with a sketch of a "worldview": a comprehensive metaphysics cast in terms of structure. As a guide to those who wish to read selectively:

The metaphysics of structure: chapters 1, 2, 6–8;

Applications: chapters 3–5, 9–12;

Metametaphysics: chapters 4–5, 9, and (to a lesser extent) 10–12;

Mix of first-order and meta- metaphysics: chapters 9–13.

I am grateful to many people for helpful discussions and feedback: Frank Arntzenius, Elizabeth Barnes, Paul Boghossian, Craig Callender, Ross Cameron, David Chalmers, David Copp, Troy Cross, Louis deRosset, Janelle Derstine, Cian Dorr, Ant Eagle, Andy Egan, Matti Eklund, Adam Elga, Matt Evans, Delia Graff Fara, Mike Fara, Hartry Field, Hilary Greaves, Liz Harman, Allan Hazlett, Eli Hirsch, Thomas Hofweber, Paul Horwich, Alex Jackson, Carrie Jenkins, Boris Kment, Tora Koyama, Uriah Kriegel, Heather Logue, Ofra Magidor, Ishani Maitra, Colin Marshall, Farid Masrour, Andy McGonigal, Ian McKay, Joseph Melia, Ulrich Meyer, Alan Musgrave, Daniel Nolan, Jill North, Tim O'Connor, Laurie Paul, Zach Perry, Agustín Rayo, Tony Roark, Dan Rothschild, Stephen Schiffer, Michael Schweiger, Adam Sennet, Alan Sidelle, David Sosa, Ernie Sosa, Joshua Spencer, Jason Stanley, Irem Kurtsal Steen, Steve Steward, Sharon Street, Zoltán Gendler Szabó, Amie Thomasson, Jason Turner, Ryan Wasserman, Brian Weatherson, Ralph Wedgwood, Bruno Whittle, Tim Williamson, Tobias Wilsch, Chris Wüthrich, Stephen Yablo, and Dean Zimmerman. I'm especially grateful to Karen Bennett, Gideon Rosen, Jonathan Schaffer, and Robbie Williams for extensive and challenging comments (which, I fear, I have not fully addressed). Thanks also to Oxford University Press and to Blackwell Publishing for permission to include bits of Sider (2003), Sider (2009), and Sider (2007a).

I'd also like to thank Kit Fine, John Hawthorne, and Phillip Bricker. I've learned much from talking to Kit about fundamentality in the past few years, and from thinking through his writings on the subject. John read large portions of the manuscript and gave me many insightful comments, as well as pushing me, years ago, to go beyond the predicate. Phil directed my dissertation, which was on Lewisian naturalness. He taught me the power of this idea, how to apply it to the philosophy of space and time, and much, much more. My intellectual debt to Phil is massive.

Finally, it should be obvious how much this book owes to David Lewis. His ideas on natural properties and relations have always seemed to me among his best: powerful, correct, revolutionary yet deeply intuitive.

Contents

1 Structure

Metaphysics, at bottom, is about the fundamental structure of reality. Not about what's necessarily true. Not about what properties are essential. Not about conceptual analysis. Not about what there is. Structure.

Inquiry into necessity, essence, concepts, or ontology might help to illuminate reality's structure. But the ultimate goal is insight into this structure itself—insight into what the world is like, at the most fundamental level.

1.1 Structure: a first look

Discerning "structure" means discerning patterns. It means figuring out the right categories for describing the world. It means "carving reality at its joints", to paraphrase Plato. It means inquiring into how the world fundamentally is, as opposed to how we ordinarily speak or think of it.

Consider three objects: two electrons in identical intrinsic states, and a cow. It is the most natural thing in the world to say that the electrons are perfectly similar to each other, and that neither is perfectly similar to the cow. The three objects should be divided into two groups, one containing the electrons, the other containing the cow. The electrons *go together*, and neither goes with the cow.

Or imagine a universe that is entirely full of fluid. A plane divides the universe into two halves, one in which the fluid is uniformly red, the other in which the fluid is uniformly blue (figure 1.1). Now imagine a group of people who encounter this universe, but accord no special status to the dividing blue-red plane. Instead of thinking of the universe as divided into the red and blue halves, they think of it as being divided in half by a different plane, marked by the dashed line in figure

Fig. 1.1. The red–blue world

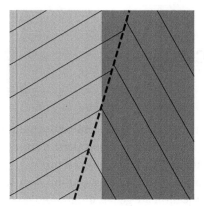

Fig. 1.2. Bizarre carving of the red–blue world

1.2. And they do not use predicates for red and blue. Instead, they have a pair of predicates that they apply uniformly within the two regions separated by their dividing plane. These predicates (whose extensions are indicated by diagonal hash lines in the diagram) cut across the predicates 'red' and 'blue'. The regions to the left of the dashed line they call "bred"; the regions to the right they call "rue".

It is almost irresistible to describe these people as *making a mistake*. But they're not making a mistake about where the red and blue regions are, since they make no claims about red or blue. And they make no mistakes when they apply their own concepts. The regions that they call "bred" are indeed bred, and the regions they call "rue" are indeed rue. The problem is that they've got the wrong concepts. They're carving the world up incorrectly. By failing to think in terms of the red/blue dividing plane, they are *missing something*. Although their beliefs are true, those beliefs do not match the world's structure.

1.2 Philosophical skepticism about structure

All is well until we encounter a philosopher, who, as usual, asks some uncomfortable questions. Why do the two electrons "go together", the philosopher wants to know? Yes, they share many features in common: each has 1.602×10^{-19} C charge, 9.109×10^{-31} kg mass, and so on. But there are plenty of features that the electrons do not share. They are in different locations, travel at different velocities, and are parts of different wholes. And why doesn't the cow go together with the electrons? If all three are located in North America, then all three share the feature *being located in North America*. And all three share the feature: *being an electron or a cow*.

The philosopher continues: what is wrong with carving the red–blue world along the diagonal plane? What is wrong with grouping the bred things together and the rue things together? All bred things really are bred; they all share the feature of *being on the left side of the diagonal plane*. One might protest that not all bred things are alike, since some are red and some are blue; but the philosopher will reply that carving the world along the vertical plane is no better on this score. Not all red things are alike, since some are bred and some are rue.

In fact, once we get the hang of the philosopher's way of thinking about "features", we can see that *any* two objects share infinitely many features, and also differ with respect to infinitely many features. For consider any objects x and y. Where F_x and F_y are any features of x and y, respectively, x and y share the feature: *being either F_x or F_y*. And they share the feature *being either F_x or F_y or 1 kg mass*. And they share the feature *being either F_x or F_y or 2 kg mass*. And so on. So they share infinitely many features. As for the infinitely many features with respect to which they differ, consider:

> *being F_x, and located at L*
>
> *being F_x-or-1-kg-mass, and located at L*
>
> *being F_x-or-2-kg-mass, and located at L*
>
> etc.

where L is some location occupied by x but not y. Object x has each of these features; object y lacks each.

The crux is obviously the philosopher's willingness to allow such "features" as *being either an electron or a cow*, and to treat them on a par with features like *being an electron* and *being a cow*. If we had nothing but the philosopher's features to go by, then indeed, we wouldn't be able to make any sense of a "correct" way to group our three objects, or of the electrons being more similar to each other than to the cow. If, on the other hand, we could make a distinction between *genuine* features—features that are fundamental, that carve nature at the joints, whose sharing makes for similarity—and the rest, then we could say what we want. Can we make this distinction?

Concepts and distinctions that resist definition in terms of the popular philosophical ideology of the day tend to be viewed with suspicion. Thus it was that throughout much of the twentieth century, philosophers tended not to speak of genuine features. Quine's extensionalism, for example, which dominated the 1950s and 1960s, allowed only a meager set of concepts to be used in drawing distinctions (roughly, those of first-order logic plus an array of scientific predicates). Noticing the presence of disjunction in the definitions of many philosopher's features, an extensionalist might begin an attempt to characterize genuineness by disqualifying features defined in this way. But what language do we use to evaluate whether a feature is "defined using disjunction"? Speakers of English must use 'or' to define the feature: *being an electron or cow*, but speakers of a language with a primitive predicate for this feature—'blurg', call it—can define the same extension without using 'or'. Indeed, if the language is strange enough, its speakers would need to use 'or' and other logical connectives to say things that in English may be said using simple predicates like 'cow' and 'electron', just as we must use logically complex predicates of English to say what they say using 'blurg'. The extensionalist attempt fails to characterize an appropriately language-independent notion of genuineness.[1]

In the 1970s, modality became kosher ideology, and there were renewed attempts to define concepts in the vicinity of structure. For instance, Roderick Chisholm (1976, p. 127) and Jaegwon Kim (1982, pp. 59-60) tried to give a modal definition of the notion of an *intrinsic property*—a property that an object has just by virtue of what it's like in itself, independently of how it is related to other objects. They proposed, roughly, that a property is intrinsic if and only if it is possibly instantiated by an object that is alone in the world. But this definition was shown to be unacceptable. The property of *being alone in the world*, and the property of *either (being alone in the world and being green) or (not being alone in the world and being blue)*, satisfy the definition but are extrinsic (Lewis, 1983a).

(The 70s' fixation on modality was doubly unfortunate. Not only are modal tools too crude;[2] they're also distant from the subject matter of most of metaphysics. It is needlessly indirect to approach the question of what the world is like by asking what it must be like and what it might have been like.[3])

Since the 1980s many philosophers have become comfortable with a richer ideology, one that includes notions in the vicinity of "genuine feature", "intrinsic property", and the like. The zeitgeist has been that these notions are legitimate even if they cannot be defined in other terms. Two Davids have led the way.[4] David Armstrong (1978a; b) used the traditional doctrine of universals to draw the distinction between genuine and nongenuine features. Some predicates, like 'is an electron', perhaps, stand for universals, Armstrong said; but others do not: there simply is no universal of "being either a cow or an electron". Through sheer force of will as much anything, he put realism about genuine features on the map. But as our second David, David Lewis (1983b) showed, Armstrong embedded this insight in a quite independent dialectic: the traditional debate over the existence of universals and their role in a general analysis of predication. According to Lewis, we can incorporate Armstrong's insight by admitting a notion of "natural properties and relations" (those properties and relations that carve nature at the joints) without thinking of these as universals in the traditional sense, and without taking on the (misguided, according to Lewis) project of giving a general analysis of predication. The notion of a genuine feature was thus freed from unwanted entanglements.

---

[1]The paradigm of first-order logic had perhaps the following additional influence. The standard model theory of first-order logic treats the semantic values of (*n*-place) predicates as subsets of the (*n*-place Cartesian product of the) domain. Viewed from a purely set-theoretic perspective, the semantic values of the predicates 'is an electron' and 'is an electron or cow' are on a par: each is a subset of the domain.

[2]On which see, for instance, Fine (1994a); Restall (1996).

[3]I also suspect that the right account of how the world might have been and must be defers to how the world *is* (chapter 12).

[4]Earlier relevant work includes Quinton (1958); Quine (1969); Putnam (1975c); Bealer (1982, chapter 8).

Of course, *everyone* can agree that there is *some* difference between *being an electron* and *being either an electron or a cow*. If nothing else, ordinary English has a single word for the former attribute. What distinguishes Armstrong and Lewis is that they regard the distinction as objective. Structure, too, is to be understood as objective. There are hard questions about what objectivity amounts to (some of which will be discussed in chapter 4), but the intuitive idea is clear: whether a property, word, or concept[5] carves at the joints has nothing to do with the place of the concept in human languages, conceptual schemes, biology, or anything like that. Thus "fundamental" (which I use more or less interchangeably with "joint-carving" and "part of reality's structure") signifies a metaphysical, rather than conceptual, sort of fundamentality. Humans may need to acquire other concepts first before they grasp joint-carving ones; and conversely, those concepts we acquire first, or most easily, may fail to carve at the joints.

1.3 Structure in metaphysics: a preview

The goal of this book is to push forward the front of realism about structure. I want to expand our conception of structure's importance, generalize the concept of structure, investigate its nature, use it as the foundation of "metametaphysics", and reconceptualize metaphysics in terms of it.

The connection to similarity is only the beginning of the importance of the notion of structure. As we will see, structure pops up throughout philosophy, in our thinking about reference, epistemology, spacetime, objectivity, and other matters.

Structure is particularly central to metaphysics. The heart of metaphysics is the question: what is the world ultimately, or fundamentally, like? And fundamentality is a matter of structure: the fundamental facts are those cast in terms that carve at the joints.

The truly central question of metaphysics is that of what is *most* fundamental. So in my terms, we must ask which notions carve *perfectly* at the joints. By using 'red' and 'blue', we carve more closely to reality's joints than do the speakers of the 'bred'/'rue' language. But we do not thereby carve perfectly at the joints; colors are presumably not perfectly fundamental. To carve perfectly, one must use the most fundamental concepts, expressing the facets of reality that underly the colors.

---

[5]Subtleties will come later, but to forestall misunderstanding: 1. Structure is a worldly, not conceptual or linguistic, matter (my informal talk of "notion/word/concept *X* carves at the joints" notwithstanding). 2. 'Structure' is not a noun; structure is not an entity or stuff (this very sentence, and phrases like "how much structure the world contains", notwithstanding). 3. 'Structure' and its variants are not predicates—not of properties, nor of any other sorts of entities ("charge carves at the joints" notwithstanding). 4. My most basic notion of structure is absolute, although I allow a derivative notion that comes in degrees. 5. Structure includes distinguished monadic features (such as charge), not just relational ones (despite what may be suggested by the term 'structure').

Which concepts are the perfectly fundamental ones? In my view, certain concepts of physics, logic, and mathematics.[6] But this thesis about structure is not built into the idea of structure, and defending it is not one of the main goals of this book. The great metaphysical disputes concern which theses of this sort are true; my goal is to explain what is at stake in such disputes, not to settle them. Is mentality part of reality's fundamental structure? (Modal theses in the philosophy of mind, such as psychophysical supervenience, are crude ways of getting at what clearly was the issue all along: whether reality is fundamentally mental.) Do mathematical entities exist, in the fundamental sense of 'there exist', and if so, what are the fundamental features of those entities? Do causal or nomic notions have any place in a fundamental description of the world? These are questions about structure.

*Meta*metaphysics—inquiry into the status of metaphysics—will be central in this book. Is the pope (or Robinson Crusoe, or a twelve-year-old boy) a bachelor? Intuitively, the question is merely verbal or conceptual. To answer it, all we need to do is investigate our concept of a bachelor; intuitively, all that is at stake is how we use the word 'bachelor'. In contrast, the question of whether there is any lithium in a certain region on Mars has nothing to do with word use or concepts; it is *substantive*. This rough and ready notion of substantivity needs to be clarified; after all, the statement that Robinson Crusoe is a bachelor is no more *about* our concept of a bachelor than the statement that there is lithium in the region is about our concept of lithium. Nevertheless, there is a strong intuitive contrast between the two questions.

The opponents of metaphysics (and even some renegade practitioners) tend to regard many metaphysical questions as being—to some extent, anyway—like the question of whether the pope is a bachelor. True believers, on the other hand, tend to think of their favorite metaphysical questions as being substantive, like the question about lithium. In my view, whether a question is substantive—in one important sense of 'substantive'—depends largely on the extent to which its terms carve at the joints; to the extent, that is, that the question concerns the world's fundamental structure. The central metametaphysical questions are about *how much structure the world contains*.

Consider two properties:

> Being an unmarried male
>
> Being an unmarried adult male eligible for marriage.

It may well be that exactly one of these properties is (determinately) what we mean by 'bachelor'. So it may be that the question of the pope's bachelorhood has an answer. But neither of these two properties carves nature at the joints better than the other. The unmarried males don't go together any more than do the unmarried males eligible for marriage. A linguistic community that used the word

---

[6]Plus the concept of structure itself! See section 7.13.

'bachelor' for the first property would not be getting at the world's structure any better than a community that used the word for the second property. And since the pope is an unmarried male who is ineligible for marriage, speakers of the first community speak truly when they say 'The pope is a bachelor', whereas speakers of the second community speak truly when they say 'The pope is not a bachelor'. So, intuitively, the only question facing us is: which sort of linguistic community do *we* inhabit? Which of two equally good ways to talk is *our* way to talk?

The question of whether there is lithium in the region near Mars has a very different status. Suppose that the region does indeed contain lithium. We can imagine a linguistic community that uses the word 'lithium' exactly as we do, but with one exception: their word does not apply to the lithium (in our sense of the word) in the region. So 'There is lithium in the region' counts as true in our language, and false in theirs. But here the parallel with the previous paragraph ends. The lithium in the region is just like the lithium elsewhere, so the imagined linguistic community fails badly to carve nature at the joints. They fail to group together things that, objectively, go together. The question of whether there is lithium in the region is *not* just a question of which of two equally good ways to talk is *our* way to talk.

Few would deny that the question of the pope's bachelorhood is insubstantial in a way that the question about lithium is not. But in metaphysics, things are far less clear. Consider questions of ontology, for example. There has been much discussion recently of whether tables and chairs and other composite material objects exist. It is generally common ground in these discussions that there exist subatomic particles that are "arranged tablewise" and "arranged chairwise"; the controversy is over whether there exist in addition tables and chairs that are composed of the particles. Is this really a substantive debate about the world? Most of the ontologists engaged in the debate think so—or really, presuppose so. But Eli Hirsch, Hilary Putnam, and other "ontological deflationists" have argued that the debate is in some sense merely verbal or conceptual. The "metaontological" question here ultimately boils down, I think, to a question of structure: whether quantificational notions like 'there exists' carve at the joints. What the ontological deflationists have in effect been saying is that reality would need fundamental quantificational structure in order for the question of whether there exist tables and chairs to be worth asking, and that this structure is, in fact, missing. I oppose ontological deflationists in chapter 9, but they deserve credit for raising an important and difficult question—a question that is in a way more foundational than the first-order question of what there is.

There are similar foundational questions throughout metaphysics. Do modal concepts carve at the joints (chapter 12)? (Here my answer is *no*; modality is not the core of metaphysics that some take it to be.) Do tensed concepts (chaper 11)? (Again, *no*; but seeing the issue as concerning reality's temporal joints helps to illuminate what are otherwise extremely perplexing questions.) Do logical concepts (chapter 10)? (Here I say *yes*. Certain debates over the "correct" logic are genuine, and are not linguistic or conceptual; they are as substantive as ontological debates.)

More generally, metaphysicians regularly speak of what is "really" or "genuinely" the case. (Often they feel guilty about it, but don't know how to stop.) As Kit Fine (2001; 2009) has emphasized, such talk is central to metaphysics, but in dire need of explication. When a nominalist says that there do not *really* exist abstract entities like properties, while granting that frogs share more properties in common with crocodiles than they share with humans, the '*really*' is essential; otherwise she contradicts herself. Those who think that "time is like space" say that there is no "genuine" or "objective" distinction between past, present, and future, but they do not deny that there once were dinosaurs. Again, if 'genuine' and 'objective' are dropped then the position becomes incoherent. These claims are not merely about what is *true*; they are about what is true at the *fundamental* level.

If the concept of structure is to play this role in metametaphysics, it must be generalized beyond Armstrong's notion of a universal and Lewis's notion of natural properties and relations. For many metaphysical questions are not about universals, properties, and relations. The crucial expressions in ontology, logic, and modality do not stand for universals, properties, or relations; these expressions are quantifiers and operators, not predicates. Our conception of structure, therefore, must allow us to ask, of expressions of any grammatical category, whether they carve at the joints.

Call a language "fundamental" if all of its expressions carve at the joints. Realism about structure leads to realism about fundamental languages. On the generalized conception of structure, in order to be fundamental, it is not enough that a language have the right predicates. It must also have the right logical apparatus. Will a fundamental language contain quantifiers? The sentential connectives of propositional logic? Modal or tense operators? The realist about structure thinks that these questions have objective answers. There is a privileged way to "write the book of the world".

2   Primitivism

I cannot define 'structure'. As we will see, a rich characterization can be given: connections to other concepts, theses about its behavior, and an official regimentation for talking about it. But none of this will add up to a definition. Indeed, I will argue in section 7.13 that structure is perfectly fundamental.

2.1   Understanding

I know from bitter experience that philosophers are wary of this primitivism. Many times I have been asked (to murmuring general approval): "What on earth do you *mean* by 'structure'??".

Let's be realistic about the extent and value of definitions. Philosophical concepts of interest are rarely reductively defined. Still more rarely does our *understanding* of such concepts rest on definitions.

On what does our understanding of philosophical concepts rest? Sometimes there is a perceptual basis: we directly experience space and time, perhaps. But the perceptual model is mostly unhelpful (think of modality, logic, laws of nature, identity over time, morality, justice, knowledge, justification, . . .). We generally "understand" philosophical concepts to the extent that we know what role they play in our thinking. (Understand "role" here very broadly, so as to include particular "cases"—we judge Gettier's (1963) Smith not to know that Jones owns a Ford or Brown is in Barcelona—as well as general inferential patterns—we think of identity as a transitive relation; we think of inability to refrain from action as an excuse.)

Philosophers sometimes slip into a magical-grasp picture of understanding. An opponent wields a crucial term. She will not be bullied into equating it with some combination of preferred terms. An inward search for a mystical mental state of UNDERSTANDING comes up empty. The opponent is pronounced confused or obscure.

Philosophical terms *can* be unclear: when they have been given no clear theoretical role to play. But 'structure' has a relatively clear role—given in this book and elsewhere. What more is wanted? The perceived magical grasp of more familiar concepts like modality, in-virtue-of, or law of nature, is due solely to the fact that we've become accustomed to talking about them. The theoretical roles backing those concepts are no richer or better specified than the role backing structure. Philosophy is not just the building of theories on previously existing concepts. We also build new concepts, by building theories that use them.

This is not to say that all there is to meaning and reference is inferential role. Meaning and reference may well be determined by external factors that transcend inferential role (see section 3.2). So even if structure's inferential role is richly specified, the concept may nevertheless fail to refer to anything. But that's true of any philosophical concept: the world may simply fail to contain anything—or any unique thing—fitting the inferential role associated with the concept. My hope is that this unhappy possibility is not realized.

2.2 Primitivism supported

And my *argument* that the unhappy possibility is not realized is simply the overall argument of this book: recognizing structure improves our understanding of the world—our understanding of:

> (Objective) similarity (chapter 1);
> Intrinsic properties (Lewis, 1986b, pp. 61–2);[1]
> Laws of nature and explanation (section 3.1);
> Reference (section 3.2);
> Induction and confirmation (section 3.3);
> The intrinsic structure of space and time (section 3.4);
> Substantivity (chapter 4);
> Epistemic value (section 4.5);
> Metametaphysics (chapter 5);
> Disputes about time, modality, ontology, logic (chapters 9–12)

(In the first four items I follow David Lewis.) Structure is a *posit*, a posit that is justified by its ability to improve our theories of these matters.

Posits are most justified when they're unifying. When a single posit can be viewed as underlying multiple phenomena, this counts in favor of the posit. But here we must distinguish two kinds of unification. Compare two unifying features of Newtonian mechanics. Newtonian mechanics contains two fundamental laws governing mass: the second law of motion, which specifies the acceleration of a body as a function of its mass and the net force acting on it, and the law of gravitation, which specifies the gravitational force between a pair of bodies as a function of their masses and spatial separation. The first unifying feature is the identification of inertial and gravitational mass: the very same notion of mass is asserted to be involved in both laws. This first unification is one of ideology, of the set of our undefined words/concepts/notions. Instead of containing two notions of mass, one for the second law ("resistance to acceleration") and one for the law of gravitation ("tendency to produce gravitational force"), Newtonian ideology

---

[1]Lewis defined "duplicates"—intuitively, perfectly intrinsically similar objects—as pairs of objects whose parts can be mapped one-to-one preserving parthood and perfectly natural properties and relations; and he then defined intrinsic properties as those that can never differ between a pair of duplicate objects, whether in the same or in different possible worlds.

contains just one notion: mass. The second unification is the derivation of the planets' elliptical orbits. Here there was unification of fundamental principles. The orbiting of the planets was shown to require no new fundamental laws, since elliptical orbits were shown to follow from the the second law and the law of gravitation. While both sorts of unification seem to count in favor of a posit, too much of the former sort without any of the latter seems rarely to be pursued. We like to keep our posits few in number, but we also want them to obey a small number of fundamental laws, from which much else can be derived.

To be sure, metaphysics isn't rocket science. In metaphysics we lack precisely formulated, sufficiently specific fundamental laws from which myriad important and precise consequences may be rigorously derived. Still, we can be guided by physics here. The posit of structure will be *un*justified if its alleged "applications"— its connections to similarity, intrinsicality, and the rest—are in the end unified by nothing beyond a bare assertion that a single notion of structure plays the needed role in each case. That would be unification of the first sort without unification of the second sort. But positing structure is not like this sort of bare assertion, since the applications are all intertwined. For example, many of the applications can be seen as flowing from a single principle connecting structure to epistemic value (section 4.5). Also, the applications just seem intuitively appropriate. Similarity, intrinsic structure of spacetime, substantivity, and the rest really do seem to be connected to fundamentality in the ways to be proposed.[2] This claim is difficult to justify, but I hope the reader will agree once the applications have been laid out.

2.3 Epistemology

A typical follow-up to "What do you *mean* by 'structure'?" is "How are we supposed to *know*—or even, reasonably believe—anything about structure?" Unless structure is defined in more familiar terms, it's thought, facts about structure become epistemically inaccessible.

The epistemic worry leads to a further worry about understanding. Suppose we reject the magical-grasp picture of understanding, as urged above. Perhaps we replace it with a more inferentialist picture. But then, if facts about structure are unknowable, structure-talk becomes inferentially isolated, in which case our understanding of such talk is again threatened.

But why think that primitivism about structure has such drastic epistemic consequences? The dialectic here is a familiar one. A "realist" resists downsizing the facts in some domain—reducing them or regarding them as subjective—and so is accused of making the facts in that domain unknowable. Her response is

[2]This vague claim raises difficult issues. The intuitive conception of structure as involving *fundamentality* doesn't seem inert; if the entire theory of this book were replaced with its ramsey sentence, omitting all mention of fundamentality, something would seem to be lost. But in what does this intuitive conception consist? Is it simply further principles connecting fundamentality to other notions? Or does it somehow resist being captured in principles?

fallibilist epistemology: the subjective or reductive facts that her opponents offer as replacements are instead fallible guides to the upsized facts.

Most philosophers are comfortable with taking the realist side of this dialectic in the most familiar case: they reject Berkeleyan idealism, phenomenalism, and other downsized conceptions of the external world, and instead regard ordinary evidence as a fallible guide to upsized facts. But their ranks dwindle as the subject matter becomes more metaphysical. The reason for this is simple: many of our models of the nature of reasonable—albeit fallible—belief about the external world do not apply straightforwardly to beliefs about more metaphysical matters. For example, we do not seem to be in causal contact with the facts debated by metaphysicians in the same way that we are in causal contact with more familiar facts about the external world.

But the models that immediately disallow reasonable belief in metaphysics are too simplistic, and as a result are in trouble anyway. Our causal contact with the facts of logic, mathematics, and particle physics, for example, is quite unlike our causal contact with the facts of the everyday external world. The ray of hope for the metaphysician is this: when the models become more sophisticated, allowing for reasonable belief in logic, mathematics, and particle physics, perhaps they will also allow for reasonable belief in metaphysics as well.

The epistemology of metaphysics is far from clear; this any metaphysician should concede. For what it's worth, as a general epistemology of metaphysics I prefer the vague, vaguely Quinean, thought that metaphysics is continuous with science. We employ many of the same criteria—whatever those are—for theory choice within metaphysics that we employ outside of metaphysics. Admittedly, those criteria give less clear guidance in metaphysics than elsewhere; but there's no harm in following this argument where it leads: metaphysical inquiry is by its nature comparatively speculative and uncertain.

This Quinean thought suggests an epistemology for structure in particular. Quine's advice for forming *ontological* beliefs is familiar: believe the ontology of your best theory. Theories are good insofar as they are simple, explanatorily powerful, integrate with other good theories, and so on. We should believe generally what good theories say; so if a good theory makes an ontological claim, we should believe it. The ontological claim took part in a theoretical success, and therefore inherits a borrowed luster; it merits our belief. This all is familiar; but a believer in structure can say more. A good theory isn't merely likely to be *true*. Its ideology is also likely to carve at the joints. For the conceptual decisions made in adopting that theory—and not just the theory's ontology—were vindicated; those conceptual decisions also took part in a theoretical success, and also inherit a borrowed luster. So we can add to the Quinean advice: regard the ideology of your best theory as carving at the joints. We have defeasible reason to believe that the conceptual decisions of successful theories correspond to something real: reality's structure.

The term 'ideology', in its present sense, comes from Quine (1951*a*; 1953). It is a bad word for a great concept. It misleadingly suggests that ideology is about ideas—about *us*. This in turn obscures the fact that the confirmation of a theory confirms its ideological choices and hence supports beliefs about structure. A theory's ideology is as much a part of its worldly content as its ontology.

The familiar Quinean thought is that we search for the best—simplest, etc.— theory that explains our evidence. My addition to this thought—though it may have been implicit all along—is that this search is ideological as well as doctrinal; we search simultaneously for a set of concepts and a theory stated in terms of those concepts. We solve for the best and most explanatory pair $\langle I, T_I \rangle$ of ideology I and theory T_I in terms of that ideology. We do not hold fixed our initial ideological choices ('fire', 'air', 'water'. . .) since there may be limits to how good a theory can be formulated in those terms. Many of the most dramatic advances in science are ideological; a new ideology (such as that of Minkowskian spacetime) can dissolve intractable problems and enable new, more powerful theories.

(Sometimes our evidence does not support a unique pair $\langle I, T_I \rangle$. This is not in itself worrisome; we do not know everything, after all. But in some cases, it is hard to see what evidence *could* be mustered in favor of one pair rather than another. For example, should our fundamental theory of part and whole take 'part' or 'overlap' as primitive? Should our fundamental logical theory take conjunction and negation, or instead, disjunction and negation, as primitive? In such cases it's hard to see how to choose, and indeed, hard to believe that there could be a single correct choice. We will return to this issue in section 10.2.)

The Quinean thought rationalizes commonly held beliefs about what is fundamental. Nearly everyone agrees that physical notions like mass and spatiotemporality are fundamental. These beliefs are reasonable because those notions are drawn from highly successful theories.

The Quinean thought also rationalizes changes in beliefs about what is fundamental. The special theory of relativity led to (at least) two such changes. First, we came to regard electromagnetism as a single fundamental force, rather than regarding electricity and magnetism as separate fundamental forces.[3] And second, we came to regard spacetime as lacking absolute spatial and temporal separation. These changes weren't ontic: changes in which entities are accepted. Nor were they merely doctrinal: changes in view, but phrased in the old terms. The changes were rather ideological: we revised our fundamental ideology for describing the world. The changes are rationalized by the Quinean thought because the fundamental ideology of the special theory of relativity differs from the fundamental ideology of Newtonian physics: in place of electrical, magnetic, spatial, and temporal ideology, the special theory has unified ideology for electromagnetism and unified ideology for spatiotemporal metrical structure.

[3] See Maudlin (1996, pp. 131–3).

The Quinean thought about ontology is sometimes put in terms of indispensability: believe in the entities that are indispensable in your best theory. The analogous thought about ideology may be similarly put: regard as joint-carving the ideology that is indispensable in your best theory. This is fine provided "indispensable" is properly understood, as meaning: "cannot be jettisoned without sacrificing theoretical virtue". The indispensability argument for mathematical entities is not refuted by just any nominalistic alternative to platonist mathematical physics. The nominalistic alternative must be attractive as a scientific theory; it must compete with the platonist theory for being simple, explanatory, and so on. Similarly, consider rewriting a given theory of mass and charge in terms of *schmass* and charge, where the schmass of an object is its mass if it has unit negative charge and twice its mass otherwise. The rewritten theory has the same consequences about charge and mass as the original, so 'charge' and 'mass' are in a sense dispensable in physics. But the resulting theory is far worse as a theory. What were syntactically simple generalizations in the old theory are no longer simple in the new.

We have been exploring the positive side of the Quinean approach to ideology: we can *support* claims about joint-carving by showing that the ideology in question is part of a good theory. The approach has a negative side too. Good theories must be as simple as possible, and part of simplicity is having a minimal ideology. So we can *oppose* claims about joint-carving by exhibiting good theories that do not contain the ideology in question.

The demand for minimal ideology recalls a familiar trade-off between ontology and ideology. We often face a choice between reducing our ontology at the cost of ideological complexity, or minimizing ideology at the cost of positing new entities.[4] If ideology is psychologized, the trade-off is one of apples for oranges: whether to posit a more complex world or a more complex mode of expression.[5] But on the present approach, both sides of the trade-off concern worldly complexity. A theory with a more complex ideology posits a fuller, more complex, world, a world with more structure. Thus ideological posits are no free lunch.

"Believe the ontology and ideology of your best theory" is schematic in various ways. One in particular is worth mentioning: should the special sciences be counted as part of our "best" theory? Saying yes leads to an expansive conception of the fundamental; saying no—my preferred answer—leads to a more austere conception. The defender of the latter answer must concede that our understanding of the world would be severely impoverished without the special sciences, but will insist that since facts about the special sciences hold "in virtue of" more fundamental facts in some sense (chapter 7), they needn't be cited in our "best" theory. This is a difficult issue, which I will not attempt to resolve here.

---

[4] See, for example, Quine (1976a).
[5] See Oliver (1996, section 2).

We have, then, an epistemology for structure. Claims about structure can be supported by evidence, and so are not inferentially isolated, and so are not in danger of unintelligibility. This epistemology is admittedly superficial and birds-eye. Then again, so are the epistemological models that are claimed to preclude reasonable belief in metaphysics. What is needed for progress in these issues is a more sophisticated and detailed understanding of the epistemology of our more theoretical endeavors, such as mathematics and theoretical physics, including their foundations.

2.4 Against reduction

Primitivism about structure would be unnecessary if structure could be reduced. This section will argue briefly against a few reductive approaches. But the matter cannot really be decided by a few quick arguments, since it turns on the question of which global metaphysics is most attractive. My primary aim in this book is to exhibit the attractions of my own approach, rather than to refute others. (Also, much of my approach could be adopted by a reductionist, provided the reduced notion of structure is sufficiently objective and capable of broad application.)

Consider first reductions to putatively fundamental concepts. One can object to such reductions in two ways: extensionally and systematically. One can argue that a reduction fails to generate a reasonable extension for 'structure'. Or one can argue, on global, systematic grounds, that structure itself, rather than the proposed reducing concept, should be taken to be fundamental.

Consider, for example, the proposal that a structural property or relation is one that figures in some law of nature, where the notion of a law of nature is taken to be fundamental. In my view, logical and mathematical notions, as well as the notion of structure itself, carve at the joints; but it is unclear whether these notions figure in the laws of nature. A notion of structure that is too closely tied to lawhood will not be general enough to do all the work it needs to do. This is an extensional objection. But there is also a systematic consideration: it is better to posit fundamental structure than fundamental lawhood. (One could posit both, but that would be overkill.) Later on I will say more against all forms of fundamental modality, including fundamental lawhood; but in brief: modal notions are generally of dubious explanatory value. Adding the notion of law to physical theory, for example, doesn't seem to enhance its explanatory power. Also, the claims of physicists do not bifurcate naturally into laws and mere facts (which is "spacetime is a four-dimensional Lorentzian manifold"?), so introducing a fundamental notion of law imposes a distinction on their inquiry that isn't there to begin with.[6]

For similar extensional and systematic reasons, we should not define structure in terms of a fundamental notion of causation. Causation is a particularly unsavory fundamental posit—at least if the posit is intended to closely match our ordinary

[6]See section 3.1 on laws and chapter 12 on modality.

concept of causation. It takes only a glance at the recent literature on causation to appreciate how arbitrary and baroque our ordinary concept of causation is.[7] One might posit a fundamental sort of causation that is only distantly related to our ordinary concept, perhaps on the grounds that the sciences demand recognition of some sort of fundamental scientific causation. The case for fundamental causation is, I suspect, strictly weaker than the case for fundamental laws of nature; but at any rate, the objections to defining structure in terms of fundamental scientific causation are the same as those in the previous two paragraphs.

Consider, next, a proposal to define structure in terms of supervenience, where supervenience is then defined in terms of a putatively fundamental notion of metaphysical necessity.[8] Call a set of properties and relations *complete* iff all properties and relations supervene (globally, across all metaphysically possible worlds) on it; and call a set *minimally* complete iff it is complete and contains no proper subset that is also complete. The proposal I want to attack is this: the set of structural properties and relations can be defined as the minimally complete set of properties and relations.

Here too there is the systematic objection that structure is a better fundamental posit than any modal notion. But there are also extensional objections. In Sider (1996*b*, section 3.3) I gave two.[9] First, it is unclear whether the structural properties and relations are complete: nonqualitative properties and relations (such as the property of being identical to Ted) may not supervene on them, and it's hard to exclude nonqualitative properties and relations in the analysis without helping oneself to some notion in the vicinity of structure. Second, and more importantly, even if the set of structural properties and relations *is* complete, it

---

[7]This literature, it seems to me, needs to make up its mind whether it is about fundamental metaphysics or conceptual analysis. (Hall (2006) and Lewis (2004) are notable for being clear which they are pursuing—the latter.) Above all, it is important not to shift uncritically between the two conceptions of the project, since they call for different methodologies. If the project is conceptual analysis, then heavy reliance on thought experiments is appropriate; but it is far less clear that one can insist on premises like: absences cannot be causes; abstract entities like facts cannot be causes; there must be uniform causal relata; causation cannot be contextual or normative or extrinsic. One could claim that these premises are part of our ordinary concept; but conceptual analysts generally regard intuitive judgments about particular cases as being far more diagnostic than intuitive judgments about such general principles. At the very least, one should evaluate these premises as alleged components of our concept, and not as if they are supported by considerations of simplicity or fit with a favored fundamental metaphysics. If, on the other hand, the project is to investigate the fundamental metaphysics of the causal relation, then it must be argued that there is such a thing—that there is a fundamental relation of causation; and heavy reliance on thought experiments must be abandoned, or else somehow justified. See also Paul (2009, section 1; 2010, sections 1–3).

[8]To say that some properties supervene on others is to say that in some sense, the former properties cannot vary independently of the latter properties. Supervenience is normally defined in terms of possible worlds and individuals, which are then defined in terms of necessity (and ancillary notions). For an overview of these issues, see McLaughlin and Bennett (2005) on supervenience and Divers (2002) on possible worlds.

[9]The proposal was there taken as a definition of Lewisian perfect naturalness. See also Lewis (1983*a*); Marshall (2009).

may not be minimally complete. Perhaps both earlier-than and later-than are structural relations, for example. Third, and still more importantly, even if the set of structural properties and relations is minimally complete, it won't be the only such set: certain other sets containing "grueified versions" of the structural properties and relations will also be minimally complete. Begin with a set containing charge and mass, say, and replace mass with schmass (see above). Since an object's mass supervenes on its charge and schmass, any set that supervenes on the former set will supervene on the latter set; so the latter set is complete. And minimally so: since it doesn't contain mass properties, removing the schmass properties would disrupt its completeness.

There is a response to my third argument that I did not consider in my (1996*b*) paper. Perhaps we can single out the set of structural properties and relations, from amongst all the minimally complete sets, as that set that "enables the best Lewisian laws", in the following sense. Lewis used his notion of naturalness to give a reductionist, "Humean" theory of laws of nature, a souped-up version of the old regularity theory.[10] Neglecting complications involving chance, he defined a law as any generalization in the "best system"; that is, in the deductive system, stated in a language whose predicates stand for natural properties and relations, that best balances the virtues of strength and simplicity. A system is strong depending on how much (in some suitable measure) information it entails; a system is simple depending on how simply (in some suitable measure) it can be axiomatized. Now, Lewis pursued this project under the assumption that naturalness was primitive (or near enough). But the suggestion I want now to consider is that we reductively define structural properties and relations in terms of goodness of deductive systems and supervenience, as follows. Say that a deductive system is *based on* a set of properties and relations iff each primitive predicate in that system expresses a property or relation in the set. And say that one set, S_1, *enables better laws than* another set, S_2, iff some system based on S_1 is better—i.e., better balances strength and simplicity—than any system based on S_2. (Perhaps the laws of the systems should also be required to nontrivially utilize all the members of the sets.) With any luck, there exists some minimally complete set that enables better laws than every other minimally complete set. If so, structural properties and relations may be defined as the members of this set.

This proposal is worth thinking about more, but the other objections given above remain. The systemic objection remains: better to posit basic structure than basic modality. And the first two of my (1996*b*) objections remain. The first might be addressed by simply taking 'qualitative' as primitive, and the second might be addressed by claiming that neither *earlier-than* nor *later-than* is structural (those who deny that time has an intrinsic direction will already want to say this). But other objections in the vicinity of the second objection remain. Since supervenience is defined modally, mathematical properties and relations

[10]See Lewis (1973*b*, pp. 73–4; 1983*b*, pp. 366–8; 1986*c*, pp. 121–4; 1994).

will supervene trivially on any set whatsoever, given the common dogma that mathematical facts are necessary. Thus, these properties and relations will not be present in any *minimally* complete set. But our conception of structure would be impoverished by their exclusion. The distribution of structural properties and relations is supposed to give the fundamental facts about the world, and we might well want to say that the fundamental facts include mathematical facts.[11]

We have considered reductions to putatively fundamental law, cause, and necessity. What of reduction to one of these notions construed nonfundamentally? The systematic objections, anyway, would be avoided. But the reduction would be circular if the nonfundamental notion were in turn reduced to structure. And I suspect it would need to be. (Consider, for example, Lewis's account of law and cause, and my account of necessity in chapter 12.)

2.5 Against subjectivity

Primitivism would also be unnecessary if structure were tied to *us* in some way—to human language, biology, history, or psychology. According to this view, what distinguishes the class of the electrons, as opposed to the class of the electron-or-cows, is just that humans have a simple predicate for the former class, find it psychologically more natural to think in terms of 'electron', and so on; it doesn't go any deeper than that. This kind of subjectivism about structure could be taken as a reduction or, alternatively, as expressivism or some other form of noncognitivism.

Speaking just for myself, this is incredible. It is really, really hard to believe that the fact that electrons go together, in a way that electrons-or-cows do not, is merely a reflection of something about us.

But this is autobiography, not argument. The *argument* here, such as it is, is that any subjectivity in the notion of structure would infect all the domains in which structure is applied. If structure is just a reflection of our language (or whatever) then so are the facts about similarity, intrinsicality, laws of nature, the intrinsic structure of space and time. . . And this is incredible.

At its last step the argument again reverts to autobiography. Certain philosophers will rightly remain unconvinced, for example "antirealists" of various stripes—pragmatists, Kantians, logical positivists, and so on.

A certain "knee-jerk realism" is an unargued presupposition of this book. Knee-jerk realism is a vague picture rather than a precise thesis. According to the picture, the point of human inquiry—or a very large chunk of it anyway, a chunk that includes physics—is to *conform* itself to the world, rather than to *make* the world. The world is "out there", and our job is to wrap our minds around it. This picture is perhaps my deepest philosophical conviction. I've never questioned it; giving it up would require a reboot too extreme to contemplate; and I have no idea how I'd try to convince someone who didn't share it.

[11] See also section 10.2.

2.6 The privilege of the physical

A final consideration in favor of primitivism about structure may be advanced. It is based on knee-jerk realism.

Let Γ be the set of true sentences in the language of completed physics, and consider two sets of propositions. The first set, P, is the set of propositions expressed by the members of Γ, under their intended interpretation. Thus P is the set of physical truths. The second set, S, consists of "scrambled" propositions. To arrive at S, reinterpret all nonlogical symbols of the language of physics under some arbitrary permutation μ of the totality of objects (see section 3.2 for a full description of this sort of reinterpretation), and let S be the propositions expressed by the members of Γ thus reinterpreted. The members of S are all true, since the members of Γ are true under their intended interpretation, and reinterpretation under a permutation preserves truth (again see section 3.2).

The consideration is then this. Even though both P and S consist of *true* propositions, knee-jerk realism requires recognizing that there is something *better* about P. Believing the members of P would be better than believing the members of S; P constitutes a better description of reality than S. To deny these things would be to admit that there's nothing mandatory about physics, that other perspectives on the world are "just different", not worse. Knee-jerk realism is incompatible with the thought that it's just *optional* to think in physical terms, that it would be just as good to pick wholly arbitrary carvings of the world (meanings under μ) and think in those terms.

Knee-jerk realism further requires that the betterness be *objective*. It isn't merely that the propositions in P have a simpler description in our language, or are more useful if one is trying to stay alive, let alone build rocket ships (though this usefulness is good *evidence* for the betterness.) The betterness, it is natural to conclude, is that only the propositions in P are cast in joint-carving terms.

Are there less metaphysical terms in which one might characterize the inferiority of S? It's hard to see what they might be. For example, P is not more "complete" than S in any interesting sense. Neither set contains all the true propositions. Granted, S is silent on questions of physics, but P is silent on questions of "shmysics" (the subject matter of S); what we need is some objective sense in which the first omission is worse.

At this point an opponent might try out some of the moves of section 2.4. She might say that P is better because it contains laws, or because it is associated with a complete set of properties and relations ("associated" in the sense that P's members are expressed by simple sentences in a language with predicates for the members of the complete set; "complete" in the modal sense introduced in section 2.4). Systematic reasons against appealing to modality—whether nomic or metaphysical—were given; but also, the appeals are intuitively off-target. The deficiency of S, surely, inheres in its categorical, real-world, nature, and should be explicable without bringing in the ghosts of what might have been.

Knee-jerk realism, then, requires that the physical description of reality be objectively privileged. And a natural account of the privilege is that physical notions carve at the joints.

3   Connections

... as I bear [the distinction between natural and unnatural properties]
in mind considering various topics in philosophy, I notice time and again
that it offers solutions to my problems.—David Lewis (1983*b*, p. 343)

Structure is central in and around metaphysics. We saw in chapter 1 how it
connects to similarity. The next three chapters explore further connections.

Each connection is a proposal, stated in terms of structure, for how to think
about a certain topic. Although none of these proposals is mandatory for the
believer in structure, each is natural and attractive.

This chapter discusses explanation and laws, metasemantics, induction, and
physical geometry. These connections (especially induction and physical geometry) will play only a peripheral role in the rest of the book. The following two
chapters discuss more central connections. Chapter 4 connects structure to questions about the status (substantivity, conventionality, objectivity) of disputes in
general, and chapter 5 connects structure to questions about the status of metaphysical disputes in particular—to metametaphysics.

3.1 Explanation and laws

Many connect laws of nature with fundamentality, in one way or another. Prim-
itivists about lawhood sometimes define fundamental properties as those that
are involved in the laws, or else claim that "fundamental properties are those
that are involved in the laws" is a substantive principle connecting two primitive notions. Conversely, a primitivist about fundamentality—in my case, about
structure—might define laws in terms of structure.

The Lewisian approach to laws of nature is an example of the final option. As
we saw in section 2.4, Lewis defined laws as generalizations in the best system—the
deductive system, cast in a language whose predicates express natural properties
and relations, that best balances the virtues of simplicity and strength. The restriction on the language of the best system is essential; otherwise, as Lewis (1983*b*,
p. 367) points out, a simple and maximally strong theory could be given with a
single, simple axiom, $\forall x F x$, where F is a predicate true of all and only things in
the actual world. All true generalizations would be counted as laws.

The metaphysical core of Lewis's theory is its Humean, negative part:
rejection of metaphysically fundamental laws of nature. Fundamentally speaki

the world is anomic. The best reason to accept this Humean core is parsimony.[1] We ought, other things being equal, to keep fundamental theories simple; and metaphysically fundamental laws would add complexity without adding to understanding. The claims of physics aren't explanatorily enhanced by adding that those claims are laws.[2]

The positive part of Lewis's theory is its definition of lawhood. This part is attractive, even more so if it is augmented as follows. Adding more content to a system generally makes it stronger but also more complex. Since the best system must balance strength and simplicity, additions are justified only if the benefit of the added strength outweighs the demerit of the added complexity. Question: how much complexity can be tolerated to gain a given amount of strength? That is, how much does complexity "cost"? Different answers correspond to different notions of law. The more expensive complexity is made, the simpler the best system will need to be, thus making fewer generalizations count as laws. Special-science generalizations, for example, are more complex than those of physics when they involve notions that carve at the joints less well than do physical notions, and when they include ceteris paribus conditions (whatever that means exactly, it surely detracts from simplicity). So let a "middling" assignment of cost to complexity be one that counts the generalizations of physics as laws, but only barely. This corresponds to a sense of 'law' in which there are laws of physics, but in which certain special-science generalizations do not count as laws.[3] If complexity is instead made cheaper, then those special-science generalizations will count as laws. (And if complexity is made expensive, so that very little complexity is tolerated, then even physical generalizations no longer count as laws; all that remain are laws of metaphysics and logic. See sections 10.3 and 12.5.)

Once augmented, Lewis's theory of law is good as far as it goes. But I doubt that the notion of law is quite as central as philosophers (or metaphysicians, anyway!) think. Consider these claims: spacetime is a four-dimensional Lorentzian manifold; the universe began with an initial singularity; the universe began in a state of very low entropy. It's a stretch to call these laws, yet they're perfectly central to physics. If the point of the notion of law is its role in a rational reconstruction of science, then we should broaden our focus, to include these non-laws as well.[4] And the

---

[1] Lewis's reason is different: metaphysically fundamental laws would require "necessary connections" (Lewis, 1983b, p. 366); but see section 12.5.

[2] See also section 12.1.

[3] I have in mind special-science generalizations that are physically contingent—perhaps because they depend on certain physically contingent "initial conditions".

[4] It might be held instead that the point of the notion of law is to play some role in systematic metaphysics. For example, laws are commonly taken to play a constitutive role in the analysis of counterfactuals: we "hold constant" the laws in determining what would have happened under a counterfactual supposition. Even so, we should still broaden our focus beyond laws, since surely we ~~hol~~d constant these non-laws when evaluating counterfactuals.

centrality of laws arguably diminishes once we move beyond physics to the special sciences. It has been argued, for example, that there are no laws of biology.[5]

The core insight of Lewis's account of laws can be generalized beyond the case of laws: good scientific theories, whether or not they cite laws, must be cast in joint-carving terms. We may put this in terms of explanation: "theories" based on bizarre, non-joint-carving classifications are unexplanatory even when true.[6] Theories whose basic notions fail badly to carve at the joints fail badly as theories, even if they are exemplary from an "internal" point of view, for their inner workings fail to mirror the inner workings of the world. We know on cardinality grounds that there are functions from the motions of the planets to past stock market performance under which the motions correspond to the fluctuations of the Dow Jones industrial average to date. But if someone were actually to produce such a function, no one would regard it as being explanatory (and no one would expect the correlation to continue). In contrast, explanations that cite facts about the geometry of spacetime or the initial singularity *are* genuine (whether or not the cited facts are laws), in part because the cited facts are stated in joint-carving terms.

This dimension of theoretical excellence is best exemplified by theories cast in perfectly fundamental terms—theories of fundamental physics, for example. But it is exemplified, to varying degrees, by special-science theories as well, since the notions of the special sciences carve at the joints reasonably well.

3.2 Reference magnetism

One of the "problems" Lewis used his notion of naturalness to solve was the problem of radical semantic skepticism (1983*b*; 1984). The problem is one in metasemantics. How do words (or thoughts—but let's stick to words) get their meanings? What "semantic glue" attaches them to the world? There are different views about the nature of the semantic glue, but on nearly all of them, the glue doesn't seem to be sticky enough; it apparently cannot secure meaning with sufficient determinacy. Most roughly put: what I mean by 'pig' is surely determined by such facts as that I've always said 'pig' when in the presence of pigs; but why do such facts determine that by 'pig' I mean pigs, rather than pigs-I've-encountered-in-the-past, or pigs-in-my-immediate-vicinity, or pigs-before-2011-A.D.-or-cows-afterwards or . . . ?[7]

---

[5] See Hamilton (2007, section 2) for a survey.

[6] Hirsch (1993, chapter 3, section 7a) argues that explanations cast in joint-carving terms can be recast, without explanatory loss, in a priori necessarily equivalent non-joint-carving terms. But the recast explanation will have "syntactic" demerits, such as being highly disjunctive. So let us refine our claim about explanation: good explanations must be cast in joint-carving terms when stated in syntactically ideal form.

[7] The problem derives ultimately from Wittgenstein (1958), and in the form presented here from Putnam (1978, part IV; 1980; 1981, chapter 2) and Kripke (1982).

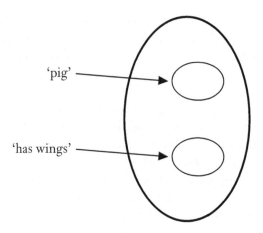

Fɪɢ. 3.1. Interpretation 1

To bring out the problem more fully, we must consider concrete proposals for the nature of the glue. Following Lewis (1984), I'll illustrate how the problem goes for a toy descriptivist theory of the nature of semantic glue. According to this descriptivism, there is a set of sentences, S, such that our words mean whatever they must in order for the sentences in S to come out true. (This theory is schematic; different versions specify different sets S. S might, for example, be taken to include "definitional sentences", whatever that means exactly.)

The sentences in S do not, on their own, provide enough semantic glue. Let (F) be an intuitively false sentence of our language that is logically consistent with S—"Some pigs have wings", say. We had better be able to say that (F) is false (otherwise, as Fodor would say, it's the end of the world). Now, (F) turns out false *in an interpretation* iff nothing is both in the extension of 'pig' and also in the extension of 'has wings' in that interpretation (figure 3.1). And (F) turns out true in an interpretation iff these extensions overlap in that interpretation (figure 3.2). So if (F) is to turn out false, the *correct* interpretation of our language must be of the former sort; interpretations like interpretation 2 are *incorrect*—such interpretations do not reflect what we really mean.[8] But if—as the descriptivist says—all that is required of a correct interpretation is that the sentences in S come out true under that interpretation, then we are pretty much *guaranteed* to be able to construct a correct interpretation like interpretation 2. All we need to do is assign extensions to predicates so that every sentence in S, plus (F) as well, turns out true. We might, for instance, begin by assigning the set of hard-boiled eggs to 'pig' and assigning the set of edible things to 'has wings'. This makes (F) true since some hard-boiled eggs are edible. Now, suppose (S) contains the sentence 'Every pig is an animal'. The interpretation we are constructing must count this sentence true as well. But this is easy to accomplish: simply assign the set of eggs

---

[8] Let us ignore the complicating factor that there will exist multiple correct interpretations, because of benign sorts of semantic undetermination like vagueness.

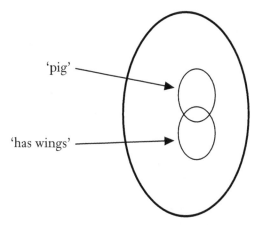

FIG. 3.2. Interpretation 2

to 'is an animal'. Since every hard-boiled egg is an egg, 'Every pig is an animal' comes out true: the bizarre assignment to 'pig' is "cancelled out" by the equally bizarre but compensating assignment to 'is an animal'. We then continue in this way, assigning compensating bizarre extensions so that every other member of S comes out true as well.

The extensions assigned by this bizarre interpretation to 'pig', 'has wings', 'animal', and other predicates are clearly not what those predicates really mean, by any ordinary standard of "really mean". But our descriptivist says that to be correct (i.e., to reflect what we really mean), an interpretation need only make every member of S come out true. So the bizarre interpretation 2 would count as a correct one, and so we could not say that 'Some pigs have wings' is false! Something has plainly gone wrong, and it is pretty clear what that is. Descriptivism is false as stated; there must be more to the correctness of an interpretation than merely making certain specified sentences come out true.

The argument assumes that it is possible to continue selecting meanings for the nonlogical expressions in our language so that *every* member of S (and (F) as well) turns out true. But this will always be possible, except in special cases. Let C be the class of entities that we are using to interpret our words, and consider any abstract model—in the logician's sense—in which (F) as well as all members of S are true, and in which the domain is no larger than C. (The only cases in which there would not exist such a model are: i) if (F) is inconsistent with S; or ii) if S and (F) are consistent but only have models that are larger than C. And we lose no important generality by stipulating that the sentences S are consistent with (F) and do not, in concert with (F), logically require the universe to be larger than C.[9]) Since the domain of this abstract model is no larger than C, it can be mapped by some one-to-one function μ onto some subset, D, of C, as in figure 3.3. But

[9]If the sentences in S and (F) are all first-order then, by the downward Löwenheim-Skolem theorem, it would be enough to stipulate that C is infinite. And even if S contains second-order

Abstract domain D

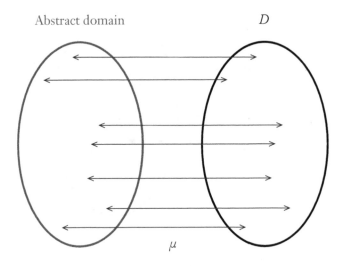

μ

FIG. 3.3. Abstract domain mapped one-to-one onto D

then we can use μ to construct our desired interpretation 2 in D. Each nonlogical symbol in our subject's language has a meaning, m, in the abstract model; let the meaning of each such symbol in interpretation 2 be the object or set of 'tuples $\mu[m]$ in D to which m corresponds under the mapping. For example, 'pig' has an extension, E, in the abstract model, so the meaning of 'pig' in interpretation 2 will be the set $\mu[E]$ of members of D to which members of E are mapped by μ (figure 3.4). Now, it is an elementary fact from model theory that if a sentence is true in a model, it is true in any model constructed via a one-to-one mapping as above. So, since all the members of S, plus (F), are true in the abstract model, they are true in interpretation 2 as well.[10]

The argument shows that a correct interpretation must do more than make specified sentences come out true. What more? Lewis's answer is that correct interpretations must, as much as possible, assign natural properties and relations (or their extensions) to predicates. The meanings under interpretation 1 are (or correspond to) at least somewhat natural properties: being a pig, being edible, and so on. But there is no guarantee that the meanings assigned by interpretation 2 are natural to any significant degree, since they were constructed from the arbitrarily chosen function μ.

Lewis's proposal must be distinguished from the proposal that the sentence 'Predicates stand for natural properties and relations' is to be included in the set, S, of meaning-determining sentences. This proposal would not solve the problem. For so long as this sentence is consistent with (F) and the rest of the sentences in S,

---

sentences, we can just stipulate that it does not contain the logically complex sentences necessary to force domains larger than C.

[10]The argument just given assumed an extensional conception of meaning. Williams (2005, chapter 5) shows how to rework it under richer conceptions of meaning.

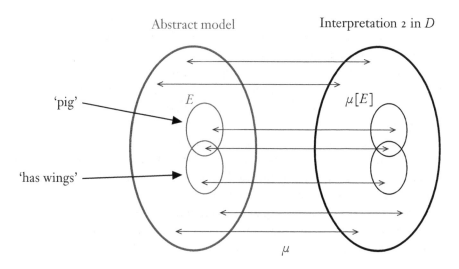

FIG. 3.4. Interpretation 2 induced by μ

we will again be able to construct our interpretation 2. The resulting interpretation will misinterpret 'predicate', 'stand for', 'natural', 'property', and 'relation' so that 'Predicates stand for natural properties and relations', like the other sentences in S, come out true. Lewis's idea is not to stick with the original descriptivist constraint on correct interpretations ("correct interpretations are those that make every sentence in S true") and add more sentences to S; it is rather to modify descriptivism by adding an additional constraint. That constraint is not that 'Predicates stand for natural properties and relations' must come out true on a correct interpretation; it is rather, and more simply, that *predicates must stand for natural properties and relations in a correct interpretation*.

Lewis's constraint on reference is "externalist"; reference is not determined merely by us. We, of course, do part of the work. Our patterns of use of language determine which sentences go into S. But the degree to which an interpretation counts sentences in S as being true is just one factor in determining whether that interpretation is correct. The other factor is the naturalness of that interpretation's semantic values. And this second factor has nothing to do with us. Natural properties and relations are "intrinsically eligible meanings"; they are "reference magnets".

The doctrine of reference magnetism has been received warily. Some regard it as an ad hoc response to a problem, with no independent backing. Others regard it as occult metaphysics, as the postulation of an irreducible "semantic force". (Perhaps the term 'reference magnetism', never used by Lewis but increasingly the doctrine's customary name, encourages this thought.[11]) Neither charge is founded. Following J. Robert G. Williams (2007, section 2), we can derive the doctrine

---

[11]The name was introduced by Hodes (1984, 135) for a related view (which he rejected).

of reference magnetism from a well-motivated and more general doctrine about theoretical virtue. This doctrine is the one defended in section 3.1: explanatory theories must be cast in joint-carving terms.

As I will develop it, the crucial assumption of the derivation is that *reference is an explanatory relation*—one can explain certain facts by citing what words refer to. But if reference were given by a bizarre interpretation, then reference-involving "explanations" would not in fact be explanatory, since they would be cast in badly non-joint-carving terms. Hence reference is not given by a bizarre interpretation.

Thus the exclusion of bizarre interpretations is of a piece with something we already do. We already regard "theories" based on bizarre classifications as being explanatorily useless; reference magnetism is just the extension of this point to metasemantics. Attempting to explain a community's linguistic behavior by citing a relation based on the permuted interpretation 2 would be like attempting to explain the behavior of the stock market in terms of an arbitrary correlation with the motions of the planets.

Let's look at the derivation of reference magnetism in more detail. Reference is a theoretical concept of a certain special science: semantics. A special science, quite generally, attempts to explain a certain target domain of facts by means of certain theoretical concepts. In the case of semantics the target domain is certain aspects of human thought, behavior, and communication, and the theoretical concepts include reference and truth. To use an example of Vann McGee's (2005, section 4), suppose a high-school teacher writes on the chalkboard the sentence 'Maiasaurs were highly social animals that traveled in herds of as many as 10,000.' Why did precisely that pattern of marks appear on the chalkboard? It clearly has *something* to do with the connection between those marks and maiasaurs. In particular, it surely involves the fact that the marks constitute words that *refer* to maiasaurs and their properties.

Some philosophers reject reference-based explanation. This is a big issue, not to be resolved here. But two small points. First, some claim that conventional meaning encodes far fewer referential properties than mainstream semantics thinks, but even they usually grant *some* explanatory role to reference—or at least to reference-by-a-speaker.[12] Second, granting the existence of deflationary concepts of truth and reference that cannot take part in explanations of the sort described above is compatible with also accepting nondeflationary concepts of truth and reference that can take part in those explanations.[13] At any rate, I will assume that some reference-based explanations are indeed explanatory.

If reference-based explanations are to be explanatory, then the reference relation must be a joint-carving one. Not a perfectly joint-carving relation, presumably; but at the very least, not a wildly non-joint-carving relation. And this excludes

---

[12] See, for example, Chomsky (2000); Pietroski (2003); Wilson and Sperber (2004).
[13] See McGee (2005).

the bizarre interpretations. For only a wildly non-joint-carving relation would relate a linguistic population to the semantic values of a bizarre interpretation.

Caveat: suppose there were a *perfectly* joint-carving reference relation. Suppose, that is, that part of the absolutely fundamental story of the world included a specification of a relation of reference between certain sounds or inscriptions made by human beings and parts of the world. Such a fundamental relation could perhaps, as a brute fact, relate words to bizarre semantic values.[14]

But reference is surely not metaphysically fundamental.[15] As a result, it's hard to see how a reasonably joint-carving reference relation could relate us to the bizarre semantic values. The point may be seen initially by making two strong, crude assumptions about "reasonably joint-carving". Assume first that a notion is reasonably joint-carving iff it has a reasonably simple and nondisjunctive definition in terms of the *perfectly* joint-carving notions, and second that the perfectly joint-carving notions are those of physics. Then surely no reasonably joint-carving relation that is to play the role of reference could relate a human population to bizarre semantic values. For the bizarre semantic values themselves have no simple basis in the physical, nor do they stand in any physically simple relations to human populations. Given any relation that does relate us to bizarre semantic values, there is surely some other relation with a simpler basis in the physical that relates us to nonbizarre semantic values.

The two assumptions of the previous paragraph are undoubtedly too crude, but the point is independent of them. Whether a notion is reasonably joint-carving—enough to take part in special-science explanations—has *something* to do with how it is based in the fundamental. So reference must have the right sort of basis in the fundamental if it's to be explanatory. It's highly unclear what exactly the "right sort" of basis is (this is in essence the question of the relation between special-science concepts and physics), but it's quite clear that a relation connecting us to bizarre semantic values would have the wrong sort of basis—for the same reason that arbitrary correlations between the motions of the planets and the stock market have the wrong sort of basis.

Conceiving of reference magnetism in Williams's way risks restricting its scope. In addition to replying to the Putnamian semantic skeptic we discussed earlier, Lewis also used reference magnetism to reply to Kripke's (1982) Wittgensteinian skeptic about the meaning of mathematical language, who asks why by 'plus' we

---

[14]A defender of this metaphysics might argue that it is *unlikely* that fundamental reference relates us to the bizarre semantic values. The simplest hypothesis, it might be claimed, is that we bear the fundamental reference relation to reasonably joint-carving semantic values; the reasoning here, it might be claimed, is analogous to any choice of a simplest hypothesis about the behavior of fundamental properties and relations. (Kripke (1982, pp. 38–9) complained that a simplicity response to his Wittgensteinian skeptic ignored the fact that the skeptical problem is not primarily epistemic, but rather is one of what constitutes semantic facts. But on the view here envisioned, semantic facts are fundamental, and the only remaining problem *is* epistemic.)

[15]See, however, Hawthorne (2006a, section 17).

mean *plus* rather than *quus*, where quus is a function like plus except that it assigns to all pairs of sufficiently large numbers the value 5. Lewis's answer is that plus is a more natural function than quus; this becomes, in Williams's hands, the claim that a semantic theory assigning quus as a semantic value is less explanatory. But now, some will claim that abstract entities cannot take part in genuine explanations, perhaps because abstracta are causally inert. For myself, I reject this conception of explanation. Explanations come in many sorts, not all of them of the "pushing-and-pulling" variety. But at any rate, the constraint on reference magnetism's scope here seems like welcome discipline, not unwanted restriction.

The problem of radical semantic skepticism was presented above as it confronts descriptivist metasemantics. But other metasemantic theories face the problem as well, and reference magnetism—understood in Williams's way—can defend these other metasemantic theories as well, so long as they conceive of reference as an explanatory relation.

For example, Ruth Millikan (1989), who thinks of reference as a biological phenomenon, also faces the problem. Why does the true reference relation, rather than numerous gerrymandered alternatives we could construct, count as the relation that has been selected by evolution for the purpose of storing and communicating information? Answer: *any* hypothesis which says that a gerrymandered relation plays a role in an evolutionary explanation is to be rejected simply because the relation is gerrymandered. The correct answer on behalf of Millikan to the skeptical worry is thus akin to any biologist's answer to the skeptical worry that it is facts about *gruegenes*, rather than genes, that explain inheritance. (The array of gruegenetic properties a thing has is determined by the physical makeup of the spatiotemporally nearest pair of bluejeans; on cardinality grounds, there are sufficiently many different gruegenetic properties to enable us to concoct "laws" of gruegenetics which really do correlate gruegenetic properties with inheritance as fine-grainedly as the real laws of genetics do with real genetic properties.) Similar remarks apply to causal theorists like Jerry Fodor (1987) (unless causation itself is taken to solve the problem[16]).[17]

---

[16] Causal theories say that reference is a certain sort of causal relation, and it's arguably built into the nature of causation that only reasonably joint-carving relations are causal. So causal metasemantics may not need reference magnetism. Even so, joint-carving remains crucial to metasemantics, via its connection to causation. See the discussion of causal theories below.

[17] These remarks defend only against the extreme undetermination threatened by the Putnamian argument, *not* against the kind of underdetermination about which Fodor (or for that matter, Quine in *Word and Object* (1960c)) is worried. The simple causal theories that Fodor rejects because they don't allow for misrepresentation generally employ notions that are just as joint-carving as those he himself employs in his own theory. Whether 'rabbit' determinately means *rabbit* rather than *undetached rabbit part* is similarly not settled by reference magnetism. (Not that reference magnetism is irrelevant; it may play a role in the story of why 'identity' means identity, which in turn is relevant to 'rabbit' meaning rabbit.) Note that subsentential underdetermination of Quine's sort wouldn't result in indeterminacy in, e.g., whether (F) is true.

When understood in the Williamsian way, we might think of reference magnetism as a thesis of *meta*-metasemantics, rather than a metasemantic theory in its own right: reference magnetism may be combined with any metasemantics you like. A metasemantics is a metaphysical proposal about the nature of the reference relation; schematically: "reference is a relation of such-and-such a type". Millikan holds that reference is a relation that was chosen by natural selection to achieve a certain goal; the descriptivist says that reference is a relation that assigns values under which sentences in S—"definitional" sentences, let us say—come out true; and so on. Each proposal faces the problem of semantic skepticism: there are many relations of the proposed type. How to cut down on this multiplicity? The answer of reference magnetism is to reinterpret a metasemantic proposal that reference is a relation of type T as the proposal that reference is a reasonably joint-carving relation of type T.

One way a relation could fit one of the modified proposals is for it to be defined in terms of the concept of joint-carving. (Assuming, that is, that the concept of joint-carving itself is reasonably joint-carving—see sections 7.11.1 and 7.13.) For example, the modified descriptivist proposal says that reference is a reasonably joint-carving relation that assigns values under which definitional sentences come out true; here is a relation that fits that proposal: $R(w, x) =_{df} w$ is a word and x is the semantic value assigned to w by the interpretation I that maximizes the combination of i) joint-carvingness of assigned semantic values; and ii) truth assigned to the sentences that are definitional in the linguistic population that uses w. But this is not the only way that a relation could fit one of the modified proposals: the relation could be defined in terms of reasonably joint-carving concepts other than the concept of joint-carving itself.

If reference magnetism is merely a thesis of meta-metasemantics, it can survive the demise of individual metasemantic theories based on it. Consider again descriptivism. To be more concrete, consider what we might call "simple charity-based descriptivism", a close cousin of the reference-magnetism-enhanced descriptivism discussed in the previous paragraph. According to simple charity-based descriptivism, the correct interpretation of a language is that interpretation that maximizes the combination of two factors, each of which comes in degrees: "eligibility"—determined by the degree of naturalness of the semantic values it assigns; and "charity to use"—the number (on some suitable measure) of sentences believed (or reasonably believed, or . . .) by the speakers of the linguistic community that come out true under that interpretation.[18] Since it's the combination

---

[18]This view is often associated with Lewis; see especially:

> . . . overall eligibility of referents is a matter of degree, making total theory come true is a matter of degree, the two desiderata trade off. The correct, 'intended' interpretations are the ones that strike the best balance. (Lewis, 1984, pp. 227–8)

> . . . we need some give and take between the eligibility of referents and the other factors that make for 'intendedness', notably satisfaction of appropriate bits of theory. (Lewis, 1983*b*, p. 372)

However, Lewis's full view, as developed in (1969) and (1975), is more complex.

of eligibility and charity that must be maximized, this theory implies that an imperfectly charitable interpretation can nevertheless be the correct interpretation, if it assigns sufficiently joint-carving properties. A highly eligible interpretation can "trump" the superior charity of rival interpretations. Now, this prediction is in some cases correct, especially for "theoretical" terms—terms that are, intuitively, *intended* to stand for joint-carving meanings. When a term like 'mass' is introduced in physics, it's intended to stand for a fundamental physical magnitude, and so if there's a joint-carving property in the vicinity then that property is meant by 'mass', even if it doesn't quite fit the physicists' theory of 'mass'. But for nontheoretical terms, the prediction of trumping sometimes seems wrong.

For example, imagine a linguistic community that uses the word 'amulet' in the same way we do, except that it just so happens that—with a single exception—the objects they call 'amulets' are all and only the instances of some highly joint-carving property—gold, say.[19] The single exception is that they call one silver ornament an amulet as well. Now, the property gold carves very well at the joints—much more so than the property *gold or silver*, or the property *ornament or small piece of jewelry thought to give protection against evil, danger, or disease*, to quote the dictionary. Moreover, nearly everything the community says about "amulets" comes out true if 'amulet' is assigned the property *gold*. So such an assignment seems to best combine the virtues of eligibility and charity; its superior eligibility trumps the superior charity of interpretations that also count the silver ornament as an "amulet". The simplistic account thus seems to imply that 'amulet' means *gold* in this linguistic community. But this is absurd. The silver ornament obviously counts as an "amulet"; the fact that it lacks a joint-carving property shared by all other objects called 'amulets' is irrelevant.[20]

Now, this particular example is easily addressed with minor refinements. For example, charity to use might be strengthened to require counterfactual robustness: charitable interpretations must make sentences that would be believed in certain counterfactual circumstances come out true in those circumstances. Since the community in question is disposed to call appropriate ornaments 'amulets' whether or not they're made of gold, the assignment of *gold* to 'amulet' no longer counts as charitable. But the underlying point of the example cannot be so easily dismissed: the fact that gold carves much better at the joints than *being an ornament or small piece of jewelry thought to give protection against evil, danger, or disease* just seems *irrelevant* to the question of which is meant by 'amulet'. No matter how "charity to use" is understood, examples of this sort will surely emerge. Consider, for instance, this example from John Hawthorne: if there just happens to be a physically special line through the Ural mountains, that line isn't thereby the determinate boundary of Europe. The candidacy of a meaning for 'Europe' that takes this line into account is not enhanced by its superior eligibility.

---

[19] *Being a maximal continuous portion of gold,* to be more exact.

[20] I learned of such examples from Matti Eklund, John Hawthorne, and Robbie Williams.

It would seem, then, that for nontheoretical terms, the joint-carvingness of candidate semantic values plays a complex role. Highly joint-carving candidates don't automatically trump; simple charity-based descriptivism is too simplistic. But on the other hand, joint-carving isn't completely irrelevant either: the gruesome candidates of the semantic skeptic must still be excluded. Fortunately, even if we reject simple charity-based descriptivism, we can still appeal to reference magnetism to exclude the gruesome candidates. We can exclude them simply because they're gruesome—simply because they carve so badly at the joints. No reference relation connecting us to the gruesome candidates could take part in an explanatory theory. And we can say this even if we're uncertain what the true metasemantic theory is. In fact, we can say this even if we doubt that the truth about metasemantics can be captured in any simple formula—not an overly pessimistic doubt, given how few simple reductive theories of complex macro-phenomena have ever been given.

I have argued that reference magnetism solves the problem of radical semantic undetermination, is a consequence of a more general claim that explanatory theories must be stated in joint-carving terms, and does not presuppose descriptivism, but rather may be combined with any metasemantic theory that regards reference as explanatory. These conclusions collectively provide a reason to recognize structure: we need structure to answer the semantic skeptic. But there is a challenge to this reasoning: a causal metasemantics also lets us answer the skeptic. According to causal metasemantics, 'pig' means pigs rather hard-boiled eggs, say, because it is pigs rather than hard-boiled eggs that cause our uses of 'pig'.[21] See? No need for reference magnetism!

But a pure causal theory is likely to be insufficiently general. We need to rule out incorrect interpretations of mathematical and logical language, for example— as put forward by Skolemite skeptics about set-theoretic language, say, or Kripke's Wittgenstein—just as we need to rule out incorrect interpretations of 'pig' and 'has wings'; and it is hard to see how a pure causal account could do this. Likewise for terms of theoretical physics for hypothesized properties that are instantiated only under conditions present only at the time of the big bang, or even conditions that have never been (and will never be) present at all.[22] Likewise for predicates for spacetime structure. Likewise for many of the concepts of philosophy, to be discussed in subsequent chapters (though how much structure there is in these areas is debatable). Reference magnetism, on the other hand, can be combined with a broader, not purely causal, metasemantics to rule out bizarre interpretations in these cases.[23] This is not to say that causation has no role to play. It's perfectly

---

[21] In its most simplistic form, anyway. See Devitt and Sterelny (1999, chapters 4–5) for a more sophisticated discussion.

[22] Note that the Ramsey-Lewis method for defining theoretical terms (Lewis, 1970b) has no hope of working unless the property quantifiers are restricted to properties that carve at the joints.

[23] See Lewis (1983b) on mathematical semantic skepticism, chapter 10 on logical joint-carving, and section 3.4 on semantic determinacy for spacetime language.

compatible with reference magnetism, construed as a metametasemantics, that causation is one ingredient of the semantic glue.

Further, the notion of causation required by causal metasemantics may presuppose the notion of structure.[24] To bring this out, consider an intuitively incorrect interpretation of our language that matches the correct interpretation up until some specified time, 3000 A.D., say, but then goes haywire afterward. For the sake of definiteness, here is one such interpretation. Indulge in the harmless simplifying assumption of "super-substantivalism", according to which the physical world consists purely of spacetime, and let v be a one-to-one mapping over points of spacetime that maps each point at or before (the first instant of) 3000 A.D. to itself, and maps each point after 3000 A.D. to the simultaneous point 10^{10} km in some one chosen direction. Thus, v leaves everything before 3000 A.D. alone, and applies a Leibnizian shift to everything afterward. Now, the intuitively correct interpretation of our physical vocabulary assigns semantic values involving points of spacetime to physical vocabulary. So v induces a "shifted" interpretation: simply replace each point p in each semantic value with $v(p)$. What makes the intuitively correct interpretation rather than the shifted one correct? The shifted interpretation is derived from the correct one by a one-to-one mapping, and therefore renders the same sentences true. Furthermore, the shifted semantic values are instantiated by exactly the same spacetime points before the year 3000 A.D. as are the correct semantic values. The interpretations diverge only in the far future. So on the face of it, the shifted values seem to be just as causally responsible for past usage as the correct ones, in which case the pure causal metasemantics fails.

Veterans of the literature on natural kinds will be quick to notice that according to a "robust" conception of causation, the shifted semantic values will not be causally responsible for past usage—indeed, not causally responsible for anything at all. On this conception, even if a property P is involved in relations of counterfactual dependence, relations of nomic necessity or sufficiency, or what have you, it still may not be causally efficacious. If I hold a *grue* emerald in front of you, you will have green sensations; my holding the grue emerald plus background conditions necessitates those sensations; if I hadn't held up the grue emerald you wouldn't have had those sensations; and so on. (An object is "grue" iff it is green and first observed before 3000 A.D. or blue and not first observed before 3000 A.D. (Goodman, 1955, chapter III).) Nevertheless, so the story goes, my holding up the grue emerald did not cause you to have the sensations. Only my holding up of the green emerald caused you to do this.[25]

What we have learned is that causation must be robustly conceived, if it's to play the needed role in metasemantics. But how is robust causation to be understood? A robust cause might be defined as a joint-carving property involved

---

[24]Compare Hirsch (1993, pp. 63–5).

[25]Davidsonians about causation must rephrase: my holding of the grue emerald did not cause the sensations in virtue of its being a holding up of a grue thing. See Davidson (1970); Kim (1989).

in an event that causes something. Or instead as any property involved in an event that causes something, where our theory of causation invokes structure.[26] Or instead as any property that figures in a law of nature, where our theory of lawhood invokes structure.[27] Each of these approaches invokes the notion of structure. Only a primitivist, structure-free approach to causation (or laws) yields a structure-free approach to metasemantics; and against such approaches, recall section 2.4.

3.3 Induction and confirmation

We need structure to make sense of learning from experience.

The simplest model of learning from experience is that we remember past experiences, we expect the future to be like the past, and so we form appropriate expectations about the future. This model requires the notion of structure to be plausible. For the philosophical skeptic of section 1.2 will be quick to point out that any possible future is "like" the past along *some* dimension of similarity. The model had better say that the future is like the past in some *genuine* dimension, some dimension that respects nature's joints.

"The future is like the past" is too crude a concept on which to base a theory of learning from experience. We do a little better with the following concept: "observation *o* confirms sentence *S*". Analogs of the above worries about similarity then confront confirmation-based theories of learning from experience.

Which observations confirm a generalization 'All *F*s are *G*s'? A natural answer is the "Nicod principle": observations of *F*s that are *G*s confirm 'All *F*s are *G*s'. But suppose that an observation confirms any logical equivalent of any sentence that it confirms. Then, as Hempel (1945) pointed out, the observation of red roses confirms 'All ravens are black' (given the Nicod principle it confirms 'All nonblack things are nonravens', which is logically equivalent to 'All ravens are black'.) And as Goodman (1955, chapter III) pointed out, Nicod's principle implies that observations of green emeralds before 3000 A.D. confirm 'All emeralds are grue' (since green emeralds observed before 3000 A.D. are grue.) But anyone who believed that all emeralds are grue would expect emeralds observed after 3000 A.D. to be blue.

These conclusions can be avoided by restricting Nicod's principle in some way—most crudely, to predicates that carve at the joints.[28] Since 'is nonblack', 'is a nonraven', and 'grue' fail to carve at the joints, the restricted principle does not apply to generalizations containing them. In Goodman's terminology, only terms that carve at the joints are "projectible".

[26]Whether in its theory of events, or its theory of the causal relation, or both. See Lewis (1986*a*; 1973*a*; 1979).

[27]Even the primitivist accounts of Armstrong (1983), Dretske (1977), and Tooley (1987) presuppose sparse universals.

[28]Compare Quine (1969), though Quine held a deflationary account of joint-carving (under the rubric of "natural kinds").

'Observation o confirms sentence S' is less crude than 'the future is like the past', but it is still too crude a concept for a realistic theory of learning from experience. A realistic theory will need to consider relative confirmation, and so surely must consider quantitative measures of confirmation, and so must surely employ the concepts of probability theory.[29] It is natural to do this within a Bayesian framework, according to which i) a rational subject's beliefs at a time consist in a probability distribution over all propositions, whose values measure the subject's "degrees of belief" ("subjective probabilities", "credences") in the propositions; and ii) the rational subject updates her degrees of belief by conditionalizing on propositions describing her experiences.[30] In this framework one can introduce various quantitative measures of confirmation, and can characterize relative confirmation.[31]

Bayesianism proper tells the rational subject what method she should use for updating whatever degrees of belief she began with: conditionalization. But it says very little about what those initial degrees of belief ought to be like (beyond the minimal demand that they must satisfy the axioms of the probability calculus, and perhaps be "nondogmatic" in never assigning the values 0 and 1 except to necessary falsehoods and truths). Now, *subjective* Bayesians say that Bayesianism proper is all there is to rationality. That is, provided a subject has updated her beliefs by conditionalization (and at each moment obeyed the minimal synchronic demands), she has done all that rationality requires. *Objective* Bayesians, on the other hand, add further synchronic requirements on credences beyond the minimal ones. One's credences must, perhaps, assign higher probabilities to "simple" hypotheses, other things being equal, or obey some sort of principle of indifference, dividing credence equally over symmetric possibilities.

This difference between objective and subjective Bayesianism matters greatly, since the effect that evidence has on a Bayesian conditionalizer depends heavily on her prior probability distribution. Bizarre prior probability distributions will result in bizarre responses to evidence. Consider, for example, making a series of pre-3000 A.D. observations of green emeralds. Intuitively, this should result in increasing confidence that emeralds observed after 3000 A.D. will likewise be green. This increasing confidence is indeed forthcoming for a Bayesian if she begins with an appropriate prior probability function Pr—one that assigns high probability to emeralds observed after 3000 A.D. being green conditional on earlier observed emeralds being green. But if she begins instead with a prior probability function Pr′ that assigns high probabilities to emeralds observed after

---

[29]Indeed, it has been suggested that if one attends to the comparative notion of confirmation, Hempel's puzzle, anyway, evaporates. See Fitelson (2006) for a survey.

[30]That is, if the subject begins with probability function Pr, and has an experience described by proposition e, then she will subsequently have a probability function that assigns to any proposition, p, the probability that Pr assigned to p conditional on e, i.e., $\Pr(p/e)$, i.e., $\frac{\Pr(p \wedge e)}{\Pr(e)}$.

[31]See Fitelson (2006); Sober (1994).

3000 A.D. being *blue* conditional on earlier observed emeralds being green, then observing the green emeralds will result in increasing confidence that emeralds observed after 3000 A.D. will be blue. Garbage in, garbage out.

The pure subjective Bayesian will say that rationality says nothing about the choice between Pr and Pr'. If one person begins with Pr, and another begins with Pr', and each then receives exactly the same evidence, which evidence includes observations before 3000 A.D. of many green emeralds (and no blue ones), and each updates her beliefs by conditionalization, then at the end of this process, neither has behaved more rationally than the other. This despite the fact that the second will become increasingly certain that emeralds observed after 3000 A.D. will be blue!

Subjective Bayesians embrace this conclusion. Fascinatingly, this descendent of Hume's notorious attitude toward induction is not uncommon in contemporary formal epistemology. Is this because the field draws the formally inclined, and the problem of constraining priors has proved formally intractable? At any rate, any Bayesian who wants to say that the second person has responded irrationally to the evidence must find fault with Pr'. (Since the subject used the correct rule of updating, the fault must lie with her prior degrees of belief.)

How might Pr' be criticized? One (vague, in need of refinement) strategy would invoke "simplicity": Pr' is worse than Pr because its description is less simple. The probabilities of Pr that concern emerald color can be given by simple rules that are uniform across all emeralds, such as: "for any emerald, the probability of that emerald being green, conditional on many other emeralds being green, is high". But to specify Pr' we need more complex rules giving different conditional probabilities for an emerald's being green, depending on the times at which earlier green emeralds were observed.

But suppose we speak the language of 'grue' rather than the language of 'green'.[32] In this language, Pr' can be specified with simpler rules, such as "for any emerald, the probability of that emerald being grue, conditional on many other emeralds being grue, is high", whereas Pr will require more complex rules, specifying different conditional probabilities for an emerald's being grue, depending on the times at which earlier grue emeralds were observed. Whether a probability function is simple depends on the language in which it is described. So a meaningful simplicity-based criticism of Pr' requires some sort of restriction on the language in which we evaluate simplicity.

Similar remarks apply to attempts to constrain priors using some version of the principle of indifference. Any version of this principle says to distribute credence equally over "symmetric" possibilities. But which possibilities count as

---

[32]This language replaces 'green' and 'blue' by 'grue' and '*bleen*', where an object is bleen iff it is blue and first observed before 3000 A.D., or green and not first observed before 3000 A.D. In a sense this language equals the 'green'/'blue' language in descriptive power; one simply says 'grue' instead of 'green' and 'bleen' instead of 'blue' for objects first observed before 3000 A.D., and 'bleen' instead of 'green' and 'grue' instead of 'blue' for other objects.

symmetric will depend on what language we use to describe the possibilities. If we use the 'grue' language, an otherwise reasonable principle of indifference might recommend Pr′ over Pr. Now, even with a suitable language picked out, there are serious obstacles. To take a familiar example, suppose a factory is making cubes of varying sizes. If I have no information specific to a given cube produced by the factory, how should I assign prior probabilities to propositions of the form *the side length of the cube is between l_1 and l_2*? In direct proportion to the difference $l_1 - l_2$, one wants to say. And how should I assign prior probabilities to propositions of the form *the face area of the cube is between a_1 and a_2*? In direct proportion to the difference $a_1 - a_2$, one wants to say. But these two answers are incompatible (van Fraassen, 1989, 303–4). So selecting the right language doesn't, on its own, solve the problem of formulating principles of indifference. But without an appropriate language, we cannot even get started on a solution.

To constrain prior probability distributions, then, we need some way to pick out appropriate languages for evaluating simplicity, symmetry, and related notions. And—to finally get to the point—it seems reasonable to pick them out by using the notion of structure. Now, even given the notion of structure, there are nontrivial questions about how exactly to pick out the appropriate languages. For example, *how* well do the predicates in the appropriate languages need to carve at the joints? Again, the appeal to structure is the beginning of a solution, not the end of one.

The argument of this section has been that structure fills a need in epistemology. A reply would be that epistemology does not demand structure objectively construed; a conception of "structure" tied to human history, biology, psychology, or interests would do. My reply to such challenges elsewhere is that subjectivity in structure would infect all notions to which structure is connected (similarity, intrinsicality, duplication, laws of nature, and so on). But in this case, the infected notion would be epistemic value. And perhaps we should embrace the idea that values in general are not objective.

But even if epistemic value is subjective along *some* dimensions, we shouldn't embrace the idea that it's subjective along all dimensions. Let Pr be a rational credence function we ought to adopt and Pr′ be one that we ought not to adopt. Intuitively speaking, we might embrace subjectivity in the "oughtiness" of the obligation while rejecting subjectivity in the distinction between Pr and Pr′. The objective facts might not mandate that we have our notion, or any notion, of epistemic obligation, but might nevertheless mandate that we choose Pr over Pr′ if we do have our notion (or anything like our notion). We will return to this issue in section 4.2.

3.4 Intrinsic structure in physical spaces

We need structure to understand talk in physics of the "intrinsic" structure of space, time, spacetime, and other spaces.[33]

---

[33] See also Bricker (1993); Sider (1993*a*, chapter 9).

NonEuclidean geometries were discovered in the early nineteenth century, proved consistent relative to Euclidean geometry later that century, and applied in physics by Einstein in the early twentieth century, in his general theory of relativity. Taken at face value, Einstein's claim that physical spacetime is curved is a substantive claim in direct conflict with the assumption of flat spacetime implicit in classical Newtonian physics (and in the special theory of relativity as well). But taken at face value, this claim raises various philosophical questions: epistemic, semantic, and metaphysical.

Let us approach the questions through the simpler case of spatial, rather than spacetime, curvature. Imagine a series of experiments, carried out with rigid measuring rods and the like, that apparently show that space in a certain region is curved. The epistemic questions arise because we do not observe space directly; what we observe is things *in* space, such as measuring rods. Effects attributable to curved space could instead result from systematic distortions to the rods. While this may at first appear to be mere Cartesian demonry, compare two alternative hypotheses. According to the first hypothesis, the measurements result from curvature. According to the second, space is flat but there are "universal forces" that affect all matter, cannot be blocked, and systematically shrink and expand the measuring rods so that their lengths are exactly as the first hypothesis predicts.[34] Unlike Cartesian skeptical hypotheses, the second hypothesis is not scientifically absurd. The epistemological question, then, is: What reason could we have for attributing distortions in our measuring rods to spatial curvature rather than to universal forces?

The semantic questions concern how the meaning of spatial language could be fixed in such a way that it would remain an open question whether space is curved. To simplify, pretend that all spatial facts may be expressed using Tarski's predicates:[35]

> point *x* is *between* points *y* and *z*
>
> points *x* and *y* are *congruent* to points *z* and *w*

One sort of semantic question arises only given an extreme empiricist philosophy of language. If every meaningful predicate must be associated with verification

---

[34] See Reichenbach (1958, chapter 1).

[35] These are the predicates from Tarski's axiomatization of Euclidean geometry; see Tarski (1959); Tarski and Givant (1999). Really, though, the fundamental metrical facts should probably not be taken to be direct point-to-point distance comparisons as in Tarski's system, but should rather be local metrical facts, from which distances along paths may be recovered. On the other hand, the standard development of a local metric should probably not be taken at face value, since it grounds metric structure in the metric tensor, a mathematical object involving real numbers. Surely the fundamental distance facts are purely about points (as they are in Tarski's account). Thus what we really want is a synthetic geometry from which one can prove representation theorems about the metric tensor (see Field (1980); Mundy (1987) for two approaches to representation theorems). I do not know whether such an account exists.

conditions for its application, then given the previous paragraph, the predicates 'between' and 'congruent' would seem not to be meaningful.

Other semantic worries will have force even for nonverificationists. If Einstein is right and Newton is wrong about curvature, then the referents of 'between' and 'congruent' must satisfy nonEuclidean rather than Euclidean axioms. But in addition to having an interpretation under which they satisfy nonEuclidean axioms, 'between' and 'congruent' also have an interpretation in which they satisfy Euclidean axioms. (The Euclidean axioms are true in the abstract model whose domain is $\mathbb{R}^3$ and in which the predicates are interpreted in the obvious way. Since the set of physical points of space has the same cardinality as $\mathbb{R}^3$, the model in $\mathbb{R}^3$ induces a model in physical space.) So if Einstein is to be right and Newton wrong, it must be that only one of these assignments is the *correct* assignment, the *intended* interpretation of 'between' and 'congruent'. But what determines that one of these assignments is the *correct* interpretation? We cannot specify the intended interpretation of 'congruent' by saying that "it is to apply to x, y, z, and w when the *distance* between x and y is the same as the distance between z and w", for 'distance' is in the same boat as 'congruent'; how is its intended interpretation determined?

The metaphysical questions concern the same issue as the semantic ones, only more directly. In what would the fact that spacetime is curved consist? In the fact that the congruence and betweenness relations satisfy nonEucledian axioms, is the obvious reply. But since there are continuum-many spacetime points, there exist "Euclidean-congruence" and "Euclidean-betweenness" relations that satisfy Euclidean axioms. So in what sense is spacetime *really* Euclidean? What makes the "real" betweenness and congruence relations, as opposed to their Euclidean counterparts, "physically significant"?

We face the same questions when reading physics textbooks on special or general relativity that speak of the "intrinsic structure" of physical space, time, and spacetime. In classical physics, we are told, spacetime is flat, and there is a "well-defined" relation of simultaneity, whereas in Minkowski spacetime there is no such relation of simultaneity—there is no "distinguished" notion of simultaneity. But of course, there are relations—sets of ordered pairs, anyway—between space-like separated points of Minkowski spacetime that foliate the spacetime; many such relations. What does it mean to say that none of these relations is "distinguished"?[36]

Geometrical conventionalists like Henri Poincaré (1952, Part II) and Hans Reichenbach (1958, Chapter 1) give a deflationary answer to the semantic questions that answers the epistemological questions, and which implicitly assumes a deflationary answer to the metaphysical questions. Return to the question of how to specify the intended interpretation of 'congruent'. According to Reichenbach, a theoretical predicate like 'congruent' requires a "coordinative" definition, a def-

---

[36] See North (2009) on structure in physics generally.

inition that correlates the predicate with something that is (relatively) observable. An example of a coordinative definition would be the definition of straight lines through spacetime as the paths of light rays in vacuum. We might think to give a coordinative definition of congruence in terms of measuring rods: points of space are congruent when they can be the endpoints of a single measuring rod. But measuring rods can be distorted by forces. Might we then define congruence in terms of measuring rods unaffected by forces? The problem is that 'force' is itself a term in need of a coordinative definition, since one can no more directly measure forces than congruence. What Reichenbach says, in essence, is that one must simultaneously give coordinative definitions of 'force' and 'congruent' in terms of measuring rods: congruent points are those picked out by the endpoints of a measuring rod that is not subject to forces. Since this coordinative definition constrains two terms, there is a certain amount of freedom in assigning meanings to those terms. One can understand 'force' and 'congruent' so that space is Euclidean but there are universal forces acting on all objects that produce the measurements that we make, or one can understand 'force' and 'congruent' so that space is nonEuclidean and there are no universal forces.[37] In fact, physicists have preferred the latter course, and so we speak of space as being curved. But this is in part a matter of arbitrary definition; physicists could have chosen the former course. They chose the latter only because the resulting physics was simpler. So according to conventionalists like Reichenbach, it is at best misleading to say that space itself is curved, that space is *intrinsically* curved. 'Space is curved' is true to say given the linguistic choices that physicists have in fact made. But those choices were arbitrary, and moreover are inextricably tied to the conventional choice of whether to speak of universal forces.

Given this view about the semantics of spatial language, the epistemological questions are immediately answered. How do we know that space is curved, rather than being flat but accompanied by compensating universal forces? We know this simply by knowing which conventions our linguistic community has adopted. (Better: knowledge of linguistic conventions plus empirical observation tells us that 'space is curved' is the right description. If different linguistic conventions had been adopted, the same observations would have called for the description 'space is flat'.)

Reichenbach (unsurprisingly) does not address the metaphysical question. But it seems clear that he would regard talk of space as being "intrinsically" flat or curved as misguided, given the need for coordinative definitions. Insofar as conventionalists have a metaphysics of spatial structure at all, it is that space is not intrinsically structured (or perhaps that talk of intrinsic structure makes no sense).

---

[37] Better: we can understand 'force' and 'congruent' so that the sentence 'space is Euclidean' comes out true, etc.

What might an anti-conventionalist—realist—account of physical geometry look like?[38] Here is what the realist *wants* to say. About semantics, spatial predicates like 'between' and 'congruent' can be understood *purely spatially*; they need no coordinative definitions. And they are attached to particular relations over physical points, which satisfy nonEuclidean axioms (assuming that Einstein is right). As for metaphysics, space is intrinsically structured; the genuine betweenness and congruence relations are privileged in a way that Euclidean-betweenness and Euclidean-congruence are not. The naïve and natural picture of physical geometry one gets from physics is thereby vindicated. The epistemological problems then confront us head-on. But these problems should be solved the way we realists solve all such problems of theory being underdetermined by observation: by appealing to criteria—"simplicity" is a common placeholder—that choose between observationally indistinguishable theories. (If such criteria do not deliver a verdict, we remain agnostic until some new test or consideration breaks the stalemate.)

A realist about structure has a clear path to this realism about physical geometry. Metaphysically, the distinction enjoyed by the genuine betweenness and congruence relations is that they are part of reality's distinguished structure: they carve perfectly at the joints, unlike any relations of Euclidean-betweenness and Euclidean-congruence. Semantically, given any reasonable metasemantics for theoretical terms, 'between' and 'congruent' attach to betweenness and congruence rather than to any Euclidean-betweenness and Euclidean-congruence relations precisely because only the former are part of the world's genuine structure. Reichenbach was led to his position by his insistence on the need for coordinative definitions, deriving ultimately from an internalist and highly empiricist approach to meaning. But a more reasonable metasemantics will allow a role for a nonobservational and externalist determinant of meaning: the world's structure.[39]

More generally, questions about metric, affine, topological, and other structure of space, spacetime, and other physical spaces are questions about the distinguished structure of those spaces. There is a substantive purely spatiotemporal fact of the matter as to whether spacetime is Galilean, neoNewtonian, Minkowskian, or a curved Lorentzian manifold.[40] The fact is given by the joint-carving features of points of spacetime. If, for example, the joint-carving features of points of physical spacetime are as described by Minkowski's theory, then physical spacetime is

---

[38]Nerlich (1976), especially chapter 9, defends realism about spatiotemporal structure, and distinguishes this realism from realism about the existence of entities (chapter 5, §6). See also Bricker (1993).

[39]Grünbaum (1973) also defended conventionalism about metric structure, but based it on metaphysical considerations rather than on an empiricist account of meaning. An intrinsic metric, Grünbaum argued, would have to be definable from facts intrinsic to the points, but if space is continuous then there are no facts intrinsic to points that suffice for the definition. The realist about structure, however, regards the distinguished structure of space as constituting facts intrinsic to points from which a metric may be defined.

[40]Or even whether there is a fundamental four-dimensional spacetime at all, as opposed to a massively dimensional configuration space; see Albert (1996); North (2009; 2010).

Minkowskian, and there is "no physically distinguished relation of simultaneity" in the sense that there is no joint-carving relation that foliates the spacetime (nor can any foliation be defined from the joint-carving relations over points).

Spacetime could have had a structure that would have vindicated a kind of geometrical conventionalism. Suppose spacetime had lacked distinguished metrical structure—suppose there had been joint-carving topological features but no joint-carving metrical features. Then no metric would have been distinguished from any other, and spacetime would have been a kind of amorphous "point soup". Reality might at the same time have lacked sufficient structure to define forces. In such a Reichenbachian world, we would have been free to choose either of a pair of coordinative definitions, simultaneously defining force and metric predicates. Neither choice would have carved reality at its joints better than the other. Metric and force predicates would require coordinative definitions in such a world, not because of general semantic considerations, but rather because the world would lack the structure needed to supply semantic determinacy. What reason do we have to think that *our* world has any more structure? The fact that physical theories with primitive metrical predicates have been so successful (section 2.3).

4 Substantivity

Structure is the key to understanding an elusive notion of substantivity.[1]

4.1 Nonsubstantive questions

Is Robinson Crusoe a bachelor? Is a water glass a cup? Is a protrusion from the floor of a deep ocean, whose tip is a tiny island, a mountain (Hawthorne, 2006*b*, vii.)? Is "some nonsense made out of sour green apple liqueur", served in a V-shaped glass, a martini (Bennett, 2009)?

Philosophers like to argue about such things at bars, but even they regard the questions as being, in some sense, *nonsubstantive* (shallow, nonobjective, conventional, terminological). By contrast, the question of whether electrons repel one another is substantive (deep, objective, nonconventional, about the world).

This is intuitively clear; but in what does the lack of substantivity consist? The answer is not straightforward. It's not a matter of mind-dependence, for example. Suppose, for the sake of argument, that Hawthorne's protrusion is indeed a mountain. Then, even if no people had existed, the protrusion would still have been a mountain; and if everyone had said 'Let such protrusions not be mountains', the protrusion would still have been a mountain. To paraphrase Lincoln, calling a tail a leg wouldn't make it one.

(The protrusion wouldn't have been *called* a 'mountain' if people had not existed, or had spoken or acted in certain ways. The linguistic fact that the sentence 'The protrusion is a mountain' is true *is* mind-dependent, since whether the sentence is true depends on what it means, and what it means is mind-dependent. But the same goes for every true sentence, even 'Electrons repel one another'. So the mind-dependence of the linguistic fact isn't what makes the question of whether the protrusion is a mountain nonsubstantive.)

Nor is the lack of substantivity due to the questions being *about* words or concepts—not in the most straightforward sense anyway. Questions such as "Is 'attorney' synonymous with 'lawyer'?" and "Does the concept of a sport include gymnastics?", which name or quantify over words or concepts, are in a straightforward sense about words or concepts; but our nonsubstantive questions are not about words or concepts in this sense. The question of whether martinis can be made of sour apple liqueur is about *martinis*, and what they can be made of. It is

---

[1] Related work includes Chalmers (2011), Fine (2001) on nonfactualist discourse, and Sidelle (2007) on verbal disputes.

no more about 'martini', or the concept of a martini, than the question of whether electrons repel one another is about 'electron' or the concept of an electron.[2]

Nor is a question's nonsubstantivity due to its having no answer—to there being no fact of the matter as to what its answer is. For the nonsubstantive questions considered above might well have answers. Edmund Gettier (1963) uncovered a surprising feature of our concept of knowledge: that justified true belief does not suffice for its application. For all we know, clever Gettiers could convince us beyond the shadow of a doubt that our concepts of bachelor, cup, and the rest yield answers to our questions. (As the case of knowledge shows, this possibility isn't ruled out by the failure of a few hours or centuries of armchair reflection.) But the questions still seem nonsubstantive.

What if there will be no Gettier-like successes in conceptual archaeology? It's arguable that our questions then have no answers. The main opposition to this conclusion comes from the epistemicists about vagueness (Sorensen, 2001; Williamson, 1994), who say that even without the facts that Gettiers uncover—at least in part, surprising facts of usage that nevertheless are readily appreciated once noticed—the questions have answers.[3] But if we reject epistemicism—as I think we should—then we may well want to say that the questions without lurking Gettiers have no answers. Where our conceptions of bachelors, cups, and mountains run out, so to speak, there are no "further facts" to be discovered. Failure to have an answer is thus sometimes symptomatic of nonsubstantivity. But since it is not necessary for nonsubstantivity, it is not the underlying cause.

The failure of the questions to be substantive, then, is hard to pin down; it's neither mind-dependence, nor a conceptual or linguistic subject matter, nor the lack of an answer. This might remind one of a problematic familiar from discussions of antirealism.[4] Begin, for example, with expressivism about morality, according to which the function of assertions about right and wrong is to convey the speaker's attitudes, rather than to "depict objective facts". But make the expressivism sophisticated, so that it applies to logically complex sentences; and further, adopt a deflationary approach to truth and related concepts. Then you will be willing to say things like "moral sentences can be true" (since "'killing is wrong' is true" boils down to "Killing is wrong", and you're willing to say the latter because you're down on killing), "there are moral facts" (since "it's a fact that it's wrong to kill" boils down to "Killing is wrong"), and "there are moral properties (since "killing has the property of being wrong" boils down to "Killing is wrong"). In what, then, does your moral antirealism consist? There are indeed analogies here with my examples. The nonsubstantivity of my questions does not consist in discourse about bachelors (cups, etc.) failing to be truth-apt, or there failing to be facts about bachelors, or there failing to exist a property of being a

---

[2]Compare Williamson (2007, chapter 2).

[3]Though they may have no "determinate" answers, given an epistemic reading of 'determinate'.

[4]See Blackburn (1993); Fine (2001); Rosen (1994); Wright (1992).

bachelor. But the analogy quickly breaks down, since an expressivist semantics for discourse about bachelors, cups, and the rest is clearly a nonstarter. Nor is J. L. Mackie's (1977) error theory a good model: our beliefs about bachelors, cups, and the like are surely not radically mistaken (not because of their nonsubstantivity, anyway).

4.2 Substantivity characterized

I think that our questions are nonsubstantive because their answers turn on which of a range of equally good available meanings we choose for the words in those questions.[5] Better (though this will need further refining): for one or more expressions E (e.g. 'bachelor') in a nonsubstantive question, the semantic candidates for E (unmarried-adult-male, unmarried-adult-male-eligible-for-marriage, etc.) are such that i) each opposing view about the question comes out true on some candidate; and ii) no candidate carves at the joints better than the others. If E uniquely means one of these candidates, this is not because that candidate is intrinsically privileged. It is only because our linguistic community happened to select that candidate rather than one of its mates as the meaning of E.[6] The situation may be depicted thus:

$$E \quad \left.\begin{array}{l} m_1 \\ m_2 \\ m_3 \\ m_4 \\ m_5 \end{array}\right\} \begin{array}{l} \text{no candidate carves at the joints better} \\ \text{than the rest; the question's answer} \\ \text{turns on which candidate is adopted} \end{array}$$

Given what we happen to mean by E, the nonsubstantive question may have an answer, but we could just as easily have meant something else by E, something equally good, one of the other non-joint-carving candidates in the vicinity, in which case the question would have had a different answer.

A substantive question is one that is not nonsubstantive. The answer to a substantive question is not sensitive to a choice amongst equally joint-carving candidates. Now, one way for this to happen is for the question to be cast in perfectly joint-carving terms (and for none of the expressions in the question to have *multiple* perfectly joint-carving candidates). Each expression E in the question may then be depicted as follows:

---

[5]The account requires there to be some way of making sense of quantification over "meanings", but not that such quantification be fundamental.

[6]How did we select the candidate? Perhaps it is the most charitable candidate given our use of E; perhaps only it is relevantly causally related to our use of E. . .—the answer depends on the truth about metasemantics.

$$E \quad \left. \begin{matrix} m_1 \\ m_2 \\ \boldsymbol{m} \\ m_4 \\ m_5 \end{matrix} \right\} \quad \text{One candidate is special; it carves at the joints much better than the others}$$

But this is not the only way for a question to be substantive. I drank no alcohol on January 1, 2011; thus, even though the question of whether I had a martini that night is not cast in particularly joint-carving terms, it is substantive because it has the same answer (no) under all candidates for its terms. Being cast in joint-carving terms is thus not the sole determiner of substantivity. Being wholly cast in perfectly joint-carving terms is normally sufficient for substantivity (since rarely does an expression have multiple joint-carving candidates), but it's not necessary.

Rival conceptions locate nonsubstantivity in some defect of the proposition in question—for example, mind-dependence, failure to have a determinate truth-value, and so on. On my conception, even questions without such defects can be nonsubstantive. The question of Hawthorne's protrusion is nonsubstantive even if 'the protrusion is a mountain' expresses a true mind-independent proposition about the physical world. The nonsubstantivity is not due to any defect of this proposition, but rather to the proposition's "metasemantic surroundings"—the other propositions that the sentence could have expressed had we meant a different candidate for 'mountain'. It is the failure of the actually expressed proposition to stand out from its surroundings (and the fact that it differs in truth-value from some of the surrounding propositions) that generates the nonsubstantivity. Put another way, the nonsubstantivity results from our process of selection of the proposition, rather than being intrinsic to the proposition itself.

What follows is a series of refinements and amplifications of this account. This process is not intended as a conceptual analysis of **substantivity**, thought of as pretheoretically given. The aim is rather to introduce a concept that sheds light on the phenomena. Also, this concept is not intended to apply to everything that might justly be called "nonsubstantive". For example, it isn't meant to apply to equivocation between distinct lexical meanings (as in a dispute over whether geese live by "the bank", in which one disputant means river bank and the other means financial bank), or disputes involving expressivist language. Nor is it meant to capture the shallowness of inquiry into whether the number of electrons in the entire universe is even or odd (an inquiry that is substantive in my sense, but pointless). My goal is simply to identify one distinctive—and neglected—type of nonsubstantivity.

On to the amplifications and refinements. First, I will speak of substantivity for many items: sentences, questions, disputes, and so on. The definition may be adjusted in obvious ways for these items. Examples: a question (construed as the set of sentences that are its possible answers—this was implicit above) is nonsubstantive iff the candidates of some expression are equistructural and each answer comes out true under some candidate; a sentence is nonsubstantive iff the candidates of some expression are equistructural and both the sentence and its negation come out true under some candidate.

Second, I said earlier that being cast in perfectly joint-carving terms normally suffices for substantivity. But being cast in *highly* albeit not perfectly joint-carving terms—a common occurrence in the special sciences—also normally suffices for substantivity. Except for questions that strain the boundaries of taxonomy (a relatively uncommon occurrence), special-science questions normally fall into one of the following two categories: i) each expression has a candidate meaning that carves far better than all other candidates; or ii) each expression has a range of candidates that carve far better than do other candidates not in the range, and the question's answer is insensitive to choices of candidates within these ranges. In either case, the question is substantive.

Third, some disputes don't seem substantive even though there is a unique joint-carving candidate, if that joint-carving candidate is of the wrong sort. Recall Hawthorne's physically significant line in the Ural mountains (section 3.2), and consider the question of whether a certain location near the line is part of Europe. The answer to this question turns on which of several candidates we mean by 'Europe'. Now, given the line, one of these candidates carves at the joints far better than the rest, and so my account classifies this dispute as substantive. But that seems wrong. The line through the Urals, though physically distinguished, isn't geographically or politically distinguished, and therefore seems irrelevant to the boundaries of Europe. The physically significant line is indeed a joint in nature, but it's the wrong sort of joint in nature, relative to a dispute over 'Europe'.

What is the "right sort"? I don't have a finished answer, but here is the beginnings of one. Suppose an expression, E, is a theoretical term, in the sense of section 3.2—a term intended to stand for a joint in nature. Suppose, further, that there is a single joint-carving meaning, m, that satisfies enough of the "core theory" that is collectively associated with E by the participants in the dispute. Then m is the right sort of joint-carving meaning. For example, in a dispute over whether any electrons are located in a certain region, R, of space, the term 'electron' is a theoretical term, and the property of *being an electron* will satisfy enough of the core theory associated with 'electron' by the disputants—a theory saying that electrons are subatomic particles that orbit nuclei, have negative charge, a certain mass, and so on. Thus, this property will be the right sort of joint-carving candidate meaning, and the dispute is substantive.

It's important that the right sorts of joint-carving meanings needn't satisfy *all* of the core theory, since there can be substantive disputes even when the core theory is somewhat mistaken. The dispute over whether any electrons are located in R remains substantive even if scientists are mistaken about the mass of an electron. The property *being an electron* remains the right sort of joint-carving meaning because it satisfies enough of the core theory. Also, there can be substantive disputes over which central principles electrons satisfy—over what the mass of an electron is, for example. In such cases the core theory that is "collectively" associated with 'electron' will be drawn from the principles not under dispute. To have a substantive dispute about electrons, there must remain enough common ground about what electrons are so that all disputants can be regarded as talking about the same thing.

What is the "wrong sort" of joint-carving candidate? Hawthorne's line is the wrong sort to render a dispute about 'Europe' substantive because 'Europe' is not a theoretical term; 'Europe' isn't intended to stand for a joint-carving meaning at all. It might be objected that 'Europe' *is* a theoretical term, albeit one of political science or geography rather than physics. But then the physically significant line will still be of the wrong sort, since it won't satisfy the associated core theory. That core theory will be a political or geographical theory, not a physical theory, and the physical line won't play a role in any distinctively political or geographical laws or explanations. (If it did, then it wouldn't be merely "physically significant", and the dispute would then be substantive.)

The revised account, then, says that a nonsubstantive question is one containing an expression E whose candidates are such that i) each opposing view about the question comes out true on some candidate; and ii) no candidate carves at the joints *in the right way for E* better than the rest. A candidate c_1 carves better "in the right way for E" than another candidate c_2, to a first approximation anyway, iff E is a theoretical term, c_1 satisfies enough of the core theory associated with E, and c_1 carves better than does c_2.

One might worry about the fact that this definition makes *all* differences in joint-carving for candidates of nontheoretical terms irrelevant to substantivity. Recall the question of whether I had a martini on January 1, 2011, which is intuitively substantive (and has the answer *no*) because I drank no alcohol that night. The current definition counts this question as *non*substantive if its answer is sensitive to the choice of candidates for its nontheoretical terms, regardless of distinctions of joint-carving amongst those candidates. But won't there be Putnam-like candidates, based on arbitrary permutations, under which the question's answer is yes? Perhaps it would be enough to reply that Putnamian semantic values are not candidates because they just couldn't be meant by any linguistic community. Or perhaps—the more likely case, I fear—a subtler definition of "the right sort" is needed, no doubt based on a subtler distinction than that between theoretical and nontheoretical terms.

Fourth, 'candidate' needs to be clarified. On the one hand, it shouldn't be taken too narrowly, to include only what supervaluationists call "precisifications". Precisifications of E are, intuitively, those semantic values that our usage of E doesn't definitely rule out. But suppose that a Gettier could show us that our usage of 'bachelor' definitely excludes Crusoe. Then semantic values under which 'Crusoe is a bachelor' is true aren't precisifications of 'bachelor', but they should count as candidates for 'bachelor' (since whether Crusoe is a bachelor is paradigmatically nonsubstantive). So candidatehood is consistent with a certain degree of "mismatch with usage". On the other hand, match with usage isn't *irrelevant*. The property of being an electron fails to be a candidate for 'bachelor' precisely because it doesn't come close to fitting our usage of that term. A candidate meaning m needn't perfectly match our usage of E; but the mismatch can't be too severe. If a linguistic community, roughly in our circumstances, *could* have used E to mean m without seeming "semantically alien"—could have used E to reach "the same semantic goal" as we use E to reach, albeit perhaps by a different route—then m is a candidate for E.

This is admittedly pretty vague. Now, it's fine if 'substantive' and related notions are rough and ready, come in degrees, admit borderline cases, and so on. Still, to firm up the notion a bit, consider another example (there will be more later). Suppose, for the sake of argument, that i) causation does not carve at the joints; and ii) in English, 'cause' has a counterfactual analysis. Now consider a linguistic community L in which 'cause' has a covering-law analysis, but in which the *conceptual role* of 'cause' is similar to its role in English, in the following sense. Causation, in both our community and L, stands in a complex network of conceptual relations to concepts of moral responsibility, control, and myriad others. Although the members of L use 'cause' differently from how we do, there are also corresponding differences in their usage of 'responsible', 'control', and other such terms, so that the network of relations is preserved. I want to count this linguistic community as not being (too) semantically alien. Given the similarity of conceptual role, speakers of L use 'cause' with the same semantic goal as we do with our word 'cause'. Thus the covering-law meaning is a candidate for 'cause'; and as a result, assuming that causation doesn't carve at the joints, the question of whether effects counterfactually depend on their causes is nonsubstantive.

Fifth, my notion of substantivity is a metaphysical one, to be contrasted with a notion of conceptual substantivity. Many expressions that fail to carve at the joints are embedded in our conceptual lives in important ways; and questions involving such expressions can have a sort of conceptual substantivity even when my analysis counts them as (metaphysically) nonsubstantive. Suppose again that the fact that causes counterfactually imply their effects is nonsubstantive in my sense. Still, discovering that causation is counterfactual dependence might reveal something important about our conceptual scheme, in contrast with a discovery that cups are glasses, which we would regard as an intellectual trifle. Given the network of connections between causation and other concepts, the discovery about causation would have far-reaching implications. And causation matters to us in ways that the concept of a cup does not—partly because of the network. True, in learning that causes counterfactually imply their effects, we are primarily learning something about ourselves; that's the metaphysically nonsubstantive part. But we're learning something important about ourselves.

Sixth, my notion of substantivity is essentially metalinguistic. Consider:

(1) Drinks with sour apple liqueur are not martinis.

In my opinion, (1) is true; 'martini' means *drink made of gin or vodka and vermouth with such-and-such proportions*. (If you disagree, replace (1), mutatis mutandis, with its negation.) But we could have used 'martini' differently, so as to include sour apple liqueur drinks, without being semantically alien or carving worse at the joints. So (1) is nonsubstantive. But now consider:

(2) Drinks with sour apple liqueur are not drinks made of gin or vodka and vermouth with such-and-such proportions.

(2) is substantive. Although the terms in (2)—'sour apple liqueur', 'drink', 'gin', and so on—do not carve at the joints, they have no candidates under which (2) comes out false. But (2) is just the result of substituting for 'martini' in (1) an expression that has the same meaning (though not the same candidates). Moral: sentences that express the same proposition can differ in substantivity. This is a feature of my account, not a bug. Notions like substantivity, depth, objectivity, and the rest have proved so elusive partly because philosophers have been looking in the wrong place: in what we say with the disputed vocabulary.[7] Substantivity, or lack thereof, is not intrinsic to semantic values. We might put this by saying that we should look to metasemantics, rather than semantics, to reveal substantivity.

Seventh, substantivity can depend on the world, and not just on the words involved and what candidates they have. Consider the question of whether there is lithium on Mars. It is natural to think that some expression in 'There is lithium on Mars' has a range of equally joint-carving candidates corresponding to the "fuzziness" in Mars's spatial boundaries. For the sake of definiteness, suppose this to involve a range of mostly overlapping candidate referents of the name 'Mars', which differ from one another by including slightly different parts near Mars's vague boundary. The question of whether there is lithium on Mars is nonsubstantive, then, if and only if some, but not all, of these candidate referents contain lithium. Now, if there is, in fact, plenty of lithium in Mars's core, so that all the candidate referents contain lithium, then the question is substantive, since its answer is yes under each candidate. But if the only lithium in the vicinity of Mars is a single lithium atom at its vague border, then the question is nonsubstantive. So the substantivity of the question depends on a fact about the world: the location of lithium. Still, regardless of the location of lithium, the question "admits" nonsubstantivity because without any change in meaning or candidates,

---

[7]Thus I deny Gideon Rosen's (1994, p. 301) claim that "if the facts in the contested class can simply be read off in a mechanical way from the facts in an uncontroversially objective class, then there can be no grounds for denying the same status to facts in the contested area." Adherence to this principle leads Rosen to his pessimistic conclusion that "it adds nothing to the claim that a certain state of affairs obtains to say that it obtains objectively" (p. 279).

the question could have been nonsubstantive: there might have been lithium just at Mars's vague borderline. In contrast, "Are there charged particles?" does not admit nonsubstantivity, and "Is it possible for a martini to be made of sour apple liqueur?" does not admit substantivity.

Eighth, it's natural to think of substantivity as depending on the interests of disputants. Suppose two scientists look at an atom through a telescope and disagree over whether it is lithium. In fact, the atom *is* lithium. Also, no other lithium atom is in the vicinity of Mars, and the scientists know this. Finally, the atom at which they are looking is in Mars's vague border. But the scientists don't know this last fact; indeed, they falsely believe that the atom is definitely on Mars's surface. As a result, they phrase their debate thus: "Is there any lithium on Mars?". For they believe (falsely) that the answer to this question is definitely *yes* if and only if the atom seen through the telescope is lithium. Now, my official account says that this question is nonsubstantive (its answer turns on which candidate for 'Mars' is meant). But intuitively, what is at issue is substantive, since the scientists don't care whether the atom is on Mars; they're just using the question of whether there's lithium on Mars to get at the question of whether the atom seen through the telescope is lithium. We might account for this by distinguishing the question the scientists actually ask ('Is there lithium on Mars?') from the question they really care about ('Is the atom seen through the telescope lithium?'), and applying the official account, as-is, to these questions. Alternatively, we might alter the official account by treating substantivity as a property of question–context pairs, rather than a property of questions simpliciter. The idea would be to make the set of relevant candidate meanings for the question depend on what issues are treated as important in the context. In the context of the scientists, different candidate meanings for 'Mars' are not relevant because the scientists don't care whether the atom is located on Mars. The difference between these two approaches seems insignificant.

Ninth, when nonsubstantive disputes have multiple expressions that fail to carve at the joints, sometimes the source of the nonsubstantivity can be localized to a proper subset of those expressions. For example, suppose 'lithium' has two candidates, $lithium_1$ and $lithium_2$. (Lithium is like jade.) And suppose that Mars is shot through with $lithium_1$, but has no $lithium_2$. Then the question of whether there is lithium on Mars is again nonsubstantive. But even though both of the terms involved, 'lithium' and 'Mars', have multiple candidates, we can place the blame for the nonsubstantivity solely on 'lithium'. For under any candidate for 'Mars', the question's answer remains sensitive to the choice of a candidate for 'lithium', whereas it's not the case that for every 'lithium'-candidate, the question's answer is sensitive to the choice of a 'Mars'-candidate (indeed: for *every* 'lithium'-candidate, the answer is insensitive to the choice of a 'Mars'-candidate).

Tenth, a question can be substantive "along some dimensions" but not along others. Contrast the following two predicates:

$Fx =_{df} x$ is more massive than all bachelors

$Gx =_{df} x$ is wittier than all bachelors

('$=_{df}$' means "means by definition that"). There is, I will say, just one dimension along which F has multiple candidates and generates nonsubstantive questions, whereas there are two such dimensions for G. F and G are alike in having multiple candidates and generating nonsubstantive questions. But in the case of F, these facts come from a single source: the fact that 'bachelor' has multiple candidates. (Let's assume for the sake of argument that 'all' and 'more massive than' carve at the joints.) F's candidates are generated by those of 'bachelor'; and there's just one way for it to be nonsubstantive whether a given thing is F: namely, for there to be some candidates bachelor$_1$ and bachelor$_2$ of 'bachelor' such that the thing is more massive than all bachelors$_1$, but not more massive than all bachelors$_2$. Along the dimension of 'more massive than' (and 'all' as well), we may say, the question of whether a given thing is F is substantive. In contrast, G's candidates are generated both by candidates of 'bachelor' and by candidates of 'wittier than'. There are, correspondingly, two ways for the question of whether a given object is G to be nonsubstantive—nonsubstantivity "along two dimensions".

Given this terminology I can clarify some cryptic remarks at the end of section 3.3. In that section I argued that even a subjectivist about epistemic value might regard the distinction between reasonable and unreasonable prior probability functions as being objective. According to this position, I said, judgments about epistemic value are subjective "along one dimension" but not along another. What I meant can now be stated more fully. Terms of epistemic evaluation do not carve at the joints. However, some of their "components" *do* carve at the joints—just as some of F's components ('more massive than', 'all') carve at the joints even though F itself does not carve at the joints. If, for example, the terms of epistemic evaluation are defined in part by "simplicity" constraints on prior probability distributions, then the joint-carving components in question would be those that state the simplicity constraint in joint-carving terms. Any nonsubstantivity in the question of whether a prior probability distribution is reasonable would *not* be due to candidates for these components (since they carve at the joints—reasonably well, anyway), but would rather be due to candidates in the rest of the components.

Eleventh, suppose some expression E has a candidate c that carves at the joints (in the right way) much better than all its other candidates, but that the actual meaning of E is not c, but rather some other candidate $c_@$ that carves much worse at the joints. (This could happen if reference magnetism is false, or if for some other metasemantic reason the joint-carvingness of c is outweighed by other factors.) Now, suppose that the truth-value of some sentence S is sensitive to the fact that E means $c_@$, rather than c. My account treats S as substantive (assuming that none of its other expressions have appropriately varying candidates), since one of E's candidates (namely, c) carves at the joints much better than the others. Nevertheless, there is an intuitive sense in which S is nonsubstantive since, intuitively, its actual truth-value is a mere reflection of a linguistic choice, not the world's structure. S, we might say, is "actual-verdict nonsubstantive" because it could have had a different truth-value *without carving worse than it actually does*—because, that is, S has a different truth-value under some candidate for one of its expressions that carves at the joints no worse than that expression's actual meaning. Something substantive is at stake here, but the actual verdict is nonsubstantive.

4.3 Conventionality

The next two sections discuss two species of nonsubstantivity. The first is a sort of conventionality. A sentence exhibits this sort of conventionality when it involves, in a sense to be explained, an arbitrary conceptual choice.[8]

The word 'convention' generally signifies an arbitrary choice amongst equally good ways to achieve a certain goal by collective action. The USA had a goal of safely organizing its motorways; that goal could have been achieved either by everyone driving on the right-hand side or by everyone driving on the left; the convention to drive on the right was a more or less arbitrary choice between these two alternative solutions.

Turning to language, there is a sort of conventionality that is both familiar and banal: the choice of symbol or sound to represent a given content. Call this: symbol-conventionality. A second sort of conventionality—call it content-conventionality—is exhibited by sentences that are *about* conventions. The notion of aboutness is admittedly slippery, but obvious examples of content-conventionality include 'there are some conventions', '"Snow" refers to snow in the dominant language of North America in 2011', and so on.

The sort of conventionality I have in mind is different. Sometimes we have a certain semantic goal; we need to introduce a word in order to accomplish that goal; and there are a number of different candidate meanings, each such that the goal would be accomplished equally well if that candidate were chosen as the meaning of the word. The choice of one of these candidate meanings to be the meaning of the word exhibits what I'll call *candidate-selection* conventionality (sometimes just "conventionality", when there's no danger of confusion).[9]

To illustrate, consider the word 'inch'. The purpose of 'inch' is to be a convenient measure for smallish things, the kinds of things we can hold in our hands. But there is a range of very similar lengths that would each have served this purpose. We chose one of these to mean by 'inch', but that choice was arbitrary; any of the others would have served our purposes equally well. This choice was one of candidate-selection convention.

By saying that each length in the range would have served our purposes equally well, I have in mind two things. First, the lengths in the range carve at the joints

---

[8] Sidelle (2009) discusses a similar sort of conventionality.

[9] Skow (2010, section 4) gives a similar account.

equally well.[10] And second, adopting any of the alternate lengths would have "achieved the same semantic goal". All length-words achieve a general semantic goal of allowing speech of absolute and relative sizes, but 'inch' has a more specific goal: to be a convenient measure of smallish things. This goal could have been achieved by many lengths within a certain range. But if 'inch' had meant *mile*, it would not have achieved exactly this goal, since measuring smallish lengths in miles would be inconvenient. And if 'inch' had meant something other than a length—for instance, if it had meant happiness—then it would not have achieved anything like its actual semantic goal.

All words for units of measure are conventional in this way. The boundaries of countries provide a further example. When countries are formed or resized, an arbitrary choice is sometimes made about where the new border will go. The corresponding choice of semantic values for words about the country is candidate-selection conventional.

Call a sentence candidate-selection conventional when its truth-value turns on a candidate-selection conventional choice. Sentence (C) is an example:

(C) My computer screen measures exactly 15 inches.

(C) is true, but would have been false if 'inch' had meant a slightly different candidate length. This is not content-conventionality: (C) is not about conventions in any interesting sense. Nor is it mere symbol-conventionality. Of course, (C) *is* symbol-conventional; all sentences are. But not all sentences contain a word for which we could have chosen an alternate meaning that would have equally well suited our purposes for that word, and which would have given the sentence a different truth-value.

It might seem odd to call (C) conventional (except, of course, in the sense of symbol-conventionality). Facts about measurable quantities like length, after all, are as objective as can be. But remember that my account of substantivity, and hence of candidate-selection conventionality, is metalinguistic. It is the sentence, not the fact, that is conventional. Moreover, recall the interest-relativity of substantivity (the eighth refinement of section 4.2). It seems odd to call (C) conventional because in typical contexts where (C) is disputed, the focus of the disputants is not on which candidate is meant by 'inch', but rather on the length of the computer screen. However, consider a context where the disputants *do* focus on which length counts as being "one inch" (and let the length of the computer screen be common ground). Then the dispute does seem nonsubstantive, and it seems natural to call the sentence conventional.[11] And if we consider sentences about measurable quantities where the second sort of context is more common,

---

[10]Or if any carves better than the others, it is of the wrong sort for 'inch'.

[11]As with substantivity in 4.2, I'm neutral on whether to relativize conventionality to context, or to say instead that although (C) is conventional in every context, for some length, l, what the disputants really care about in the first context is not (C), but rather the nonconventional sentence 'the screen has length l'. (The variable 'l', under a given assignment, is intended to lack alternate candidates.)

the label 'conventional' no longer seems odd at all. A dispute between an American and someone from England over whether a certain container of milk measures "one gallon", where the container's volume is not under dispute, is quite naturally thought of as nonsubstantive; and it's natural to call sentences in the dispute as being conventional, since their truth turns on the conventional decision of whether to adopt the U.S. or imperial standard for the gallon.

(Even paradigm nonsubstantive sentences exhibit the sort of relativity just discussed. 'The pope is a bachelor' could be the subject of a substantive-seeming dispute if, say, the disputants knew little about Catholicism and were in effect arguing about whether the Pope is married.)

Our definitions ensure that conventionality (of the candidate-selection variety) implies nonsubstantiality; but the converse does not hold. Both involve a sentence whose truth-value depends on which of several equally joint-carving candidates is assigned to one of its terms. But for conventionality, there must be a selected candidate (or a vague selected range, in the case of vague conventionality), and that selection must be made by arbitrary choice. If no selection is made (whether because of vagueness or some other form of semantic indeterminacy), or a selection is made nonarbitrarily (see section 4.4), there is no conventionality. Also, 'conventional' seems most apt when the arbitrary choice is made more or less consciously, when alternative choices stare us in the face, and when those choices accomplish *exactly* the same semantic goal; it seems less apt when the choice has been made implicitly and collectively, over time, when no one thinks much about the alternatives, and when the alternatives accomplish slightly different semantic goals. Supposing the question of whether Crusoe is a bachelor to have an answer, perhaps we should not call it "conventional".

Everyone agrees that the boundaries of countries and units of measure are in some sense conventional. But claims of "conventionality" have been made in more controversial domains: for physical geometry (recall section 3.4), morality, and so on.[12] Candidate-selection conventionality is a useful tool for articulating such doctrines.[13] For some of these conventionalists do not want to claim that sentences about the target domain are *about* conventions, nor do they wish to merely make the trivial claim that the sentences exhibit symbol-conventionality.

---

[12]The geometric conventionalism of philosophers like Reichenbach should not be confused with conventionalism about units of measure. The former concerns even unitless length predicates such as Tarski's 'congruent'.

[13]Not in all cases, however. Some such doctrines are best understood as claims of content-conventionality. Conventionalism (or social constructionism) about works of art, artifacts, or gender and race might be construed as the view that sentences about these subject matters express propositions that are in some sense about social conventions. Were our conventions different or nonexistent, there would exist different (or even no) sculptures, tables and chairs, men and women, and so on, since what it is to be a work of art, etc., involves social conventions. (Compare Haslanger's (1995, p. 98) notion of constitutive construction.) Other such doctrines are not clearly instances of any of my three sorts—the logical conventionalism discussed in section 6.5, for instance.

Consider, for example, the view that moral sentences are candidate-selection conventional. According to this view, society had an interest in introducing moral vocabulary, attached to some norms or other; but within certain limits, various norms would have equally well served the purpose. Thus, there were various candidate meanings available for normative words, each of which would have achieved those words' semantic goal. Moreover, none of these candidate meanings carves at the joints better than the others. One of these was selected, more or less arbitrarily—a candidate-selection convention. Now, this view is not a mere claim of symbol-conventionality. By claiming that the meanings we have actually selected for moral language are on a par with alternate meanings—both metaphysically and concerning the satisfaction of the goal of morality—this view really does downgrade morality (a part of it, anyway) in a way that a mere claim of symbol-conventionality would not. But nor does this view imply that moral sentences are about conventions. Thus it allows that (for example) murder would have been wrong even if we had chosen different norms (since the conventionality of the choice of norms is not built into the propositions we express using moral words).

4.4 Subjectivity

The second species of nonsubstantivity may be called subjectivity. Like convention-ality, it occurs when a linguistic community chooses one of several candidates. But in the case of subjectivity, the choice is not arbitrary; rather, it reflects something important about the linguistic community.

As with conventionality, this sense of subjectivity must be distinguished from others. Consider the following toy semantic theories of aesthetic sentences:

Expressivism By uttering 'x is beautiful', a speaker communicates no proposition, but rather gives expression to a certain positive aesthetic attitude, A, to x.

Indexicalism By uttering 'x is beautiful', a speaker, S, communicates the proposition that S **bears attitude A to x**.

Aesthetic sentences express attitudes, given the first semantics, and communicate propositions about attitudes, given the second. Either way, there is a straightfor-ward kind of subjectivity. But the kind of subjectivity I have in mind is different. It is brought out by a third semantics:[14]

Projectivism By uttering 'x is beautiful', a speaker, S, communicates the proposition that x **is P**, where the property *being P* is a certain physical property that is the linguistic meaning of the predicate 'is beautiful' in S's language; *being P* is the linguistic meaning of 'is beautiful' because members of S's linguistic community bear attitude A to Ps.

---

[14]I am using 'projection' nonstandardly; it usually signifies the mistaken attribution of mental features to the external world.

Under this semantics, aesthetic sentences are not subjective in the straightforward sense. Accordingly, they pass common tests for "objectivity". For example, sentences about beauty make mind-independent claims: beautiful mountains would still have been beautiful even if no humans had ever existed. Nevertheless, there remains a clear sense in which the aesthetic is subjective. For *which* physical properties aesthetic predicates stand for is determined by the attitudes of the speaker's community, and any attitudes are as good as any other.[15] Even though the properties ascribed by aesthetic predicates are wholly mind-independent, response-independent, and so on, the *selection* of *these* features as the features to be expressed by aesthetic predicates is accomplished solely by our having the attitudes that we do. Imagine a range of linguistic communities, each with different aesthetic attitudes. The predicate 'is beautiful' expresses different—equally joint-carving—properties in these different linguistic communities.[16] Where we call a mountain beautiful, speakers of another language withhold that predicate, and instead call the mountain 'ugly'. In such cases, everyone speaks truly; no one is making a mistake. The mountain has the property B_E that is expressed in English by 'beautiful', and lacks the property B_O that is expressed in the other language by 'beautiful'.[17] The appropriateness of the language of subjectivity in this case is manifest.

Shine a light down on a piece of paper suspended over a table. If the paper has a geometric shape cut from it—a circle, say—the light will shine through the hole and project that shape onto the table below. Let X be the illuminated portion of the table. X is circular. Moreover, X—that portion of the table—would still have been circular even if a square rather than a circle had been cut from the paper (though X would not then have been exactly illuminated). But there is nothing special about X. The square region that would have been illuminated, had the cut-out hole been square, is just as good a region. The illuminated region is a projection of the hole. An observer of the illumination will learn something more important about the hole than about the table, even though circularity is an intrinsic feature of the illuminated part of the table. Aesthetic features are like the shape of the illuminated region X, the selection of meanings for aesthetic predicates like the selection of the shape of the hole in the paper. If projectivism is true, then aesthetic features are not "about" us, and would persist even if there were no humans. But assuming there are no aesthetic joints in nature, nothing beyond our aesthetic attitudes constrains the aesthetic categories picked out by

---

[15]Compare Street (2006, section 7).

[16]If predicates are individuated by the properties they express, then we cannot say that each community uses the same predicate 'beautiful'; what we must say instead is that each uses a predicate that plays the role that 'beautiful' plays in our language. Allow me the liberty of speaking of each community as having "aesthetic" predicates, "aesthetic" attitudes, and so on.

[17]This variation in the meaning of 'beautiful' is not just the mundane sort of variation that is possible because of symbol-conventionality. In each language, 'beautiful' plays the same role; it is a word for the things picked out by the aesthetic attitudes of that language's speakers.

aesthetic language; an observer who watches us label things 'beautiful' and 'ugly' will learn as much about our attitudes as they will about the things, even if these predicates ascribe intrinsic properties of the things. Aesthetic predicates express the properties they do because of our attitudes; aesthetic features are projections of our attitudes.

I do not claim that projectivism is true; it is, I suspect, an overly simplistic model of the semantics and metasemantics of 'beautiful'. Its point, rather, is to establish a general fact about the nature of subjectivity: there is a kind of subjectivity that results, not from statements in the target discourse being about our values, but rather from our values selecting one from a range of equally good meanings. The importance of this fact for metaethics should be clear. To earn titles of objectivity and realism (together with the associated imagery of externality, discovery, and so on), it is not enough that evaluative language be assigned "objective content". For projectivism assigns *physical* contents, which are as objective as can be; yet it merits neither the names nor the imagery. The objective content must also stand out from its metasemantic surroundings. It must enjoy some sort of privilege over alternate candidate contents.[18]

A sentence is subjective, then, in the sense illustrated by the projectivist semantics, if and only if its truth-value depends on which of a range of equally joint-carving candidates is meant by some term in the sentence, where the candidate that we in fact mean was selected in a way that is not arbitrary, but rather, reflects something important about us, such as our values.[19] As with conventionality, it is appropriate to speak of this sort of subjectivity only if no one candidate carves at the joints (in the right way) better than the rest. If there *were* aesthetic joints in reality—vindicating the very strongest form of aesthetic realism—then one of the communities from our earlier example might match those joints with their usage of 'beautiful'. This lucky community would then be *uniquely right* about aesthetics, and talk of "subjectivity" would seem out of place. They might be uniquely right in the straightforward sense of being the only community that speaks truly, if 'beauty' in every community has the same, joint-carving sense (this might happen because of reference magnetism). But even if the communities mean different things by 'beautiful', so that every community speaks truly, the lucky community remains uniquely right in the sense that only their term 'beautiful'

---

[18]Moral realists sometimes implicitly support such a privilege, even if their explicit focus is on the contents of moral sentences (see, for instance, Boyd (1988) on homeostatic property-clusters and Railton (1986) on feedback). Note also that the appropriateness of the language and imagery of realism and objectivity comes in degrees. Even if contents for moral language are selected by facts about us, morality seems more realistic and objective if those facts are counterfactually robust and universal across different societies—if they reflect the human condition rather than historical accident.

[19]What if our actual values are so hard-wired into our brains that it would be difficult or even impossible to adopt others? I still want to count other values as picking out "candidates" for the term in question; those candidates are not "semantically alien" even if we could not adopt them. Thus it's not always right to say (as I have been) that "we could just as easily" have adopted alternate candidate meanings.

gets at the distinguished aesthetic structure of the world. The other languages are metaphysically second-rate. In such a circumstance, the language of subjectivity again seems out of place, even though the unlucky communities all speak truly given what they mean by 'beautiful'.

The kind of subjectivity we have been discussing results from the projection of our values. But perhaps 'subjective' is also appropriate when we project important features of ourselves other than values. Suppose causation does not carve at the joints, and that there are a number of candidate semantic values for 'cause', none of which is metaphysically distinguished. Suppose that one of these is in fact the actual semantic value, for some reason that reflects something important about us. Suppose, for instance, that it's essential to the role that 'cause' plays in our conceptual scheme that it have a counterfactual analysis. Like 'beautiful', the semantics of 'cause' reflects an important feature of ourselves, not an arbitrary semantic decision, but unlike 'beautiful', the feature has nothing to do with value.

Whether or not 'subjective' is appropriate here, this sort of projection is opposed to "objectivity". If, contrary to what I think, there is a joint-carving relation of causation, then it would be natural to describe this by saying "there are objective facts about causation", or "one description of the facts of causation is objectively correct". Objectivity is opposed to subjectivity, conventionality, or any other sort of nonsubstantivity.

Philosophers often make inchoate claims that are best understood as concerning this notion of objectivity. To take one example, consider the criticism made by Armstrong (1983, pp. 40–59) and others that Lewisian laws of nature are not genuinely necessary and cannot explain regularities. Everyone agrees, after all, that mere regularities do not explain regularities, and need not be necessary; but Lewisian laws are just glorified regularities, regularities that are integrated into the simplest and strongest system. Lewis's reply always seemed elusive and unconvincing:

Some familiar complaints seem to me question-begging . . . If you're prepared to agree that theorems of the best system are rightly called laws, presumably you'll also want to say that they underlie causal explanations; that they support counterfactuals; that they are not mere coincidences; that they and their consequences are in some good sense necessary; and that they may be confirmed by their instances. If not, not. It's a standoff—spoils to the victor. (1994, pp. 478–9)

Lewis's response is in essence to define 'nomic necessity', 'explanation', and so on, in terms of 'law', and then to claim that if you don't think that necessity and explanation, thus defined, are *genuine*, that must be because you are just resisting his analysis of lawhood. What is really going on, I think, is that Armstrong is bothered by the fact that on Lewis's account, laws (and so everything defined in terms of them) are not objective. For Lewis there is no distinguished structure in the vicinity of laws of nature. (This is the whole point of Lewis's Humeanism.[20]) This rankles some; they believe that laws "run deep"; they cut at the joints; they are objective. Likewise for necessity, explanation, and the rest: Lewis provides analyses of these concepts that to some degree fit our ordinary concepts, but are not particularly objective. This is what really bothers Armstrong (and Lewis's reply is not responsive).

4.5 Epistemic value

I have been arguing for connections between joint-carving and a range of concepts. Many of these connections can be unified by a single thesis about epistemic value: it's *better* to think and speak in joint-carving terms. We ought not to speak the 'grue' language, nor think the thoughts expressed by its simple sentences.

The goal of inquiry is not merely to believe truly (or to know). Achieving the goal of inquiry requires that one's belief state reflect the world, which in addition to lack of error requires one to think of the world *in its terms*, to carve the world at its joints. Wielders of non-joint-carving concepts are worse inquirers.

Recall the community that divides the red–blue world along the diagonal plane (section 1.1). They are *missing out*; they do worse than we do as inquirers. Of course, if they explicitly form false beliefs *about* structure, then there is a perfectly obvious sense in which they are doing worse. But even if neither they nor we form such beliefs, they still do worse, simply by thinking of the world in the wrong terms.

Joint-carving thought does not have merely instrumental value. It is rather a constitutive aim of the practice of forming beliefs, as constitutive as the more commonly recognized aim of truth. Nor is joint-carving a conscious goal, at least not of most inquirers. It is rather a standard by which beliefs and believers may be evaluated, whether or not it is consciously acknowledged.

(Strong and weak versions of this thesis about epistemic value can be distinguished.[21] The strong version is what I have been advocating: it's worse to employ non-joint-carving concepts. The weak version says merely that it's worse to believe non-joint-carving *propositions*, where a proposition is joint-carving to the extent that it can be simply expressed using joint-carving concepts, given some appropriate notions of simplicity and proposition. (The strong version implies the weak, more or less, given the perhaps plausible additional assumption that anyone employing joint-carving concepts ought to believe propositions simply expressible in terms of them.) The weak version allows one to employ 'grue' and 'bleen', provided one does not believe propositions like *all emeralds in this room are*

---

[20]See Lewis (1986c, introduction), Lewis (1994). In this respect, Lewis is just like the traditional regularity theorist. Each agrees that the world is *fundamentally* anomic; the difference is that Lewis does a better job of approximating in extension the ordinary notion of a law of nature. Matters are very different for Armstrong (1983), whose relation of nomic necessitation is a universal, and so is part of reality's fundamental structure.

[21]Thanks to Steve Steward.

grue, but rather believes instead propositions like *all emeralds in this room are either grue and first observed before 3000 A.D. or bleen and not first observed before 3000 A.D.*—the idea is that this latter proposition is relatively joint-carving because it can be expressed by "all emeralds in this room are green". Both versions are correct, I think, and so I stick with the strong. But one might reject the strong version while accepting the weak; and much of what I go on to say could be reformulated to appeal only to the weak.)

In his book *Dividing Reality*, Eli Hirsch argues effectively that it is intuitively compelling that we ought to speak and think in joint-carving terms; but he also argues effectively that this position is difficult to support. Although the epistemic value of joint-carving inquiry is, I think, a basic one and hence not derivable from other values, I do think it can be supported in several ways. First, the aim of joint-carving can be seen as having the same source as the aim of truth: beliefs aim to *conform to the world*. Here is a simplified but intuitive picture. The realist about structure thinks of the world as coming "ready-made" with distinguished carvings. By analogy with the notion of a mathematical structure, think of The World as a structure: a set E of entities together with a set R of relations over E (think of the relations here simply as 'tuples of members of E). Now, ignoring partial belief, it is natural to think of the beliefs of a subject, S, as consisting of the representation of a structure: the subject represents there being objects, E_S, together with a set R_S of relations over E. Given this picture, it is utterly natural to think of full conformity to The World as requiring $\langle E_S, R_S \rangle$ to be identical to $\langle E, R \rangle$. Conformity requires the believer to represent the structured world exactly as it in fact is, and thus requires the represented relations R_S to be identical to the world's structuring relations R. Thus if belief aims to conform to the world, and if belief and the world are both structured, belief aims not just at truth, but also at the right structure—truth in joint-carving terms.

Second, we think of scientific discovery as satisfying the aims of inquiry particularly well; why? Answer: it is because scientific discoveries are phrased in particularly joint-carving terms. Relatedly, we think of truths that are stated in extremely non-joint-carving terms—for example, the scrambled propositions of section 2.6—as being comparatively worthless. Relatedly, imagine (or recall) first coming to believe that morality, beauty, justice, knowledge, or existence is a mere projection of our conceptual scheme—that the truth in these domains is conventional, subjective, or otherwise nonsubstantive. Why does that feel so deflating; why does it diminish the urgency of finding the truth; and why does it diminish the value of the truth once found? Answer: though we might not put it exactly thus, our original picture in these lofty domains is that of joint-carving. Morality, beauty, and the rest are built into the nature of things, we naïvely think, rather than being mere projections. Giving up on objectivity means giving up on joint-carving, and hence diminishes the value of truth.

Third, consider the following series of scenarios. Scenario 1: the physical world is pretty much the way we think it is; it includes physical objects in addition to spacetime. Scenario 2: the physical world consists of nothing more than propertied points and regions of spacetime. Scenario 3: the physical world consists of a wave function in a massively dimensional configuration space. Neither three-dimensional space nor four-dimensional spacetime exist, fundamentally speaking. Scenario 4: our ordinary beliefs are caused by The Matrix, a computer simulation that directly stimulates our brains while our bodies lie in stasis.[22] Scenario 5: I am a disembodied brain floating in an utterly empty space; the changes in my brain that give rise to my "mental states" happen purely by chance. In Scenario 1 my ordinary beliefs about myself and my surroundings are true. The same holds in Scenario 2, I think, though some would disagree. This is less clear in Scenario 3, since the structures in the world that ordinary beliefs would need to pick out in order to be true—patterns in the wave function—are so far from the joints in reality. Matters are worse in Scenario 4: our ordinary beliefs would be true only if interpreted as picking out aspects of the computer program, which are (we may stipulate) quite distant from reality's joints in the world that houses the program. And once we get to Scenario 5, if I can be said to have any mental states at all, nearly all of them are clearly untrue. They would be true only if they had contents defined on the world's empty space (or parts of my brain); but no assignment of such content could be regarded as being more correct than other assignments on which the mental states would come out false. Now, in this series of scenarios, the match between our beliefs and reality's joint-carving structure is gradually eroded. The erosion is severe enough to disrupt truth only late in the series. But even earlier in the series, at stage 3, say, much of what we care about has been lost, even if what we normally say is still true. We are a partial intellectual failure if we live in configuration space or The Matrix, even if we believe truly. Moreover, even if the transition from truth to falsity in our ordinary beliefs is abrupt, what we care about in inquiry seems to be more continuously eroded in the series. These facts suggest that what we care about is truth in joint-carving terms, not just truth.

The thesis about the value of joint-carving inquiry unifies many of the connections I have forged between joint-carving and other concepts. The unification takes the form of a recurring theme, rather than a derivation from first principles. Here are a few sweeping lines of thought.

Duplication: Lewis defined duplicates as objects whose parts have the same natural properties and stand in the same natural relations. But why *care* about duplication? A partial answer emerges from this section's thesis: if it's good to classify objectively alike things together, then duplication should be of interest to us. (This is only a partial answer, because it does not address why duplicates in particular, rather than merely objects that share natural properties, would be of interest. In particular, why are we interested in objects whose *parts* have the

---

[22]Compare Chalmers (2005).

same natural properties and stand in the same natural relations? The answer here, I think, somehow concerns the distinctive status of parthood in our thought.[23])

Explanation: here we have a direct connection to the thesis of this section. Explanation is an epistemic achievement. There are many views about explanation, and no doubt many species of explanation; but on all views, explanation is an attempt to improve our epistemic position in some way, to make the world more intelligible. But the epistemic achievement will be diminished if cast in non-joint-carving terms, given this section's thesis.

Laws: given the Lewisian theory of laws, on which laws must be phrased in joint-carving terms, it follows that laws are propositions in which we ought to take an interest. Concern with what science says is not epistemically optional.

Reference: Lewis himself defended reference magnetism by saying that it is constitutive of reference that reference goes to the most natural candidate. But this just invites the question of why we should care about reference. What's better about reference than "reference*", which does not always go to the most natural candidate? Answer: reference carves better at the joints than reference*; given the thesis of this section, that is why we should care about it.[24]

Induction: in Bayesian terms, the problem of induction is to characterize the correct prior probability distributions. Now, here is a way of thinking about this notion of correctness. In worlds like ours, human beings have survived, and thrived, in part because of how they formed beliefs about their environment. Taking for granted that they updated by conditionalization (more or less), they survived because they had appropriate priors. So an explanation of why humans survived will cite certain general features of human prior probability functions. These general features cannot be too specific if they are to explain why humans in general (as opposed to on this continent or that) survived; but they cannot be too general either if they are to robustly explain the survival. They will surely include such features as this: humans tend to project reasonably joint-carving properties (like blue) more than badly non-joint-carving properties (like grue). Note further that having these features explains why humans survive *in worlds like ours*. If our world contained few regularities involving joint-carving properties, then projecting such properties wouldn't lead to survival. So: there are general features of human priors that explain why we survived. These features, according to this line of thought, just are the features that make priors correct. Correctness just is: having the features that explain humans' survival. This is just one crude story, at best incomplete and at worst on the wrong track; but my point could be made under refined or alternate stories. My point is this: epistemic notions—such as the notion of a correct prior probability distribution—have their source in what explains certain facets of our epistemic success. Thus those notions must respect nature's joints in certain ways, since explanations quite generally must be

---

[23] See Sider (2007*b*).

[24] Thanks to Robbie Williams.

cast in reasonably joint-carving terms. Given the crude story imagined above, for example, the features of our prior probability distributions cited by the explanation of our survival would need to be cast in reasonably joint-carving terms. (Similar points could be made under alternate stories in which the explanation of our epistemic success cites features of the present, say, rather than our evolutionary past.)

Space and time: the intrinsic structure of space and time is given by the spatiotemporal notions that carve at the joints. But why is uncovering this structure the goal of science? Because science—like all inquiry—aims to correctly represent the world, and this requires representing the world "in its own terms"; it requires carving at the joints.

Objectivity: why do we prize substantivity and objectivity, and downgrade the subjective, conventional, nonsubstantive? Because it's better to think in joint-carving terms; and the more one does, the more one's meanings "stand out from the metasemantic background", yielding substantive, objective claims.

4.6 Objectivity of structure

We have uncovered a web of connections between structure and various notions. This web of connections yields the primary argument against Goodman's claim that structure is merely the projection of our interests or biology: subjectivism about structure leads to subjectivism about the other notions in the web. We could not formulate an appropriately objective form of Bayesianism. We could not rebut conventionalists about physical geometry. We could not believe in objective semantic determinacy.

But the most significant fallout from Goodmania, to my mind, arises from structure's connections with epistemic value and with objectivity.

Epistemic value: joint-carving languages and beliefs are better. If structure is subjective, so is this betterness. This would be a disaster. Recall section 2.6. If there is no sense in which the physical truths are objectively better than the scrambled truths, beyond the fact that they are propositions that we have happened to have expressed, then the postmodernist forces of darkness have won.

Objectivity: whether questions are substantive, nonconventional, objective, and so on, depends on whether they are phrased in terms that carve at the joints. Given subjectivism about structure, we would have subjectivism about substantivity, depth, conventionality, objectivity. No discourses would be objectively objective. Another disaster.

The knee-jerk realist thinks that the world is "out there", waiting to be discovered rather than constructed—all that good stuff. Everyone agrees that this picture rules out views according to which all truth is mind-dependent in the crudest ways, but it requires more. After all, under the projectivist semantics (section 4.4) one can truly say that "the mountain would still have been beautiful even if humans had never existed". The realist picture requires the "ready-made world" that Goodman (1978) ridiculed; it requires the world to *really* be as physics says; it requires objectivity; it requires objective distinguished structure. To give up on structure's objectivity would be to concede far too much to those who view inquiry as being merely the investigation of our own minds.

5 Metametaphysics

Metametaphysics is inquiry into the status of metaphysics. It is of the nature of the beast that one is led to ask: are metaphysical disputes substantive? Are they objective, genuine, deep? Or are they nonsubstantive in some way: conventional, subjective, merely verbal or conceptual? Must there be a fact of the matter about who is right?

The answers to these questions depend on which metaphysical dispute is at issue. The crucial factor is whether the dispute is phrased in terms that carve at the joints. This connection to metametaphysics is the final part of the role I envisage for the notion of structure.

5.1 The challenge of metaphysical deflationism

Metaphysics has always had critics. The most extreme base their critique on sweeping views about language (logical positivism, ordinary language philosophy) or knowledge (naïve empiricism). But such views are in trouble on independent grounds. Their oversimplified conceptions of how we make semantic and cognitive contact with the world notoriously threaten the science of unobservables as much as they threaten metaphysics.

A more formidable challenge comes from a more modest critic, whom I'll call a (metaphysical) *deflationist*.[1] A deflationist about question Q says that Q is in some sense merely verbal or conceptual. Its answer (if it has an answer) is determined by linguistic or conceptual rules. What is at issue is not "the world", but rather *us*—how we think and talk. (We will need to refine this rather vague characterization, but it will do for now.) This critique, moreover, is based, not in a sweeping conception of language or epistemology, but rather in considerations specific to Q.

My deflationist has a favorite "go-to move". The move is schematic, and can be made in service of various antimetaphysical conclusions, but in each case its form is the same:

1. The deflationist observes a certain metaphysical dispute, in which one of the contested views is expressed by a certain sentence S.

---

[1]Not to be confused with a deflationist about truth such as Paul Horwich (1990). Although my metaphysical deflationist is not any specific person, Eli Hirsch's work on metaontology—certain facets of it anyway—may be kept in mind as a model.

2. He argues that there is an interpretation of the language of S—a way of assigning meanings to the sentences of that language—under which *everyone* can agree that S is true.

3. And he argues for a certain *parity* between this and rival interpretations.

The go-to move may be summarized thus: "There's a perfectly good way to talk under which S is clearly true."

Before discussing the meaning of 'parity' in step 3 and how the move might lead to antimetaphysical conclusions, let me give some examples. Confronted with a dispute over whether the relation of part to whole is reflexive, the deflationist might point out that the following defines a reflexive relation:

x is part* of $y =_{df} x$ is part of y or $x = y$.

Even if 'part' in English is not reflexive, 'part*' is. So under an interpretation of English words that is just like actual English except that 'part' means part*, the sentence 'Everything is part of itself' obviously comes out true. Moreover, this interpretation is very similar to English since 'part' and 'part*' have exactly the same extension except perhaps for pairs of the form $\langle x, x \rangle$—parity.

Second example: with respect to the same dispute, the deflationist might construct a related interpretation, also very similar to English, in which 'Nothing is part of itself' comes out true, by letting 'part' mean part**:

x is part** of $y =_{df} x$ is part of y and $x \neq y$.

Third example: confronted with a dispute over whether holes exist, a deflationist might construct an interpretation of quantificational sentences in which 'There is a hole in object x' means that x is perforated. Even an opponent of holes will agree that some such sentences are true in this interpretation, since the opponent agrees that some things are perforated.

The deflationist can use the go-to move within various dialectical strategies. Many of the strategies appeal to the fact that meaning is largely determined by use. For example, a large part of why 'bachelor' means (something like) *unmarried adult male* is that we tend to call something a 'bachelor' if and only if it is an unmarried adult male. This is oversimplified; but rather than trying to refine it, let's just employ the code: "Our use of 'bachelor' favors the hypothesis that it means unmarried adult male." Here, then, are some of the strategies:

Common-sense strategy Suppose a metaphysician argues for a noncommonsensical position. Argue first, using the move, that sentences expressing a more commonsensical rival position can be truly interpreted. Argue, second, that our use of the crucial terms favors the commonsensical interpretation over any interpretation on which the noncommonsensical position comes out true. Conclude that the noncommonsensical position is not true. (For example, our use of sentences like 'There is a hole in that piece of cheese' clearly favors interpretations under which the sentence comes out true whenever the piece of cheese in question is perforated. So, nominalism about holes is false—and this conclusion was secured simply by reflecting on language.)

Indeterminacy strategy Argue first, using the move multiple times, that each of a range of views about some metaphysical question comes out true under some interpretation. Argue, second, that our use of the crucial terms does not favor any of these interpretations over the others. Conclude that it is indeterminate which view is true. (For example, our use of 'part' favors neither part* nor part** over the other; so it's simply indeterminate—and therefore pointless to debate—whether parthood is reflexive.)

Deflationary strategy As with the indeterminacy strategy, argue first that each of a range of views about some metaphysical question comes out true under some interpretation. But now, rather than taking a stand on whether actual usage favors one interpretation, simply conclude that the question is "merely conceptual", because which view is true depends on which interpretation is favored by our usage. (For example, both the question of whether parthood is reflexive, and the question of whether there are holes, are merely conceptual. Since each view about these questions comes out true under some interpretation, the only question is which interpretation fits English usage.)

I think of the third strategy as the core of metaphysical deflationism, since it seems presupposed by the first two strategies, and is potent even if unaccompanied by either of the first two.

The deflationist's arguments are pretty unimpressive if step 3 of the go-to move is omitted. Let p be a particle in some distant galaxy. The sentence 'particle p is an electron' is a paradigm of the kind of sentence for which no form of deflationism is true. And yet, we can construct an interpretation on which it is true and an interpretation on which it is false, each of them very similar to English: let the first be like English except with p removed from the extension of 'electron', and let the second be like English except with p added. Step 3 is crucial; the rival interpretations must in some sense be on a par with one another and with other competing interpretations (such as English).

If the deflationist is a realist about structure then he can construe step 3 as requiring at least that the constructed interpretation must carve at the joints (in the right way—recall section 4.2) as well as its rivals. The rival interpretations of 'electron' do not lead to deflationism about whether particle p is an electron because, whereas the actual, English, meaning of 'electron' carves at the joints, one of the two constructed meanings does not. But when a deflationary stance is correct, the rival interpretations carve at the joints as well as one another and as well as English.

A deflationist who rejects realism about structure, on the other hand, will need some other way to explain why the go-to move has a deflationary upshot for metaphysical questions but not for the question of whether particle p is an electron; and he will need some other way to construe step 3. It is hard to see how this could be done.[2] So I think the way to defend a targeted deflationism is to be a realist about structure. At any rate, this is the form of deflationism on which I'll focus.

The deflationist should also, I think, take step 3 as requiring that the rival interpretations not be "semantically alien", in the sense of section 4.2. That is, although the rival interpretations might determinately differ from English, speakers using those interpretations should use the words in question to accomplish the same semantic tasks as do English speakers. For the deflationist about a question Q wants to conclude that the answer to Q depends on how we use words, but not in the trivial sense in which *all* truth depends in part on meaning. The idea should rather be that Q's answer depends on usage in the nontrivial sense that it depends on which *nonalien* interpretation is actual.[3]

Thus what the deflationist is saying is in essence that Q is *nonsubstantive*, in the sense of chapter 4. The deflationist's nonalien interpretations result from multiple *candidates* for the crucial terms in Q. For example, part* and part** are candidates for 'part', and generate interpretations under which different answers to the question "Is parthood reflexive?" come out true. If each carves at the joints as well as the other (and as well as any other candidate for 'part'), then this question is nonsubstantive. As we saw, this is not to say that Q is *about* how we use words. The question of whether appletinis are martinis is not about words, and yet it too is nonsubstantive in the same sense.

What are the ways for a metaphysician to respond?

Sometimes metaphysicians should embrace deflationism. And sometimes this requires admitting that the debate is just silly, and should be discontinued. (Even a partisan needn't fight *every* battle.) But not all nonsubstantive debates are silly. As we saw in section 4.2, questions that are nonsubstantive in my metaphysical sense may yet be conceptually deep and thus important if their answers reveal important facets of our conceptual scheme. Perhaps questions about causation are like this.

But sometimes the true believer in metaphysics will want to oppose the deflationist. This is particularly true when the believer wants to defend a revisionary position, since such positions are hard to regard as reflecting our ordinary concep-

---

[2]Hirsch tries to target his deflationism by applying it only when the disputed metaphysical proposition is regarded by one disputant as being a priori necessarily equivalent to one undisputed proposition, and by another disputant as being a priori necessarily equivalent to another undisputed proposition. But the disputants need make no such claims about a priority and necessity. Most metaphysicians nowadays regard their views as theoretically supported conjectures, not as propositions knowable by anyone who understands them. And some of Hirsch's targets regard their subject matter as contingent (Cameron, 2007). Moreover, a priori necessary equivalence seems relevant only if one thinks of it as a kind of sameness of meaning, whereas surely it is no such thing. For a more comprehensive (and very insightful) discussion of Hirsch, see Hawthorne (2009).

[3]Note also that if the interpretations are alien, then there is no hope of carrying out the common-sense and indeterminacy strategies.

tual scheme.[4] It is also true when the believer regards herself as doing fundamental metaphysics.

In the case of fundamental metaphysics, the most straightforward way to resist deflationism is to claim that the crucial expressions in the debate carve perfectly at the joints. As we saw in section 4.2, the relation between substantivity and joint-carving is a complex one. However, a *sufficient* condition for substantivity (or near enough, anyway) is that the dispute be cast in perfectly joint-carving terms. Such a dispute concerns the nature of fundamental reality. In such a dispute, the existence of alternate interpretations has no more deflationary import than it had in the question of whether particle p is an electron.

(Why is the condition only "near enough" sufficient? Because there might be multiple joints in the vicinity, and because the joints might be the "wrong sort", in the sense of the third refinement of section 4.2. I'll mostly be ignoring these complications.)

There are other ways to resist the deflationist, but they are unappealing. One might try to argue that the alternate interpretations simply do not exist. For example, the deflationist about the ontology of holes claimed to produce an interpretation under which 'There is a hole in x' means that x is perforated. But the dispute over holes does not involve that sentence form alone; it involves sentences with many different syntactic forms, for example:

There is a circular hole in x.

There are fifteen holes in x.

The hole in x is identical to the hole in y.

In light of this, it might be argued that there is no way to give a *general* antinominalist interpretation of quantification over holes. But this is a slender reed on which to rest one's hopes. (I argue in chapter 9 that in the case of the ontological deflationist, the hope is in vain.)

It is also possible to grant the existence of multiple equally joint-carving interpretations, but claim that those interpretations are semantically alien and thus not candidates. Consider the question of whether "Magnesium is more plentiful on Earth than carbon." This sentence comes out true if 'magnesium' means oxygen, but this does not support deflationism about the question since this alternate meaning for 'magnesium' is not a candidate (despite carving at the joints). The semantic goal we are trying to achieve with 'magnesium' is not so unspecific that it could just as well have been achieved by letting 'magnesium' mean oxygen. However, this kind of response to deflationism seems inapplicable in cases of philosophical interest. For what is distinctively puzzling about philosophical questions is closely connected with the fact that we *can* imagine ourselves speaking

---

[4] Hard but not impossible; perhaps certain internal tensions in our conceptual scheme are best resolved by preserving some aspects at the expense of others.

in any of a number of different ways using the disputed term, without thereby being semantically alien.

One might instead make a big deal out of the fact that the candidate meanings for the crucial term differ from its actual meaning:

"Who cares whether there are ways to interpret 'There is a hole in x' so that it comes out true? What I care about is whether *there is a hole in x*; and if you define 'There is a hole in x' to mean that x is perforated, it no longer says that there is a hole in x!"

This performance is oblique, since it rejects none of the deflationist's claims. It does not challenge the claim that the interpretations exist, nor does it deny that they carve at the joints equally well, nor does it claim that they're semantically alien. And the deflationist never claimed that 'There is a hole in x' still means that there is a hole in x when it means that x is perforated. What is conveyed by the agitated speech is that the "deflationist's" claims do not deserve the name 'deflationism', that the status quo in metaphysics is unthreatened by the existence of the interpretations.

This is a hard attitude to maintain. Most metaphysicians at least sometimes think of themselves as *not* being engaged in conceptual archaeology. (From this point of view, Peter Strawson's (1959) "descriptive metaphysics" is a near oxymoron.) Instead, they think of their project as being rather like speculative science. This self-conception isn't always articulated, but it is often subconsciously present. It reflects itself in the willingness to take noncommonsensical positions seriously, and to be guided by theoretical virtues that are prized in science (such as "simplicity"). This self-conception cannot survive the admission that rival answers to one's question come out true under equally joint-carving candidate interpretations. Imagine we live on the shore of a gigantic lake, around which there are numerous other isolated linguistic communities. None of these is semantically alien with respect to the others, but the different communities do use ontological language differently: in one, 'There are holes' is true, in another it is false; in another 'There are numbers' is true; in another it is false; and so on. And suppose further that none of these languages carves better at the joints than any of the others. If we metaphysicians learned of all this, it would seem perverse for us to continue to regard our ontological questions with the original, quasi-scientific attitude. Granted, in some of these other languages, 'There are holes' does not mean that there are holes. But so what? Speakers of those languages could make parallel true statements about us in their language: "Your sentence 'There are holes' does not mean that there are holes." Look out over the lake—the parochiality of our conception of there being holes is staring us in the face. The metaphysical attitude requires a more transcendental view.

5.2 Personal identity, causation

Let's make all of this a little more concrete. Consider a group of proponents of the doctrine of temporal parts who disagree over the criterion of personal identity. Their dispute is over which relation between person stages is the "unity relation" for persons—that is, over which relation holds between all and only the person stages that are part of some one continuing person. Some of them think that the unity relation is that of psychological continuity; others think that it is the relation of bodily continuity (i.e., spatiotemporal continuity under the sortal: human body).

Never mind which group has the right answer. Let us instead ask the metametaphysical question: Is the dispute substantive?

A deflationist about personal identity could argue as follows. First, there is no perfectly fundamental unity relation over person stages. There are numerous relations over person stages in the vicinity: the relation of psychological continuity, the relation of bodily continuity, and so on. But none of these carves at the joints perfectly, and none carves better than the others. Moreover, these are candidates for our talk of personal identity. Neither a community who spoke of personal identity as being governed by psychological continuity, nor a community who spoke of it being governed by bodily continuity, would be semantically alien. So the question of personal identity is nonsubstantive. There is no objective, substantive, deep answer as to whether I would survive certain transformations— those in which my psyche is transferred to a new body, for example, or in which I abruptly lose all my memories. Which answers are correct is largely a question about our conceptual scheme, not a question of reality's fundamental structure (and our conceptual scheme might be silent about some cases).[5]

For another example, return to causation. If there is a perfectly fundamental relation of causation, then there must be objective, deep answers to questions like: Is causation two-place or four-place? Does it relate facts or events? But otherwise, deflationism about some questions about causation will presumably be true, since linguistic communities differing over whether 'cause' expresses a two-place or four-place relation, for example, do not seem linguistically alien. The questions about causation may have no answers at all; and insofar as they do have answers, those answers will be a mere reflection of our concept of causation.

The distinction between conceptual and metaphysical substantivity (section 4.2) is particularly important in metametaphysics. Even if questions about personal identity and causation are not metaphysically substantive, they clearly are conceptually substantive, given how deeply the concepts of sameness of person and causation are embedded in our conceptual scheme. These concepts play a role in many central aspects of our thought: thought about ourselves, moral responsibility, deliberation, control, prediction, explanation, and myriad others. Even if this entire edifice rests on metaphysical sand, understanding its inner workings is a crucial part of understanding ourselves.

Disputes over causation, personal identity, and the like are conceptually deep, even if metaphysically shallow; this is a significant part of their philosophical

[5]See Sider (2001a).

interest. Conversely, and ironically, some of the metaphysically deepest disputes—certain ontological disputes, for example (see chapter 9)—are conceptually shallow in that they have few implications outside rarified metaphysics. This, I suspect, contributes to the common distrust of those disputes.[6]

5.3 The metaphysics room

Sometimes fundamental metaphysics can be conducted in ordinary language. But not always. Metaphysicians need a plan B.

Suppose we attempt to ask a question of fundamental metaphysics using some ordinary, natural-language expression E. Suppose further that there is some joint-carving meaning m "in the vicinity" (see below). The problem is that E might not mean m. Various metasemantic scenarios discussed in section 3.2 could have this result; here are three. 1. Reference magnetism is false in all its forms, and E is not a theoretical term—like 'amulet' it is not "trying" to stand for a joint-carving meaning. 2. Some form of reference magnetism other than simple charity-based descriptivism is true, and E is not a theoretical term. 3. Simple charity-based descriptivism is true, but m fits badly with the use of E. (According to simple charity-based descriptivism, the correct interpretation must maximize the combination of charity and eligibility; thus a highly joint-carving interpretation might nevertheless be incorrect if it is too uncharitable. Not all words carve at the joints, after all!)

If E does not stand for m, then it might instead stand for some non-joint-carving meaning that reflects a more-or-less arbitrary choice of usage that our linguistic community has made—a choice of one amongst a range of equally non-joint-carving candidate meanings. Thus the question would be nonsubstantive in that its answer would turn on linguistic usage, not reality's structure. (More accurately, the answer would be actual-verdict nonsubstantive in the sense of section 4.2.)

That is, the *ordinary, natural language* question, phrased in terms of the ordinary, natural-language expression E, would be nonsubstantive. But we could discard E, and enter the metaphysics room, so to speak. We could replace the ordinary expression E with an improved expression E^* that we stipulate is to stand for the joint-carving meaning in the vicinity. The question we ask in the metaphysics room, cast in terms of E^* rather than E, is substantive. Indeed, it is *superior* to the original question, for it concerns reality's fundamental structure, rather than its merely conventional or projected aspects. This is plan B.

Early on in philosophy we are taught not to abandon ordinary language on the battlefield. If a novel language had to be stipulated in order to carry on a debate, we're warned, there could not be open questions about what is true in that language, since the answers would need to be settled by stipulation. Arguing about what is true in the novel language would be like arguing about how the queen

---

[6]Thanks to Eric Funkhouser here.

ought to move in a new version of "chess" whose rules are unconstrained by the existing rules. The traditional debate over whether freedom is compatible with determinism, for example, would be trivialized if we had to stipulate a meaning for 'free'. If we stipulated that 'free' means 'undetermined by the laws and past' then there would be nothing worth debating: "freedom" thus understood is obviously incompatible with determinism. And if we instead stipulated that 'free' means 'not in chains', then again we would have nothing worth debating; "freedom" thus understood is obviously compatible with determinism. The only way to have a meaningful debate, so we are taught, is to abandon such stipulations, and mean by 'free'. . . *freedom*!—freedom in the ordinary sense.[7]

Abandoning ordinary language is indeed often a bad idea, but when it is, that is because there is no *other* way to anchor the debate, no other way to explain the meanings of the crucial words without trivializing the debate. But joint-carving meanings give us another anchor. We can then introduce new words with a *minimum of semantic pressure*, with only minimal stipulations on their behavior. Of course the stipulations must be strong enough to pick out unique meanings (by picking out the relevant "vicinity"); but this aside, we stipulate nothing that settles disputed claims. We nevertheless succeed in securing unique meanings because joint-carving meanings are sparse—there is usually at most one joint-carving meaning in a given "vicinity". (To suppose otherwise would be to needlessly attribute complexity to the world.) Picture introduction of terms with minimal semantic pressure as something like definition by ostension. We are saying "Let us introduce words for *these* meanings, so that we can disagree about how *they* behave." If there are indeed (unique) joint-carving meanings in the vicinity—the anchor—then the words in question will have determinate meanings even though the stipulations were so minimal. The answers to the disputed questions will not be settled by the stipulations, and inquiry into those questions—questions about reality's fundamental structure—will be worthwhile.

Let's consider an example. Suppose there is a fundamental relation C that is a lot like causation, except that it holds only between events at the subatomic level. Macro events, such as the throwings of rocks and the breakings of windows, never stand in C. Now, the ordinary English term 'cause' may well not mean C. For i) C fits terribly with ordinary usage of 'cause' (or at least with usage of simple causal sentences such as 'the throwing of the rock caused the window to break'); and ii) 'cause' may well be a nontheoretical term in English. Rather than standing for C, 'cause' may instead stand for that non-joint-carving relation that best fits our usage of 'cause'. A debate involving 'cause' would then not be (actual-verdict) substantive. But we could enter the metaphysics room, and coin a new term, 'cause*', for the joint-carving relation in the vicinity of causation.

---

[7] Qualification: *some* stipulation might be allowed, if it is ultimately grounded in ordinary terms ('free' could be stipulatively tied to 'moral responsibility' in its ordinary sense).

'Cause*' will stand for *C*—fundamental causation, we might call it—and our new debate about causation* will be substantive.

How, exactly, will we fix the meaning of 'cause*'? It is to stand for the joint-carving meaning "in the vicinity of" causation. Thus its metasemantics should be like that of 'cause' except that joint-carving is paramount. Any general metasemantic presumption that non-joint-carving candidates may be assigned is suspended in the case of 'cause*'; carving perfectly at the joints is an absolute requirement. 'Cause*' should stand for that meaning which i) carves at the joints (perfectly); ii) fits our use of 'cause' better than any other joint-carving meaning; and iii) fits our use of 'cause' well enough. If nothing satisfies all three of these conditions—if, that is, there is no fundamental causation, or if there is more than one sort—then 'cause*' stands for nothing, and debates about causation* are ill-posed. Conditions ii) and iii) are admittedly vague, but harmlessly so. What might we actually do to coin a new term with this metasemantics? I see no reason to deny that the following performance would do the trick: "Let 'cause*' be a theoretical term for that perfectly joint-carving relation (assuming there is such a thing) that is in the vicinity of the ordinary notion of causation, but which (since it carves at the joints) may differ somewhat from that ordinary notion."

The metaphysics room gambit requires that successful stipulations of the envisaged sort be possible. It may be objected that new languages or terms can be introduced only by translation into existing natural languages or terms.[8] But that can't be right. Natural languages themselves had to bootstrap; they had to somehow latch onto the world in the first place. So why can't we bootstrap now? It may be thought that the stipulation could not succeed if reference magnetism is false, or worse, if some radically nonreferential conception of meaning—some form of deflationism or inferentialism, perhaps—is true. But even such views must allow for the introduction of new theoretical terms in science. If they don't, then they are thereby refuted. And if they do, then given realism about joint-carving they surely also allow the introduction of theoretical terms in the metaphysics room. The cases really are parallel: in each case we introduce new terms with minimal semantic pressure, we intend to mean "whatever is in the vicinity", and semantic determinacy is achieved (if it's achieved) primarily because the world contains an appropriate meaning, not primarily because of facts about us.

The gambit also requires that semantic interpretation—at least for terms stipulated to carve at the joints—be under our control. But it does not require that grammar be under our control in the same way. Consider, for example, the fact that natural language quantifiers are grammatically binary, whereas first-order logic's quantifiers are monadic. It might be argued that for this reason, the first-order quantifiers are in some sense grammatically impossible for us. Even if we try to pronounce "$\exists x$" in a monadic-looking English form, "For some

---

[8]Hofweber's (2009) critique of "esoteric" metaphysics—metaphysics done using distinctively metaphysical rather than ordinary concepts—is related.

x . . .", we nevertheless continue, despite ourselves, at some psychologically basic level, to represent the quantification binarily: "For some *object x . . .*". Binary quantificational grammar is built into our minds in a way that's difficult or even impossible to change. But even if this view is correct, it is no obstacle to introducing the language of first-order logic in the metaphysics room and giving it a monadic *semantics*. The formal sentences of this language would describe fundamentally monadic facts; it's just that we couldn't think about those facts "natively". There would be a mismatch between the structure of the facts and the structure of our thoughts (though not between the facts and the sentences of the formal language).

5.4 Substantivity in nonfundamental disputes

The simplest way to regard a dispute as substantive is to regard it as being phrased in terms that carve *perfectly* at the joints. But sometimes one wants, instead, to regard a dispute as substantive because it concerns reality's less-than-perfectly fundamental joints.

To illustrate, it is natural to wonder whether anything substantive is at stake in the dispute over the location of the semantics/pragmatics border. Everyone agrees that context supplies an enormous amount of information that is relevant to communication. But is that information part of the *semantics* or the *pragmatics*? For there to be any interesting issue here, we must fix the notions of semantic and pragmatic without begging any disputed questions. For example, if it is to be an open question whether the semantic contents of sentences are (complete, truth-conditional) propositions, we must not simply define the semantic content of a sentence as a proposition that is conventionally associated with that sentence.

To secure substantivity, the debate should be regarded as being about the way to carve the subject matter of communication at its natural joints—about the form that a good theory of communication ought to take. Two participants in this debate might advocate their positions as follows. *Participant one:* "A good theory of communication divides the processing of communicated information into two stages. At stage 1, a fairly simple level of content is associated with each word. This level of content is memorized by the competent speaker. Stage 2 combines the output of stage 1 with all the information provided by the context, resulting in truth-conditions of the utterance. In computing stage 2 content, the speaker appeals to her general world-knowledge. Further, stage 1 associates a complete proposition—something with truth-conditions—with each grammatical sentence."[9] *Participant two:* "I agree about the two stages, but I disagree with your final claim. Stage 1 does not associate a complete proposition with each

[9]The two-stage process is oversimplified; a more realistic account would divide linguistic processing into multiple stages (phonological, syntactic, logical form. . .), and contextual information might intrude at multiple points. The point still stands: there can be substantive dispute about the semantics/pragmatics border if the disputants can agree on a sufficiently detailed skeleton of a theory of linguistic processing so that they can disagree over where, in that skeleton, truth-conditions figure in.

grammatical sentence; sometimes it instead associates what Kent Bach (1994) calls a 'proposition radical'." We can think of this dispute as being over whether semantic contents are always complete propositions, since we can think of stage 1 as semantics and stage 2 as pragmatics. And the dispute isn't terminological since 'semantic' and 'pragmatic' have been picked out by their role in a good theory of communication, and not by a definition that begs the question of whether semantic contents are propositions.

The story I just told in effect picks out the semantics/pragmatics divide via its role in the Ramsey sentence for a theory of communication. This pattern—a term of philosophical interest is picked out by its role—recurs all over philosophy.[10] Think of debates over perception. How much is contained in "the content of visual experience", it is asked.[11] Information about real-world objects, or just their appearances? Causal information? This debate can seem puzzling to outsiders; how is the meaning of 'the content of visual experience' to be fixed so that the questions remain open? The answer must be that the participants in this debate are attempting to carve the subject matter of perception at its joints. A good theory of this domain, they believe, will appeal to a certain notion of the content of visual experience; and their debate is about *that notion*—the notion that appears in a good theory of perception. (The role might be expansive. Some, for example, pin down the notion of the content of experience by its role in epistemology.)

Construing a dispute in this way doesn't on its own secure substantivity, because it might be that no joint-carving theory takes the shape that the disputants envisage. In the dispute over the border between semantics and pragmatics, a third participant might deny the claim shared by participants one and two, that a good theory of communication has anything like the two stages. If she is right, then in a sense there would be no substantive questions about semantics and pragmatics, since the distinction is based on a false theory. Either our uses of 'semantic' and 'pragmatic' are empty of meaning, or they are massively indeterminate, or their meanings are determined simply by how they are casually used in ordinary speech.[12] (Even so, a substantive three-way debate over the shape of a good theory of communication would remain.)

So: substantivity, in these questions of perception and meaning, turns on the nature of reality's joints. (Likewise for questions of substantivity in the special sciences, although this is less often in dispute.) But reality presumably contains no *perfectly* fundamental perceptual or meaning structure. So we must make sense

---

[10] See also Chalmers (2011).

[11] See Siegel (2006).

[12] The following can happen. (a) A philosophical debate began when there was no decent scientific theory of a certain domain. (b) Subsequently a good scientific theory was developed. (c) No good rival philosophical theory was developed; the concepts of the original philosophical debate were simply badly chosen; they carved nature at its joints badly. Nevertheless, (d) the philosophical debate continues uncritically, in the old terms.

of joint-carving in domains that are not perfectly fundamental. We will revisit this issue of imperfect fundamentality in section 7.11.

5.5 A test case: extended simples

To illustrate my approach to metametaphysics, let us look in detail at the recent dispute over "extended simples".[13] My guess is that many readers suspect that this dispute is not substantive (as I myself did initially). Is this suspicion justified?

"Extended simples" are defined as spatially extended objects without proper parts. For example, if *I* am an extended simple then I have no proper parts. Not only do I lack "philosophers' parts" such as a "right half", I also lack such ordinary parts as a head, arms and legs, internal organs, molecules, atoms, and subatomic particles. There is, in my vicinity, but a single thing—me—which occupies an extended, person-shaped region of space.[14] A limiting case would be existence monism, in Jonathan Schaffer's (2007; 2010c) terminology, according to which the entire world is a single extended simple.[15] The dispute is over whether there are, or could be, such things.

The status of this dispute is tied up with general questions about space and ontology. Are ontological questions in general substantive? Do there exist such entities as points and regions of space? If so, are objects in space to be identified with points or regions? If not, how are objects in space related to space? The answers to these questions affect whether disputes over extended simples are substantive.

To illustrate, suppose for the sake of argument that the following answers to the general questions—call them, collectively, the *occupation picture*—are correct:

1. The notions of logic, mereology, and physical geometry (quantification, identity, parthood, sum, point, region, . . .) carve perfectly at the joints.
2. Substantivalism is true: there exist points and regions of space.
3. Supersubstantivalism is false: objects in space ("inhabitants") are not identical to points or regions of space.
4. Spatial facts about inhabitants emerge from the holding of a perfectly joint-carving relation of *occupation* between inhabitants and space.

Now, the question of whether there are any extended simples, given the occupation picture, becomes a question about the pattern of instantiation of the occupation relation:

> Does there exist something that lacks proper parts but occupies more than one point of space (i.e., occupies multiple points or a sum or region of points)?

---

[13] See Hudson (2006, chapter 4); Markosian (1998; 2004a; b); McDaniel (2003; 2007a; b); Parsons (2003).

[14] In this example we have a qualitatively heterogeneous extended simple, which goes beyond the bare definition of an extended simple. See Sider (2007b, section 1).

[15] See also Horgan and Potrč (2000; 2002).

And given my metametaphysics, this question is substantive, since it is phrased in terms that carve perfectly at the joints.

I have seen philosophers roll their eyes when extended simples come up. They regard that topic as "spooky metaphysics" (in a bad sense, it would seem)—as being somehow misguided. But what is the complaint?

In fact, there are a number of complaints that one could be making. The list of possible complaints, I hope, challenges both the extended-simple enthusiasts and the eye-rollers. The enthusiasts must check that they avoid each complaint. The eye-rollers must check they can genuinely embrace one of them, and they must specify which one that is (the eye-rolling tends to be scattershot and uncritical).

One complaint is purely epistemic. It admits that the dispute is substantive, but claims that the considerations offered by the enthusiasts are inadequate to resolve it. We do not know whether there exist extended simples, it is alleged, and the enthusiasts' arguments aren't helping. Such allegations may or may not be right, but one cannot make them without actually entering into the fray. (Eye-rolling tends to come from the sidelines.) Also, this complaint does not demand that the enthusiasts cease and desist. The enthusiasts might instead take it as an exhortation to do better.

A second complaint concedes that the question of whether extended simples *actually* exist is substantive, but notes that some enthusiasts address primarily the question of whether they *possibly* exist. This shift makes a big difference to the tenability of deflationism about the debate. Given my metametaphysics, a deflationist about an issue must locate a nonfundamental term essentially involved in its statement. Once the issue becomes the *possibility* of extended simples, it is open to claim that the nonfundamental term is 'possibly'. In particular, suppose that there are, in fact, no extended simples. One could then claim that the question "Is it possibly the case that there exist extended simples?" is nonsubstantive, on the grounds that its answer is *yes* under some candidate meanings of 'possibly' and *no* under other equally joint-carving candidates.

The theory of possibility to be defended in chapter 12 could sustain such a claim. Very roughly, the theory says that for a proposition to be necessarily true is for that proposition to be i) true; and ii) of the right sort. What is the "right sort"? This is given by a list of properties of propositions, a list including the property *logical truth*, the property *mathematical truth*, and certain others. Moreover, the list is determined more or less arbitrarily, rather than by some deep criterion. *Our* meaning of 'necessity' is tied to *our* list; but other linguistic communities could choose different lists and thus different meanings for 'necessarily'. They wouldn't thereby carve at the joints worse than we do; they would just be different—like a linguistic community that counted the pope as a "bachelor". Given this theory of modality, different candidate meanings for 'necessary' arise from different choices of lists. If the true proposition that there are no extended simples falls under some of these lists but not others, then 'necessarily there are no extended simples' counts as true under some candidates and not others; and so, 'possibly, there are extended simples' counts as true under some candidates and not others.[16] Intuitively: extended simples would depart from actuality in certain ways; the question of whether they are possible is the question of whether these departures are too drastic; whether the departures are too drastic turns on the metaphysically shallow question of what we have decided to mean by 'possible'.

Our first two complaints interact. Given the second complaint, the only substantive issue can be the question of the actuality of extended simples. But much of the literature on extended simples has discussed only their possibility. If this portion is omitted, the first complaint becomes more powerful.

A third class of complaints results from rejecting one facet or another of the occupation picture. An *ontological deflationist*, for example, who thinks that quantifiers do not carve at the joints, could claim that the sentence 'there are extended simples' is true under some candidate meanings for 'there are' and false under others, and that all such candidates carve at the joints equally well. Thus the sentence is nonsubstantive.

There are many questions here. There is first the question of whether ontological deflationism is true; I will argue in chapter 9 that it is not. There is also the question of whether ontological deflationism is behind the eye-rolling; I think that in most cases it is not. Most of the people I have caught rolling their eyes are not skeptical of ontology in general (though perhaps their eye-rolling is a sign of an underlying malady that would lead to ontological deflationism, or worse, if not treated). And there is, finally, the question of whether ontological deflationism is enough to deflate all of the disputes in the vicinity. It's hard to tell, because ontological deflationists tend not to say what they think the fundamental structure of reality *is*; they merely say what they think it *isn't* (namely, quantificational). Once the deflationist has developed his fundamental language—which must be able to completely describe the world, including its scientific aspects—who knows? Perhaps we will be able to raise, in its alien terms, a substantive question that is akin to the question of whether there are extended simples.[17]

A fourth and final sort of complaint amounts to simply rejecting extended simples—perhaps all extended simples, or perhaps only certain kinds. This may not seem like a metametaphysical complaint, but it feels more like one if the reasons for the rejection are sufficiently general. Consider, for example, what Kris McDaniel (2003) calls "spanners": extended simples that occupy an extended region, rather than occupying each of the many points in that region. One might object to spanners because they violate a sort of micro-reductionism, namely, the view that all fundamental properties and relations relate mereologically simple entities. (One might, in turn, base this on the view that only mereologically simple entities exist, in the fundamental sense of 'exist'; see chapter 13.)

---

[16] As is customary, I define "possibly ϕ" as "not necessarily not-ϕ".

[17] See also section 9.6.2.

We have seen four different sorts of complaint about extended simples.[18] Notice that, with the exception of the first, each presupposes a substantive thesis of metaphysics. The second depends on the claim that there are no modal joints to reality; the third depends on the claim that there are no quantificational joints to reality; and the fourth assumes micro-reductionism. No complaint wholly sustains the common attitude of the eye-rollers that the extended-simple enthusiasts are making a *methodological* error. The complaints mark a difference of opinion about metaphysics. As we will see in the next section, this is a general feature of metametaphysical critiques.

5.6 Metametaphysics as just more metaphysics

One worry about metaphysics is that we have no way to answer metaphysical questions. But is metaphysics so much worse off than the rest of philosophy?[19] Many scattershot critics move from the difficulties of metaphysical epistemology to the conclusion that metaphysics is something like meaningless, without realizing how close this comes to assuming a crude form of verificationism. Often these critics have a blind spot: they are verificationist when thinking about metaphysics, but not when thinking about other matters (especially about their own bit of philosophy!). A sensible attitude is that metaphysics, like much of philosophy, is just hard. Its epistemology is hard too, but this is no cause for panic.

A different (though related) worry is the feeling that metaphysicians see substantive issues where there are really just different equally good ways to talk. It is on this strand—metaphysical deflationism—that I have focused.

Details aside, my crucial claim has been that a sufficient condition for substantivity is being cast in joint-carving terms. An important consequence is that metametaphysical critiques are distinctively metaphysical in nature. Whether they

---

[18] A fifth complaint might target the dispute only when extended simples are construed as having "pseudo-parts"—further extended simples that are not genuine parts (i.e., parts in the joint-carving sense) but are located where genuine parts would be located. This dispute might be claimed to be nonsubstantive because the truth of 'there are extended simples' turns on whether 'part' means genuine parthood or pseudo-parthood. The claim might be correct if 'part' is not a theoretical term; for then, even though exactly one candidate meaning for 'part' carves at the joints, that candidate might be the "wrong sort"—recall the third qualification of section 4.2. But if 'part' is a theoretical term then the dispute remains substantive, for it is then cast in purely joint-carving terms of the right sort. Thanks to a referee. A sixth complaint might be that the question just isn't significant. (The old joke about angels dancing on the head of a pin combines this and the first complaint.) And a seventh complaint might be that the answer is obvious in some sort of Moorean way. Neither the sixth nor seventh complaint challenges the substantivity (in my sense) of the question. Moreover, each seems wrong. Why wouldn't a question about the fundamental relationship between objects and space be significant? And why should the nature of this relationship be obvious to "common sense"? (See also the critique of Mooreanism in Sider (2011).)

[19] Timothy Williamson (2007) gives a compelling account of the epistemology of philosophy (and of the sociology of pessimism about philosophy) with which I mostly agree, except that for the epistemology of metaphysics I would stress continuity with scientific explanation rather than counterfactual reasoning.

are correct is a *function of the facts*—a function of what joints reality in fact has. One cannot do metametaphysics simply by examining metaphysical language and reasoning. For given the sufficient condition, in order to claim that a question is nonsubstantive, one must claim that it is not cast purely in joint-carving terms, and such a claim cannot be supported solely by reflecting on language and reasoning. For example, we saw in the previous section that a sufficient condition for the extended-simples debate being substantive is that a certain metaphysical thesis be *true*: the occupation picture. Thus, in order to decide whether that debate is substantive, one must directly engage in metaphysics.

It may be objected that this conclusion—that metametaphysical critiques are metaphysical in nature—is simply an artifact of *my* way of conceiving of metametaphysics. The objection is partly correct. An austere metametaphysician who rejected realism about structure could perhaps introduce some sensible notion of substantivity that doesn't presuppose the notion of carving at the joints. But even so, his metametaphysical critiques could not be wholly ametaphysical. For imagine a metaphysician who shrugs off a purely methodological or linguistic critique by saying that *she* is a realist about carving at the joints, and that she believes her ideology to carve at the joints. Surely the austere critic couldn't simply concede these claims. For, I hope, this book provides a *model* of metaphysics; a model of how, in a world with objective structure, language could be attached to that structure and metaphysicians could reasonably speculate on its nature. So even the austere critic should agree that *given* the realism about structure, metaphysics would make sense, both linguistically and methodologically. So the austere critic must oppose the metaphysician's claims. Granted, he could oppose them by rejecting the realism about joint-carving, rather than by accepting this realism while denying that the metaphysician's ideology carves at the joints. But this rejection of joint-carving is just more metaphysics.

Many are drawn to metaphysical deflationism because they want the epistemic high ground. They want to rid the world of difficult-to-answer substantive questions. But their very metaphysical deflationism costs them the high ground. For since metametaphysical critiques are just more metaphysics, they raise all the old epistemic questions. This is certainly true if the critic embraces realism about structure and claims that the crucial notions in the targeted debate do not carve at the joints—the epistemology of such a claim is as hard as can be. But it's even true if the critic is austere, since *rejecting* realism about joint-carving raises the same old epistemic issues.

This does not mean that metaphysical deflationism is never reasonable. It's often attractive to avoid some bits of metaphysics, some difficult questions. But it does mean that no one should adopt metaphysical deflationism with the goal of avoiding metaphysics, or difficult questions, in their entirety.

Nor should one adopt deflationism about a metaphysical question merely because the ideology needed to state that question differs from one's own. This should go without saying, but in fact, many critics have a blind spot here too. They notice that the crucial term T in a metaphysical question can be understood in multiple ways in terms of their own ideology, which they regard as fundamental, never stopping to think that the participants in the debate regard T itself as being fundamental. In the dispute over holes, certain critics keep complaining that they don't see the question. "Is it whether holes are causally efficacious? Is it whether some of their properties fail to supervene on the presence of matter and its arrangement?" No, the question is simply: Do holes *exist*?!

6   Beyond the predicate

Structure is more general than its kin, Armstrong's universals and Lewis's natural properties and relations, along two axes.

The first axis is ontological. Call a predicate "sparse" when it marks a joint in nature. For Armstrong, a predicate is sparse when there exists a corresponding universal; for Lewis, a predicate is sparse when there exists a corresponding natural property or relation.[1] Each assumes the existence of abstracta. But the idea that the world has a distinguished structure—that electrons go together and not together with cows, that it is better to think in terms of electrons than in terms of electron-or-cows, and so on—does not require this assumption. (Nominalists could surely embrace the idea.[2]) The notion of structure is to be free of commitment to abstract entities.

The second—more important—axis concerns the scope of structure. Armstrong and Lewis's accounts are confined to properties and relations. Linguistically speaking, their focus is on the predicate. Structure, on the other hand, is not to be restricted to any particular grammatical category. Just as Lewis and Armstrong ask which predicates get at the world's structure, we can also ask which function symbols, predicate modifiers, sentence operators, variable binders, and so on, get at the world's structure.

One might force these expressions into the Armstrong/Lewis mold, by analyzing them using predicates and then assessing the predicates for sparseness as before. Sometimes this is harmless; one can treat function symbols as standing for relations, for example. But in other cases, it foists unwanted commitments on us. For example, if sentence operators for negation and disjunction are to be predicates, they must presumably be predicates of propositions. Thus there must exist propositions; and further, even friends of propositions might doubt that the most fundamental negative and disjunctive facts are facts *about* propositions. (We will return to this last point.) And in still other cases the predicate strategy is unavailable. Variable binding expressions, for example, seem impossible to treat as predicates. (One can take quantifiers to be predicates rather than variable binders, but this just moves the bulge in the carpet: new variable binders must then be introduced. Stalnaker (1977), for example, treats quantifiers as not binding vari-

---

[1]Lewis (1983*b*, 347–8) considers replacing his primitive predicate of natural sets with a primitive multigrade predicate of similarity amongst possible individuals. But this proposal does not generalize along the second axis, and it arguably requires Lewis's modal realism.

[2]Not that Armstrong and Lewis claim otherwise. They simply formulate the idea in their own terms.

ables, but his variable-binding operation of complex predicate formation cannot be thought of as predication. Similar remarks apply to Montague's treatment of quantification.[3])

The two axes are connected. For Armstrong and Lewis, a predicate is sparse when it stands for an appropriate sort of abstract entity. When we move beyond the predicate, for instance to sentential connectives or quantifiers, it becomes increasingly strained to think in terms of abstract entities. So, insofar as one is wedded to abstract entities (first axis), it is hard to move beyond the predicate (second axis).

6.1 The reason to generalize

Why move beyond the predicate? Because the connections with the notion of structure that we have been exploring are not confined to the predicate.

For example, I have argued that a dispute's substantivity—whether it concerns reality or just how we conceptualize reality—depends on how well its crucial expressions carve at the joints. Sometimes those crucial expressions are indeed predicates; disputes over causation, for example, are usually cast in terms of predicates of facts or events. But other times the crucial expressions are not predicates, and the question of substantivity can be posed nevertheless. In certain disputes over ontology, time, modality, and classical logic, for example, the crucial expressions are quantifiers (or perhaps names), tense operators, modal operators, and negation and other sentential connectives, respectively. (These disputes will be discussed in subsequent chapters.) As before, one can attempt to force-fit the predicate mold. But often this can be done only given the existence of disputed entities (such as propositions); and with disputes involving quantification, predicate reinterpretation seems unavailable.

Advocates of restrictive ontologies will be particularly loathe to formulate their distinctive claims using predicates. Rejectors of both events and facts, for example, cannot construe causal claims as involving a predicate of events or facts; they might instead use a sentence operator: "that ϕ causes it to be the case that ψ". Rejectors of propositions cannot regard modal and temporal claims as involving predicates of propositions; they might instead use sentential modal and tense operators. Rejectors of sets cannot define generalized quantifiers such as 'finitely many' and 'most' in terms of set theory; they might instead take them as primitive.

And even defenders of more permissive ontologies often require nonpredicates in subtle ways. For example, someone who regarded modal and tense operators as really being predicates of semantic entities might still require primitive nonpredicates such as 'the proposition that ϕ' and 'the property of F-ing' to characterize the space of semantic entities. (These are not predicates; their grammar is to turn sentences and predicates, respectively, into terms.)

---

[3] See Montague (1973) (Dowty et al. (1981) makes it go down easier).

To assess the substantivity of disputes whose crucial terms are nonpredicates, then, we need to go beyond the predicate. Such disputes also introduce a further need for doing so, within epistemology. As we saw in section 2.3, ideological simplicity is part of what makes a theory choiceworthy. Further, in choosing a fundamental theory we often face the choice of whether to adopt increased ideology or ontology. But theories which forgo ontology at the cost of increased ideology often do so precisely by introducing distinctive non-predicate ideology. The function of predicates, after all, is to combine with singular terms—which denote entities—to make statements; renouncing certain entities can thus call for distinctive modes of expression other than predicates. So to evaluate proposed trades of ontology for ideology—which we must do in order to choose which fundamental theory to believe—we need to speak of joint-carving for expressions other than predicates.

We have seen two ways in which the proposed "applications" for the notion of structure are not confined to the predicate. There are many more. (To mention just two: the doctrine of reference magnetism should be extended to nonpredicates; and in the Lewisian theory of laws, the logical expressions in the lawmaking language must be required to be joint-carving; otherwise cheap simplicity can be obtained with rigged logical expressions just as through rigged predicates.) The domains in which we need to speak of structure are not confined to the predicate. We need a broader conception than that of Armstrong and Lewis.

But this broad conception of structure often meets resistance. The following sections examine various sources of this resistance, and argue in each case that the resistance is misguided.

6.2 Inapplicability of the similarity test

One common source of resistance is the apparent failure of a similarity conception of structure to apply to expressions other than predicates. Armstrong and Lewis tie their accounts to similarity. Lewis, for example, says of his perfectly natural properties:

Sharing of them makes for qualitative similarity, they carve at the joints, they are intrinsic, they are highly specific, the sets of their instances are *ipso facto* not highly miscellaneous . . . (1986*b*, p. 60)

For many, this "similarity criterion" is the only handle they have on Lewisian naturalness. But it seems inapplicable to quantifiers and sentential connectives, for example. Quantifiers and sentential connectives aren't "shared", nor do they have instances, so we can't assess whether their sharing makes for qualitative similarity or whether the sets of their instances are highly miscellaneous. As for "carving at the joints", that metaphor suggests a similarity-theoretic reading: i) *do* carve where there's a joint, i.e., assign different natural properties to dissimilar objects; and ii) *don't* carve where there's no joint, i.e., assign similar things the same natural properties. And neither i) nor ii) seems to apply to quantifiers or sentential connectives. So it's easy to see how someone whose only entrée to naturalness is similarity would be baffled by the more general notion of structure.

Worse, insofar as the similarity criterion can be applied in these cases, it seems to deliver the wrong results. Does the existential quantifier carve at the joints? I will argue in chapter 9 that it does. But every two things, no matter how dissimilar, share the feature of *existing*; so doesn't that mean that the existential quantifier in some sense fails the similarity criterion?

The worry is not that since natural properties are *defined* as similarity-makers, the notion of naturalness cannot be generalized to quantifiers. Lewis doesn't *define* 'natural' at all.[4] The worry is rather the following. As an undefined theoretical term, 'natural' is understood through its theoretical role (section 2.1). The theoretical role consists of principles specifying how naturalness relates to certain other notions, such as similarity. My term 'structure' has its theoretical role fixed by many of these same principles, and more besides. If the theoretical role of 'structure' is exhausted by its connection to similarity, and if this connection is restricted to predicates, then we have no understanding of how 'structure' could apply to expressions in other grammatical categories.

But the theoretical role that Lewis offers for naturalness is *not* exhausted by the similarity criterion. Still less is the theoretical role for the more general notion of structure exhausted by the similarity criterion. The connection to similarity is just one of a network of theoretical connections that give the notion its life.[5] These are the connections we have been exploring, the connections to laws, explanation, metasemantics, epistemology, physical geometry, substantivity, objectivity, and epistemic value. None of these further aspects of structure's theoretical role relies on similarity. So even if we set aside similarity, structure has a rich enough remaining theoretical role to be intelligibly applied beyond the predicate.

But in fact, we needn't set aside similarity. The connection to similarity can be maintained, even for expressions other than predicates, if that connection is properly understood.

First we must expose a confusion. A putative reason for doubting that the existential quantifier carves at the joints was the observation that every two objects, no matter how dissimilar, share the feature of existence. But this observation is irrelevant. It concerns the *predicate* 'exists', whereas our question concerns the existential quantifier.

Next we must change our focus, from object-similarity to fact-similarity. The connection between similarity and structure, in the case of the existential quantifier,

---

[4]Nor *could* he have defined natural properties as similarity-makers, at least not without some serious chisholming (along the lines of Hirsch (1993, chapter 3, section 3, and appendix 2)). He doesn't count extremely specific intrinsic properties—for example, the property shared by all and only perfect duplicates of a certain porcupine—as being perfectly natural, but their sharing certainly makes for similarity. Indeed, their sharing makes for *more* similarity than the sharing of the properties that Lewis does count as being perfectly natural: the fundamental properties of particle physics.

[5]See also Sider (2004, p. 682).

should be understood thus: if existential quantification carves at the joints, then whenever two facts are existential facts, that is a genuine similarity between them. The fact that *there is a donkey* and the fact that *there is an electron* are genuinely similar in that each is an existential fact. Similarly, to evaluate whether 'or' ensures similarity, we must ask whether any two disjunctive facts are *ipso facto* similar; to evaluate whether modal operators insure similarity, we must ask whether all facts of the form *possibly*, ϕ are *ipso facto* similar; and so on.

Language is no more a guide to fact-similarity than it is to similarity in general. Just as the applicability of 'grue' to each of a pair of particulars does not guarantee the similarity of those particulars, the recurrence of 'there is' in the sentences used to state a pair of facts does not on its own guarantee the similarity of those facts. If all existential facts are indeed similar, this is because of something about quantification: being existential is a genuine, not merely nominal, feature of facts. (We can invent words with the same grammar as quantifiers for merely nominal features of facts. "There schmexists an F", recall, means that the property of being an F is expressed by some predicate in some sentence of this book. It is a fact that there schmexists a donkey, and also a fact that there schmexists a brilliant Republican president born in New Haven, but these facts share nothing in common.)

Why this move to fact-similarity? The idea of a genuine similarity is that of a real commonality. Here we have a negatively charged thing; there we have another negatively charged thing; has something in nature recurred? Is there a real commonality between the negatively charged things? We think so. The recurrence was within objects in this case, but that is inessential to the legitimacy of the question. There exists a donkey; there exists an electron—has anything recurred? Is there something in common between there existing a donkey and there existing an electron? If I am right that quantification carves at the joints, then the answer is yes; these facts share a real commonality. But if I am wrong (as defenders of "quantifier variance" think—see chapter 9) then the answer is no; quantificational facts do not particularly "go together".

It has been convenient to speak of facts in order to introduce this broad conception of similarity, but the similarity judgments in question don't really require reifying facts.[6] The idea of a genuine commonality, of recurrence, requires no *things* in which the recurrence occurs. Such nonontic similarity judgments can be regimented using a sentence operator: "When ϕ, it's like when ψ".[7] Thus we can say, for example, that when there exists a donkey, it's like when there exists an electron. I don't claim that we already speak this way (though it's not clear to me that we don't; consider "When it sleets, it's like when it snows"). What I do claim

---

[6]Better: it does not require that there are facts in the fundamental sense of 'there are'; see section 9.3.

[7]Jason Turner suggested this regimentation, pointing out that we can think of the 'it' as being like the 'it' in 'It is raining.' (The suggestion is not that this sentence operator is fundamental.)

is that there are coherent judgments that can be thus expressed, and that they're similar enough to ordinary ontic similarity judgments to be thought of as being in the same species.

6.3 No entities

We have already touched on a second source of resistance to going beyond the predicate. Armstrong/Lewis sparseness—the most familiar game in town—is "entity-based". For Lewis, in order to evaluate whether a predicate carves at the joints we must look at a certain entity—the set of the predicate's actual and possible instances—and ask whether the entity is natural. And for Armstrong, we must ask whether a certain entity exists—a universal corresponding to that predicate. To extend their strategy to expressions like quantifiers or sentential operators, we would need to identify corresponding entities. But there seem to be no such entities.

One might reply that the entities do exist after all. In the usual model theory of first-order languages, quantifiers and sentential connectives are taken to be syncategorematic: the definition of truth in a model fixes their contributions to truth-conditions without appealing to entities associated with them. But one can instead associate entities with these expressions as their semantic values. One can treat quantifiers as denoting second-order properties of (or relations between) properties (Montague, 1973), and one can treat sentential connectives as denoting truth functions or relations between propositions.[8] And then joint-carving for quantifiers and sentential connectives can be treated in Armstrong and Lewis's way, as turning on the existence or nature of denoted entities.

But this does not get to the heart of the issue—at least, not if we are looking for an account of what structure *is* (please read with the appropriate cadence), as opposed to merely seeking a systematic way to talk about structure. For the treatment of quantifiers as expressing second-order properties or relations, however appropriate in linguistic theory, does not ring true at a metaphysical level. Let $\exists^2$ be the second-order property of *having at least one instance*. That there exist cows does not seem to be a second-order fact. It surely concerns the concrete world directly, rather than through abstract intermediary entities like $\exists^2$. But if quantificational facts are not about $\exists^2$, then surely facts about quantificational structure are not about $\exists^2$ either.

Similarly, it may be appropriate in linguistics to treat 'and' as a relation between propositions; but metaphysically speaking, the fact that I am human and I am typing surely concerns neither propositions nor relations between them. I'd even like to say the same about predicates. Even if linguistics is right to associate 'is human' with a semantic value, the ultimate metaphysics of my being human has

---

[8]Indeed, one can treat all expressions as standing for entities, as in categorial grammars (Gamut, 1991, chapter 4), although then there is a meaningful syntactic operation—concatenation—that stands for no entity.

nothing to do with this semantic value.[9] And if conjunctive and predicational facts don't involve the semantic values of 'and' and predicates, then surely the corresponding facts about structure don't involve these semantic values either.

The view that structure facts do not concern semantic values is certainly intuitively compelling; but it's best not to rely solely on intuitive compulsions. Fortunately, there is a systematic consideration as well: semantics is, like other special sciences, not fundamental. Our most fundamental level of theorizing should no more recognize distinctively semantic entities and ideology than it should recognize distinctively economic or psychological entities and ideology.[10] This is not to say that the statements of semantics are untrue, only that they are not fundamental (see section 7.8). But if semantics isn't fundamental, the facts about carving at the joints can't fundamentally involve semantic entities.[11]

It's a mistake, then, to think of structure as concerning semantic values. For similar reasons, it would be a mistake to think of structure as concerning linguistic items. The fact (if it is a fact) that 'is negatively charged' carves at the joints isn't in the first instance a fact about the predicate 'is negatively charged'. The fact is simply a fact about the concrete, nonlinguistic world—about its "charge aspect", so to speak. Likewise, the fact (if it is a fact) that the first-order quantifiers carve at the joints isn't a fact about the linguistic items 'there is' and 'for all'. It's a fact about the world—specifically, its quantificational aspect. (Not to reify aspects.)

The no-entities worry can seem inescapable given a certain regimentation of structure-talk, which takes the core locution to be a predicate. In Lewis, for example, the core locution is the predicate 'is natural'. But predicates must be ascribed to *entities*; for Lewis, the entities were the semantic values of predicates; this then leads to taking the facts about structure to involve semantic values.[12] (And it's no better to take the core locution to be a predicate of linguistic items.) This suggests a way to answer the no-entities worry: introduce a regimentation in which the core locution is not a predicate, so that we can talk about structure without bringing in entities of any sort.[13]

We want a locution, call it "$\mathscr{S}$", with which to make statements about structure. What should its grammar be? Here we face an obstacle. Since we are going beyond the predicate, $\mathscr{S}$ must somehow combine with expressions α of arbitrary

---

[9]See Melia (1995; 2000).

[10]By "distinctively semantic ideology" I do not mean metasemantic ideology like 'refers', which relates semantic entities to human populations (though such ideology is surely not fundamental either). I mean, rather, ideology that gives the intrinsic structure of the domain of semantic entities (for instance: notions of conjunction, entailment, and the like, over propositions; or a fundamental predicate functor 'the property of ϕ-ing').

[11]More needs to be said about this argument; see chapter 13 for a fuller discussion.

[12]Caveat: Lewis takes properties to be sets of possible individuals; and set-theoretic ontology and ideology can be viewed as earning their keep in physics, not semantics, which answers my argument against taking the facts of structure to involve semantic values. See the fuller discussion of this argument in chapter 13.

[13]Thanks to Robbie Williams for discussion of the following issues.

grammatical category—with quantifiers, sentential operators, and so on, as well as predicates—to form sentences. But what kind of expression has this sort of grammar? (The attraction of the predicate regimentation is that it avoids this problem: we first convert each such α into a singular term, t_α, to which a predicate for structure may be applied. But what would t_α be? The only possibility seems to be a quotation name of α itself, or a name of α's semantic value; but then we'd be back to treating the facts about structure as involving linguistic items or semantic values.)

We might overcome this obstacle by taking $\mathscr{S}$ to have a very flexible grammar, so that it attaches *directly* to α, regardless of α's grammatical category. I don't know of any natural language expressions with this sort of grammar, but I don't see that as a problem. Some philosophers think that we can understand only what can be defined using the pre-existing resources of natural language; but this stultifying doctrine is inadequate to the evident fact of linguistic innovation within science, as well as to the initial emergence of natural language itself. If the inferential role of a novel expression has been made tolerably clear, and if the world contains structure corresponding to the new expression, then surely the introduction of the novel expression has been successful.

So on this way of overcoming the obstacle, the core locution for talking about structure is an "operator" $\mathscr{S}$, which can attach to an expression of any grammatical category α to form a grammatical sentence $\mathscr{S}(\alpha)$. Thus, we can say "$\mathscr{S}$(is negatively charged)", "$\mathscr{S}(\exists)$" (or "$\mathscr{S}$(there is)"), "$\mathscr{S}(\wedge)$" (or "$\mathscr{S}$(and)"), and so on. Since nothing in English really matches this regimentation, I'll tend to revert informally to a predicate of linguistic items or abstract entities; I'll speak of 'is negatively charged', 'and', and 'there exists'—or negative charge, conjunction, and existential quantification—as "carving at the joints" or "being fundamental". But the facts of structure are more faithfully represented using $\mathscr{S}$.[14]

To say $\mathscr{S}$(and) is not to say something about an alleged object Conjunction. It is not to say anything about any thing at all. It is nevertheless to say something true, something objective, something about reality. Nowhere is it written in stone that all facts must be entity-involving. In Graham Nerlich's phrase, "realism need not be ontic".[15] To be sure, the entity-based ideology of predicate logic is simple, beautiful, and well-behaved, and it's best to stick to it whenever possible. But the realist about structure, it would seem, cannot live by predicate logic alone.

There are hard questions about $\mathscr{S}$, thus taken. I said that it can attach to expressions "of any grammatical category". What, exactly, does that mean? $\mathscr{S}$

---

[14]In a fundamental language, all and only primitive expressions carve at the joints. Thus $\ulcorner\mathscr{S}(\alpha)\urcorner$ will be true iff α is a primitive expression. One might worry that this somehow makes the $\mathscr{S}$ operator metalinguistic or trivial. But that would be a mistake. First, it doesn't follow that $\ulcorner\mathscr{S}(\alpha)\urcorner$ *says* that α is a primitive expression. Second, you can't learn that $\ulcorner\mathscr{S}(\alpha)\urcorner$ is true simply by observing that α is a primitive expression; you would also need to know that your language is a fundamental one.

[15]Nerlich (1982, p. 274). See also Putnam (1975*d*, p. 70); McGinn (1981, 169–70); Yablo (2000, section IX).

must at least be able to attach to all primitive expressions of the language in question; but what about complex expressions? (As we will see in section 7.13, we need to be able to query complex expressions for joint-carving.)

We might say that $\mathscr{S}$ can attach to any "grammatical unit"—intuitively, any string that is either a primitive symbol or a complex symbol that is generated at some point by the language's recursive formation rules. This has certain limitations, depending on the grammar of the fundamental language we're using to talk about structure. Suppose we want to ask whether a certain conjunctive predicate, the conjunction of predicates F and G, carves at the joints. If our language has a predicate functor **c** for predicate conjunction then this is straightforward. Our formation rules will include a clause for complex-predicate formation; one of the expressions formed via that clause will be the conjunctive predicate $F\,\mathbf{c}\,G$; so we can form the sentence $\mathscr{S}(F\,\mathbf{c}\,G)$. But suppose (as I suspect is more likely) that our fundamental language is grammatically simpler. Suppose, for example, that its grammar is that of predicate logic (without function symbols), with the addition of the operator $\mathscr{S}$. In that case, there simply are no complex predicates, since the only rules of formation are for the grammatical category of sentence. So the only complex strings we can query for structure are sentences (including those with free variables). But then, we can achieve our goal of evaluating the conjunction of F and G for structure only indirectly, by forming the open sentence $\mathscr{S}(Fx \wedge Gx)$.[16] And the querying becomes even more indirect for, say, complex operators. Suppose, for instance, that the only primitive sentential connectives in the language are $\sim$ and $\vee$, and we want to query for structure a complex expression with the truth table of the material conditional. We can query the various sentences of the form $\sim\phi \vee \psi$ (for example, $\sim Fx \vee Gy$, $\sim Ha \vee \forall x \forall y Rxy$, and so on); but each of these sentences also queries certain other expressions; namely, the expressions occurring inside ϕ and ψ.

We might just live with the fact that we can't query complexes directly. We could say that the question of whether "the material conditional carves at the joints" is not a matter of the truth of any one sentence in our fundamental language; rather, it emerges from the totality of sentences of the form $\mathscr{S}(\sim\phi \vee \psi)$.[17] Alternatively, we might pursue a different method for overcoming the obstacle to constructing a grammar for $\mathscr{S}$.[18] According to this method, $\mathscr{S}$ no longer has a flexible grammar; now it is a one-place sentence operator. However, we include in our fundamental language a collection of dummy variables. There are dummy variables of every grammatical category: individual dummy variables, sentential dummy variables, predicate dummy variables, sentence-operator dummy variables,

---

[16] And even this does not fully isolate the complex predicate, since one is also querying the variables.

[17] We might introduce a nonfundamental language with grammatical resources to directly query the material conditional. A metaphysical semantics (see section 7.4) for such a language might assign to the query the truth-condition that each sentence of the fundamental language with the form $\mathscr{S}(\sim\phi \vee \psi)$ be true.

[18] Compare Sider (2009, section 8).

and so on. Dummy variables are not bindable. Their purpose is to combine with other expressions to form complete sentences, so that the sentence operator $\mathscr{S}$ may then be applied. The expressions other than dummy variables in such sentences are those that are queried for carving at the joints. So we no longer query sub-sentential primitive expressions by directly attaching $\mathscr{S}$ to them; instead, we attach those primitive expressions to appropriate dummy variables to obtain a sentence, and then attach $\mathscr{S}$ to that sentence. For example, we query the predicate G, the name a, the quantifier $\exists$, and the operator $\Box$, with the following sentences, respectively (dummy variables are in sans serif):

$\mathscr{S}(G\mathsf{x})$

$\mathscr{S}(F\mathsf{a})$

$\mathscr{S}(\exists\mathsf{x}P)$

$\mathscr{S}(\Box P)$.

Complex expressions are now straightforward to query. We can query the material conditional, for example, using the sentence $\mathscr{S}(\sim P \vee Q)$.

I have argued that we should not think of judgments about structure as concerning entities. Judgments about structure concern ideology, not ontology. Let us close with a discussion of an opposing, ontic approach.[19]

This opposing approach is modeled on Armstrong, rather than Lewis. Lewis's approach to regimenting talk of structure was to posit an abundant group of entities (for him, sets of 'tuples of possibilia) and regard only some of them as being structural (natural). The Armstrongian approach, by contrast, does away with the abundant entities, and posits only a sparse group of entities. Given a sparse entity, there is no further question of whether it carves at the joints; sparse entities automatically carve at the joints, so to speak. But given a *linguistic* entity, there is a further question of whether it stands for a sparse entity. The sparse entities, for Armstrong, were universals; thus on his view, a predicate carves at the joints iff it stands for some universal.

The sparse entities of this approach are not to be thought of as semantic values. (After all, most meaningful expressions do not stand for sparse entities.) Thus the approach is immune to the objection that semantics is nonfundamental.

Call this approach ontologism, since it insists that fundamental metaphysical commitments be ontic. Distinguish two forms: methodological and metaphysical. The defender of methodological ontologism says that his opponents are making some sort of methodological or conceptual mistake. It's somehow conceptually confused to think of a fundamental metaphysics as being given by anything other than a list of entities. The defender of metaphysical ontologism, on the other hand, puts forward her position as a substantive hypothesis about the nature of fundamental reality.

---

[19] Thanks to Jonathan Schaffer for discussion here, though the opposing approach should not be attributed to him.

Methodological ontologism seems hopeless. Earlier in this section I put forward a conception, using the operator $\mathscr{S}$, of what non-ontic claims of fundamental metaphysics might look like. It's hard to see how this position is conceptually or methodologically confused. Further, it's tempting to view the defender of methodological ontologism as arbitrarily privileging his own ideology. *His* ideology includes the quantifiers and a special predicate that singles out the sparse entities; *my* ideology includes $\mathscr{S}$ and various other expressions; what makes his ideology the sole intelligible vehicle for giving fundamental descriptions of reality?

Quine's terminology—to return to my rant—has perhaps contributed to methodological ontologism appearing more plausible than it really is. 'Ideology' suggests a purely arbitrary, conceptual matter; ideology and ontology are supposed to be exhaustive; thus, the only nonconceptual question is that of one's ontology. Quine's terminology is so ingrained that this reasoning can seem built into the very concept of metaphysics.[20] Simply appreciating the possibility of an alternative, of ontology-free but nevertheless worldly metaphysics, should break this spell.

Metaphysical ontologism is a much more likely proposition. The attitude here is that the alternative is inferior, not unthinkable; the best metaphysics of fundamentality is entity-based.

Ontologism could, in principle, sustain much of the project of this book. For in many cases, talk of joint-carving ideology can be replaced with talk of sparse entities. In a discussion of whether causal disputes are substantive, for example, instead of asking whether $\mathscr{S}$(causes), the defender of ontologism could ask whether there exists a causal universal. But problems begin when the defender of metaphysical ontologism tries to go beyond the predicate. Whenever she wants to speak of joint-carving she faces a choice: either posit a corresponding sparse entity, or else do not speak of joint-carving at all.

For example, if she wanted to say that modal operators carve at the joints, she would have to posit an appropriate entity and claim that the modal facts ultimately boil down to the facts about this entity. Candidates for the entity might include i) a modal universal that is instantiated by other universals;[21] ii) a modal universal that is instantiated by propositions (which would themselves need to be reified—a very unArmstrongian move); or iii) a modal entity of a different sort, call it a "modal monad", that plays a role in instantiation: the necessary possession of a universal U amounts to the instantiation of U by a particular *with respect to the modal monad*, whereas the merely contingent possession of U is the instantiation *simpliciter* of U by the particular. If she is unwilling to say any of these things—to underwrite the claim of modal structure by positing a sparse modal entity—then she cannot speak of modal structure at all.

[20] In fact, one can discern a usage of 'ontology'—particularly prevalent in the philosophy of physics literature—as a synonym for 'metaphysics'.

[21] Compare Armstrong's (1983) own approach to laws of nature.

I myself do not believe in modal structure (chapter 12), so I don't regard this limitation as unwelcome. But consider, next, the case of quantification. As we saw, it is artificial to take a quantifier, in one's ultimate metaphysics, as standing for an entity. So the defender of ontologism must choose between an artificial metaphysics of quantification and forgoing talk of joint-carving for quantifiers. And the latter would be a real limitation: as we will see in chapter 9, the thesis that quantifiers carve at the joints is the best way to defend the substantivity of ontological questions. This limitation is the chief problem with metaphysical ontologism.

The previous paragraph's line of thought is especially dialectically effective because the defender of ontologism has a particular reason to regard quantificational questions as being substantive. After all, questions about the nature of fundamentality, for her, turn on whether *there are* appropriate sparse entities. She, of all people, cannot acquiesce to the Carnapian thought that talking as if sparse entities do not exist is just as good as talking as if they do. Thus metaphysical ontologism is "unreflexive": given its strictures on what can be evaluated for fundamentality, its own apparatus cannot be ratified as fundamental.

Armstrong's own theory is similarly unreflexive. With good reason, Armstrong refrains from positing a universal of instantiation (1978*a*, chapter 11, section 1). Thus, although 'instantiates' is an ineliminable part of his ideology, he cannot recognize 'instantiates' as fundamental, in the way that he recognizes fundamental physical predicates as fundamental. But claims specifying which particulars instantiate which universals are clearly part of Armstrong's fundamental theory of the world. Merely to list the universals and particulars, without specifying which particulars instantiate which universals, would be a woefully partial description of what, according to him, the world is fundamentally like. There is, therefore, overwhelming pressure on Armstrong to recognize, somehow, that talk of instantiation is fundamental; but he is barred from doing so by his ontologism.[22]

The defender of ontologism might, in Wittgensteinian fashion, reply that one cannot *say* the whole truth about fundamentality. The whole truth can only be *shown*, by quantifying over entities, saying that particulars instantiate universals, and so on. If this position is uncomfortable, that is a reason to reject ontologism, and to adopt a broader conception of metaphysical commitment.

6.4 Unclear epistemology?

A third reason to fear going beyond the predicate is epistemic: how could we ever tell when attributions of structure to nonpredicates are justified? But in fact, the generalized conception of structure raises absolutely nothing new, epistemically. Questions about how much nonpredicate structure the world contains are

---

[22]To be fair, Armstrong is not really asking the same set of questions as I am, so it is somewhat misleading to describe him as accepting ontologism.

substantive metaphysical questions, just like the most substantive questions of first-order metaphysics, and can be addressed in the same way.

Section 2.3 presented a broadly Quinean approach to the epistemology of metaphysics, and to the epistemology of joint-carving in particular. It is reasonable to regard the ideology of our best theory—"best" by the usual criteria for theory choice, such as simplicity—as carving at the joints. This approach is not bound to the predicate. Successful theories justify belief in *all* of their ideological posits. I will, for example, argue in chapter 9 that since our most successful theories employ quantification, we have reason to believe that quantifiers carve at the joints—that quantificational structure is fundamental. This argument is exactly parallel to the argument for fundamental spatiotemporal structure: quantification is no less part of the ideology of fundamental physics than are spatiotemporal notions.

When a conceptual decision has become wholly familiar, it is easy to forget that it is nevertheless a decision. Such are the overwhelmingly successful conceptual decisions of modern logic. Thinking in terms of *and*, *or*, *not*, *all*, *some*, and *identical* has led to great strides in the foundations of logic and mathematics, and so, less directly, in the foundations of all other disciplines as well. The success of these conceptual choices justifies belief in the existence of corresponding structures in the world. Once "ideology" is purged of its psychological connotations, there is no barrier to recognizing a theory's logical ideology as a coequal part of that theory's portrayal of the world, and thus as being as good a candidate for carving at the joints as the theory's nonlogical vocabulary.

6.5 Logical conventionalism

A fourth source of resistance to going beyond the predicate, and in particular to speaking of joint-carving logical notions, is vaguer, more primordial, and (I think) widespread. It is the thought that it is appropriate to evaluate expressions for carving at the joints only when they are "contentful". *Predicates* are paradigmatically contentful. But logical expressions, on the other hand, are purely "formal", so the thought goes. They do not describe features of the world, but rather are mere conventional devices. Since logical expressions are not "worldly", it is inappropriate to speak of the world as containing structure corresponding to those expressions.

This is picture thinking. But behind the picture, I suspect, there lies an identifiable—and mistaken—philosophical doctrine: the doctrine of logical conventionalism.

Actually, what I really think is widespread is not so much an *acceptance* of logical conventionalism as a failure to fully repudiate it. The status in contemporary philosophy of logical conventionalism and the related doctrine of "truth by convention" is curious. On the one hand, few people self-identify as logical conventionalists. If pressed on why not, I suppose most would gesture at Quine's famous critique in "Truth by Convention". But on the other hand, the picture thinking described above really does have staying power, which would be explained by latent logical conventionalism. Moreover, the *language* of truth by convention persists: one still hears the phrase "true purely by virtue of meaning", logical truths are still described as being "trivial" or "empty" (and are thus thought of as being epistemically unproblematic), and so on.[23]

Against logical conventionalism, I uphold Russell's (1919, p. 169) diametrically opposed position: "logic is concerned with the real world just as truly as zoology, though with its more abstract and general features". Evaluating logical expressions for joint-carving is therefore not different in kind from evaluating any other expressions for joint-carving.

All I have to offer in support of Russellian realism about logic is a critique of conventionalism; discussion of intermediate positions remains a lacuna.

Logical conventionalism originated in the "linguistic theory of the a priori", popularized by A. J. Ayer in *Language, Truth and Logic* (1936):

Like Hume, I divide all genuine propositions into two classes: those which, in his terminology, concern "relations of ideas," and those which concern "matters of fact." The former class comprises the *a priori* propositions of logic and pure mathematics, and these I allow to be necessary and certain only because they are analytic. That is, I maintain that the reason why these propositions cannot be confuted in experience is that they do not make any assertion about the empirical world, but simply record our determination to use symbols in a certain fashion. (p. 31)

A proposition (sentence) is analytic, Ayer goes on to say, "when its validity depends solely on the definitions of the symbols it contains . . .". Analytic propositions can be known a priori because they are "devoid of factual content" (p. 78), because they merely "record our determination to use words in a certain fashion". Something like this view was once widely held, by logical positivists, Wittgensteinians, and ordinary language philosophers.[24] The core of the view is that an analytic truth, for instance the truth that all horses are horses, is true purely by virtue of linguistic conventions. By adopting certain rules governing the use of logical words like 'all', language users somehow make 'all horses are horses' true.

Quine famously objected to the doctrine of truth by convention as follows. (B) is allegedly true by convention:

(B) An object is a bachelor iff it is an unmarried man.

Pretend that, as a matter of convention, 'bachelor' means the same as 'unmarried man'. Thus, (B) means the same as the following logical truth:

(A) An object is an unmarried man iff it is an unmarried man.

---

[23] Ironically, one source of the lingering conventionalist strain may be a backlash against Quine's critique of analyticity. Quine's overarching critique contained, as a part, the empirical assertion that there are no facts of meaning (1951*b*). The manifest inadequacy of this view may have led to a failure to appreciate the most powerful part of the critique, namely, his attack on truth by convention (1936; 1960*a*). See also Boghossian (1997).

[24] Conventionalists include Ayer, Britton (1947), Carnap (1937, §69; 1950), and Malcolm (1940). Pap (1958, chapter 7) contains a thorough (critical) discussion of conventionalism. See also Lewy (1976, especially chapter 5), and Boghossian (1997).

The introduction of the convention governing 'bachelor' therefore makes (B) have the same truth-value as (A); but this on its own, Quine pointed out, does not make (B) true. The truth of (B) requires the "prior" truth of (A). As Quine says, ". . . definitions are available only for transforming truths, not for founding them" (1936, p. 81).

(B) *would* be rendered true by convention if the logical truth (A) itself were in some sense true by convention. But as Quine went on to argue, logical truths do not in any interesting sense owe their truth to conventions. In particular, he considers the thought that we can legislate a logical truth T by proclaiming "Let T be true." He points out a problem (one that arises even before the pressing question of how such proclamations are supposed to do the trick). A would-be legislator of logical truth cannot individually legislate each logical truth, for there are infinitely many of them. He might think to make general legislations to the effect that every sentence of a certain form is to be true, such as:

(I) Let every instance of the following schema be true: $\ulcorner$If ϕ then $\phi\urcorner$.

But any such legislation results in truths of a single fixed logical form, whereas logical truths can take infinitely many forms. So, he might think, a second type of general legislation is required, which specifies that *if* certain statements are true, then others are to be true as well. Here is an example:

(II) If a statement ϕ and a statement $\ulcorner$If ϕ then $\psi\urcorner$ are true, then let ψ be true as well.

The conventionalist's hope, as Quine imagines, is to make true all the truths of propositional logic using legislations of types (I) and (II). For there exist complete axiomatizations of propositional logic with finitely many axiom schemas in which the only rule of inference is modus ponens; each axiom schema could be legislated in style (I), and modus ponens could be legislated into effect by proclaiming (II). One could then go on to legislate the truths of (first-order) predicate logic in a similar fashion.

According to Quine, the problem for conventionalism thus understood is that logic is needed to apply the conventions, and cannot therefore be grounded in the conventions. Suppose that statements ϕ and $\ulcorner$if ϕ then $\psi\urcorner$ have been legislated to be true by legislations of sort (I). (II) now says that *if* these sentences are true, *then* ψ is to be true as well. To derive from this the result that ψ is indeed true, we must perform modus ponens—we must use logic. But logic is exactly what the legislations are supposed to ground.

For various reasons, it seems to me that Quine's objection—that logic will be needed to legislate the infinity of logical truths—does not get to the heart of what is metaphysically problematic about conventionalism.[25] Imagine a finitary

---

[25] It does a better job of showing that conventionalism cannot epistemically justify logic: we already need to be justified in using logic before we can gain the justification that the conventionalist is trying to supply.

conventionalist, who tries to introduce conventional truth in a language whose set of well-formed formulas is finite. Or imagine a conventionalist with an infinitary mind, who can legislate each of the infinitely many logical truths individually. Logic would surely not be true by convention even in these cases, but in neither case does Quine's objection apply.

Moreover, the conventionalist might reply to Quine that legislations of form (II) are *conditional legislations* rather than *legislations of conditionals*. (Compare the distinction between conditional probability and the probability of a conditional, or between conditional obligation and an obligation to see to the truth of a conditional.) Quine's objection is actually pretty elusive, but one way of taking it is as follows:

After legislations of type (I) are made, for certain sentences ϕ and ψ, both sentence ϕ and the sentence ⌜if ϕ then ψ⌝ are true by convention; and after legislation (II) is made, the following conditional sentence is also true by convention: ⌜If ϕ and ⌜if ϕ then ψ⌝ are both true, then ψ is also true⌝. But we cannot pass from the fact that these three sentences are true by convention to the conclusion that ψ is true by convention unless we make the further assumption that the truths by convention are closed under modus ponens (and also under conjunction-introduction, truth-introduction, and truth-elimination). Since that further assumption is precisely what (II) was supposed to accomplish, (II) is ineffective.

This objection, notice, assumes that the effect of legislation (II) is that a certain conditional sentence (namely ⌜If ϕ and ⌜if ϕ then ψ⌝ are both true, then ψ is also true⌝) is true by convention. But the conventionalist might reply that its effect is instead that it be the case that if ϕ and ⌜If ϕ then ψ⌝ are both true by convention, then ψ is also true by convention. The conventionalist might reply, that is, that his claim all along was that (II) results directly in the set of truths by convention being closed under modus ponens, and not that it results in a conditional sentence corresponding to modus ponens being true by convention. (II) is not an unconditional legislation that a certain sentence (a conditional sentence) be true by convention. It is rather an irreducibly conditional legislation, which results in its being the case that if certain sentences are true by convention, then so is a certain further sentence. The latter sentence is legislated conditionally on the former sentences being legislated. Quine in effect grants the conventionalist for the sake of argument that the words pronounced in (I), "Let any statement of the following form be true . . ." have their desired effect. But the words are not magic: something about the pattern of beliefs and dispositions in the linguistic community that results from the pronouncement of those words is what allegedly does the trick: certain sentences individually become true by convention. If Quine is willing to grant that the words in (I) have this effect, why is he not also willing to grant that different words, the words in (II), which result in a different pattern of beliefs and dispositions, have a different effect, that of a conditional legislation?

Quine's argument does not go far enough. An adequate critique must challenge the very idea of something's being "true by convention". Even an infinite mind, or a conventionalist with only finite aspirations, or a conditional legislator, could not make the logical truths, or any other sentence for that matter, true by convention (unless the sentence is *about* conventions). The components of this critique are not new, but are nevertheless worth repeating.

Part of the critique consists in pointing out that it is no easy task for the conventionalist to specify an appropriate sense in which logical truths are "true by convention". There is a mundane sense in which *all* true sentences are partly true because of convention, since all sentences exhibit symbol-conventionality (section 4.3). Even a synthetic sentence like 'Snow is white' is true partly because of its meaning; it would not have been true if it had meant that grass is green. Of course, in order for 'Snow is white' to be true, the world must also cooperate: the world must really be as the sentence says. Snow must really be white. So, it might be thought, the conventionalist could claim that the requirement of worldly cooperation is not present for logical truths. But on the face of it, this is wrong. By convention we make it the case that the sentence 'If it is raining then it is raining' means that if it is raining then it is raining; but in order for the sentence to be true, the world must also cooperate; the world must really be as the sentence says. It must really be that if it is raining then it is raining. It is easy to overlook the requirement of cooperation in this case because it is so obvious that if it is raining then it is raining. But no sense has yet been given to the idea that the requirement is not present.

A conventionalist might reply that 'If it is raining then it is raining' "automatically" becomes true upon being endowed with its meaning; that is the sense in which there is no further requirement that the world cooperate. But what does 'automatically' mean here? It could be understood in terms of necessity: it is necessarily true that if 'if' and 'then' mean what they do then 'If it is raining then it is raining' is true. Thus understood the claim is correct, but it does not secure a truth-making role for the convention. The mere fact that it is necessarily true that it is raining if it is raining ensures that 'If it is raining then it is raining' is "automatically"—in the current sense of 'automatically'—true once it has been given its meaning. Conventionalism thus understood says little more than that logical and other analytic truths are necessary; nothing is left of the intuitive idea of their truth being grounded in conventions.

We are still in search of an appropriate sense in which logic is true by convention. Ayer's claim that analytic truths "simply record our determination to use symbols in a certain fashion" is unhelpful. It suggests that analytic truths make statements *about* linguistic conventions. But this is a nonstarter; statements about linguistic conventions are contingent, whereas the statements made by typical analytic sentences are necessary (Broad (1936, p. 107), Lewy (1976, p. 9)). Ayer's claim that analytic truths "say nothing about the empirical world" is similarly unhelpful: it is hard to attach any sense to it that advances his cause. 'If it is raining then it is raining' *seems* to say something about the empirical world: that the empirical world contains rain if it contains rain. Of course, the thing it says is a logical truth. We might define "about the empirical world" to exclude logical truths, but what would be the point?—the claim that logical truths "say nothing about the empirical world" could then play no role in explaining the epistemology or metaphysics of logical truth.

To further reinforce the difficulty of finding an appropriate sense of 'true by convention', consider that the phrase is intended to indicate an intimate sort of *dependence* of truth on convention. But what sort, exactly? The conventionalist will surely deny counterfactual or temporal dependence, at least of the sort that would imply absurd statements like the following:

> Before we introduced our conventions, not all green things were green.

> If we had introduced no conventions, not all green things would have been green.

Of course, metalinguistic counterfactual and temporal statements such as the following are unproblematic:

> Before we introduced our conventions, the sentence 'all green things are green' was not used to express a truth.

> If we had introduced no conventions, the sentence 'all green things are green' would not have been used to express a truth.

But *all* truths depend on conventions in this metalinguistic way; before we introduced our conventions, the sentence 'Snow is white' was not used to express a truth. It remains unclear just what sort of dependence of truth upon conventions is supposed to be distinctive of conventionalism.

Here are two further failed attempts to understand what the defender of truth by convention has in mind. Return to the would-be truth-legislator, who says "Let every sentence of the form 'If ϕ then ϕ' be true." What is this performance intended to accomplish? On the one hand, the legislator could be resolving to use the word 'true' in a new way; he could be listing the sentences to which this new term 'true' applies. But this obviously isn't what the conventionalist wants. On the other hand, the legislator could be constraining the intended meaning for conditional constructions. He could be placing a necessary condition on the function from sentences to the propositions that they mean: this function must assign a true proposition to each sentence of the form 'If ϕ then ϕ'. Any function that violates this constraint, the legislator is saying, is not the means-in-English function. This, too, is not what the conventionalist wants, for it assumes an antecedent notion of propositional truth that has not been shown to depend in any way on convention.

This last point bears emphasis. We should all agree that one way to constrain the meaning of an expression, E, is to stipulate that E be interpreted so that certain sentences containing E turn out true, or that certain inferences involving E be truth-preserving. It can seem that such stipulations create truth, or truth-preservation, on their own. But this is not the case, as was illustrated by

Arthur Prior (1960) in dramatic fashion. Prior imagined the introduction of a new sentential connective 'tonk', stipulated to obey a disjunction-like introduction rule "From ϕ infer ϕ-tonk-ψ", as well as a conjunction-like elimination rule "From ϕ-tonk-ψ infer ψ." The stipulations do not result in the two rules being truth-preserving, for the rules would allow us to infer any statement ψ from any other statement ϕ (first infer ϕ-tonk-ψ from ϕ using the introduction rule, and then infer ψ using the elimination rule). 'Tonk' is stipulated to stand for a meaning that obeys the two rules; but there simply is no such meaning; 'tonk' cannot be interpreted so as to obey the rules. Now, we do not believe the usual logical connectives to be like 'tonk'. When we stipulate that conditional sentences are to be so interpreted that every sentence of the form 'If ϕ then ϕ' is true, or when we stipulate that 'and' and 'or' obey their usual introduction and elimination rules, we believe that these expressions *can* be understood so as to obey the stipulations. But the case of 'tonk' shows that the stipulations do not, on their own, create the truth, or truth-preservation.

The critique so far has not produced an argument against conventionalism; it has merely cleared away obstacles to understanding, by enumerating various things that conventionalists cannot mean by 'true by convention'. Now, this sort of clarification can be effective. For some, conventionalism will lose whatever appeal it had, once the scales fall from their eyes. Nevertheless, direct arguments against conventionalism would be welcome.

It is difficult to argue against a doctrine that has not been clearly articulated. But what we can do is formulate the doctrine in schematic terms, and then argue that so long as those schematic terms behave in a certain way, the doctrine must be false. I will give two arguments of this form, assuming the following schematic understanding of the doctrine of truth by convention: "We can *legislate-true* the truths of logic."

The first argument assumes that sentences that are *about* certain parts of the world cannot be legislated-true. These are the parts of the world that I cannot affect simply by wishing or pronouncing or legislating. I cannot, for example, make true the sentence 'My computer monitor has been thrown out the window' by wishing or pronouncing or legislating; I must defenestrate the monitor myself, or pay or incite someone else to do it. Indeed, given my lack of magical powers, the *only* statements that I can affect by mere wishing or pronouncing or legislating would seem to be sentences *about* conventions or related matters, such as which noises I make. We nonmagical humans can legislate-true such sentences because they are about *us*. The first argument, then, is this. Sentence (O) is not about us:[26]

(O) Either it is raining or it is not raining.

---

[26]This could be regarded as a stand-alone premise; or it could be supported thus: 'It is raining' is not about us; 'It is not raining' is not about us; the statements that are not about us are closed under disjunction. Supporting the premise in this way would draw this first argument closer to the second.

Since the only statements that we can legislate-true are those that are about us, we cannot legislate-true the logical truth (O).

Talk of "aboutness" is admittedly slippery. Now, all the first argument needs is that there is *a* sense of 'about' on which (O) is not about us, and on which only sentences about us can be legislated-true. Still, an argument that makes no appeal at all to aboutness may be welcome.

The second argument fits the bill. What it assumes about the schematic notion of legislating-true is that i) I cannot legislate-true 'It is raining'; and ii) I cannot legislate-true 'It is not raining'; and iii) if I cannot legislate-true ϕ, nor can I legislate-true ψ, then I cannot legislate-true the disjunction $\ulcorner\phi$ or $\psi\urcorner$. In defense of iii): a disjunction states simply that one or the other of its disjuncts holds; to legislate-true a disjunction one would need to legislate-true one of its disjuncts. (To know (believe, promise, . . .) a disjunction, one needn't know (believe . . .) one of its disjuncts; but this needn't undermine iii), which is specific to legislating-true.) Given premises i)–iii), I cannot legislate-true (O).

It is open, of course, for the defender of truth by convention to supply a notion of legislating-true on which the argument's premises are false. The challenge, though, is that the premises seem correct given an *intuitive* understanding of "legislate-true".

7　Questions

Friends of fundamentality face some abstract questions about its nature. My way of thinking about fundamentality—in terms of structure—is distinctive in large part because of how I answer the questions. My answers: the fundamental is complete, pure, subpropositional, absolute, determinate, and fundamental.

7.1　Complete?

It is natural to assume that the fundamental must be "complete", that the fundamental must in some sense be responsible for everything.

Completeness seems definitive of fundamentality. It would be a nonstarter to say that the fundamental consists solely of one electron: thus conceived the fundamental could not account for the vast complexity of the world we experience.

A preliminary formulation of completeness might run as follows: *every non-fundamental truth holds in virtue of some fundamental truth*.[1] But the exact content of this formulation is far from clear. What do 'in virtue of' and 'fundamental truth' mean here? There are subtle issues about how to understand these notions in terms of my official notion of structure. I want to postpone discussion of those subtleties, however; so for now let us leave completeness stated in this intuitive way. A fundamental truth (or fact), intuitively, is a metaphysically basic or rock-bottom truth (fact). Facts about the positions of subatomic particles would be, on most views, fundamental facts, whereas the fact that some people smile when they eat candy would presumably not be. 'In virtue of', intuitively, stands for the relationship whereby the fundamental facts underwrite or give rise to all other facts. The fact that some people smile when they eat candy holds in virtue, perhaps, of certain facts about the states of subatomic particles (or, given a less materialistic outlook: in virtue of these subatomic facts plus certain fundamental mental facts).

Though I will be leaving 'in virtue of' at an intuitive level for now, I should say up front that it is *not* to be understood in terms of modality, truthmaking, or fact-identity. Thus I reject these conceptions of completeness:

"All truths are necessitated by (or, supervene on) a fundamental description of the world."

"Every truth has a fundamental truthmaker."

"Every fact is identical to a fundamental fact."

[1] A refined principle would allow a nonfundamental truth to hold in virtue of multiple fundamental truths taken collectively.

The modal gloss imposes no meaningful requirement of completeness for necessary truths, the truthmaking gloss requires a commitment to truthmaking, and the fact-identity gloss requires a commitment to facts, individuated in an appropriate way. (I'll have more to say about truthmaking and facts in chapter 8.) A less objectionable way to cash out "in virtue of" would appeal to the—currently very popular—notion of ground: "all truths are grounded in fundamental truths".[2] To say that the existence of a city is grounded in certain facts about subatomic particles is to say that the latter facts produce or account for or explain the existence of a city, in a distinctively metaphysical way. Although ground implies necessitation, necessitation is insufficient for ground. (Examples like the following are often given: snow's being white does not ground its being the case that either grass is green or grass is not green, even though it's necessary that if snow is white then grass is either green or not green; what grounds the truth of grass's being either green or not green is its true disjunct: grass's being green.) Thus the grounding approach lays down a meaningful requirement of completeness for necessary truths.[3] Further, properly understood, speaking in terms of ground requires no commitment to truthmaking, or to facts, propositions, or any other abstract entities. I will indeed sometimes speak of the grounding of propositions or facts (and will likewise speak of in-virtue-of relations amongst facts and propositions), but such talk is dispensable: one can always construe 'ground' (and related locutions) as a sentence operator: "That ϕ grounds its being the case that ψ" (Fine, 2001). Later on I will criticize the ground-theoretic interpretation of completeness, and propose a different gloss of "in virtue of". But the ground-theoretic gloss is much closer to my own than are those in terms of modality, truthmaking, or fact-identity, so if it is familiar, it can serve as a working heuristic: "Every nonfundamental truth is grounded by some fundamental truth."

7.2 Pure?

There is a second assumption about structure that I think we ought to make—what I call "purity": *fundamental truths involve only fundamental notions*. When God was creating the world, she was not required to think in terms of nonfundamental notions like city, smile, or candy.

As with completeness, there are subtleties about how exactly to understand purity in my preferred terms. "Fundamental notion" is easy (it means "carves at the joints") but "fundamental truth" remains to be explained. Let us postpone discussion of these subtleties just a little longer. (But do notice that purity concerns two distinct concepts of fundamentality: the concept of a fundamental *notion*, and the concept of a fundamental *truth*.)

---

[2] On grounding see Fine (2001; 2010; 2011); Rosen (2010); Schaffer (2009a); Schnieder (2011); and the papers in Correia and Schnieder (2012).

[3] This is just one way in which ground improves on the coarser-grained notion of modality; see especially Fine (2001).

Suppose someone claimed that even though cityhood is a nonfundamental notion, in order to tell the complete story of the world there is no way to avoid bringing in the notion of a city—certain facts involving cityhood are rock-bottom. This is the sort of view that purity says we should reject. This might seem obvious and uncontroversial. But in fact, purity has some very striking consequences.

Here is a truth: there exists a city. Since the notion of a city is not fundamental, purity says that this truth is not fundamental. No surprises so far. Completeness then says that this truth holds in virtue of some fundamental truth T—perhaps some truth of microphysics. So we have:

(1) There is a city in virtue of the fact that T.

Still no surprises.

But now consider (1) itself. Just like 'There are cities', (1) is a truth involving the notion of a city. And so, given purity, it cannot be a fundamental truth. And so, given completeness, it must itself hold in virtue of some fundamental truth.

Now, I accept this consequence (given the way I will eventually understand "in virtue of"). (1) is not itself fundamental (nor is any other in-virtue-of truth, in my view). So (1) must itself hold in virtue of other truths. But this is a nontrivial claim; and it is a claim that some people are going to want to resist. A certain sort of primitivist about in-virtue-of, for example, will refuse to explain truths like (1) in other terms. Purity stands in the way of this sort of primitivism; it requires facts about the *relationship* between the fundamental and the nonfundamental to be themselves nonfundamental. Thus purity brings a heavy explanatory burden: it requires there to be facts in virtue of which in-virtue-of-facts hold. But this is a burden we ought to shoulder. The rock-bottom story of the world ought not to mention cityhood at all, not even in sentences like (1). The primitivist about in-virtue-of who opposes this is in an awkward position. On the one hand she must surely acknowledge that *most* truths involving cityhood—truths such as "There is a city", "Philadelphia is a city", "Candy can be purchased in most cities", and so on—are not fundamental; and she must surely feel the force of the thought that this is in some sense because such truths involve the nonfundamental notion of being a city. But then why the special exception for truths like (1)? Admitting that (1) is a fundamental truth would drag the notion of cityhood itself into the realm of the fundamental, since the admission concedes that the fundamental story of the world cannot be told without bringing in cityhood.

Let's think a little more about purity, and in particular, how it relates to forms of primitivism. Consider the doctrine of modalism, which I understand as the claim that necessity is a fundamental notion (in my terms, carves at the joints). Now, many modalists would, I think, take this a step further, and say also that modal truths are fundamental truths. But given purity, it cannot be that *all* modal truths are fundamental. The modal truth that it is necessary that all cities are cities, for example, must be nonfundamental given purity, since it involves the nonfundamental notion of cityhood. But then given completeness, "Necessarily, every city is a city" must hold in virtue of some further fundamental truth N; and N cannot, given purity, involve the notion of cityhood. Notice, though, that N *can* involve the notion of necessity, if modalism is true. N might, for example, have the form "Necessarily, all Cs are Cs", where C involves only fundamental notions. (Think of C as a "metaphysical definition" of the notion of being a city.)

So what we have learned is this: even if the modal notion of necessity is fundamental, purity prohibits modal truths involving nonfundamental notions from being fundamental. The only fundamental modal truths are an array of "austere" or "pure" modal truths that give the necessary connections amongst fundamental notions. (The array will include necessitations of logical truths that contain only fundamental notions—such as "Necessarily, all Cs are Cs"—but it will presumably include further truths; perhaps: "Necessarily, nothing is both negatively and positively charged", "Necessarily, if x is more massive than y and y is more massive than z then x is more massive than z", and the like.)

I myself reject modalism (chapter 12); but I accept other sorts of primitivism for which purity has analogous consequences. Negation, on my view, is a fundamental notion; but since 'eats', 'candy', and 'smile' are nonfundamental notions, purity implies that the truth "It is not the case that something eats candy without smiling" is not a fundamental one. It holds, perhaps, in virtue of some fundamental truth of the form "It is not the case that something Es some Y but does not S", where E, Y, and S are "metaphysical definitions" of 'eats', 'candy', and 'smile', respectively. Likewise, I think that quantifiers are fundamental (they carve at the joints); but given purity, such truths as "There exists a city" are nonfundamental, and hold in virtue of quantificational truths (perhaps of the form "There exists a C") that involve only fundamental notions. As with modality, even if negation and quantification are fundamental *notions*, the only fundamental *facts* involving those notions are pure—they involve those notions in combination only with other fundamental notions.

The issue of purity can be further explored by discussing a particular example— one that, I hope, an opponent of purity will agree is a sort of crucial experiment, on which the issue turns. First some setup. Let C_0 be a predicate that describes New York City at the subatomic level in complete detail (relationally as well as intrinsically). The following is presumably true:

(2) Necessarily, every C_0 is a city.

("City-zombies" are impossible.[4]) Finally, assume for the sake of argument (what I do not myself believe) that modalism is true—necessity is a fundamental notion.

Purity implies that (2) is not a fundamental truth, since it contains 'city'. An opponent of purity, I think, will take this as a good place to draw a line in the sand. She will say that (2) *is* a fundamental truth; the modal connection between C_0 and cityhood is incapable of further explanation. (This is a good place to draw

---

[4] Cf. Bennett (2006).

the line in the sand because the modal connection between macro-predicates like 'city' and their micro-realizations is particularly resistant to reduction.[5]) I, on the other hand, accept purity's consequence that (2) is not fundamental (even under the pretense of modalism). My argument has been simply that the fundamental story of the world ought not to mention cityhood at all, not even within sentences like (1) and (2). ("When God created the world, she did not need to use 'city'.") But this can be brought out more vividly.

Think of a sentential operator like 'necessarily' as a machine. You feed it a statement (proposition, interpreted sentence), and it spits out a truth-value. The output *true* means that the input statement is necessarily true; the output *false* means that the input statement could have been false. Think of the fundamental facts of the form "Necessarily, ϕ" and "It's not the case that: necessarily, ϕ" as corresponding to the inputs ϕ that the machine is equipped to handle—the inputs for which the machine "knows what to do". If it's a fundamental fact that it's necessary that all electrons are electrons, the machine "knows what to do" with the input 'all electrons are electrons'; it spits back *true*. The thought in favor of purity is then this: the machine should *not* know what to do with the input 'Every C_0 is a city'. If the machine did know what to do with this input, it would "know" how to inspect the notion of a city, and figure out what its microphysical modally sufficient conditions are. And this is an inappropriate capacity for the machine to have. When God created the fundamental notion of necessity, she needed to endow it with the fundamental capacity to interact with other fundamental notions (perhaps: all, and, not, electron, and the like), but *not* with notions like city, smile, and candy. (After all, fundamentally speaking there are no such notions.) This is not to deny that (2) is true; it is only to deny that (2) is fundamentally true. Demanding that (2) be fundamentally true demands more of a fundamental notion of necessity than it has to give.

7.3 Purity and connection

In the previous two sections I formulated completeness and purity in intuitive terms—"fundamental fact", "in-virtue-of"—rather than in my own official terms. This was not only for ease of digestion: it was also because the issues are not particular to my own metaphysics of fundamentality. The question of whether facts about the relation between the fundamental and the nonfundamental (like (1)) are themselves fundamental, for example, confronts everyone who takes the notion of fundamentality seriously. But ultimately I want a formulation of completeness and purity in my own terms. The next few sections head in that direction.

What is the relationship between the fundamental and the nonfundamental? In what sense do all fundamental matters "boil down to" or "derive from" or "hold in virtue of" fundamental matters, as completeness says they do? How does the nonfundamental *connect* to the fundamental?

[5] See Lewis (1986*b*, pp. 150–7) and section 12.9 of this book.

We learned something important about the nature of the connection in section 7.2. As we saw, purity implies that claims like (1) and (2), which describe in-virtue-of and modal connections, respectively, express merely nonfundamental truths. But purity lets us draw a more general conclusion. On *any* conception of the nature of the connection, connecting truths—true statements expressing the distinctive connection between fundamental and nonfundamental matters—are going to, like (1) and (2), involve nonfundamental notions. (This is so by definition; connecting statements relate *nonfundamental* notions to fundamental ones.) So on any conception of the nature of the connection, the connecting truths are going to have to be nonfundamental.

This in turn tells us something about how to attack the question of the relationship between fundamental and nonfundamental: we should *not* attack it using the method of metaphysical posit—by positing a metaphysically fundamental notion (such as in-virtue-of, necessity, or truthmaking) for the connection. The point of using the method of posit would be to claim that the connecting truths involving the posited notion are fundamental truths, thereby obviating the need to say in virtue of what such connecting truths hold. But purity implies that the connecting truths could not be fundamental.

(Although purity tells us that it's pointless to posit fundamental notions like in-virtue-of, necessity, or truthmaking *in order to attack the question of the connection*, it does not prohibit such posits per se.[6] One could, for example, posit a fundamental notion of in-virtue-of, and claim that in-virtue-of truths involving only fundamental notions—for example, "There exist things that are either negatively or positively charged in virtue of the fact that there exist things that are negatively charged"—are fundamental truths. But such truths are not connecting truths, and do not help with the problem of how the fundamental relates to the nonfundamental. And absent some independent motivation, there would be no reason for the posit.)

We have been focusing on the relationship between the fundamental and the nonfundamental, worrying about whether facts about this relationship are fundamental, and so on. It's a little tempting (though only a little) to dismiss such concerns by saying something like this: "Given the fundamental facts, nonfundamental facts follow *automatically*; they're not *extra* facts, somehow *over and above* the fundamental facts; so there's no need for facts connecting the fundamental to the nonfundamental." But the problem with this thought is pretty transparent. What do the italicized phrases mean here? It's natural to construe them all in terms of in-virtue-of.[7] To say that nonfundamental facts "follow automatically" from, and are neither "extra" relative to nor "above and beyond" the fundamental facts is simply to say that they hold in virtue of fundamental facts. But then it becomes clear that the concerns have not been dismissed at all, only relabeled. The fact

---

[6] Thanks to Bruno Whittle for this point.

[7] Similar remarks apply if we construe them in terms of necessitation or truthmaking, etc.

that there being cities follows automatically from, etc., a certain fundamental fact is exactly the sort of fact whose status we have been questioning.

A related attempt to dismiss the concerns is a little more tempting: "The fact that there is a city *just is* the fact that there is a C; so there is no need for any fact connecting the 'two'. The relationship between so-called fundamental facts and nonfundamental facts is simply identity (so really we shouldn't call some of them fundamental and others nonfundamental); and the status of identity facts is unproblematic." It's worth spending a little time discussing this, since it illustrates a way of hiding metaphysical commitments that will be important later (section 8.5). The objection's crucial claim is that the relationship between fundamental and nonfundamental is unproblematic because it consists simply of identities like these:

(*) The fact that there is a city = the fact that there is a C.

Now, I agree that identities are in a sense unproblematic. But notice that the singular terms flanking '=' in (*) are not names, but are rather complex singular terms, formed using the locution 'the fact that'. This is important. Grammatically, this locution combines with a sentence ϕ to form a singular term, 'the fact that ϕ'. Metaphysically, the locution functions as a connector between whatever ideology is allowed to occur within ϕ and certain entities (the facts). The use of this locution marks a serious metaphysical commitment; intuitively, it is this locution, not the identity sign, that both does the work in connecting the fundamental to the nonfundamental and also creates problems with purity. This is clearest if we break (*) into the following three components (where a and b are proper names of facts):

(i) the fact that there exists a city $= a$;

(ii) the fact that there exists a $C = b$;

(iii) $a = b$.

When the objector says that identities between facts raise no problems, this is partly right: purity does not conflict with (iii)'s being a fundamental truth.[8] Nor does it conflict with (ii)'s being fundamental (provided our fan of facts regards 'the fact that' as a fundamental notion). But purity does rule out (i)'s being a fundamental truth, since (i) contains 'city'—even if 'the fact that' is taken to be a fundamental notion. Return to the metaphor of the machine: 'the fact that ϕ' is a machine that takes ϕ as input and picks out the corresponding fact. If (i) expresses a fundamental fact, then the machine knows how to pick out the appropriate fact when ϕ contains 'city'; this is an ability that one of reality's basic building blocks should not have.

---

[8] So long as facts are taken to exist in the fundamental sense, anyway; otherwise it might be objected that names like a somehow bring in nonfundamental notions.

7.4 Metaphysical semantics

As we saw in the previous section, we cannot attack the problem of the relationship between fundamental and nonfundamental by the method of posit—by positing a fundamental notion for the connection. We should instead take facts about the connection to be nonfundamental facts, which may ultimately be explained in terms of fundamental facts that do not involve a fundamental notion of connection.

This is not to say that we should require ourselves to actually specify what those fundamental facts are, in terms of which facts about connection may be explained, before we are willing to speak of the connection. That would require us to possess a metaphysical reduction of the connection; and metaphysical reductions are quite generally very hard to come by. (More on this methodological issue in section 7.6.) Instead, we should introduce a suitable undefined but nonfundamental notion for the connection. We should explain and clarify the suitable notion as best we can, and there should be reason to believe that it could *in principle* be metaphysically reduced; but we need not ourselves possess a reduction.

What is this suitable notion to be? ("In virtue of" has been a mere placeholder.) Earlier I mentioned reasons not to construe it in terms of necessity, truthmaking, or fact-identity. Might the suitable notion be that of ground, regarded as a non-fundamental notion? This is a close relative of my own proposal; but for reasons to be given in section 7.9, I prefer a slightly different, linguistic approach. The suitable notion, in my view, is that of a *metaphysical semantics*—a certain sort of semantic theory. As we will see, completeness may then be understood roughly as the claim that every language has a metaphysical semantics.

A metaphysical semantics is a semantic theory with two distinctive features. First, meanings are to be given in purely joint-carving terms. For example, if the semantic theory takes the form of a truth-theory, then the truth-conditions must be stated in perfectly joint-carving terms. More on this below.

Second, the explanatory goals differ from those of linguistic semantics. In one way they are more ambitious, and in another, more modest. Metaphysical semantics is more ambitious in that by giving meanings in fundamental terms, it seeks to achieve something not sought by linguistic semantics: to show how what we say fits into fundamental reality. Metaphysical semantics is more modest in that it tries to explain a narrower range of phenomena. The semantic theories of philosophers of language and linguists attempt to explain a broad range of phenomena, psychological and social, as well as narrowly linguistic. According to a traditional conception (largely associated with Frege), meaning plays a broad theoretical role: the meaning of a sentence is conventionally encoded by that sentence, grasped by anyone who understands the sentence, is communicated when the sentence is used; sentence-meanings are the objects of thought and other propositional attitudes, and so on. Successor theories have in some cases bifurcated this role, but in other cases have expanded it, by taking semantics to interface with adjoining theories of cognitive science, both linguistic (such as syntax) and psychological. The metaphysical semanticist seeks to explain *some* of the same phenomena as does the linguistic semanticist. For example, just like the linguistic semanticist, she wants to help explain why English speakers will point to the salient horse, rather than the salient car, when they hear the sounds "Point to the horse!"; and like the linguistic semanticist, she will invoke concepts like truth and reference to do so. But she is not concerned to integrate her semantics with other linguistic or psychological theories. Thus she is not trying to integrate her semantics with syntactic theory, for example. And she is free to assign semantic values that competent speakers would be incapable of recognizing as such, for she is not trying to explain what a competent speaker knows when she understands her language. She might, for example, assign to an ordinary sentence about ordinary macroscopic objects a meaning that makes reference to the fundamental physical states of subatomic particles. And she might simply ignore Frege's (1952/1892) puzzle of the cognitive nonequivalence of co-referring proper names, since she is not trying to integrate her semantics with theories of action and rationality.

Returning to the first distinctive feature of metaphysical semantics: suppose a metaphysical semantics for a language L takes the form of a truth theory—a theory issuing in theorems of the form:[9]

Sentence S of L is true in L iff ϕ.

The requirement that meanings be "given" in purely joint-carving terms amounts to the requirement that ϕ be phrased in purely joint-carving terms. ('Sentence of L' and 'is true in L' are, of course, not purely joint-carving. Remember that the notion of metaphysical semantics is not intended to be a fundamental one.)

A truth theory is just one form that a metaphysical semantics might take. A metaphysical semanticist might conclude that, rather than assigning truth-conditions, a more explanatory approach would be to assign expressivist assertion-conditions to normative discourse, say, or proof-theoretic assertion-conditions to mathematical sentences. In the former case, the metaphysical semantics would issue in theorems of the form:

Normative sentence S of L, as uttered by speaker x, is expressively appropriate for x in L iff $\phi(x)$

where $\phi(x)$ is a condition on speaker x's attitudes. Here the requirement that meanings be given in purely joint-carving terms requires $\phi(x)$ to be stated in purely joint-carving terms. If psychological language is fundamental then $\phi(x)$ may contain such language; otherwise (the more likely case, to my mind) $\phi(x)$ will need to be phrased in the terms one would use for giving metaphysical truth-conditions for factualist discourse about psychology.

Expressivism thus construed is immune to a common dilemma. Suppose we extend the expressivist semantics to encompass a disquotational truth predicate

---

[9]There is no need for 'iff' to have a sense that is somehow distinctive of metaphysical reduction. It can have the same sense that it has in any explanatory theory—the material biconditional, say.

(and related vocabulary). Expressivism is supposed to be a form of nonfactualism; but the claims one can assert in L (such as "The sentence 'It is wrong to kill' is true") now sound just like the claims that factualists make. What happened to the nonfactualism?[10]

The answer is that the metaphysical semantics for factual discourse (say, discourse about chemical or biological phenomena) has a different shape from the metaphysical semantics for discourse about value. To a speaker's sentence, the former assigns a condition on the world—a closed sentence—whereas the latter assigns a condition on the speaker—an open formula applied to a variable to which the speaker is assigned; and this condition, moreover, concerns the speaker's mental state.[11] True, this difference disappears if one states a semantics for L from within L (provided L contains, or is enhanced to contain, the appropriate semantic vocabulary). Such a (nonmetaphysical) semantics might then take the form of a truth theory, issuing in theorems like:

'It is wrong to kill' is true in L iff it is wrong to kill.

But the difference remains at the level of metaphysical semantics. A metaphysical semantics could not take this form, assuming that 'wrong' and 'kill' fail to carve at the joints. And the expressivist who is opposed to reductive naturalism will argue that no metaphysical semantics issuing in truth-conditions of the form:

'It is wrong to kill' is true in L iff ϕ

where ϕ is a condition on the world (rather than the speaker) phrased in fundamental terms, is adequate to our use of normative language.

Returning to metaphysical semantics of the truth-theoretic form: what exactly is required of a fundamental truth-condition ϕ for a sentence S in such a theory? We know from the literature on Donald Davidson's (1967b) approach to semantics that sentences ϕ and ϕ' can have the same truth-value, even necessarily so, despite the fact that ϕ is an appropriate truth-condition for S while ϕ' is not.[12] 'Snow is white' is an appropriate truth-condition in a (nonmetaphysical) semantics for 'Snow is white'; neither 'Grass is green' nor 'Snow is white and $2 + 2 = 4$' is appropriate. A metaphysical semantics must successfully explain the linguistic behavior of the population in question, and a truth-theory with necessarily true conjuncts tacked onto each of its truth-conditions is presumably not explanatory, though it's a hard question why not. I have no particular answer to the question, though I suspect that the approach of section 3.2 is applicable. And if the question

[10]See Dreier (2004); Fine (2001). My solution to the problem is in the vicinity of Dreier's and Fine's: we all agree that the reason expressivism is nonfactualist (Dreier says "irrealist") has something to do with expressivism's implications for how value relates to the fundamental. I prefer my approach to Fine's for the reasons given in section 7.9 below.

[11]There are other differences between truth-conditional and expressivist semantics, especially when they are integrated with a broader theory of the mind. For example, truth-conditions and expressive appropriateness conditions play different roles in communication and deliberation.

[12]See Soames (1992) against the Davidsonian approach.

proves intractable, the metaphysical semanticist could abandon the Davidsonian approach. I have chosen that approach largely because it's simple, not because metaphysical semantics is wedded to it.

What I have said about metaphysical semantics falls far short of a full characterization, and it could surely be improved in various ways. However, it is unlikely that there is any single best way to improve it. The notion of a metaphysical semantics for a language, after all, is a high-level notion—a notion posited in the course of explaining a high-level phenomenon, the phenomenon of language-use by flesh and blood people; and there are often different, equally good ways to explain such phenomena, as well as equally good ways to carve the world into groups of phenomena to be explained. Given our discussion of purity, this is a virtue. We should take a nonfundamental, no doubt vague, and perhaps not even uniquely correct, approach to the question of the relationship between fundamental and nonfundamental.

7.5 Completeness and purity reformulated

We can now, at last, take up the question of how to formulate completeness and purity in my preferred terms. Those theses were, recall, initially formulated as follows:

Completeness Every nonfundamental truth holds in virtue of some fundamental truth.

Purity Fundamental truths involve only fundamental notions.

The theses involve three crucial notions: fundamental truth, in-virtue-of, and fundamental notion. A fundamental notion is just one that carves at the joints; and in-virtue-of I am going to explain in terms of metaphysical semantics. But how to understand the notion of a fundamental truth?

Here we encounter something interesting. There are two natural definitions of fundamental truth in terms of the other two notions; what is interesting is that on each definition, one thesis comes out trivial and the other comes out nontrivial. The first natural definition of a fundamental truth is that of a truth involving only fundamental notions. On this definition, purity comes out trivial while completeness comes out nontrivial. The other natural definition of a fundamental truth is that of a truth that does not hold in virtue of any truth. Now purity becomes nontrivial while completeness becomes—somewhat—trivial. I say "somewhat" because completeness does not follow solely from the definition; but it does follow from the definition together with a natural assumption about how in-virtue-of behaves, namely that it is transitive and "well-founded" in the sense that if a truth holds in virtue of any truth at all, then it is connected by an in-virtue-of chain to some truth that does not hold in virtue of any truth ("no unbounded descending chains of in-virtue-of").[13] So it would seem that completeness and purity are in

---

[13]Thanks to Karen Bennett here. For more on well-foundedness, see section 7.11.2.

some sense not wholly independent, at least when the notion of a fundamental truth is regarded as being definable in terms of the other two notions.

My—somewhat arbitrary[14]—decision for how to define 'fundamental truth' will be the first: a fundamental truth is a truth involving only fundamental terms. Thus understood, purity becomes trivial. But notice that its upshot has not disappeared. Completeness now says the following: "Every truth that involves at least one nonfundamental notion holds in virtue of some truth that involves only fundamental notions"; and this has implications that are analogous to the distinctive implications of purity discussed in section 7.2. Completeness, as it's now understood, implies that even if a notion is fundamental, any fact involving that notion together with some nonfundamental notions must hold in virtue of pure or austere facts about that notion, which do not involve any nonfundamental notions. (It implies, for example, that even if necessity is a fundamental notion, the truth that every C_0 is a city must hold in virtue of truths that involve only fundamental notions.)

So: completeness, as we're now understanding it, says that every truth that involves at least one nonfundamental notion holds in virtue of some truth that involves only fundamental notions. It remains to eliminate "in virtue of" in favor of metaphysical semantics. Actually, I wish simultaneously to generalize completeness a little, to handle the case of expressivist and other such language:

Completeness (new version) Every sentence that contains expressions that do not carve at the joints has a metaphysical semantics.

By a metaphysical semantics for a sentence, I mean either a truth-condition, an expression-condition, a proof-condition, or perhaps some other sort of semantic condition, that is assigned to that sentence by some metaphysical semantics for its language. This principle constrains the notion of carving at the joints in accordance with the issues we have been discussing in this chapter. There is no need for a further principle of purity, since the distinctive implications of that principle discussed in section 7.2 are implied by this new version of completeness. (But when I wish to emphasize these implications, I will speak of "purity".)

7.6 Metaphysics after conceptual analysis

How much should we expect from ourselves, if we attempt to actually give metaphysical truth-conditions? Not much, I think.

We certainly should not expect to be able to give truth-conditions that are intuitively correct in every possible world or conceivable circumstance. Judging from the history of conceptual analysis, that is unattainable. In retrospect, we

---

[14]I could instead adopt the second definition of 'fundamental truth', rendering completeness (somewhat) trivial. The corresponding version of purity would then be: truths that do not hold in virtue of any truth involve only fundamental notions. That is: any truth that involves a nonfundamental notion must hold in virtue of some other truth. Modulo the assumptions of transitivity and well-foundedness of in-virtue-of, this is equivalent to the result of the other decision.

should never have expected that project to succeed. Why should there be any simple definitions, preserving intuitive or cognitive significance, of any of our words in any other terms? Words aren't generally introduced as definitional equivalents of pre-existing phrases, and even then they subsequently take on semantic lives of their own. Current meaning derives from a long, complex history of use, which would seem unlikely to result in neat equivalences. Our failure to come up with counterexample-free definitions of 'cause', 'knows', and 'good' is not due to the philosophical depth of these concepts. We'd have no better luck with 'city', 'smile', or 'candy'. Words just aren't neatly equivalent to other words, and there's no reason to expect them to be.

And it only gets harder if the truth-conditions must be stated in absolutely fundamental terms, as metaphysical truth-conditions must be. Our ignorance of the facts of physics then compounds our ignorance of the facts of meaning. We have no chance of actually giving a metaphysical semantics for any significant fragment of a natural language.

A more reasonable goal is the construction of "toy" metaphysical truth-conditions. These will be toy in at least two ways. First, they needn't match with intuitively correct usage in absolutely all possible worlds or conceivable circumstances. The mesh need only be approximate (the more mesh, the better). Second, they needn't be stated in perfectly fundamental terms. Rather, they must be stated in terms that are fundamental enough for the purpose at hand (and again, the more fundamental the better).

What is the point of toy metaphysical truth-conditions? One point is to convince us that real, non-toy metaphysical truth-conditions exist.[15] Consider, for example, the controversy over whether causation is fundamental. To help resolve this controversy, we might try to produce reductive (i.e., not involving 'cause') toy metaphysical truth-conditions for 'cause'. If all attempts fail, then the case for fundamental causation will receive a nice boost, especially if we discern in-principle reasons for the failures. For if reductive metaphysical truth-conditions for 'cause' do not exist (and if 'cause' lacks an expressivist or otherwise non-truth-conditional metaphysical semantics), then completeness forces us to say that causation is fundamental. But if a toy semantics *can* be produced, we needn't recognize fundamental causation (not because of completeness, anyway). The toy needn't be perfect. For its purpose is not to *be* a real metaphysical semantics, but rather to convince us that *there is* a real metaphysical semantics, even if that metaphysical semantics is too complex for us to discover. The purpose of the toy is to convince us that the unfathomable workings of history and usage can do their thing with 'cause', as well as with 'city', 'smile', and 'candy'. The reason philosophers obsess over the definition of 'cause' is not that they think that a

---

[15]Another is to study how our concepts relate to one another. Even a simplistic semantics might illuminate the overall shape of a network of concepts consisting of wrongdoing, blame, guilt, shame, and the like.

word must be defined before it's legit (otherwise no philosophers would speak of cities, smiles, or candy). It's rather that it's a live issue whether causation is part of the fundamental furniture of the universe. We don't obsess over the definition of 'candy', not because we could easily define it if we wanted to (we couldn't), but rather because no one seriously contemplates fundamental candy.

Conceptual analysis is out of fashion in metaphysics, but there is uncertainty about what its replacement should be. Reduction? Supervenience? Realization? The proposed replacements have tended to be either inadequate or unilluminating (or both). The recent trend is to think in terms of a kind of purely metaphysical analysis. There's a bad idea in here mixed in with a good one. The bad idea is that we should posit a fundamental gizmo for the relationship between analysans and analysandum (truthmaking, necessity, fact identity, ground). The good idea is Armstrongian: metaphysical analysis is not linguistic analysis.[16] But that leaves a big gap: if not linguistic analysis then what? I say: metaphysical truth-conditions—toy models of them, at any rate.

7.7 Metaphysical semantics for quantifiers

Metaphysical semantics are not required by definition to take any particular form. They must presumably be compositional in some sense (since they must be explanatory and hence cast in reasonably joint-carving terms, and must contend with infinitely many sentences). But this still allows considerable variation.

In particular, the form of metaphysical truth-conditions can depend on what is fundamental. After all, metaphysical truth-conditions must be stated in perfectly fundamental terms; thus which terms are in fact fundamental, and what is true at the fundamental level, will affect what metaphysical truth-conditions can look like.

An illustration comes from ontology. If fundamental ontology is abundant, then the metaphysical truth-conditions for existential claims in nonfundamental languages can be existential in form; but if fundamental ontology is sparse, then these metaphysical truth-conditions need to take some other form.[17] To bring this out I will consider an example at length. I will give (toy) metaphysical truth-conditions for certain statements of chemistry, first assuming classical mereology, and then assuming mereological nihilism.

Assume classical mereology. More fully, assume for the sake of argument that the joint-carving notions are those of logic: $\exists$, $\forall$, $\sim$, $\wedge$, $=$, etc.; a predicate $<$ for mereological parthood; and the following physical predicates: E ("is an electron"), P ("is a proton"), N ("is a neutron"), R ("orbits"), and U ("is a nucleus"). (U is to apply to fusions of protons and neutrons that are bound together into a nucleus by

---

[16] See, for example, Armstrong (1978a; b).

[17] This corresponds to Fine's (2003) distinction between proxy and non-proxy reductions.

the strong nuclear force.[18]) Our fundamental language is thus one in which only these notions are primitive. One can then define, in the fundamental language, various mereological notions using $<$ in well-known ways. For example, one can define Oxy ("x overlaps y") as meaning $\exists z(z < x \land z < y)$. And for any fixed positive integer n, one can define an $n+1$-place fusion predicate $x\mathrm{Fu}^n y_1 \ldots y_n$ ("x is a fusion of $y_1 \ldots y_n$") thus:

$$x\mathrm{Fu}^n y_1 \ldots y_n =_{\mathrm{df}} y_1 < x \land \cdots \land y_n < x \land \forall z(z < x \rightarrow (Ozy_1 \lor \cdots \lor Ozy_n))$$

And assume further that classical mereology's principle of "unrestricted composition" is true. For present purposes we may take this as the assumption that for each n, '$\forall y_1 \ldots \forall y_n \exists x \, x\mathrm{Fu}^n y_1 \ldots y_n$' is true.

Now consider a very simple language of chemistry, which is just like the fundamental language except for containing new predicates: H ("is an atom of hydrogen") and L ("is an atom of helium").[19] Thus, this language contains sentences like:

(1) $\exists x H x$

"There exists an atom of hydrogen."

(2) $\exists x L x$

"There exists an atom of helium."

We can give metaphysical truth-conditions for these sentences by, in essence, defining atoms as fusions of their subatomic particles. Say that a sentence ϕ in the fundamental language "translates" a sentence χ in the language of chemistry iff ϕ results from χ by replacing occurrences of H and L according to the following definitions:

$$Hx =_{\mathrm{df}} \exists y \exists z(Ey \land Pz \land Ryz \land x\mathrm{Fu}^2 yz)$$

"x is a hydrogen atom iff x is a fusion of an electron and proton where the electron orbits the proton."

$$Lx =_{\mathrm{df}} \exists y_1 \exists y_2 \exists z_1 \exists z_2 \exists w_1 \exists w_2 \exists v(Ey_1 \land Ey_2 \land y_1 \neq y_2 \land Pz_1 \land Pz_2 \land z_1 \neq z_2 \land Nw_1 \land Nw_2 \land w_1 \neq w_2 \land Uv \land Ry_1 v \land Ry_2 v \land v\mathrm{Fu}^4 z_1 z_2 w_1 w_2 \land x\mathrm{Fu}^3 y_1 y_2 v)$$

"x is a helium atom iff x is a fusion of two electrons and a nucleus, where the nucleus is a fusion of two protons and two neutrons, and the electrons orbit the nucleus."

We could say, then, that the metaphysical truth-condition of any sentence in the language of chemistry is its translation. Thus, the metaphysical truth-conditions of (1) and (2) are, respectively:

$$\exists x \exists y \exists z(Ey \land Pz \land Ryz \land x\mathrm{Fu}^2 yz)$$

---

[18] On a more plausible view, U would nonfundamental, and defined in terms of mereology and a fundamental predicate for the strong nuclear force. The approach in the text is for simplicity.

[19] I have in mind hydrogen-1 and helium-4, respectively.

$$\exists x \exists y_1 \exists y_2 \exists z_1 \exists z_2 \exists w_1 \exists w_2 \exists v (Ey_1 \wedge Ey_2 \wedge y_1 \neq y_2 \wedge Pz_1 \wedge Pz_2 \wedge z_1 \neq z_2 \wedge Nw_1 \wedge Nw_2 \wedge w_1 \neq w_2 \wedge Uv \wedge Ry_1 v \wedge Ry_2 v \wedge v\mathrm{Fu}^4 z_1 z_2 w_1 w_2 \wedge x\mathrm{Fu}^3 y_1 y_2 v)$$

This was a particularly simple example of metaphysical truth-conditions. Given classical mereology, our fundamental ontology already contained helium and hydrogen atoms, so to speak; all we lacked was primitive predicates classifying them as such. So the definition of translation was quite easy; all we needed to do was define the predicates L and H in fundamental terms. Things get more complex if a sparser fundamental ontology is true, as we'll now see.

Assume next that mereological nihilism is true—no mereologically composite things exist. More fully, assume that $\forall x(Ex \vee Px \vee Nx)$ is true in our fundamental language—nothing exists other than electrons, protons, and neutrons (these lack proper parts, let us pretend). Drop $<$ from the fundamental language (it is unneeded since nothing has proper parts). The fundamental language must no longer speak of nuclei (there aren't any); let us replace, therefore, the predicate U with a two-place predicate B ("bonded") holding between the protons and neutrons that we formerly called the parts of nuclei. Similarly, instead of speaking of electrons orbiting nuclei, let us now speak of electrons as orbiting protons and neutrons. Let us assume that B is transitive and symmetric, and reflexive over protons and neutrons, and that if Rxy and Byz then Rxz—if an electron orbits one subatomic particle "in a nucleus" then it orbits each subatomic particle "in that nucleus".

What form must metaphysical truth-conditions for sentences of chemistry now take? We can no longer translate claims of chemistry into fundamental claims simply by giving definitions, in fundamental terms, of the predicates H and L. If we proceeded that way, then the translation of sentence (1), i.e., $\exists x Hx$, would have the form $\exists x \psi(x)$, where $\psi(x)$ is the proposed definition, in fundamental terms, of Hx. Since only subatomic particles exist, and since we want (1) to come out true in the language of chemistry, $\psi(x)$ must apply to subatomic particles. But $\psi(x)$ was supposed to be the definition of 'x is a hydrogen atom.'[20]

We need a different strategy of translation. A natural approach is to translate (1) and (2) into:

(1_N) $\exists x \exists y (Ex \wedge Py \wedge Rxy)$

(2_N) $\exists x_1 \exists x_2 \exists y_1 \exists y_2 \exists z_1 \exists z_2 (Ex_1 \wedge Ex_2 \wedge x_1 \neq x_2 \wedge Py_1 \wedge Py_2 \wedge y_1 \neq y_2 \wedge Nz_1 \wedge Nz_2 \wedge z_1 \neq z_2 \wedge By_1 y_2 \wedge By_1 z_1 \wedge By_1 z_2 \wedge Rx_1 y_1 \wedge Rx_2 y_1)$

On this approach, the translation of 'There exists a hydrogen atom' is: 'There exist an electron and a proton, the first of which orbits the second'. The translation

---

[20]Well, one *could* (at the price of artificiality) specify a tricky translation scheme in which $\psi(x)$ does indeed apply to subatomic particles, namely, those subatomic particles that are "part of" hydrogen atoms: $\psi(x) =_{\mathrm{df}} \exists y \exists z (Ey \wedge Pz \wedge Ryz \wedge (x = y \vee x = z))$. One would need to make adjustments elsewhere. For example, the language of chemistry's predicate P could not be translated as the fundamental language's predicate P; otherwise $\exists x(Px \wedge Hx)$ ("something is both a proton and a hydrogen atom") would be translated as a truth.

omits reference to the hydrogen atom itself; it states the nihilistic basis for the entire sentence 'There exists a hydrogen atom.'[21]

In such a metaphysical semantics, the truth-conditions for sentences of the form $\exists x F x$ do not have the form $\exists x \psi(x)$, with ψ a translation of the predicate F. Quantification over Fs disappears when we move from the chemical sentence to its metaphysical truth-condition. Given this, it is natural to say that the existential quantifier in the language of chemistry does not mean what it means in the fundamental language used to give metaphysical truth-conditions. Quantification in the language of chemistry is nonfundamental quantification. We might make this explicit by using 'there is' in the language of chemistry, reserving '$\exists$' for fundamental quantification.[22]

Quantifiers in many languages—for example, ordinary languages in which we quantify over tables and chairs—might in this way express nonfundamental quantification, if fundamental ontology is sparse. Granted, the metaphysical semantics for a more complex language will need to be more complex than the toy semantics just mentioned. And particularly austere views about fundamental ontology or ideology might make it impossible to give metaphysical truth-conditions for some high-level language—which might be a reason for abandoning such austere views. The point here is just to demonstrate some of the resources available for giving metaphysical truth-conditions, and to show how a sentence's metaphysical truth-conditions might look quite unlike that sentence, as with the truth-conditions (1_N) and (2_N).

---

[21]Here is a general translation scheme of the desired sort. Let F be the set of sentences in the fundamental language that express the assumptions we are making about our fundamental predicates. F thus includes the claim that B is transitive, symmetric, and reflexive-over-protons-and-neutrons. So in any model, M, of F, $M(P) \cup M(N)$ is, if nonempty, partitioned into equivalence classes under the relation $M(B)$ (I use "$M(\pi)$" for the extension of predicate π in M). Think of these equivalence classes as "nuclei" (they obviously aren't really nuclei; M is only a model). For each such equivalence class, c, call the ordered pair $\langle c, h \rangle$ an "atom", where $e \in h$ iff: $e \in M(E)$ and $\langle e, o \rangle \in M(R)$ for some $o \in c$. Each "atom" is an ordered pair of a "nucleus"—a set of "protons" and "neutrons"—and the set of "electrons" that "orbit" the members of the "nucleus". Next we construct an augmented model, M', by adding the "atoms" to M's domain. (The added "atoms" are to be new; so if any are already present in M's domain, first pair them with some arbitrarily chosen object not in the transitive closure of M's domain.) Let the extensions of E, P, N, B, and R in M' be as they were in M. And let M' also interpret the extra predicates of the language of chemistry: let the extension in M' of $<$ include all pairs $\langle d, \langle c, h \rangle \rangle$ where $\langle c, h \rangle$ is an "atom", and either $d \in c$ or $d \in h$, plus further pairs so that $<$ satisfies the axioms of mereology; and assign extensions to H and L in the obvious way. (Place an "atom" $\langle c, h \rangle$ in $M'(H)$, for example, iff h has exactly one member, and c has exactly one member, which is a member of $M'(P)$.) Finally, say that ϕ in the fundamental language translates χ in the language of chemistry iff for every model M of F in which ϕ is true, χ is true in the corresponding augmented model M'. Notice that a given sentence might now have more than one translation. (Notice also the use of set theory to specify the translations, even though the fundamental theory in question was nominalistic. There's no immediate conflict since only metaphysical truth-conditions themselves, not the description of how to arrive at them, must be stated in purely fundamental terms.)

[22]See also section 9.3.

7.8 Metaphysics and the study of language

Suppose that mereological nihilism is true. Should linguistic semanticists—not metaphysical semanticists, but rather, real live semanticists in linguistics departments—then follow the lead of last section's metaphysical semanticist, and assign truth-conditions like (1_N) and (2_N) to sentences of the language of chemistry? It might be thought that they should; otherwise, they would count the chemist's sentences as being false.

There is an alternative. If the language of chemistry can have a metaphysical semantics that allows its sentences to be true despite mereological nihilism, then why not the metalanguage used by linguists? Linguists could then use sentences quantifying over atoms of hydrogen, helium, and the like, rather than sentences like (1_N) and (2_N), to give truth-conditions for the sentences of chemistry. The chemist's 'There exists a hydrogen atom' would then have, as a *linguistic* truth-condition, the linguist's homophonic sentence 'There exists a hydrogen atom.' This linguistic truth-condition must be distinguished from the *metaphysical* truth-condition shared by both sentences: '$\exists x \exists y (Ex \land Py \land Rxy)$' (i.e., (1_N)). Similarly, linguists might assign to ordinary sentences about tables and chairs, truth-conditions that themselves quantify over tables and chairs, provided the sentences of their metalanguage have appropriate metaphysical truth-conditions.

There is a tradition in the philosophy of language according to which linguistic and metaphysical inquiry should tightly constrain each other. Davidson (1977) is a representative example. According to Davidson, a good semantic theory must count ordinary sentences as being, for the most part, true. Suppose the best semantic theory for a discourse assigns truth-conditions to ordinary sentences that quantify over entities of a certain sort. Then, since the ordinary sentences must be counted as true, the assigned truth-conditions must be true; and so, the entities in question must exist. For example, Davidson argued, the best linguistic theory of adverbial modification assigns truth-conditions quantifying over events (1967a); thus we must embrace an ontology of events. This is an example of linguistic theory constraining metaphysics, but there is no reason in principle, given this tradition, to resist the reverse direction of influence: that of metaphysics constraining linguistic theory. Powerful metaphysical arguments that events do not exist, for example, would give us reason to reject Davidson's approach to adverbial modification.

An advantage of the metaphysical semantics approach, as against the Davidsonian tradition, is that it allows for a looser relationship between metaphysics and linguistics. We can agree with Davidson that linguistic semantics ought to count ordinary sentences as being mostly true, without needing to embrace an ontology of events, tables and chairs, or atoms of chemistry, because ontology concerns fundamental existence, whereas linguistic semantics is given in the metalanguage of linguistics, whose quantifiers need not be fundamental. The linguist's sentences about events, atoms, and tables and chairs can be true even if such entities do not fundamentally exist, given an appropriate metaphysical semantics for those sentences.

The approach allows, more generally, for a looser relationship between metaphysics and the special sciences. That relationship may be pictured thus:

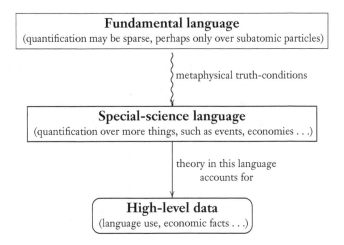

Linguistics, psychology, economics, and other special sciences may be carried out in their own languages—largely natural languages, enhanced here and there with special-purpose vocabulary. Sentences of special-science languages have metaphysical truth-conditions, but these are of no more concern to the special scientist than the underpinnings of her discipline in fundamental physics. Explanations of high-level data are given in the language of these special sciences, not in the underpinning languages of physics or metaphysics.

The advantage of this approach is that it allows linguists, psychologists, and economists to be guided by considerations internal to linguistics, psychology, and economics. It would be inappropriate to complain to an economist that economies don't really exist, or to insist that an engineer rewrite her book on repairing potholes to reflect the fact that holes do not really exist. Likewise, it would be inappropriate to require linguists to warp semantics around metaphysical scruples about molecules of helium, or tables and chairs, or events.

Conversely, it allows metaphysicians to be guided by considerations internal to metaphysics. It has always seemed odd that insight into the fundamental workings of the universe could be gained by reflection on how we think and speak. Of course, such reflection can provide *some* constraint on metaphysics. Human thought and speech are real phenomena, and so must fit somehow into any adequate metaphysics. But this is a far cry from reading off one's fundamental metaphysics directly from the structure of thought and talk.

Thus we have a limited Carnapian (1950) spirit of tolerance. Special sciences can conduct their business without interference from metaphysics, if their languages can be given a metaphysical semantics. (The same point from another angle:

metaphysics can be relatively free from interference from the special sciences. Note how structure opens up breathing room for metaphysics.) The tolerance is limited for two reasons. First, the metaphysical semantics must not be too complex; otherwise one might question whether the science is genuinely explanatory. Whether, and if so when, an alleged science is unexplanatory for this sort of reason is a difficult question about special-science explanation.[23] Second, it cannot be just assumed that a metaphysical semantics can be given. In particular, Carnap's insouciance about the ontological status of mathematical entities is *not* justified, since it is particularly hard to see how mathematical language can be given a metaphysical semantics if, fundamentally speaking, mathematical entities do not exist. It is comparatively easy to see how chemistry and biology could rest on top of physics, since the world of physics is fine-grained enough to supply sufficiently many facts to underlie chemistry and biology. But the infinitary nature of mathematics presents a special challenge. If one's conception of the fundamental is overly sparse—if it contains for example, neither mathematical entities nor a correspondingly rich structure of modal or higher-order logical facts—then there may simply be no way to give a metaphysical semantics for mathematical language.

7.9 Nonfundamental ground

I have given a linguistic account of connecting facts—facts connecting nonfundamental to fundamental. It might be urged, against this, that the matter of how chemistry, biology, economics, and so forth, relate to the fundamental does not *seem* to concern language, and hence that we ought to regard connecting facts as involving some nonlinguistic notion such as ground. As we saw, purity requires connecting facts to be nonfundamental; but a friend of ground might embrace this.

The friend of ground that I have in mind shares my main approach to fundamentality: his basic notion is that of structure, and he embraces purity; it's just that he accounts for the connection between fundamental and nonfundamental in terms of ground, not metaphysical semantics.[24] Given his embrace of purity, he must say that ground-theoretic connecting facts—facts like: there being C_0s grounds there being cities—are themselves grounded in facts that do not involve nonfundamental notions; and he presumably cannot produce reductive definitions of 'ground', 'city', and other relevant terms that demonstrate compliance with purity. However, I am in the same boat: I am committed to the existence of a metaphysical semantics for sentences containing 'metaphysical semantics', but I cannot produce that metaphysical semantics.

---

[23] As pursued, for example, by Fodor (1974) and Kim (1992).

[24] In chapter 8 I consider views that *replace* the notion of structure with ground and/or related notions.

It would be easy to overstate the difference between this approach and my own. After all, a metaphysical semantics is supposed to explain linguistic phenomena in purely fundamental terms, and the sort of explanation required is distinctively metaphysical in nature since the meanings must be given in fundamental terms. Still, there is a reason to prefer my approach: it handles nonfactual discourse more smoothly.

Given my approach, there is a simple and natural way to distinguish factual from nonfactual discourse: the difference is one of the "shape" of the metaphysical semantics. The shape is truth-conditional in the former case, and some other shape in the latter. For example, an expressivist metaphysical semantics for evaluative discourse might take the form of an assignment of expressively appropriate assertion conditions; and a formalist metaphysical semantics for mathematical discourse might take the form of assertion conditions that are sensitive to the proofs that the speaker possesses.

How will the friend of ground distinguish factual from nonfactual discourse? I see two main possibilities. The first would be to exclude nonfactual discourse from the scope of grounding. One way to implement this would be to say that grounding only concerns *facts*; and since nonfactual sentences do not express facts, grounding does not apply to them. But the notion of fact thus invoked is in need of explanation (it cannot be disquotational), and surely the explanation ought to have something to do with grounding. So let us understand talk of facts disquotationally from now on, and implement this first possibility differently: nonfactual sentences do express facts, alright—call these "nonfactual facts" (sorry)—it's just that those facts are ungrounded. Moreover, nonfactual facts are not fundamental (that is, they are not cast purely in joint-carving terms), which is what distinguishes them from, say, physical facts, which are also ungrounded.

The problem here, however, is that the approach has nothing to say about *how* nonfactual facts relate to the fundamental. Various sorts of nonfactual facts (moral and mathematical, perhaps) are all lumped together as being ungrounded and nonfundamental. My approach, in contrast, makes distinctions within the class of nonfactual sentences, depending on the "shape" of their metaphysical semantics.

To be fair, the friend of grounding can make distinctions within the class of nonfactual facts by an indirect method, following Fine (2001). Unlike mathematical facts themselves, facts about our beliefs about mathematics, and metalinguistic facts about mathematical language, are grounded in the fundamental, and may be thus grounded in a different fashion from how facts about our beliefs in value, or metalinguistic facts about evaluative language, are grounded in the fundamental. Perhaps the former facts are grounded in facts involving proof whereas the latter are grounded in facts involving our attitudes. So the friend of grounding can draw the distinctions that need to be drawn. But they must be drawn so indirectly, and so differently from how analogous distinctions are drawn in the case of factual discourse.

A second possibility for treating nonfactual discourse would be to allow nonfactual facts to be grounded. This is Fine's approach (2001). Some nonfactual facts are grounded in others: the fact that either murder or snorkeling is wrong is grounded in the fact that murder is wrong. But not all nonfactual facts are grounded: the fact that murder is wrong is perhaps an example. This fact is ungrounded, but is distinguished from the physical facts in that it is not fundamental.[25] This second possibility is the more attractive one, I believe, but it faces the same problem as the first. It has nothing to say about *how* ungrounded nonfactual facts are related to the fundamental; it lumps all ungrounded nonfactual facts—moral, mathematical, say—together. As with the first possibility, distinctions can indeed be made, by examining how moral beliefs and metalinguistic facts about moral language are grounded; but these distinctions would be drawn indirectly.

My objection, then, is not that the grounding approach cannot draw the distinctions that need to be drawn. It is that it does not draw them in the most perspicuous way.

The root of the problem is the connection between the grounding approach and the disquotational conception of fact. Think of the grounding approach as follows. We begin in natural language, a language that is highly heterogeneous in that it contains both factual and nonfactual discourse. We then introduce a disquotational notion of fact, which applies to all asserted sentences, whether factual or no. Finally, we apply the notion of grounding to facts thus understood.[26] Now, disquotational notions of fact, truth, property, and the like are prized because of their ability to obliterate metaphysical differences. When I lack information about what my neighbor has said—including information about its status as factual or nonfactual—it helps to have catch-all notions of fact, truth, and so on, by which I may express agreement, disagreement, or otherwise make cognitive contact with my neighbor. But however valuable this metaphysical neutrality of disquotational notions is for ordinary purposes, it is a liability in the present, metaphysical, context, for here we are trying to highlight differences in how our thought and talk connect with fundamental reality. In the present context, it's best not to adopt such a catch-all conception of fact, for doing so already obscures many of the differences we wish to capture—even if those differences can be accounted for, down the line, in some indirect way.

There are other—related—reasons to prefer metaphysical semantics over grounding. I'll mention two. First, consider the approach to the liar paradox according to which both the liar sentence and its negation must be rejected (where rejection is not the same thing as assertion of the negation). On a grounding approach, we seem not to be able to say anything at all here. Since neither the liar

---

[25] To say that this fact is grounded in our attitudes, for example, would turn moral expressivism into a form of descriptivism.

[26] Fine (2001) ultimately prefers to regard 'ground' as a sentence operator rather than as a predicate of facts (or propositions); but similar remarks apply since the sentences to which this sentence operator may be applied are heterogeneous; they may be either factual or nonfactual.

sentence nor its negation is assertable, we can say nothing of the form "ϕ grounds L", where L is either the liar sentence or its negation (assuming 'grounds' to be factive). But a natural approach can be taken if we speak in terms of metaphysical semantics rather than ground; see section 10.6.

Second, consider nonfundamental natural language quantification. Suppose that in the fundamental sense of 'there is', there are no such things as statues or lumps of clay, but that natural language is governed by a metaphysical semantics specifying that if some clay is appropriately shaped, then the following sentence is true in English: "There exists a lump made from that clay with modal properties m_L, and there also exists a distinct statue made from that clay, which has modal properties m_S." If we do not semantically ascend, and ask simply after the grounds of facts construed disquotationally, we will be led to an awkward place, as follows. Since there exist a lump and statue as described, there must exist a pair of singular facts, the fact that L has m_L and the fact that S has m_S, where L and S are the lump and statue in question. Further, if these are distinct facts, there must surely be some fundamental ground of one that is not a ground of the other—something fundamental that grounds their distinctness. But no such differential ground can be located.[27] Now, it's not as if the friend of ground has no response. He might claim that although no ground differentiates the pair of facts, the complex fact that L and S are distinct and instantiate m_L and m_S, respectively does have a ground: namely, the fact that the clay exists and is appropriately shaped.[28] But it remains awkward that the facts in question lack differential grounds. Intuitively, one wants to say, there really is no such fact as that L has m_L, or that S has m_S, because there really are no such things as L or S. A more satisfying picture of the situation is achieved by semantic ascent. The metaphysical semantics for English provides metaphysical truth-conditions for various statements about statues and lumps of clay, but it does not do so by associating referents to singular terms like 'S' and 'L'. It rather does so by associating complex truth-conditions for whole sentences containing quantifiers over, or singular terms for, both statues and lumps. These truth-conditions render 'Lump L has m_L and the distinct statue S has m_S' true, despite the absence of distinct metaphysical truth-conditions for the sentences 'L has m_L' and 'S has m_S.'[29]

These examples—of evaluative discourse, the liar paradox, and nonfundamental quantification—illustrate how adopting the disquotational notion of fact and asking after the grounds of facts thus understood can obscure what is important about the metaphysics of nonfundamental matters. We *can* speak of facts and ground in these contexts, but a clearer view is attained if we semantically ascend and describe how our discourse about values, truth, and nonfundamental entities relates to fundamental reality.

---

[27] Compare Sider (2008*b*). deRosset (2010) raises related issues about grounding.

[28] Compare Dasgupta (2010) on plural ground and Fine (1994*b*) on reciprocal essence.

[29] Depending on details, this might call for a refinement of the completeness principle.

7.10 Subpropositional?

Conceptions of fundamentality may be *propositional* or *subpropositional*—they may be notions that apply to entire propositions, or to constituents of propositions. To avoid reifying propositions and their constituents, we can put it linguistically: a locution for talking about fundamentality might be *sentential*—applying to entire sentences—or *subsentential*—applying to parts of sentences.

Lewisian naturalness is subpropositional: it is properties and relations, rather than entire propositions, that are evaluated for naturalness. The notion of a fundamental truth is propositional: truths are entire propositions, not proposition-parts. The notion of ground is propositional: entire propositions ground one another.

Structure is subpropositional. In my official regimentation, judgments of structure take the form $\mathscr{S}(\alpha)$, where α may be a subsentential expression (such as 'is an electron' or 'and'). Thus the ultimate locus of fundamentality is for me subpropositional. (I have no objection to propositional notions of fundamentality—such as various notions of fundamental truth—so long as they are defined in terms of the subpropositional notion of structure.)

There are both systematic and intuitive reasons for taking structure to be subpropositional. The systematic reasons will emerge in section 8.3: a subpropositional notion is explanatorily more powerful. The intuitive reason is that subpropositionality is tied to the following attractive picture: there are some fundamental "building blocks"—the "ultimate constituents of reality"—and the nature of reality is given by the arrangement of those building blocks.

7.11 Absolute?

Conceptions of fundamentality may be *comparative* or *absolute*. Lewisian perfect naturalness, for example, is absolute: one says of a property or relation that it is perfectly natural (or not) simpliciter. Lewis also spoke of properties and relations being more or less natural; this is an example of comparative fundamentality. (Lewis defined comparative naturalness in terms of perfect naturalness and length of definitions; but an alternate approach would be to take the former as basic and define the latter in terms of it.[30])

Structure is absolute: I say 'is structural' rather than 'is more structural'. (In my official regimentation, the structure operator attaches to a single expression rather than to a pair of expressions: "$\mathscr{S}$(is an electron)", "$\mathscr{S}$(and)", and so on.) (I have no objection to comparative notions of fundamentality so long as they are defined in terms of the absolute notion of structure. More on this below.)

The main reason for taking structure to be absolute is that facts about structure (in interesting cases, anyway) are fundamental, whereas facts about comparative fundamentality are nonfundamental. Why regard facts about structure as being

---

[30]I discuss this variant in Sider (1993a, chapter 3).

fundamental? Because structure is itself structural (section 7.13). While this allows *some* facts about structure to be nonfundamental, in interesting cases, claims about structure cannot be further explained. Why regard facts about comparative fundamentality as being nonfundamental? Because of purity. The point of a comparative conception of fundamentality would largely be to connect fundamental to nonfundamental matters; but given purity, such comparisons could not be fundamental facts.

There is a further reason in favor of absolutism. As before, in interesting cases the facts of structure are fundamental; and fundamental facts are always determinate (section 7.12) and objective (chapter 4). But in many interesting cases, it's hard to believe that the facts of comparative fundamentality are determinate and objective—consider, for example, the question of whether geological notions are more fundamental than biological ones.

7.11.1 *Absolutism and comparative structure*

I have not been practicing what the previous section preaches. Throughout this book I have spoken of comparative structure: of carving "reasonably well" at the joints, carving "equally well" (though not perfectly) at the joints, carving "badly" at the joints, and so on. Examples: a nonsubstantive question was characterized as one whose answer depends on which of various candidate meanings we adopt, where the candidates are *equally* joint-carving, and where no other candidate is *more* joint-carving (section 4.2). The doctrine of reference magnetism appealed to imperfect joint-carving (section 3.2). Explanations were required to be cast in joint-carving terms, and in the case of special-science explanation, "joint-carving" cannot mean *perfectly* joint-carving (section 3.1). Relatedly, think of the traditional "levels" picture of the sciences, with physics at the bottom, chemistry next, and the other sciences arranged in some order or other on top. This ordering can be thought of as corresponding to the comparative fundamentality of the notions of those sciences.

Thus we need a comparative notion of structure in many of the applications. This may be reconciled with absolutism by distinguishing the fundamental notion of structure from the notion of structure in those applications; it is only the fundamental notion which is absolute. (Or we may rephrase thus, to avoid putting weight on notion-identity: the fundamental facts about structure involve only absolute structure; all facts about comparative structure are nonfundamental.) Talk of comparative structure must have metaphysical truth-conditions in terms of absolute structure (and other fundamental notions).

How to give such metaphysical truth-conditions? How to define comparative structure? I do not know. But I can suggest several elements to employ in a definition.

One element comes from Lewis. Lewis's notion of a perfectly natural property or relation is absolute; but he went on to define a comparative notion. A property or relation is more or less natural, he said, depending how short a definition it can be given in a perfectly natural language—a language in which all predicates stand for perfectly natural properties and relations (1986*b*, p. 61). This approach could be generalized in the case of structure: one notion is "definitionally more structural" than another, let us say, iff it has a shorter definition in a fundamental language—a language in which all expressions are structural.

Lewis's approach has been thought to face serious challenges (Hawthorne, 2007; Sider, 1995; Williams, 2007), chief among which is that it counts every two properties that require an infinite definition (of the same cardinality) as being equally natural.[31] But this is a limitation only when properties require infinite definitions, and it is far from clear that properties of interest do. It might appear otherwise because such properties have infinitely many realizations. A complete specification of a certain kangaroo, in perfectly natural terms, down to the last microphysical detail, is just one realization of the property of being a kangaroo; and there are infinitely many such realizations, since (for example) kangaroos can vary continuously in length. So, let us grant, the property of being a kangaroo has an infinite definition in a perfectly natural language: the disjunction of its realization-predicates. But this needn't be the shortest definition. The property of being a kangaroo might also have a finite functional definition:

> x is a kangaroo $=_{df}$ x has some realization (property) or other that plays role R

if the perfectly natural language allows quantification over properties, and if role R is finitely definable in that language.

The class of finitely definable properties is particularly rich if quantification over arbitrarily high-order properties and relations is available. Begin with an initial class of finitely definable properties. Then give finite definitions of further, higher-order, properties, that make reference to the initial properties. (For example, one might define a space S of the initial properties, as well as a geometry on S, and then define properties of the form: *having some member of region R of space S*, where R is finitely definable. Also one might make use of causal notions— viz., *having some member of region R which plays such-and-such causal role*—provided causal notions can themselves be finitely defined.) Next give finite definitions of still higher-order properties, which can make reference to the previously defined properties. And so on. Given higher-order resources, there is reason to be optimistic that properties of interest are finitely definable in perfectly natural and fundamental languages.

(The procedure requires quantification over properties, but such quantification needn't be fundamental. Suppose, for example, that the language in which the definitions are cast includes no quantification over properties, but does include quantification over sets. Then we could simulate quantification over properties by

---

[31]There is a parallel worry about a Lewisian account of special-science laws: Lewisian laws must be simple; unnatural properties detract from simplicity; special-science properties are equivalent to infinite disjunctions of physical properties and hence highly unnatural.

identifying fundamental properties and relations with their extensions, and other properties with quasi-linguistic set-theoretic constructions out of fundamental properties. The conjunction of p and q, for example, could be identified with the triple $\langle \wedge, p, q \rangle$, where $\wedge$ is a symbol standing for conjunction.[32])

A further worry about the Lewisian approach is that mere length of definitions is an inadequate measure. Shouldn't the degree to which a definition is "disjunctive" render the defined notion less natural? But there are strategies for refinement available here. One might, for instance, require all definitions to be in some standard form (prenex disjunctive normal form, say, if the language is a first-order predicate calculus); and one might evaluate definitions, as given in this standard form, by a more complex measure that takes more into account than length (the number of disjuncts might, for instance, be taken to count against a definition more than the average number of conjuncts per disjunct).

The first element, then, is the notion of being definitionally-more-structural-than. A second element is "lawlikeness": the degree to which a notion figures into simple and strong generalizations. Green is more lawlike than grue because green figures in simpler and stronger generalizations than does grue. (As with Lewis's account of laws, the relevant notions of simplicity and strength must be spelled out.)

Lawlikeness has little utility on its own, since one can cook up simple and powerful generalizations with even highly non-joint-carving notions—recall Lewis's (1983b, p. 367) "law" $\forall x F x$, which implies everything true because F is a predicate true only of things in the actual world. But suppose we restrict our attention to somewhat definitionally structural notions—green, grue, kangaroo, being-a-snail-or-a-kangaroo, and the like. With respect to such notions, lawlikeness is an interesting measure—green, for example, is more lawlike than grue. It is only when applied to *extremely* definitionally unstructural notions, such as F in Lewis's "law", that lawlikeness is uninteresting. (It doesn't matter how exactly we sharpen the idea of a "somewhat" definitionally structural notion; on any reasonable sharpening, lawlikeness will generate an interesting ordering.)

The third element is really a class of elements. Philosophers of science have done much subtle and detailed work on explanation in the special sciences. Lawlikeness is one concept they use to characterize how the special sciences are explanatory, but there are many others: probability, unification, cause, and so forth.[33] These concepts can be understood without distinctive fundamental metaphysics; indeed, much of this work is designed to show how the special sciences can be explanatory in an ultimately physical world. So any of these concepts could play a role in a definition of a comparative notion of structure. The degree to which a notion plays a role in causal statements, for example, could be appealed to

---

[32]There is obviously some arbitrariness in this construction. For a defense of such arbitrariness in another context, see Sider (2006, section 2).

[33]See Strevens (2006) for an overview.

in such a definition, provided the notion of causation is itself given a metaphysical semantics.

So far the elements have been more or less "objective" (modulo some arbitrariness around the edges). A fourth element is more subjective. Perhaps economics deserves its place in the hierarchy of "levels" partly because of its value to us as a tool for prediction and control of things we care about. Disinterested Martians who for this reason do not develop economic theory would not be *missing out* in the way that they would if they did not develop chemistry or physics. In general, the comparative structuralness of a notion might be in part a function of how important it is to us. Section 2.5 argued against subjectivism about structure. But the opponent there was a *general* subjectivist about structure, including absolute structure. It would be really bad if there were no objective privilege at all to the physical conceptual scheme—recall "knee-jerk realism". But all I am allowing here is a partial subjectivism about one facet of comparative structure. This is comparatively benign, and does not conflict with knee-jerk realism, at least of the sort I find in myself. Absolute structure provides a bedrock of objectivity, on top of which a modicum of subjectivity in comparative structure may be overlaid.

I can supply, then, these elements. A nice project would be to actually produce a definition of comparative structure from them. I'd like to do this, but I don't know how. To anyone trying this at home: if you get discouraged, remember three things. First, remember that what you are attempting is a definition of a complex high-level notion in perfectly fundamental terms. No one can give a fully adequate definition of this sort for *any* complex high-level notion. A reasonable goal in such endeavors is persuading ourselves that *some* metaphysical semantics exists, by producing toy accounts that work well in a decent number of cases and have no in-principle defects. (Producing the elements of the definition is a start.) Second, don't be alarmed if a certain amount of vagueness or arbitrariness creeps into your attempts. These can be tolerated since comparative structure is not intended to itself be structural. Third, remember that there is no need to settle on a single definition once and for all; perhaps different applications call for different definitions of comparative structure. Granted, my case for primitivism about structure has been that positing a single notion of structure illuminates multiple domains (chapter 2, and see also section 7.13). But that single posited notion is absolute structure, which can be used to define multiple sorts of comparative structure.

Comparative structure, as defined from these elements, will not itself carve perfectly at the joints. But it can nevertheless carve reasonably well at the joints, provided the definition from the elements is a reasonable one. Thus its explanatory value needn't be compromised. While good explanations must be cast in reasonably joint-carving terms, they needn't be cast in perfectly joint-carving terms (there can be good explanation outside of physics, after all). Some vagueness or arbitrariness may enter the definition, which introduces the potential for nonsubstantive questions. But it does not follow that *all* questions about comparative structure are nonsubstantive. Only the questions whose answers turn on the vagueness or arbitrariness are rendered nonsubstantive. This is as it should be; some questions about comparative structure *are* nonsubstantive. For example, it may not be a substantive question whether geological notions are more structural than biological ones. It is compatible with this that the usual hierarchy of "levels" of special-science notions is by-and-large objective; the nonsubstantivity is only "around the edges".

7.11.2 *Absolutism and infinite descent*

It might be objected that absolutism requires a "ground floor". For the alternative to a ground floor is some sort of infinite descent of ever more fundamental facts or notions, and making sense of infinite descent seems to require a comparative notion of fundamentality.

Distinguish three sorts of "ground floor": ideological, mereological, and propositional. Only the first is demanded by my absolutism; but the first is unobjectionable.

The first sort of ground floor is ideological. The alternative is infinite *ideological* descent—a chain of ever more fundamental notions, with no notions more fundamental than every member of the chain. My account does indeed require an ideological ground floor. For me, the facts about fundamentality are in the first instance facts of the form "Notion α is structural" ($\mathscr{S}(\alpha)$); and it's hard to see how to construct a metaphysical semantics for talk of comparative notion-fundamentality in terms of such facts that would allow infinite ideological descent. (Certainly the account of definitional structure in section 7.11.1 does not allow it.) But infinite ideological descent is a seriously weird hypothesis, and seems unproblematic to deny. The hypothesis denies the existence of a book of the world, a complete perfectly fundamental description of reality, since for any chosen concepts, more fundamental concepts could be chosen.

Infinite *mereological* descent—a.k.a. the metaphysician's beloved hypothesis of "gunk"—is comparatively mundane. An object is gunky if each of its parts has further proper parts; thus gunk involves infinite descent in the part–whole relation. The corresponding sense of 'ground floor' is mereological: atomism. My theory of fundamentality does *not* require atomism, because gunk can be described using perfectly structural ideology.[34] Suppose, to take a toy example, that a certain gunky patch varies continuously in color from one wavelength to another. As Frank Arntzenius and John Hawthorne (2005, section V.2) show, the color facts about this patch could be taken to emerge from the totality of facts of the form *the average wavelength of part x of the patch is λ*. And there are various bits of fundamental ideology one could introduce to characterize these facts about average wavelength (such as 'x has a higher average wavelength than y' and

---

[34]I myself reject gunk (for independent reasons); see Sider (2011).

'x's average wavelength together with y's average wavelength equals z's average wavelength'—the details will depend on one's general approach to quantities.) For a more physically realistic example, Jeffrey Sanford Russell (2010) shows how to characterize the topology, mereology, and measure-theoretic facts about gunky space using a finite list of primitive notions; his primitive notions could be taken to carve at the joints.[35]

The final sort of ground floor is propositional, or factual: a ground floor of facts. A propositional ground floor is opposed to infinite propositional descent— an infinite descending chain of the in-virtue-of relation over facts or propositions. Now, as we've seen, "in-virtue-of" is not my preferred way of talking about fundamentality. Still, we can ask: Can I accommodate—in terms of structure—the kinds of scenarios that would be described by the friend of in-virtue-of as involving infinite propositional descent? The answer depends on which of two kinds of scenario is alleged. In the first sort, each level in the chain is a new "sort" of proposition—a proposition involving new ideology that is more fundamental than ideology involved in propositions higher up in the chain. I cannot accommodate this scenario, since it would require infinite ideological descent. But I can accommodate a tamer scenario, in which the propositions throughout the descending chain are all of the same sort—they all involve the same ideology. For example, it might be claimed that the proposition that a certain gunky object has a certain mass is true in virtue of a proposition about the masses of its parts under some finite decomposition, that the latter proposition is true in virtue of propositions about the masses of still smaller parts under a more fine-grained but still finite decomposition, and so on infinitely:

> a is 1 g mass in virtue of ...
>
> ... b being 0.5 g and c being 0.5 g (where $a = b + c$), which holds in virtue of ...
>
> ... d being 0.25 g and e being 0.25 g and f being 0.25 g and g being 0.25 g (where $b = d + e$ and $c = f + g$), which holds in virtue of ...

("+" signifies fusion). Even though this scenario would be described by the friend of in-virtue-of as one of infinite propositional descent, my description of it does not require infinite ideological descent. I can simply state all the propositions involved in the chain:

> a is 1 g
>
> b is 0.5 g
>
> c is 0.5 g
>
> $a = b + c$
>
> etc.

leaving out the in-virtue-of claims (since I renounce them), and add the only relevant claim about fundamentality, which is that the ideology common to all the

---

[35] See also Arntzenius (2008).

propositions—namely, mereological and mass-theoretic—is absolutely structural. (The exact nature of the mass-theoretic ideology common to all the propositions depends on one's views about the nature of quantity. One view would be that the ideology is comparative: "x is more massive than y", or "x's mass together with y's mass equals z's mass".)

So: the only limitation stemming from the absoluteness of structure is that I cannot accommodate infinite ideological descent. This is no real limitation, I say, because there is no reason to suppose that this weird scenario obtains.

"Objection: there *is* reason, namely empirical inductive reason, to believe in infinite ideological descent. Physicists once thought that everything depended on the features of molecules. But molecules gave way to atoms, which gave way to protons, neutrons and electrons, which have given way to quarks, leptons, and gauge bosons. Each time a new type of particle was discovered, physicists posited new features of the newly discovered particles, whose distribution accounted for, but could not be accounted for in terms of, the distribution of the distinctive features of the older particles. This historical progression of theories will probably continue forever, so there are no ultimate features on which everything depends."— This is a bad argument, for a few reasons. First, it is an induction from only four cases. Second, by moving from "finite" observations to an "infinite" conclusion, the argument makes a big leap. Compare it to the argument that there must be infinitely many people, since for each person we've observed, there exists a taller person.[36] Third, the argument fails by drawing a conclusion that is drastically dissimilar from the initially observed pattern. The initially observed pattern is an historical progression of physical theories:

Theory 1: The fundamental features are those of molecules.

Theory 2: The fundamental features are not those of molecules, but are rather those of atoms.

Theory 3: The fundamental features are not those of atoms, but are rather those of protons, neutrons, and electrons.

Theory 4: The fundamental features are not those of protons, neutrons, and electrons, but are rather those of quarks, leptons, and gauge bosons.

The conclusion drawn is that there are no fundamental features, since for any physical feature had by any particle, there are further features (had by smaller particles) that do not depend on the first feature. But this conclusion isn't inductively suggested by the initial pattern. The conclusion has the superficial appearance of a kind of limit point of the initial pattern, if that pattern were infinitely extended. By moving through Theories 1–4, so the idea goes, scientists have been moving closer and closer to the conclusion. But this impression vanishes upon closer inspection. Each Theory in the progression does not *add* a new layer of fundamental features, but rather *ditches* the previous Theory's layer (since it regards

---

[36]Thanks to Cian Dorr here.

the previous layer as just depending on the newly hypothesized layer). Extending the pattern indefinitely results in a series that simply has no intuitive limit. For comparison, imagine a countably infinite series of chairs: $c_1, c_2, \ldots$. Suppose first that in scenario 1, c_1 is filled; in scenario 2, chairs c_1 and c_2 are each filled; in scenario 3, chairs c_1, c_2, and c_3 are each filled; and so on. I suppose there's some sense in which the limit of this series is a scenario in which all the chairs are filled. But consider a second series in which only c_1 is filled in scenario 1, *only* c_2 is filled in scenario 2, *only* c_3 is filled in scenario 3, and so on. This series has no intuitive infinite limit. The imagined infinite extension of the progression through Theories 1–4 is like the second series.

This third criticism of the inductive argument depends on the fact that I construed Theories 1–4 in terms of "fundamental features", by which I meant absolutely fundamental features. Suppose they were construed instead in terms of comparative fundamentality:

Theory 1a: Molecules have certain distinctive features.

Theory 2a: Atoms have certain distinctive features, which are *more fundamental than* those of molecules.

Theory 3a: Protons, neutrons, and electrons have certain distinctive features, which are more fundamental than those of atoms.

Theory 4a: Quarks, leptons, and gauge bosons have certain distinctive features, which are more fundamental than those of protons, neutrons, and electrons.

If continued infinitely, this progression *does* seem to have an infinite limit (it's like the first chairs series): that for every feature, there are more fundamental features—infinite ideological descent. But this is not dialectically effective against absolute fundamentality, since comparative fundamentality was assumed from the start, in the characterizations of Theories 1a–4a.

"Even if there is in fact no infinite ideological descent, infinite ideological descent is *epistemically possible*, and hence should be allowed by any good theory of fundamentality."—If infinite ideological descent is epistemically possible then my theory of fundamentality is not epistemically necessary. That's ok! My theory is intended to be an educated guess about the nature of the world, not as some sort of a priori deduction that must hold with certainty. Neutrality on "first-order" questions like that of infinite ideological descent is not a reasonable constraint on the metaphysics of fundamentality. A metaphysics of fundamentality is supposed to give the truth about the nature of fundamentality, not provide a dialectically neutral framework in which to conduct first-order debates.

"Even if infinite ideological descent is not actual, it is nevertheless *metaphysically possible*, so a good theory of fundamentality should permit it."—As we will see in section 12.5, the Humean theory of modality to be defended undermines such arguments from possibility. In brief, the impossibility of infinite descent amounts to little more than its nonactuality, so there is no distinctively modal way to support it.

7.12 Determinate?

In addition to being pure, complete, subpropositional, and absolute, I hold that the fundamental is also determinate.

"The fundamental is determinate" is not particularly clear, and improving on the situation is difficult because there are so many different ways to understand what "determinacy" amounts to, but perhaps we can put it thus. First, no special-purpose vocabulary that is distinctive of indeterminacy—such as a determinacy operator or a predicate for supertruth—carves at the joints. Second, fundamental languages obey classical logic. The combination of these two claims is perhaps the best way to cash out the elusive dogma that vagueness and other forms of indeterminacy are not "in the world".

This is not to deny the value of determinacy-theoretic vocabulary, or supervaluationism, or nonclassical logic; it is just to deny them a place at the fundamental level. They might yet play a role in explaining vagueness in nonfundamental languages (see section 10.6).

7.13 Fundamental?

Last question: is fundamentality fundamental?

There are two questions here. First, is fundamentality a fundamental *notion*? And second, are facts about fundamentality fundamental *facts*? Given my subpropositional approach to fundamentality, the first question is primary. In my terms it is the question of whether structure is itself structural—of whether carving at the joints carves at the joints. In the official regimentation: is it the case that $\mathscr{S}(\mathscr{S})$?[37] My answer is yes.

My answer to the second question is: not all of them. In my terms, the question is whether facts about structure are fundamental facts. Facts about structure that involve only structural notions are indeed fundamental facts; but facts about structure that involve nonfundamental notions cannot be fundamental facts, given purity. For example, the fact that grue does not carve at the joints involves the nonfundamental notion grue, and so cannot be a fundamental fact. Thus it must, given completeness, have a metaphysical truth-condition stated in purely fundamental terms. But that truth-condition can mention structure, since structure is a fundamental notion. The truth-condition might have the form "G does not carve at the joints" (officially: "not $\mathscr{S}(G)$"), where G is a "metaphysical definition" of 'grue'.

Back to the first question. My reasons for saying that structure is structural emerge from considering an opposing viewpoint.

[37] On some regimentations of talk of structure, one might raise a worry about the intelligibility of the question: "Being structural is a property of semantic values; the question would be about the proposition that the property of being structural instantiates itself; there is no such proposition." I'm not sure if I accept any part of this objection, but at any rate, my preferred regimentation for talking about structure avoids the worry because $\mathscr{S}$ is an operator.

A vivid test for whether a given expression, E, carves at the joints is this: did God need to think in E-terms when creating the world? Clearly, she needed to think in terms of quantification, mass, distance, and so on; accordingly, those notions carve at the joints. But did she need also to think in terms of structure? It is natural, I must admit, to say no. All she needed to do was decide which objects to create, how massive to make them, and where to put them; she didn't need also to consider whether quantification, mass, distance, and the rest were structural.

If structure is not structural, then completeness requires all statements about structure to have metaphysical truth-conditions. Since those truth-conditions must be stated in perfectly structural terms, they cannot contain 'structure'; but they can contain terms that are structural—terms of physics, perhaps. What might such truth-conditions look like? I will sketch an answer that I will call "Melianism", since it contains elements of an intriguing view due to Joseph Melia.[38]

Let's simplify by discussing Lewisian (perfect) naturalness, rather than the more general notion of structure. We are after a definition of 'natural' in terms of natural properties and relations (by hypothesis these do not include natural-ness itself). Where $N_1, N_2 \ldots$ are the natural properties and relations, the Melian definition is:

P is natural $=_{df}$ $P = N_1$ or $P = N_2$ or $\ldots$

This is a highly disjunctive definition. The Melian embraces this. There is no need for a nondisjunctive, explanatory notion of naturalness, he says, because naturalness itself is never invoked in explanations. Whenever Lewis would cite naturalness in an explanation, the Melian cites particular natural properties. Why are these two electrons exactly alike? Because they have exactly the same natural properties, Lewis says. The Melian says instead: because they both have charge c, mass m, and spin s.

Objection: "We may not know which natural properties the electrons possess."—The Melian reply is that this is an epistemic limitation of ours, not a deficiency in the proffered explanation. The best explanation of the electrons being duplicates cites the particular natural properties they share, even if we do not possess that explanation.[39]

Objection: "The Melian's definition is circular since 'natural' was used to pick out the list $N_1 \ldots$"—There would be objectionable circularity only if 'natural' occurred on the right hand side of the definition. But it does not. 'Natural' was used to pick out the list by description; and perhaps our only access to the list—and thus to the definition—is via this description. Nevertheless, the definition itself contains only the list, not the description. Further, the Melian could avoid appealing to 'natural' in even this indirect way if he accepted the epistemology of section 2.3. He could then pick out the list by the description 'properties that figure in our best theory'. (This would not be an identification of naturalness with

---

[38] Melia put this forward in conversation, so please don't blame him for what follows!

[39] Compare Melia (1995; 2000).

the property of figuring in our best theory. Naturalness would remain identified with a disjunctive property of the form *being N_1 or N_2 or . . .*; the description would represent our best guess as to the identity of the disjuncts.)

"Objection: Melianism diminishes the significance of duplication, intrinsicality, lawhood, and other notions defined in terms of naturalness." Here we approach a more telling objection. Since Melian naturalness is highly disjunctive, so will be the defined notions. So although the Melian agrees with Lewis on the first-order questions—on which objects are duplicates of which, which properties are intrinsic, what the laws are, and so on—he must regard Lewis's focus on *these* first-order questions—questions of duplication, intrinsicality, law, and so forth—as being arbitrary, because based on highly disjunctive notions. This is a strange predicament. The Melian is trying to achieve Lewis's aims on the cheap, but his theory implies that these aims are metaphysically arbitrary and not particularly worth pursuing.

And the predicament is worse than strange; Melianism undermines all of the applications of naturalness. The Melian admits that a notion so disjunctive as Melian-naturalness cannot be explanatory, and tries to get around this by claiming that explanations can always cite particular natural properties rather than naturalness itself. We can explain why two electrons are exactly alike, he said, by pointing out that each has charge c, mass m, and spin s. But that is no explanation; explanations must cite generalizations. Explanations of similarity-facts require generalizations about similarity; explanations of meaning-facts require generalizations about meaning; explanations of substantivity-facts require generalizations about substantivity; and so on. Moreover, explanations must cite generalizations of sufficient scope. It would be no good to cite the generalization that any two electrons sharing charge c, mass m, and spin s are similar; the generalization is too specific. The generalizations must cite naturalness—or better, structure. But then structure cannot have a Melian definition, if the generalizations are to be explanatory.

The argument of this book is that the explanatory power of our overall theory is enhanced by positing structure. Must the posited notion be itself (perfectly) structural, or could it have a definition in structural terms? What we have seen so far is that it could not have a Melian, disjunctive definition, for that would undermine its applications.

Could it have a nonMelian, nondisjunctive definition? Then even though structure would not be structural, it might still be capable of figuring in explanations, just like notions of the special sciences.

But it is hard to see how a definition of structure could avoid being disjunctive. Chemical kinds have nondisjunctive (metaphysical) definitions because instances of chemical kinds are reasonably physically alike, and physical notions are structural. Biological kinds have nondisjunctive definitions because instances of biological kinds are functionally, if not physically, alike; and functional notions have reasonably nondisjunctive definitions in structural terms. But consider the instances of the notion of structure. These include notions of mass, charge, spatiotemporal distance, set membership, conjunction, disjunction, and universal quantification, let us suppose. This class of notions is neither physically nor functionally unified. Nor does it seem to be unified in any other way that would allow a nondisjunctive definition.[40] Other than the fact that all its members are structural, the class is highly heterogeneous.

Relatedly, consider the notions to be defined in terms of structure—similarity, intrinsicality, laws and explanation, meaning, induction, physical geometry, and substantivity. The instances of any one of these notions are heterogeneous in physical and functional and other "first-order" ways. When x is similar to y and x' is similar to y', there needn't be any physical or functional or other first-order commonality between the pairs $\langle x, y \rangle$ and $\langle x', y' \rangle$; there needn't be any physical or functional or other first-order commonality between any two laws of nature; and so on. What unifies all the pairs of similar objects, and all the laws, is just the fact that they involve structural notions in certain ways; and the structural notions themselves are neither physically nor functionally unified.

The "first-order heterogeneity" of structure, and of structure-involving notions, is an in-principle obstacle to a nondisjunctive definition of structure. Thus the choice is stark: either adopt extreme realism about structure—holding that structure is itself structural—or else give up altogether on explanations that invoke structure, which is tantamount to giving up on structure itself. My choice is for the former.

The status of metaphysics itself hangs on this choice. In their loftiest moments, metaphysicians think of themselves as engaged in a profoundly important and foundational intellectual enterprise. But if fundamentality is highly disjunctive, the field of metaphysics itself—which is delineated by its focus on fundamental questions—would be an arbitrarily demarcated one.

Although it offers explanatory power (and a pleasing self-conception for metaphysicians), extreme realism about structure raises some difficult questions. I'll mention three.

First, the argument for saying that structure is structural was that this is needed to insure that structure can take part in genuine explanations. But look at the notions other than structure involved in the putative explanations: simplicity, correctness of interpretation, candidate meaning, and so on. These do not seem structural either. Doesn't this already undermine the genuineness of the explanations? And if it doesn't—if the genuineness of the explanations is compatible with their involving nonstructural notions—then why can't the explanations remain genuine if structure isn't structural?

---

[40] Or better: that would allow a nondisjunctive and objective definition. The class does seem unified by the fact that its members are all indispensible in our best theories.

This can be answered. Genuineness of explanation does not require *perfectly* structural notions, as we see from the special sciences. It is enough that simplicity, correctness of interpretation, and the rest, are somewhat structural. The reason for thinking that structure cannot be merely somewhat structural is its first-order heterogeneity—if structure is not perfectly structural then it is disjunctive and therefore highly nonstructural.

The second question I find more challenging. In section 6.3 we considered two possibilities for regimenting talk of structure, each involving the operator $\mathscr{S}$. On one, $\mathscr{S}$ had a very flexible grammar, and on the other, the language needed to be supplemented with dummy variables. Neither smacks of fundamentality. Each seems to require our fundamental languages to be much more complex than they would otherwise need to be. The complexity could be avoided by taking talk of semantic values as fundamental; $\mathscr{S}$ could then be a predicate of semantic values. But semantics does not smack of fundamentality.

The third question is also challenging. Realism about structure requires a fundamental posit, and such posits are generally to be avoided. The concern is particularly pressing given my own preference, expressed many times in this book, for simplicity. I have been disdaining, and will continue to disdain, primitive modality, law, cause, tense, logical consequence, higher-order quantification, and other such luxuries. But when it comes to my own pet concept, structure—it might be alleged—my scruples go out the window.

It's not that I have no answer to this charge. My answer is that structure is no luxury, since it cannot be reduced without loss. Still, it smells fishy, doesn't it? This is a serious challenge facing the audacious doctrine of realism about structure.

8 Rivals

A metaphysics of fundamentality consists of some distinctive concepts for characterizing fundamentality and a theory of how those concepts behave. I have been
defending one such metaphysics, whose distinctive concept is structure. In this
chapter we will discuss some rival approaches, based on rival concepts. These
rivals are close cousins of my own approach, in that much of the work I do with
structure could be done using my rivals' concepts. Thus the criticisms I will make
should be viewed as sparring amongst friends.

8.1 Fine's concepts

Let us begin with the two concepts introduced by Kit Fine in his article "The
Question of Realism". The first is that of one proposition's *grounding* another.[1]
When *p* grounds *q* then *q* holds *in virtue of p's* holding; *q's* holding is *nothing
beyond p's* holding; the truth of *p* *explains* the truth of *q* in a particularly tight
sense (explanation of *q* by *p* in this sense requires that *p* necessitate *q*). Fine
also considers the possibility of taking the fundamental locution to be a two-
place sentence operator, "ϕ because ψ", rather than a two-place predicate of
propositions, "*p* grounds *q*". I'll alternate between these formulations.

The second concept is that of a proposition's being *real*. A proposition is real
if it is *fundamentally* the case, if it describes reality's *intrinsic structure*.[2] As with
ground there is a sentence-operator formulation: "In reality, ϕ."

The next few sections discuss two views about the metaphysics of fundamentality based on Fine's concepts: one based on ground and reality, the other based
solely on reality. Now, although there are elements of these views that Fine himself
would endorse, it should not be assumed that he would endorse the whole of either
of them (hence I call them merely "Finean"). For one thing, I am particularly
interested in the versions of these views according to which facts about fundamentality are themselves fundamental; but Fine does not commit himself to such a
view.[3] For another, Fine's purpose for introducing his concepts was not primarily
to provide a metaphysics of fundamentality, in the sense at issue here. It was rather
to clarify what is at stake in debates over "realism". Fine views such debates as

---

[1] Fine (2001, p. 15–16). I'll ignore certain complications Fine discusses, such as multiple propositions
on the "left-hand side" ("$p_1, p_2, \ldots$ grounds q") and the nonfactive sense of ground.

[2] Fine (2001, p. 26).

[3] He does say that "there is a primitive metaphysical concept of reality, one that cannot be understood in fundamentally different terms" (p. 1). But "primitive" here could have a conceptual or
methodological sense (note the words 'concept' and 'understood').

concerning what is *factual*, where a factual proposition is one that is either real, or grounded in propositions that are real. The difference between anti-realists and realists cannot be articulated in less "metaphysical" terms, according to Fine, since anti-realists about a subject matter S may well accept truth, bivalence, and so on, for statements about S. But what they do not accept is that statements about S are factual in his metaphysical sense. Today's ethical anti-realists are not so crude as to deny that murder is wrong, or that 'murder is wrong' is true; but on Fine's view they must deny that the proposition that murder is wrong is factual: it is neither real nor is it grounded in what is real.

8.2 First Finean view: grounding and reality

One rival conception of fundamentality makes use of both of Fine's notions. According to this conception, the facts about fundamentality consist of the facts of the forms: "In reality, ϕ", and "ϕ because ψ", or the corresponding facts in the propositional formulation.

(Following Fine, we can define a basic proposition as one that is grounded in no proposition.[4] This raises the possibility of a simplification: might we define a real proposition as a basic one? Fine rejects this identification, for two reasons. First, a nonfactual proposition—for example, an ethical proposition according to the moral expressivist—might lack a ground and thus count as basic, but being nonfactual, it would not be real.[5] Second, Fine allows that some real propositions might ground others, for example if matter were infinitely divisible (2001, p. 27). Thus, for Fine, basicness is neither necessary nor sufficient for reality. My discussion will be independent of this issue.)

8.2.1 *Ground and purity*

Consider grounding facts involving nonfundamental notions, such as:

(1) The proposition that there is a C_0 grounds the proposition that there is a city.

Are such facts fundamental?

Some defenders of the present approach will want to say that they are. After all, it's very hard to say in any reductive way how facts about cities relate to the fundamental. This is the main form of this first Finean view that I wish to consider.

---

[4]This definition uses the predicate-of-propositions formulation. In the operator formulation, we might define "basically ϕ" as "for no sentence ψ is $\ulcorner\phi$ because $\psi\urcorner$ true", or, alternatively, as "$\sim\exists P(\phi$ because $P)$". Neither is ideal. The first renders 'Basically ϕ' too weak—it could be true if ϕ had a ground that our language cannot express; the second requires quantification into sentence position.

[5]Fine's proposition b) (Fine, 2001, p. 17) commits him to this conclusion.

And my main argument against it is that it violates purity (section 7.2). Purity prohibits fundamental facts that involve nonfundamental notion, and (1) involves the nonfundamental notion of being a city.[6]

This argument must be put carefully in order to avoid begging the question. My original statement of purity was this: "Fundamental facts involve only fundamental notions." But 'fundamental notion' is *my* term—it means joint-carving—and the dispute with the Finean is over whether to use his terms or mine. A dialectically appropriate challenge must be formulated in Finean terms, in terms of ground and reality rather than in terms of carving at the joints. Rephrased, the argument is as follows. The Finean view under consideration says that true propositions about ground and reality are themselves real. So if (1) is true, then the proposition it expresses is real. But, I say, no proposition about cities—that is, no proposition involving the notion of being a city—is real. (This premise plays the role of purity.) Thus the Finean view under consideration is false. It is false because it implies that the fundamental story of the world includes facts about cities, namely, facts about how propositions about cities are grounded.

The argument assumes that no propositions about cities are real. Intuitively, the property of being a city is not the kind of subject matter that would show up in a fundamental description of the world. The Finean might reject this assumption by saying that, while propositions about cities *that do not involve ground* are indeed never real, propositions of ground about cities are sometimes real.[7] In particular, he might say, the proposition expressed by (1) is real. This move is intuitively very unsatisfying. What would motivate the special exception?

The problem with this first Finean view, then, is that it does not heed the lesson of section 7.3: facts about the *connection* between the fundamental and the nonfundamental should not be taken themselves to be fundamental; otherwise the domain of fundamental facts becomes infected with facts about cities, smiles, and candy. The problem arises because the view embraces two things: i) a *comparative* (recall section 7.11) distinctive concept—ground; and ii) fundamental facts in which that comparative concept connects fundamental to nonfundamental matters. There are other rival views that also embrace i) and ii). Consider Cian Dorr's (2004; 2005) theory of metaphysical analysis, for example. Dorr's key locution for talking about fundamentality, "to $R(x_1 \ldots)$ is to $\phi(x_1 \ldots)$" (as in "to be a city is to be a C") is comparative. So any follower of Dorr who also held that facts like "to be a city is to be a C" are fundamental would face the problem as well. Similarly, a view based on the notion of truthmaking, which held additionally that facts about truthmaking are fundamental, would also face the problem (see section 8.5).

---

[6]For another interesting objection to the grounding approach to fundamentality, see deRosset (2010).

[7]This move is formally available because the Finean needn't accept the combinatorial principle of section 8.3.

It is natural to think of grounding as a kind of metaphysical causation. As a Humean I'm suspicious of metaphysical pushings and pullings; but it's awfully hard to stop thinking in terms of them. It's overwhelmingly tempting to say that it is either raining or snowing because it is raining (Fine, 2001, p. 22), or that my being a philosopher makes it the case that someone is a philosopher. But we reductionists can take the same attitude towards metaphysical causation as towards everyday causation: it reduces in some way to facts that don't involve metaphysical causation. As a first pass at the cases of disjunction and existential quantification, there is a sort of "metaphysical covering law" underwriting each case. In the first, the law is that whenever p is true, so is $p \lor q$; in the second, it is that whenever a is F, something is F. Most crudely: metaphysical causation occurs when an instance is subsumed under such a metaphysical law. No doubt the account will need to be refined ad nauseum in familiar ways; but the possibility of such a project largely dispels the temptation to admit *fundamental* metaphysical causation. I'm also inclined to reject fundamental laws of metaphysics, and so to regard the covering metaphysical laws as being mere regularities (the regularities are *metaphysical* laws because they involve only the abstract and general notions of interest in metaphysics). Opposition to metaphysical laws is of a piece with opposition to primitive logical consequence and primitive modality, on which see chapters 10 and 12.

I have been opposing the Finean who says that propositions like (1) hold in reality. What if the Finean denies this?

If propositions like (1) are not real, they must be grounded in real propositions (for surely they are factual). It will be difficult to say what the grounding propositions are. But I am in the same boat: it is similarly difficult to provide a metaphysical semantics for sentences about metaphysical semantics.

If propositions like (1) are not real, then what about propositions about reality? Do they too fail to be real? Answering yes would put the Finean in the same boat as the Melian of section 7.13. It would then be hard to avoid saying that facts about ground and reality are grounded disjunctively, in which case no good explanations could be given using those notions.

But the Finean might say that unlike propositions about ground, propositions of the form "In reality, ϕ" *are* real. This view does not face the purity problem, since in true propositions of this sort, ϕ will presumably not involve notions like city, smile, or candy. Thus, a powerful position remains to be considered: the position that the fundamental facts about fundamentality are those involving Fine's concept of reality. I discuss this position in section 8.3.

8.2.2 *Ground and infinite descent*

Friends of ground face the question of whether there could be an infinite descent of ground, a chain of propositions $p_0, p_{-1}, p_{-2} \ldots$, where p_{-1} grounds p_0, p_{-2} grounds $p_{-1} \ldots$, and where no proposition grounds the whole sequence. Many think that there is something deeply incoherent about the idea. As Schaffer (2010c) puts it, "Being would be infinitely deferred, never achieved."[8]

Suppose for the sake of argument that infinite descent of ground ought indeed to be banned. Compliance with the ban might seem easy. It is only exotic metaphysical hypotheses (such as gunk), one might think, that would result in infinite descent of ground; and such hypotheses may safely be rejected. But as we will see, some perfectly ordinary phenomena involve an infinite descent of ground. Or rather, the ground-theoretic description of the phenomena involves infinite descent; the *structure*-theoretic description does not. Thus the notion of ground gives rise to a sort of paradox that is immediately dissolved by thinking instead in terms of structure.

Consider first the facts of distance. It's arguable that distances, fundamentally, are not direct connections between points, but are rather path-dependent.[9] (Distance is treated this way in general relativity, for example.) Suppose distance is indeed path-dependent, and consider the fact that a certain path through space is one meter long. It's surely overwhelmingly natural for the friend of ground to say that the path is one meter long *because* it is made up of two (nonoverlapping) half-meter long parts. (This is consistent with saying that it's *also* the case that the path is one meter long because it's made up of a quarter-meter part and a three-quarter meter part.) But now, the half-meter long parts of the initial path have the lengths that they do because they are made of quarter-meter parts, which themselves have their lengths because of the lengths of still smaller parts, and so on. There is no end to this descent of grounds, *even if space is atomic*, provided space is not discrete. For even if space is atomic (nongunky), there are no shortest paths.[10]

An analogous argument can be given for the topological notion of continuity. A friend of ground should describe a continuous curve as being continuous *because* its left and right halves are continuous (and continuously connected). Those halves are themselves continuous because their parts are continuous, and so on. As before, even if space is atomic, provided it is not discrete there is no end to this descent of ground, because there are no "atoms of continuity"—there are no smallest continuous paths.

These examples do not call for infinite ideological descent. Metrical and topological facts can be stated using perfectly fundamental notions ('open set', in the latter case, and terminology from the mathematics of differential manifolds in the former). The demand for infinite descent has a distinctively fact-theoretic source. Intuitively, the source lies in the way the facts in question are quantifi-

---

[8] See also Cameron (2008).

[9] See Bricker (1993); Maudlin (1993, p. 196).

[10] A priority monist like Schaffer (2010c) can escape by denying that a path has its length because of the lengths of its parts. A friend of entity-grounding might try to escape by grounding facts about path length in the plurality of points in the path, rather than in any fact or facts about distance. This strikes me as an illustration of the evils of entity-grounding; see sections 8.5 and 8.6.

cationally defined in terms of the distribution of the fundamental ideology over infinite collections of points. Actually this can be illustrated by a simple mathematical example. Just like topological and metric facts, set-theoretic facts can be stated with perfectly fundamental notions (perhaps just a single predicate for set-membership). Set theory thus does not call for infinite ideological descent. But using the primitive notions of set theory, we can define the notion of an infinite set. And on the face of it, the *facts* about infinite sets call for infinite descent of ground. For example, it would seem that a certain countably infinite set, $A = \{a_1, a_2, \ldots\}$ is infinite because it is the union of $\{a_1\}$ and the infinite set $\{a_2, a_3 \ldots\}$; and the latter is infinite because it is the union of $\{a_2\}$ and the infinite set $\{a_3, a_4 \ldots\}$; and so on.

8.3 Second Finean view: reality

A second rival conception of fundamentality dispenses with ground (thus avoiding the objection from purity[11]), and invokes only Fine's notion of reality. On this second Finean view, the facts about fundamentality consist of the facts of the form "In reality, ϕ." (I particularly have in mind the version that adds that all such facts themselves hold in reality.)

Call a sentence *structural* iff each of its words carve at the joints. Call a proposition structural iff it is expressed by some structural sentence. And call a proposition (or sentence, depending on context) a structural truth iff it is true and structural. Structural truths behave very much like Fine's real propositions. Each can be thought of as a way of cashing out the intuitive notion of a *fundamental truth*. Nevertheless, there are important differences. The notion of a fundamental truth behaves differently under the two conceptions.

8.3.1 *Explanation of fundamental truths*

The differences come from the fact that structure is subpropositional, whereas reality is propositional (recall section 7.10). The locus of fundamentality for the Finean is the whole proposition, whereas for me it is the proposition-part. Fundamentality is holistic for the Finean, atomistic for me. Suppose, for example, that it is a fundamental truth that there are electrons. For me, this boils down to the fact that i) there are indeed electrons; and ii) electronhood and existential quantification carve at the joints. For the Finean, it amounts simply to the fact that the entire proposition that there are electrons is real.

The subpropositional locus does seem more intuitive. One wants to say that it's a fundamental truth that there are electrons *because* of something about electronhood and existential quantification. Now, I cannot lean too heavily on the thought in this form since the 'because' surely has the sense of ground. But the thought has an epistemic/explanatory reading that has real bite.

---

[11]But the objection from infinite descent still threatens, insofar as real propositions are to be intuitively thought of as ungrounded.

There are patterns in the fundamental truths. Perhaps the following are all fundamental truths:

e_1 is an electron;

e_2 is an electron;

There is an electron;

There is a quark;

and perhaps none of the following truths are fundamental:

New York is a city;

Tokyo is a city;

There schmexists an electron;

There schmexists a quark.

(There schmexists an F, recall, iff the property of being an F is expressed by some predicate in some sentence of this book.) On my account, we can *explain* why this is so: the predicates 'electron' and 'quark', the quantifier 'there is', and the names 'e_1' and 'e_2' carve at the joints, whereas the predicate 'city' and the variable-binding expression 'schmexists' do not. My theory of fundamental truth is unified by these claims. On the Finean view, on the other hand, the patterns remain unexplained; they are brute patterns in the propositions that are real.

8.3.2 *Combinatorialism about fundamentality*

The propositional/subpropositional difference between the second Finean view and my own thus leads to a difference in explanatory power. As we will see in the next three sections, it also leads to differences in flexibility.

My subpropositional, atomistic account implies a sort of combinatorial principle of fundamental truth:

If S is a fundamental truth, and S' is any true sentence containing no expressions other than those occurring in S, then S' is a fundamental truth as well.

A fundamental truth, for me, is a structural truth; and a structural truth is just a true sentence composed only of joint-carving expressions; so any true sentence composed only of expressions drawn from some structural truth must itself be a structural truth. The combinatorialism is due to the atomism. But Fine's holistic account does not imply the combinatorial principle; Fine need not accept that if ⌜In reality, S⌝ is true and S' is a true sentence containing no expressions other than those occurring in S, then ⌜In reality, S'⌝ must be true as well.

Are there reasons to deny the combinatorial principle? One might, for example, want to hold that some sentence $\sim\phi$ is fundamentally true but that $\sim\sim\sim\phi$ is *non*fundamental (though true).[12] Now, this particular example doesn't worry me much, since its force would seem to derive from considerations of ground: the

---

[12] Thanks to Kit Fine for this example.

intuitive reason for saying that $\sim\sim\sim\phi$ is nonfundamental is presumably that it is grounded, in a fundamental sense, in $\sim\phi$. So if I am right that we should reject a fundamental notion of ground, we have no reason to accept the example. The claim that $\sim\phi$ grounds $\sim\sim\sim\phi$ in some *non*fundamental sense of 'ground' would not justify the claim that $\sim\sim\sim\phi$ is nonfundamental; the "covering law" account of metaphysical causation/ground mentioned above, for example, would make it unremarkable for some fundamental truths to ground others.

But there are quite different, and systematic, reasons one might have for denying the combinatorial principle. Consider, for example, the following version of "ontological semi-realism":[13]

Some ontological facts are fundamental and others are not. Facts about the existence of subatomic particles (such as electrons and quarks) are fundamental. But there is no fundamental fact, one way or the other, about whether there exist further things, things like composite material objects, holes, numbers, and so on.

This semi-realist will presumably grant that the following is a fundamental truth:

(1) $\sim\exists x(\text{electron}(x) \wedge \text{quark}(x))$
   Nothing is both an electron and a quark.

But then, given the combinatorial principle for fundamentality, each of the following is fundamentally true if true at all:

(2a) $\exists x(\sim\text{electron}(x) \wedge \sim\text{quark}(x))$
   There is something that is neither an electron nor a quark.

(2b) $\sim\exists x(\sim\text{electron}(x) \wedge \sim\text{quark}(x))$
   Nothing is neither an electron nor a quark.

For both (2a) and (2b) contain only expressions occurring in (1): variables, '$\exists$', '$\sim$', '$\wedge$', 'electron', and 'quark'. Thus whether there exists anything other than electrons and quarks is a fundamental matter. If we indulge in the harmless assumption that electrons and quarks are the only sorts of subatomic particles, this is precisely what our ontological semi-realist wanted to deny.

The conflict with semi-realism might be regarded as unwanted flexibility in my subpropositional approach. I view it instead as a powerful argument against semi-realism!

There are ways to square semi-realism with the combinatorial principle. The semi-realist could distinguish two quantifiers: i) a quantifier over subatomic particles, $\exists_{\text{part}}$; and ii) an ordinary quantifier. When '$\exists$' is replaced with '$\exists_{\text{part}}$', (1) is a fundamental truth. Accordingly, any true statement containing just variables, '$\exists_{\text{part}}$', '$\sim$', '$\wedge$', 'electron', and 'quark' is also fundamentally true. So when '$\exists$' is replaced with '$\exists_{\text{part}}$', whichever of (2a) and (2b) is true, is fundamentally true. In particular, the semi-realist could claim, it is (2b) that is true—only electrons and quarks exist in the sense of $\exists_{\text{part}}$. But it is the ordinary quantifier, not $\exists_{\text{part}}$, that the semi-realist has in mind when she says that there is no fundamental fact, one way

---

[13] Chalmers (2009) is sympathetic to this sort of view.

or the other, as to whether there are any things other than subatomic particles. When '∃' is replaced with the ordinary existential quantifier, the semi-realist will say, (1) and (2a) are true but not fundamentally true, whereas (2b) is simply false.

But this ontological semi-realist faces a challenge: to remain distinct from an ontological *realist* (see chapter 9) who accepts mereological nihilism—the denial of mereologically complex entities. Cian Dorr (2002; 2005), for example, accepts a fundamental sort of quantification, which he uses to state his nihilism; but he grants that 'There are composite entities' is true in ordinary English. For Dorr as for the purported semi-realist, (1) and (2b) are true in the fundamental sense of '∃', whereas under the ordinary English sense, (1) and (2a) are true but not fundamentally true and (2b) is false.

There are ways to meet the challenge. The semi-realist might say that there are several joint-carving quantifiers, $∃_1 \ldots ∃_n$.[14] Under each quantifier, there are electrons and quarks (that is, for each i, $\ulcorner ∃_i x \, \text{electron}(x) \wedge ∃_i x \, \text{quark}(x) \urcorner$ is true). Under $∃_1$, only electrons and quarks exist; under the others, various other objects exist in addition (so to speak). $∃_{\text{part}}$ is $∃_1$; the ordinary existential quantifier is semantically indeterminate over two or more of the $∃_i$s. And it is the ordinary "there is" under which "There is no fundamental fact of the matter, one way or the other, whether there are anything other than electrons and quarks" is true. This is a consistent position, and is distinct from Dorr's position; but the semi-realist may feel at this point that he has drifted far from where he began.

The general moral is that the combinatorial principle rules out certain views about fundamentality: views on which the fundamental level is distinguished, not by a distinctive vocabulary, but rather by a distinctive set of claims in a more inclusive vocabulary. One is always free to make such a view combinatorialism-friendly by "splitting" the inclusive vocabulary. Whenever one previously used a term T to state both a fundamental truth and a nonfundamental truth, one now distinguishes a term T_f which occurs exclusively within fundamental truths from a term T_n which occurs exclusively within nonfundamental truths. But the result of doing so may not preserve the spirit of the original view.

8.3.3 *Combinatorialism about determinacy*

My view implies a further combinatorial principle:

> If S is a fundamental truth, and S' is any sentence containing no expressions other than those occurring in S, then S' is determinate—either determinately true or determinately false.

For given my definition of 'fundamental truth', such an S' contains only joint-carving expressions, and thus must be determinate given section 7.12's claim that there is no indeterminacy at the fundamental level.

The continuum hypothesis is sometimes said to be indeterminate. But suppose that mundane set-theoretic truths, such as the axiom of extensionality, are

---

[14] See McDaniel (2009); Turner (2010*b*) on "ontological pluralism".

fundamental. Then by the combinatorial principle, the continuum hypothesis must be determinate, since it can be stated using only expressions that occur in mundane set-theoretic truths (namely, logical expressions and the predicate ∈). Thus we have a surprising result: the fundamentality of mundane truths of set-theory requires the non-mundane continuum hypothesis to be determinate.

The surprise is due to my account's subpropositionality. To say that a set-theoretic claim is fundamental, given my account, is to attribute the status of joint-carving to its constituents, and so to set-membership in particular. For the Finean, by contrast, to say that a set-theoretic claim is fundamental is not to attribute any particular status to set-membership. Thus the Finean has no particular reason to say that other set-theoretic claims, such as the continuum hypothesis, are determinate.

8.3.4 No fundamental truths

We have been exploring ways in which the Finean account is more flexible than mine. But there is also a small way in which the Finean account is less flexible: its positive statements of fundamentality require whole propositions to be fundamental.

Consider "quantifier variance" (chapter 9). This view is based on the thought that objecthood, and facts about objects, are not fundamental. A Finean might want to put this by saying that no propositions involving object-theoretic concepts are real.[15] But there may not be any non-object-involving propositions at all (or no real ones, anyway). For, one might think, to build up a sentence for a (real) proposition, one needs to begin with predicates, whether applied to names or quantified variables; but predication, naming, and quantification are all object-involving concepts. Thus, the Finean would be forced to admit, there are no real propositions at all, in which case nothing positive whatsoever can be said about fundamentality.

With the concept of structure, by contrast, a quantifier variantist could still say something positive about fundamentality. She could claim that conjunction, disjunction, negation, and necessity (say) carve at the joints. Since structure is subpropositional, she wouldn't need to build up to an entire fundamental truth in order to attribute structure.

Thus the second Finean view does not combine easily with this sort of quantifier variance. Not that this is especially damning.

8.3.5 Nihilism and deflationism

A final point about the second Finean account is that it conflates certain nihilistic and deflationary positions.

For example, consider on the one hand a *causal deflationist*, who thinks that causality is not fundamental, and on the other hand a *causal nihilist*, who is a

---

[15] The view *might* be put differently since the Finean view does not imply the combinatorial principle; my point is just that the Finean might put it this way.

causal anti-deflationist with the additional view that, fundamentally speaking, nothing causes anything. Each, let us suppose, thinks that everyday statements about causation are true. How to distinguish these positions?

It is clear how my approach distinguishes them. Each thinks that 'Some things cause other things' and other ordinary English sentences about causation are true. Each thinks that the ordinary English word 'cause' fails to carve at the joints. The causal deflationist thinks additionally that *no* causal locution carves at the joints. The causal nihilist, on the other hand, thinks that there is a joint-carving causal locution, 'causes*', in terms of which it is true to say: "Nothing causes* anything" (recall section 5.3).

But how could the Finean distinguish the causal deflationist from the causal nihilist? On the face of it, each agrees that:[16]

> Some things cause other things, but it is not the case that in reality, some things cause other things.

There are various moves the Finean might make here. I can't conclusively refute any of them, but none seems wholly satisfactory. The first is to say that the nihilist is distinguished by her additional belief that in reality, nothing causes anything. But this would involve denying that 'in reality' is factive. I cannot find an explicit claim of factivity in Fine (2001), but surely that was his intention.

The second is to make a distinction like my own between fundamental and nonfundamental languages. (Perhaps the Finean could define a fundamental language as a language in which ⌜In reality, ϕ⌝ is true whenever ϕ is true.) In terms of this distinction, the Finean could say that the disagreement is over whether 'nothing causes anything' is true in a fundamental language: the causal nihilist thinks it is, and the causal deflationist thinks it is not. But this seems to go against the spirit of Fine's approach. That spirit is to do fundamental metaphysics within an enhanced version of English (English with the addition of 'in reality'— and perhaps also 'grounds') rather than to give up on English and do fundamental metaphysics in a different, fundamental language.

The third was suggested by John Hawthorne: say that only the causal nihilist admits that certain general laws governing causation are real, such as the proposition that causation is transitive. The suggestion is intriguing, but it requires that the nihilist accept some laws of causation. It would not work, for example, if the causal nihilist denied the transitivity of causation, and further, that any other general principle about causation is lawlike enough to merit being real. More generally, it would not work for nihilists about other matters who are unwilling to accept such laws.

Intuitively speaking, the problem is that deflationisms—of the sort I have been considering, anyway—are attacks on language, whereas the Finean ideology is resolutely "object-language" rather than metalinguistic. Faced with a question Q?,

---

[16]Let us assume that the causal deflationist and the causal nihilist are both ontological realists, so the quantificational language here is not a distraction.

the deflationist wants, in the first instance, neither to give a positive nor negative answer, but rather to accuse the question of being faulty in some way. Likewise, the anti-deflationist's primary goal is not to take a stand on Q's answer, but rather to defend Q itself. Now, in Fine's ideology, if we don't want to just answer Q, our remaining option is to ask whether the proposition that Q is real. But *that* question doesn't correspond to the question of the status of Q. Since reality is factive, to answer it in the affirmative is to answer Q in the affirmative.

8.4 Truthmaking

According to the doctrine of truthmaking, each truth has a *truthmaker*—an entity whose very existence "makes-true" that truth.[17]

What are these truthmakers? Sometimes they can be perfectly mundane entities. I, for example, serve as a truthmaker for the truth that there exists at least one thing. My very existence makes it true that there exists at least one thing. (In fact, anything at all is a truthmaker for this truth; the truthmaking relation is not one-to-one.) But other kinds of truths require distinctive entities as their truthmakers. I cannot serve as a truthmaker for the truth that I am five feet nine inches tall, since I could have existed but had some other height. (Truthmaker theorists disagree over the exact nature of the truthmaking relation, but they all agree that the existence of the truthmaker must necessitate the truth.) Nor is that truth made true by the property of being five-nine, since that property could have existed without my instantiating it. Nor is it made true by the ordered pair of me and the property, since that ordered pair could have existed without my instantiating the property.[18] Nor does there seem to be any other particular, property, or set-theoretic construction therefrom whose existence is sufficient for my being five-nine. So what is the truthmaker here? When mundane entities don't suffice, truthmaker theorists tend to posit new entities that are fit to serve as truthmakers—entities that simply could not have existed if the truths in question had not been true. Different sorts of entities could be posited; I'll focus on "states of affairs". (Other entities that might be posited include tropes and "thick particulars".) The state of affairs of my being five-nine is the truthmaker for the truth that I am five-nine; it is to be thought of as a contingent entity, an entity that, necessarily, exists if and only if I am five-nine. (States of affairs thus construed are like facts on a "concrete" conception. But I have been using the term 'fact' more neutrally, so I will avoid using that term for truthmakers. Note

---

[17] See Armstrong (1997; 2004); Cameron (2010; 2011).

[18] Whatever one thinks of truthmakers, it should not be thought that they are required to "distinguish facts from mere lists"—to distinguish i) the scenario in which I instantiate the property of being five-nine from ii) the scenario in which I and the property both exist but I don't instantiate the property. Without truthmakers, we cannot say that the scenarios contain different entities. But we can say simply that I instantiate the property in i) but not ii). Instead of appealing to an ontological difference, we state the difference with a piece of primitive ideology ('instantiates').

that the truthmaker theorist's "concrete" states of affairs must be distinguished from necessarily existing "abstract" states of affairs, as in Plantinga (1974).)

In the next section I will discuss an approach to fundamentality based on truthmaking; but first I want to distinguish, primarily in order to set them aside, two vague ideas that are often cashed out in terms of truthmaking.

First, there is the quite plausible idea that there can be a gulf between fundamental metaphysics and ordinary truth. According to this idea, a metaphysician who takes the world ultimately to consist of nothing more than atoms in the void, or of a wavefunction in statespace, or of The One, does not conflict with common sense or science. For common sense and science do not concern themselves with questions of fundamental reality, and the truth of ordinary and scientific beliefs is compatible with a range of positions on the underlying metaphysics of those beliefs. This idea is often put in terms of truthmaking: truths of common sense and science are made true by fundamental states of affairs about atoms or wavefunctions or Ones. The truthmaking relation needn't be one-to-one and isn't tied to ordinary meaning; thus a state of affairs specifying an appropriate configuration of atoms can make true both the truth that those atoms are thus configured and the truth that I am five-nine, and it can make the latter true even though the ordinary meaning of 'Ted is five-nine' does not concern atoms. But truthmaking isn't the only way to accommodate the gulf. A Finean could say that propositions of common sense and science are grounded in propositions about atoms, wavefunctions, or Ones; and I could say that the metaphysical truth-conditions of sentences of common sense and science make reference only to atoms, wavefunctions, or Ones.[19]

I have a bone or two to pick with the second idea: that truthmakers are needed in order to catch "ontological cheaters"—those ne'er-do-well metaphysicians (such as presentists, phenomenalists, or solipsists) who refuse to countenance a sufficiently robust conception of the fundamental (as containing past entities, physical objects, other persons) to underwrite the truths they accept (that there once existed dinosaurs, that there exist external physical objects arranged thus and so, that there exist such and such people other than themselves), and who instead state truths using suspect ideology (tense operators, statements about possible experiences, Arthur Prior's (1968b) "person-tenses"). What is wrong with the presentist's tensed claim that there once existed dinosaurs, according to this second idea, is that the claim has no truthmaker. The presentist rejects the existence of past dinosaurs, and so accepts no entities whose existence would suffice for the truth of the tensed claim—the claim "lacks a basis in reality". But there is a different, more direct way to object to the cheaters: simply reject their fundamental ideologies. These include tense operators, counterfactual constructions, and the like; and one can simply argue, on grounds of parsimony, that ideologically leaner (though

[19] See also Horgan and Potrč (2000) on indirect correspondence.

more ontologically committed) rival views are more attractive.[20] (It's important to this assessment that ideological commitments are coequal with ontological commitments.) This is not intended as a "methodological" critique of the cheaters; it is a squarely metaphysical objection. Nor is it intended to be a mechanical recipe; we must enter the trenches and argue, on a case-by-case basis, that it's better to posit merely past things, external physical objects, and the like, than to introduce tensed, counterfactual, and other ideology.

Similar remarks apply to Truthmaker 2.0, "truth supervenes on being" (TSB), according to which any two possible worlds that are alike in what objects exist and what properties and relations they instantiate are alike in every way whatsoever.[21] Its point is to catch the cheaters while avoiding certain perceived problems with the truthmaker principle. As we saw, the truthmaker principle requires the existence of distinctive entities (for example, states of affairs) in the case of predicational truths (like the truth that I am five-nine). And even more distinctive entities (to put it mildly) are required for negative statements: one needs negative states of affairs (entities whose existence somehow suffices for its *not* being the case that such-and-such) or "totality" states of affairs (entities whose existence suffices for certain entities being *all* the entities). TSB, on the other hand, requires no such distinctive entities, because the truth values of negative and predicational sentences about properties and relations do not vary between worlds that are alike in what objects there are and what properties and relations they instantiate. But a more direct response to the cheaters is just to object to their ideology.

Indeed, there is a satisfyingly simple thesis about fundamental ideology that has essentially the same upshots regarding cheaters as TSB: *the correct fundamental ideology is that of predicate logic*. Like TSB, this thesis rules out primitive tense operators and counterfactual conditionals, since the only sentence operators in predicate logic are 'and', 'or', and so on, and the quantifiers; and it allows predications and negative statements without requiring the existence of states of affairs, since 'not' and predications are again part of predicate logic ideology. TSB's similarity to the simple thesis is hidden by the way the formulation of TSB *uses* the ideology of predicate logic. To say that worlds are "alike in what objects exist and what properties and relations they instantiate" is to say that the worlds contain the *same objects* (quantification and identity), and that an object *has a property* (predication) in one world *if* and *only if* (propositional-logic sentential connectives) it has that property in the other. As a consequence, true sentences containing this ideology automatically supervene on being, and thus pass the TSB test. But if we used other ideology to state the constraint, this other ideology would automatically pass the test as well. For example, sentences containing primitive

---

[20]Sider (2001*b*, chapter 2, section 3) argued for a general prohibition of 'hypothetical' fundamental ideology. The present approach seems superior.

[21]The doctrine is from Bigelow (1988, 130–3) and Lewis (1992, 215–19). For other criticisms see Merricks (2007, chapter 4); Sider (2001*b*, chapter 2, section 3).

tense operators would pass the test of a tensed TSB, *viz.*, "Worlds that are alike in which objects instantiate, or used to instantiate, or will instantiate, which properties and relations, are alike in every way." TSB has, therefore, an implicit commitment to the ideology of predicate logic; better to make this commitment explicit with the simple thesis.[22]

Further, it is important to appreciate that the truthmaker principle and TSB are *not* mere generic assertions that the facts must be grounded, somehow, in fundamental reality. Still less is either claim "certain *a priori*", as Lewis claims of TSB (1994, 473). Each is a substantive and distinctive claim of metaphysics. Consider, for example, what the two principles have to say about primitivism about laws of nature. The truthmaker principle requires this primitivism to take the form of the postulation of a distinctive sort of entity.[23] TSB requires it to take the form either of the postulation of a distinctive sort of entity, or of the postulation of a distinctive sort of property or relation.[24] But neither allows a third form, a view that takes as primitive a sentence operator 'it is a law that'. On this third formulation, there are no distinctive entities called laws, nor are there distinctive properties and relations corresponding to laws; two worlds might contain the same distribution of properties and relations over objects, but might nevertheless differ in that in one, it's a law that all Fs are Gs, whereas in the other, all Fs are indeed Gs but it's not a law that all Fs are Gs. This third form, in fact, seems to be the most natural form for primitivism about laws to take; and it's inconsistent with both TSB and the truthmaker principle.[25] Now, I don't myself defend primitivism about laws, but my preferred form of primitivism about structure—based on the primitive operator $\mathcal{S}$ described in section 6.3)—conflicts with both TSB and the truthmaker principle for essentially the same reason that the third form of nomic primitivism did. So it's important for me to point out that TSB—or better, the thesis that the correct ideology is that of predicate logic—is a substantive thesis of metaphysics. It's admittedly attractive, but it can be given up if total theory demands it.

---

[22]Another problem with TSB is that it is modal. As is often the case, unwanted consequences result from trying to say indirectly, via modality, what would be better said directly, in terms of fundamentality. In this case, the problem is that statements about necessary subject matters trivially supervene on being. Anyone willing to say that mathematical claims are noncontingent can, for example, deny that the fundamental level contains anything mathematical, but can nevertheless say that mathematical statements are true, without violating TSB.

[23]Tim Maudlin seems to accept this view when he calls laws "fundamental entities in our ontology" (2007*b*, p. 18), but I suspect he cares more about antireductionism than reifying laws.

[24]Armstrong (1983) and Michael Tooley (1987), for example, hold views of the latter type: laws arise from the holding of a relation between universals.

[25]Note also that all three formulations seem on a par, insofar as cheater-catching is concerned. The thought that it's illegitimate for presentists to take tense seriously and illegitimate for phenomenalists to speak of counterfactuals about experiences doesn't lead to finding the third formulation any more repugnant than the first two.

8.5 Truthmaking as a theory of fundamentality

The notion of truthmaking can be used to formulate a third rival view about fundamentality, according to which the realm of the fundamental is exceedingly sparse.

Fineans and I allow fundamental facts of arbitrary logical forms: predicational, negative, quantificational, and so on. (We *can* defend more restrictive views—a Finean, for example, might deny that disjunctive truths are ever real (Fine, 2012). But our theories of fundamentality per se do not restrict what sorts of truths can be fundamental.) The truthmaking theory of fundamentality I have in mind, on the other hand, countenances far fewer fundamental facts. The only fundamental facts, on this view, are certain singular existential facts, facts of the form "x exists", where x is a truthmaker. (It's an open question whether such facts should be construed quantificationally, or as consisting of the attribution of a primitive notion of existence. Alternatively, one could sidestep the question of the nature of these facts and construe the theory as rejecting the idea of a fundamental fact altogether, holding simply that the fundamental consists solely of entities.) Predicational truths ("a is F"), negative truths ("It is not the case that ϕ"), quantificational truths ("Everything/something is ϕ"—with the possible exception of assertions of the existence of truthmakers) are all of them nonfundamental. How do these nonfundamental truths fit into fundamental reality? They are *made true by* truthmakers. Thus the making-true relation is the distinctive concept for this theory. It both distinguishes the realm of the fundamental—that realm consists of truthmakers, i.e. things that stand in the truthmaking relation to something—and also connects the fundamental to the nonfundamental.

It is very difficult to abide by this restrictive conception of fundamentality. And in fact, truthmaker theorists in practice almost never abide by it (not that they all intend to). What in fact happens is that by making ineliminable use of certain bits of ideology, they smuggle in fundamental facts beyond those allowed by their theory.

One smuggling route is through the *canonical names* given to truthmakers, such as 'the state of affairs of grass's being green'. These names are formed by means of distinctive ideology, 'the state of affairs of ϕ', which is a functor that turns a sentence into a singular term naming a state of affairs. This functor acts as a cache for smuggling unacknowledged fundamental facts. To illustrate, David Armstrong objects to fundamental predicational facts, claiming that it is unacceptable simply to include a predicational sentence 'a is F' in one's fundamental description of reality. To do so without reifying universals is to be an "Ostrich nominalist" (Armstrong, 1978*a*, pp. 16–17); but even realists about universals are forbidden simply to attribute universals to particulars using a predicate of instantiation; the existence of states of affairs must instead be asserted (Armstrong, 1997, chapter 8). Armstrong himself, however, apparently smuggles predication into his own fundamental theory of the world, when he employs canonical names like 'the state of affairs of a's instantiating U'. Armstrong provides no metaphysical explanation of facts like:

(A) There exists a state of affairs of a's instantiating U

and it's hard to see what explanation could be given. So he apparently accepts that facts like (A) are fundamental. But such facts involve predication, since 'instantiates' is a two-place predicate. So Armstrong accepts fundamental facts involving predication after all. (Nominalist truthmaker theorists who reject fundamental predicational facts smuggle in a similar way when they canonically name their states of affairs thus: 'the state of affairs of a's being F'.) Armstrong might grant a special exemption to (A) because the predication in (A) occurs within the scope of 'the state of affairs of ϕ'; but it's hard to see why this exemption would be justified. Alternatively, he might say that his use of canonical names is not part of his fundamental theory; but in fact I suspect that the canonical names are indispensable (see below). At any rate, if a truthmaker theorist allows fundamental predication-involving facts like (A) in this way, then his conception of the fundamental draws closer to that of the Finean and my own, since we too allow fundamental predication-involving facts.

A similar smuggling route is employed by those who reject the existence of fundamental facts involving negation or universal quantification, and in their place posit negative or "totality" states of affairs. These smugglers tend to make ineliminable use of canonical names like "the state of affairs of not-ψ" or "the state of affairs of $a_1 \ldots a_n$'s being all the objects", which suggests that facts like "There exists a state of affairs of not-ψ" or "There exists a state of affairs of $a_1 \ldots a_n$'s being all the objects" are fundamental facts, thus violating their own view.

Truthmaker theorists may respond that these facts are not fundamental because the canonical names are eliminable: the canonical name possessed by x is determined by the array of truths that x makes true. x counts as *the state of affairs of a's being F*, rather than *the state of affairs of not-ψ* or the state of affairs $a_1 \ldots a_n$'s *being all the objects*, because x makes it true that a is F, and does not make it true that not-ψ or that $a_1 \ldots a_n$ are all the objects.

But this just moves the smuggled cargo. The sorts of truthmaking claims just cited involve predication, negation, and quantification:

(T1) x makes-true that a is F.

(T2) y makes-true that not-ψ.

(T3) z makes-true that $a_1 \ldots a_n$ are all the objects.

So if they express fundamental facts then they too violate the truthmaker theorist's standards. And there is now particularly strong pressure to say that truths like (T1)–(T3) are indeed fundamental. The only strategy for reductively defining 'makes-true' would have been to somehow make use of canonical names. A first attempt might have been:

x makes true that $\phi =_{\mathrm{df}}$ for some ψ that entails ϕ, $\ulcorner x =$ the state of affairs that $\psi \urcorner$ is true.

This strategy may be doomed, if 'entails' is too restrictive and there is nothing to put in its place. But it seems like the only possible strategy. And it is unavailable here since it uses the canonical names to define 'makes-true'; the goal was to use 'makes-true' to define the canonical names.

One way out remains for the truthmaker theorist. She might deny that (T1)–(T3) are fundamental facts, even in the absence of any way to explain their truth in terms of other facts, simply by insisting that they have truthmakers, and that having a truthmaker is sufficient for not being a fundamental fact. Now, the truthmakers of (T1)–(T3)—call them t_1, t_2, and t_3, respectively—raise questions like those above. They have canonical names (t_1, for example, might be the state of affairs of x's making-true that a is F); they enter into relations of truthmaking (t_1 makes (T1) true); and there is pressure to say that at least one of these two facts is fundamental. But this charge the truthmaker theorist will again stubbornly deny: each of the two facts has some further truthmaker and hence is not fundamental. (One could then raise similar questions about these further truthmakers, and receive a similar response.)

Thus the truthmaker theorist can simply dig in, and cite further truthmakers whenever she appears to require fundamental facts involving ideology she is trying to avoid (predication, negation, quantification). While this entrenchment may be a stable position, it is very explanatorily unsatisfying. To bring this out, consider how it would look as offered by a *monistic* truthmaker theorist, who accepts only a singular truthmaker: the Cosmos.[26] According to this monist, fundamental reality consists merely of the existence of a single thing, the Cosmos, X, so that the only fundamental fact is a fact asserting the existence of X. Now, suppose we ask her to give us *ultimate explanations* of various matters. We want her to explain to us, in terms that require no further explanation, why there are cities, why no one can eat candy without smiling, and why electrons repel one another. To such questions she will always give the same answer: because of X. But this is manifestly *un*explanatory. You cannot give satisfying explanations without citing detailed general laws or patterns or mechanisms. But no detailed general laws or patterns or mechanisms can be given by someone whose fundamental conception of reality is so unstructured, consisting solely of the existence of a single entity.[27]

The monistic entrencher can give more satisfying explanations by staying away from the absolutely fundamental level—by appealing to facts other than X's existence. She can say that no one eats candy without smiling because people

---

[26] Compare Schaffer (2010*b*), except that Schaffer is not (I take it) entrenching.

[27] This is not to object to monism per se; a monist might give satisfying ultimate explanations that terminate in facts about the Cosmos, so long as there is a sufficiently rich set of facts about the Cosmos (for example, higher-order facts about the properties instantiated by the Cosmos, as discussed in Sider (2008*a*)).

smile when they're happy and candy makes people happy; she can say why candy makes people happy by citing their taste buds and candy's chemistry; and she can explain taste buds and chemistry in terms of physics. But these explanations are not ultimate, since their explananda can be further explained by citing X. And the monist's ultimate explanations always consist simply of citing X. There's something wrong with a story about fundamental reality that precludes satisfying ultimate explanation.

It's tempting to respond that the monist's ultimate explanations are satisfying after all because their explanans, X, is a very complex entity, a state of affairs specifying the entire configuration of the world. But this talk of what X "specifies" is another instance of smuggling via canonical names. X "specifies" that the world is configured in a certain way—that, say, a_1 is F and a_2 is G and a_3 Rs a_4 and . . .—only in the sense that X is the state of affairs of a_1's being F and a_2's being G and a_3's R-ing a_4 and . . . ; and this latter fact is not fundamental, but rather has a further explanation: namely, X. So the complexity of X, as captured in its canonical name, cannot be cited in ultimate explanations.

The position of the nonmonistic entrencher is unsatisfying for the same reason, albeit not *quite* so unsatisfying. Ultimate explanations always terminate in the citation of entities; but since a mere list of entities is so unstructured, these "explanations" cannot be systematized with detailed general laws, patterns, or mechanisms.

Think of the point this way. Suppose God hands you a collection of entities: Alexander, Buffy, Cordelia, Dawn. . . , and asks you to work out the rest. Are there helium molecules? Are there cities? Why did *Buffy the Vampire Slayer* end after season seven? You wouldn't have any idea how to respond. (The problem is most acute given monism; the collection then has just one member. What are you supposed to do with *that*?) But according to the entrenched truthmaker theorist, the fundamental facts consist just of facts citing the existence of entities. It's hard to see how all the complexity we experience could possibly be explained from that sparse basis.

(A symptom of this sparse basis is a certain lack of discipline in the practice of citing truthmakers, which we might call the "truthmaker free-for-all". A paradigm case is Armstrong's discussion of modality in section 10.1 of *A World of States of Affairs*. There Armstrong tries to show that irreducibly modal states of affairs need not be recognized since modal truths can be given nonmodal truthmakers. The truthmaker for 'Necessarily, anything that is 1kg mass has a part that is 1 pound' is, he says, the fusion of the universals *1kg mass* and *1 pound mass*. The truthmaker for "It is possible that aRb and also possible that bRa" is said to be the fusion $a+R+b$. Other modal truths are similarly accorded truthmakers that are simply fusions of the involved entities. The problem isn't that Armstrong's claims are *wrong*. It's rather that they are manifestly unexplanatory. The giving of truthmakers is the truthmaker theorist's proposed form of metaphysical explanation, but the entities Armstrong cites clearly do not help to explain modality.[28] This is no accident; it is a natural result of the fact that truthmaking is an unsatisfactory tool for metaphysical explanation. It is entities that make-true, and entities are too unstructured to explain. To mention just one other instance of the free-for-all: in response to the question "What makes it true that *a* makes *S* true?"—this is the analog, for truthmaker theorists, of the question "What grounds facts about grounding?"—one often receives the unenlightening answer "*a*"!)

Unlike the entrenching truthmaker theorist, Fineans and I can give satisfying ultimate explanations. For we accept structured and plentiful fundamental truths, and can tell detailed stories about how they ground (Fine) or are metaphysical truth-conditions for (me) various nonfundamental truths.

In sum, the truthmaker theorist is caught in a dilemma. Either she accepts fundamental facts beyond those that merely cite the existence of truthmakers, thus giving up on her theory, or she entrenches (by simply citing further truthmakers when faced with certain explanatory demands), thus leading to an unexplanatory theory.

One final point. Recall the two caches for smuggling fundamental facts: the ideology for giving canonical names, and the ideology of truthmaking itself. With each piece of ideology, the truthmaker theorist is going to want to make claims that involve nonfundamental notions, claims like these:[29]

> *x* is the state of affairs of there existing a city.
>
> *x* makes-true that there is a city.

Now, given purity, claims like these cannot express fundamental facts. (Otherwise, telling the fundamental story of the world would require bringing in the notion of a city.) But truthmaker theorists regularly make claims like these without giving any hint of how they might be reductively explained.

8.6 Schaffer: entity-grounding

Another rival account of fundamentality is that of Jonathan Schaffer (2009*a*). Schaffer's central concept is a relation of *entity-grounding*. Unlike Finean grounding, Schaffer's grounding relation relates entities of arbitrary sort. Thus we may speak of concrete particulars, properties, states of affairs, tropes, facts, and other entities grounding and being grounded. When *x* grounds *y*, *x* is "prior to" *y*; *y* "ontologically depends on" *x*; *y* is a "derivative entity". Schaffer's picture is of reality as an ordered structure, a "hierarchy of being":

---

[28] To be fair, Armstrong says a lot more about modality, in the same book and also in his earlier book *A Combinatorial Theory of Possibility*. But what he says is more explanatory when he he attempts to *analyze* modality, and not just cite truthmakers.

[29] Here I treat 'makes-true' as taking a sentence on its right-hand side. If it were taken instead as a two-place predicate '*x* makes proposition *p*' true, the purity problem would be relocated to facts involving proposition-theoretic ideology such as 'the proposition that ϕ'.

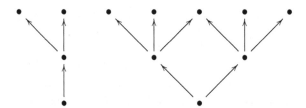

The entities at the bottom of this hierarchy—those entities that are not grounded by anything—are the *fundamental entities*, or *substances*; all else derives from them.[30] On this conception of fundamentality, the grounding relation is the distinctive concept for talking about fundamentality, the fundamental facts consist solely of facts asserting the existence of substances (though see below), and it is the grounding relation that connects the nonfundamental to the fundamental.

Schaffer tells us how *entities* are grounded. But a theory of fundamentality must also address questions like the following: What, in the realm of the fundamental, makes it the case that a is F? In virtue of what is it the case that not-ψ? What grounds the fact that $a_1 \dots a_n$ are all the objects? We do not only, or even primarily, want to know *why x*; we want to know *why ϕ*, where ϕ is a sentence. (We might put this point by saying that Schaffer addresses only entity-grounding, not propositional grounding, but this is misleading—see below.)

Finean grounding is built for such questions; with it we can say "the proposition that χ grounds the proposition that a is F". Truthmaking is also built for such questions: "x makes it true that a is F". (As we saw, it is doubtful whether a mere entity x is a suitable explanans; but the question here concerns the explanandum.) I can answer the questions as well; I can supply a metaphysical truth-condition for 'a is F'. On the face of it, however, Schaffer cannot answer these questions, since his grounding relation relates only entities.

Schaffer's grounding relation applies to *all* entities. So in particular it applies to propositions. So, it might be thought, Finean ground is just a special case of Schaffer's. But this isn't right; Schaffer and Fine's grounding relations have different significance when applied to propositions. Schaffer's grounding relation essentially involves its relata *as entities*. He characterizes grounding as "the metaphysical notion on which one entity depends on another for its nature and existence" (2010*a*, p. 345). Thus when proposition p Schaffer-grounds proposition q, the existence and nature of q are due to p. Finean grounding, on the other hand, is not particularly focused on its propositional relata as entities, but rather on their *subject matters*. (Indeed, Fine is happy with a sentence-operator regimentation, "ϕ because ψ", which dispenses with relata altogether.) If the proposition that snow is white Fine-grounds the proposition that either snow is white or snow is blue, this is a fact about snow and its color, not about the existence and nature of propositions. (For Fine, the ground of the existence of a

---

[30] Schaffer thinks that there is but a single fundamental entity (2009*b*; 2010*c*), but this monistic view is detachable from his theory of grounding as such.

proposition, p, would be a proposition that grounds the proposition that p exists; and the ground of p's nature would be a proposition that grounds the proposition that p has such-and-such features.)

So on the face of it, Schaffer cannot answer the question of what makes a be F by listing the entity (or entities) that ground the proposition that a is F. That would explain the existence and nature of that proposition, a certain abstract entity. It's hard to say what would ground the existence and nature of an abstract entity like a proposition, since we know so little about the natures of propositions (what is important to us about propositions is their theoretical role, not their innards). Perhaps the proposition's constituents? Perhaps nothing? But whatever the answer, it is surely distant from what we were asking about, which was a, and why it's F.

I can think of two ways to respond.[31] The first is, I take it, not Schaffer's own response. It is to become more like Fine, by recognizing a distinctive sentential/propositional grounding relation. The most natural way to do this would be to invoke, in addition to entity-grounding, a further relation of proposition-grounding like Fine's, which is understood to concern the content, not the existence and nature, of propositions.[32] In that case my objections to the first Finean theory of section 8.2 apply. Further, once proposition-grounding is introduced, entity-grounding would seem to be superfluous: instead of speaking of the entity-ground of x, we could speak instead of the proposition-grounds of propositions about x's existence and nature.

The second way is, I believe, Schaffer's preferred way. It is to become more like the truthmaker theorist, by sticking with entity-grounding but invoking states of affairs (or other suitable entities) to bridge the gap between the sentential explanatory questions we want to ask and the explanations of entities that his grounding relation delivers. Where x is the state of affairs of a's being F, the existence of x is tightly bound to a's being F in at least this sense: it's necessarily true that x exists if and only if a is F. So, Schaffer could say, explaining why x exists (and has the nature that it in fact has) explains why a is F.

If Schaffer does take the second way, he faces some of the same questions as the truthmaker theorist. What do ultimate explanations look like? Do they always terminate in the mere citation of entities? If so then his position is as explanatorily unsatisfying as the entrenching truthmaker theorist. Or can they also cite fundamental facts involving canonical names, such as the fact that x is the state of affairs of a's being F? If so then the view no longer holds that all fundamental facts consist of the existence of substances (and the facts of fundamentality no longer consist solely of the holding of the grounding relation over the class of

---

[31]A third way would be to say that when its arguments are propositions, grounding concerns their subject matters rather than their existence and nature. But this would implausibly fragment the relation.

[32]If the notion takes the form 'entity x grounds proposition p' rather than 'proposition q grounds proposition p', then this would move him closer to truthmaker theory rather than to Fine.

entities). My guess is that Schaffer will follow the second course. His purpose in introducing entity-grounding is expansive rather than reductive. He's not trying to make do with the leanest possible tools for talking about fundamentality; rather, he's trying to make sure that we have enough tools to make sense of all sorts of grounding, including entity-grounding.

It's worth appreciating the structural role that states of affairs play, both for Schaffer and for the truthmaker theorist. Schaffer's grounding relation relates entities to entities:

> x grounds y.

Truthmaking is like the grounding relation on the left, but is propositional on the right:

> x makes-true that ϕ.

(And Fine's grounding relation is propositional on both sides: ϕ because ψ.) Mere entities are too unstructured either to serve as explanans or explanandum in proper explanations; we need instead to appeal to entire sentences/propositions. Thus the appeal to states of affairs, which bridge the gap between mere entities and full propositions: given free use of canonical names, whenever one wishes to use a full sentence ϕ in an explanation, one can instead cite a corresponding entity: the state of affairs of ϕ. Schaffer requires the states of affairs to bridge the gap both on the left- and the right-hand sides of his grounding relation, whereas the truthmaker theorist needs them only for the left-hand side of the truthmaking relation. (Fine needs them on neither side.)

One final point. Like the truthmaker theorist, Schaffer needs to appeal to facts about states of affairs, phrased using canonical names, that involve nonfundamental concepts. For example:

> x is the state of affairs of there existing a city.

But again, purity[33] disallows these facts from being fundamental. So like the truthmaker theorist, if Schaffer wants to respect purity, he faces an explanatory burden: to explain such facts. And this burden cannot be discharged simply by citing grounding entities—that would be a return to entrenching.

8.7 Entity-fundamentality

Finally, I'll briefly discuss a rival approach that has not (as far as I know) been defended in print, but which seems to underlie much casual talk of fundamentality. On this approach, the distinctive concept is that of a fundamental *entity*. Fundamental entities are like Schaffer's substances: they are the entities on which all else is (in some sense) based. Electrons, perhaps, are fundamental entities, whereas tables and chairs are nonfundamental.

---

[33] Side point: purity is the claim that all notions involved in fundamental facts are fundamental notions. Schaffer's ideology allows a related claim of "substance-purity" to be formulated: all entities involved in fundamental facts are substances. Is there pressure on him to accept it?

The approach is usually extended to cover the fundamentality of properties and other abstract entities. The property grue, for example, is said to be a nonfundamental entity, whereas unit negative charge is a fundamental entity.

It would be easy to confuse this approach with my own. Both approaches, it might be thought, can allow talk of the fundamentality of entities of arbitrary sort: properties, quantifier meanings, and so on. But my approach is very different. My official notion of structure ("$\mathscr{S}$") is an operator, not a predicate. To be sure, I often speak casually of properties, words, and "bits of ideology" as carving at the joints, but this is loose talk. Moreover, there are several reasons to reject this approach to fundamentality, and they do not apply to my account.

First, extending the account to properties requires thinking of abstract entities as the locus of fundamentality. This is especially problematic if we want to go beyond the predicate; recall section 6.3.

Second, once the approach is extended to abstract entities, it mixes together two things that are best separated: the fundamentality of an abstract entity "as an entity" and the fundamentality of what it "represents"; recall section 8.6.

Third, even when applied just to concrete entities, the approach mixes together two further things that ought to be kept separate: the fundamentality of an entity's existence and the fundamentality of its nature. To illustrate: what is the status of tables and chairs and other mereologically complex entities according to a mereological universalist like David Lewis (1986b, 212–13; 1991, 79–81)? As I see it, it is the following. The *existence* of tables and chairs is just as fundamental as the existence of electrons (in contrast, perhaps, with smirks and shadows, which do not exist fundamentally). However, tables and chairs have nonfundamental *natures*.[34] These claims are easily distinguished on my own approach: in the fundamental sense of the quantifier 'there are', there are tables and chairs as well as electrons (whereas 'There are smirks and shadows' is true only under a nonfundamental sense of 'there are'); but unlike electrons, tables and chairs satisfy no monadic joint-carving predicates. It is unclear how to make these claims if we speak only of entity-fundamentality.

Fourth, the entity-fundamentalist seems to conceive of the fundamental as consisting solely of a collection of entities; but a theme of the preceding sections has been that mere entities cannot generate satisfying explanations. If the entity-fundamentalist responds in certain ways (such as invoking states of affairs), my objections to the truthmaker theorist and to Schaffer will apply.

---

[34]Notice that substance-purity (note 33) is hostile to this sort of mereological universalism. For surely this universalist will want to say that singular mereological facts are fundamental; but when x is part of y, surely x and y are not both substances. My own framework, by contrast, is friendly to the position. The ideology in mereological claims can be held to carve at the joints; and since my framework allows no notion of substance, substance-purity cannot be formulated.

9 Ontology

"Is there evidence for the existence of black holes? Indeed there is."—Roger Penrose

"I turned to speak to God, About the world's despair; But to make bad matters worse, I found God wasn't there."—Robert Frost

"No definite evidence is yet available to confirm or disprove the actual existence of unidentified flying objects as new and unknown types of aircraft."—United States Air Force

"The Cosmos is all that is or ever was or ever will be."—Carl Sagan[1]

Ordinary ontology is no more remarkable than wondering about the weather. We ask whether there is ice-cream in the freezer, whether there is a twenty for a cab, whether there is a game on television. In more expansive moments we ponder the existence of black holes, gods, UFOs, or anything at all beyond the world of space and time. We understand these questions, and we know, more or less, how to go about answering them.

Extraordinary, or philosophical, ontology, on the other hand, is perplexing. Consider the question of whether holes exist. Not black holes. Holes. Like in Swiss cheese. "Of course holes exist", one is inclined to respond; "I have one in my sock right now." "Well," the philosopher says; "I see the sock. And I see that it 'has a hole in it', so to speak. But why think that, in addition to the sock, there really exists another entity, the hole? What sort of strange entity would that be? Why not think instead that only the perforated sock exists?"

The question of holes is perplexing partly because it's unclear how to answer it. It's hard to see how to tell by experiment or the senses whether the hole exists, in addition to the perforated sock. Then again, the same can be said for all philosophical questions. Part of what makes them philosophical is that they strain our usual methods of inquiry. The most promising thought about methodology in ontology, to my mind, is Quine's (1948) exhortation to believe locally by thinking globally—to evaluate local ontological claims by assessing global merits of theories that contain them. These global merits include such factors as "simplicity", as well as fit with and prediction of our evidence. We should believe in the existence of mathematical entities, says Quine, because our best theories include mathematical physics, which says (assumes) that there exist such entities as real numbers and

[1] Penrose (2005, p. 711); Frost (1936); USAF Maxwell Blue Book 1, p. 8; Sagan (1980, p. 4).

functions over real numbers. Others reject this claim while accepting the Quinean dialectic. Hartry Field, for example, agrees that if our best theories said that there are numbers, that would be a good reason to accept numbers; but he formulates a nominalist version of physics which he claims to be superior to the usual platonistic version (1980). One finds this methodology, in one form or another, throughout contemporary writing on ontology.

But our concern here is a different respect in which the question is perplexing. It can seem unclear just what is at stake. When philosophers ask whether there exist holes in addition to perforated objects, just what are they asking? In ordinary circumstances no one hesitates to say "There is a hole in that sock" if the sock is perforated. By ordinary standards, the sentence would seem to be true. Yet some philosophers think that it is false. And many others think that it isn't *obviously* true; they think that it's an open question whether a perforated sock contains a hole. These philosophers, apparently, understand the question of whether there exist holes in some extraordinary sense. But what does it mean to say that *there exists a hole*, in this extraordinary sense? What does it take for a sock to contain a hole, over and above being perforated? The existence of the hole makes no clear difference to reality. The question itself, rather than our methods for answering it, is unclear. Or so say many.

9.1 Ontological deflationism

Failing to see what is at stake in philosophical ontology, some are led to *ontological deflationism*.[2] According to this view, the philosopher's question of whether holes exist is confused, because the extraordinary, philosophical sense of the existence of a hole has not been, and cannot be, clearly specified. The only coherent question is the more mundane one of what exists according to ordinary standards. And this mundane question can be settled by a conceptual analysis of ordinary standards; there is no need to resort to the Quinean methodology. Likewise for the other questions of philosophical ontology—questions about the existence of numbers, propositions, events, past and future objects, tables and chairs, and so on. As the leading ontological deflationist, Eli Hirsch, puts it:[3]

... many familiar questions about the ontology of physical objects are merely verbal. Nothing is substantively at stake in these questions beyond the correct use of language. A derivative claim is that, since they are verbal, the proper way to resolve these questions is by appealing to common sense or ordinary language.

The most viable form of ontological deflationism, in my view, holds that ontological questions are not substantive, in the sense of chapter 4. Their answers turn on which of the equally nonfundamental candidate meanings we adopt for their crucial terms. (We'll discuss other forms in section 9.7.)

---

[2] See Carnap (1950); Chalmers (2009); Hirsch (2002a; b; 2005; 2007; 2008; 2009); Hofweber (2009); Putnam (1987); Sidelle (2002; 2010); Sosa (1999); Thomasson (2007; 2009).

[3] Hirsch (2005, p. 67). Hirsch is a deflationist about only some of philosophical ontology.

According to one subspecies of this sort of ontological deflationism, the crucial terms in ontological questions are semantically defective.[4] Since the ontologists do not judge sentences like 'There are holes' by ordinary standards, they fail to use the crucial terms in their ordinary senses. They have supplied no replacement senses; and there are no perfectly fundamental candidate meanings supplied by the world; so no replacement meanings have been supplied at all. The crucial terms are therefore semantically empty, or else semantically indeterminate over a wide range of candidate meanings. Thus ontological questions are semantically defective, and have no determinate answers.

According to a second subspecies, the crucial terms have their ordinary senses. The defender of this second subspecies agrees with the first that ontologists do not judge ontological sentences by ordinary standards, and that the world supplies no perfectly fundamental candidate meanings for crucial ontological terms; but he holds that ontologists nevertheless use the crucial terms in their ordinary senses—despite themselves, so to speak. After all, surely the ontologists mean to be speaking English (or another natural language)![5] The ordinary senses of the crucial terms are whichever candidate meanings best fit ordinary usage. (The terms may be vague over a small range of the candidates, but the indeterminacy is less drastic than envisioned by the first subspecies.) Thus, ontological questions have answers, but the answers may be ascertained simply by reflecting on the ordinary use of ontological language.[6] The Quinean methodology is as out of place for such questions as it would be in a dispute over whether an innocent factual mistake is a lie. It would be hopeless to argue that a globally simpler theory could be had, if we only regarded Newton as having lied when he said that space and time are absolute. Any competent speaker of English knows that the word 'lie' just doesn't work like that, simplicity nonwithstanding.[7]

Both subspecies agree on the bottom line: ontological questions have multiple equally nonfundamental candidates. Intuitively, there are lots of things we could mean by ontological questions, none of them better than the rest, so the only real issue is linguistic/conceptual: which of these is meant in *our* language?

9.2 Ontological realism

Opposing ontological deflationism is *ontological realism*, according to which ontological questions are "deep", "about the world rather than language". In my view, the most viable form of ontological realism holds that ontological questions are substantive in the sense of chapter 4. I further think that the best way to secure this substantivity is to hold that ontological questions can be posed in perfectly

---

[4]Compare the indeterminacy strategy of section 5.1, and see Chalmers (2009).

[5]Compare the common-sense strategy of section 5.1, and see Hirsch (2005).

[6]The second deflationist would presumably turn into the first if ontologists were to enter the philosophy room, and introduce new ontological vocabulary stipulated to carve at the joints (section 5.3).

[7]Although see Weatherson (2003).

joint-carving terms. This is the position I will defend (and it is usually what I mean by "ontological realism"). It is the doctrine of true believers in ontology.

Ontological realism is a claim about "metaontology"—a claim about the nature of ontological claims and disputes. As such it is consistent with all positions on first-order ontology. It is consistent both with the existence and with the nonexistence of holes, with the existence and with the nonexistence of numbers, and so on. This is not to say that it is wholly neutral on first-order ontology. To take just one example, existence monism (according to which only a single entity exists, the Cosmos) is a nonstarter if ontological questions are settled by ordinary usage of ontological language. The monistic denial of the existence of nearly every entity of common sense would then be like the claim that Newton's mistakes were lies. But if ontological realism is true, monism cannot be so quickly dismissed.

Ontological realism meshes with the Quinean methodology for ontology; ontological deflationism does not.[8] Quine says to believe in the ontology of one's "best" theory, where one of the determinants of bestness is "simplicity". But as we have seen, simplicity is cheap if one is free to choose any vocabulary one likes. That simplicity is cheap given free choice of *predicate* meanings is familiar: recall again Lewis's (1983b, 367) point that the theory $\forall x F x$, where F is a predicate true only of things in possible worlds exactly like ours, is a massively powerful and syntactically simple theory. But a similar point holds about free choice of meanings for logical constants. Let $\forall^*$ be an expression with the same grammar as $\forall$, but interpreted so that $\forall^* x \phi$ is true iff everything satisfying ϕ is such that the world is exactly as it actually is; in that case, "$\forall^* x$ electron(x)" is again a syntactically simple and massively powerful theory. The moral is that Quinean simplicity is a sensible goal only for theories with appropriate logical vocabulary. It seems reasonable to draw a further moral: simplicity is a sensible goal only for theories with joint-carving logical vocabulary.[9] Thus, simplicity is a good guide to *ontology* only if ontological language carves at the joints.[10]

Recent work on ontology nearly always relies on the Quinean methodology. Nowhere is this more explicit than in Lewis's *On the Plurality of Worlds*, which argues that the best systematic theory of a range of philosophical and linguistic phenomena requires an ontology of possible worlds. Another pillar is Peter van Inwagen's *Material Beings*, which argues that there exist no nonliving material objects with proper parts. Although there exist subatomic particles "arranged

---

[8]Another connection to Quinean methodology: why follow Quine's advice to regiment in first-order terms before assessing ontological commitments? One possible answer is that i) first-order quantifiers carve at the joints; ii) second-order quantifiers do not (section 9.15); and iii) ontological commitments are given in terms of joint-carving quantifiers (section 9.12).

[9]Compare section 3.3.

[10]Further, if ontological language doesn't carve at the joints, then why think that positing more entities would be worse? Occam's (ontological) razor is based on the thought that "emptier" possibilities are prima facie more probable than "full" possibilities. But the measure of the fullness of a possibility should depend on its description in fundamental terms; if ontological language doesn't carve at the joints, then a possibility with more entities might not be fuller in the relevant sense.

tablewise" and "arranged chairwise", as van Inwagen puts it, there do not exist any tables or chairs. Where one billion subatomic particles are arranged tablewise, there is no billion-and-first entity, the table; there are only the billion particles. Van Inwagen relies more heavily than Lewis on intuitive verdicts about thought-experiments—for example, the intuitive conviction that the following is not the case: a composite object made up of two people is formed if and only if the people shake hands (1990, chapter 3). But like Lewis, van Inwagen seeks the simplest theory that accommodates the "data", which in his case are his intuitive judgments plus a range of theoretical presuppositions (1990, preface). Since the Quinean methodology is appropriate only given ontological realism, ontological realism seems to be an unacknowledged presupposition of recent ontology.

Recent ontology presupposes ontological realism in a further way. It's commonly assumed that a metaphysical theory is given by its ontology and its ideology. But this is an apt schema only given a certain substantive view: that ontological notions are fundamental ideology. Otherwise one might better say that a metaphysical theory is given by its set of *possibilities* and its ideology, or its *substances* and its ideology, or some other schema, if one thinks of modal or substance-theoretic or some other notions as being more fundamental than ontological notions. Given ontological realism, the ontology/ideology division is indeed natural, but this should not be assumed from the start. (A more general schema: a metaphysical theory is given by its ideology and its *doctrine*—its claims phrased in terms of its chosen ideology.[11])

Ontological realism (in my preferred form anyway) says that the crucial terms in ontological questions carve perfectly at the joints. But what exactly are these "crucial terms"; what is the form of fundamental ontological assertions? Alternate views will be discussed in section 9.14, but for now I will take fundamental ontological assertions to be quantificational:[12]

$\exists x F x$

There are Fs.

The crucial expression here is the first-order existential quantifier, which, according to this form of ontological realism, carves at the joints. If F carves at the joints as well, the question of whether $\exists x F x$ is guaranteed to be substantive. Inquiry into what there is, is inquiry into the fundamental facts.

To head off a potential misunderstanding, on my conception, the ontological question is *not* "Are Fs fundamental?"[13] Thus conceived, 'fundamental' would be a predicate of entities, and ontology would be the task of sorting entities

---

[11] I take this use of 'doctrine' from Fine (2005).

[12] Compare Quine (1948), though he would reject the backdrop of realism about metaphysical structure. The first formulation is in first-order logic, the second in English; but English quantifiers have a different syntax from those of first-order logic. I'll take the official formulation to be the first, though I'll often paraphrase in English.

[13] As it is according to Jonathan Schaffer (2009a).

(understood under a non-joint-carving sense of the quantifier?) into two groups, the fundamental entities and the nonfundamental ones. On my conception, the ontological question is rather "Are there Fs?", where 'there are' is understood as having a fundamental sense. (I do not speak of entity-fundamentality at all; recall section 8.7.) Thus one should not say to me: "Your fundamentality-based approach to ontology would make it absurd to accept tables and chairs in one's ontology, since tables and chairs are obviously not fundamental entities." This commits the misunderstanding just described. On my conception, to accept an ontology of tables and chairs is not to say that tables and chairs are "fundamental entities", but rather to say that there are, in the fundamental sense of 'there are', tables and chairs. And saying this is not absurd. For one can say this while conceding that the *property* of being a table, the property of being a chair, and indeed, all other properties of tables and chairs, are not particularly fundamental. Intuitively speaking, although the natures of tables and chairs are nonfundamental, their being is perfectly fundamental.

9.3 Ontologese

There is a wrinkle. Suppose that, fundamentally, there are very few things. Suppose with Cian Dorr (2005), for example, that there exist, in the fundamental sense, nothing but subatomic particles.[14] Given such a sparse ontology, the most plausible view about natural language quantifiers might be that they do *not* carve at the joints. The best metaphysical semantics of an ordinary sentence like 'There is a table' might not be a strict semantics that interprets it as making the false claim that there exists, in the fundamental sense, a table, but rather a tolerant semantics, which interprets it as making the true claim that there exist subatomic particles appropriately arranged. The English 'there is', according to such a semantics, would not express fundamental quantification. (Section 7.7 gave an example of such a metaphysical semantics.)

Or suppose that in the fundamental sense of the quantifiers, there are no holes. The best metaphysical semantics of 'There is a hole in that sock' might not interpret 'there is' as expressing fundamental quantification, but might instead count the sentence as being true if the sock in question is perforated.

So even if there is *a* joint-carving sort of quantification, the quantifiers of ordinary language might not carve at the joints. We must therefore refine our construal of ontological realism. Ontological realism should not claim that ordinary quantifiers carve at the joints, or that disputes using ordinary quantifiers are substantive. All that's important is that one *can* introduce a fundamental quantifier, which can then be used to pose substantive ontological questions.[15] Similarly, ontological deflationists should not hold merely that ordinary-language ontological disputes are nonsubstantive. They must hold, in addition, that no sense of

---

[14]I defend a similar view, except that I accept sets in addition. See chapter 13 and Sider (2011).

[15]Compare Dorr (2007, section 1).

the quantifier can be introduced on which ontological questions would become substantive.

The question of whether ordinary quantifiers express joint-carving quantification is a difficult one. At what point in the following series should a metaphysical semantics start counting the sentences as false?: 'There are hydrogen atoms', 'There are dogs', 'There are tables', 'There are economies', 'There are events', 'There are smirks', 'There are holes', 'There are fictional characters', 'There are gods'? To avoid getting embroiled in this question—which is after all metasemantic, not metaphysical—ontological realists might conduct their ontological debates in the metaphysics room rather than the marketplace (section 5.3). They might introduce a new language—"Ontologese"—whose quantifiers are *stipulated* to carve at the joints. Ontological questions in Ontologese are substantive, even if those in ordinary language are not. Moreover, Ontologese is a better language, since its structure better matches reality's structure.

How is Ontologese to be introduced? The crucial thing is to stipulatively remove any normal metasemantic pressure towards tolerant interpretations that assign non-joint-carving meanings to quantifiers. Ontologese quantifiers are to have meanings that carve at the joints, but are otherwise as similar as possible (in inferential role, for instance, as well as in extension), and similar enough, to the meanings of the ordinary quantifiers.

Of course, ontological deflationists will think that the attempted introduction of Ontologese misfires, since the world lacks the necessary structure. They might compare the attempted introduction of Ontologese to a failed attempt to introduce 'dirt' as a natural kind term: "by 'dirt' I shall mean the element of the periodic table in which trees grow, which forms mud when combined with water, and which is flattened to make country roads". Whether the introduction of Ontologese succeeds depends on the facts, on whether there is a joint-carving sort of quantification, just as the imagined introduction of 'dirt' depends on whether the periodic table contains an appropriate element.

The shift to Ontologese is an instance of the following schematic reply to ontological deflationism: "While it may be absurd to deny that there's *any* sense in which—for example—there is a hole in a perforated sock, it's not absurd to deny that in 'a metaphysical sense' there exist holes." Anyone pursuing this schematic reply needs to characterize the alleged metaphysical sense. I do this by appealing to a metaphysical notion, the notion of carving at the joints. Others attempt to do this using more linguistic notions. For example, the ontological question of whether there are holes is sometimes put as the question of whether there *strictly speaking* exist holes, or whether there *literally* exist holes. But I doubt these notions of linguistic theory are up to the task. "Literal" is opposed to things like metaphor and hyperbole; "strict" casts off things like quantifier domain restriction and loose talk (as when people who live in Cherry Hill, New Jersey say they're "from

Philadelphia").[16] But 'There are holes' is neither metaphorical nor hyperbolic nor restricted nor loose.

In what follows I will generally continue to speak as if the metaontological question concerns ontological disputes in English; but take it as read that we may need to construe it instead as concerning disputes conducted in Ontologese.

9.4 Predicates not the issue

Ontological deflationists say that questions of philosophical ontology are nonsubstantive. These questions, let us continue to assume, have the form: $\exists x F x$? Now, a (near enough) sufficient condition for a question to be substantive is for all of its terms to carve at the joints. So in the cases in question, the ontological deflationist must argue either that the predicate F fails to carve at the joints, or that the quantifier fails to carve at the joints. I will argue in this section that they must make the second choice. They cannot rely solely on claims about predicates.[17]

To take a concrete example, consider the dispute over the ontology of composite material objects. Van Inwagen (1990) claims that there are no tables; his opponents claim that there are. And the ontological deflationist says that this is not a substantive dispute. There are multiple equally joint-carving candidates for ontological language; under some, 'There are tables' is true; under others it is false. (The sentence is false under strict candidates that require the parts of would-be composite objects to satisfy some strong condition—being "caught up in a *life*", say—and true under lax candidates that make no such requirement.) Now, could the ontological deflationist grant that the quantifiers carve at the joints, but claim that these candidates are for the predicate 'is a table'?

It is intuitively clear that he could not. The deflationist's thought is *not* that the nonsubstantivity is merely about how to *classify* things—that there substantively is a certain thing, x, which counts as a "table" under some conceptions of tablehood but not under others. The deflationist's thought is rather that it is not a substantive matter whether x exists at all, never mind how it is classified.

Distractingly, the predicate 'table' does indeed fail to carve at the joints, and has multiple candidate meanings. But this noise can be eliminated. We can simply drop the predicate 'table', and instead construe the dispute as concerning whether $\exists x \tau(x)$ is true, for some appropriate τ stated in purely fundamental terms. τ might specify the exact mass, or exact boundaries, or exact arrangement of parts, of some particular putative table. Van Inwagen will reject the existence of τs; his opponents will accept the existence of τs; and the ontological deflationist will want to claim that the dispute is nonsubstantive. Since τ carves at the joints, this requires the deflationist to say that $\exists$ does not carve at the joints.

---

[16]See Sperber and Wilson (1986); Wilson and Sperber (2004).

[17]To be sure, *some* ontological disputes are nonsubstantive or equivocal because of their predicates—for instance, a dispute over whether "God" exists in which some mean by 'God' the center of mass of the universe. But this is not so in the disputes to be discussed.

Many ontological deflationists seem to be tempted to resist this conclusion, to blame the predicates instead, and to say things like this:

The dispute over whether "there are tables" (or "there are τs") is nonsubstantive because its resolution depends on whether one adopts a strict or lax definition of 'table'. The lax definition takes 'table' to mean "collection of appropriately arranged particles", while the strict definition adds some further requirement (being alive, say). It's obvious that 'There are tables' is true under the lax definition and false under the strict definition, so what is the dispute about?

Meta-ontology 101: never say such things. The problem is with the phrase 'collection of appropriately arranged particles'. What does it mean? This is a predicate, so we can rephrase: what must something, x, be like in order to count as a "collection of appropriately arranged particles"? A natural answer is: x must be an object containing parts that are appropriately arranged. Given this understanding, it is not at all "obvious" that there exist tables in the lax sense. The debate between van Inwagen and his opponents is precisely over whether there exist things whose parts are appropriately arranged. Van Inwagen's claim is that there simply are no such things.

It would not help to take 'collection of appropriately arranged particles' as instead meaning '*set* of appropriately arranged particles', for this would not support deflationism about a debate between ontologists who have stipulated that they intend 'table' in a mereological, rather than set-theoretic sense. Van Inwagen and his opponents would be happy to stipulate $\tau(x)$ to mean that x is composed of (i.e., made up from parts that are) appropriately arranged particles, and to recast their debate as being over whether $\exists x \tau(x)$. Indeed, that is how they understood the debate all along. (Also, the disputants might not accept the existence of sets.)

A further reason not to blame 'table' is that van Inwagen and his opponents also disagree over how many entities there are, and such disagreements do not concern 'table'. Consider a world in which there exist exactly two subatomic particles. Of that world, van Inwagen would reject, while some of his opponents would accept:

$$\exists x \exists y \exists z(\sim x=y \wedge \sim x=z \wedge \sim y=z)$$

—that is, "There exist at least three things."[18] (Van Inwagen may think that subatomic particles are invariably accompanied by abstract objects—sets for example—in which case he too would accept the displayed sentence. But we could simply restrict the sentence's quantifiers to concreta.) This sentence contains only quantifiers, truth-functional connectives, and the identity sign. Surely the deflationist

---

[18]Could the crucial expression be the predicate 'is a thing'? In that case, the deflationist would have to admit that a metaphysical dispute could be reinstated simply by recasting the debate as being over whether there exist tables at all, as opposed to tables that are things. Van Inwagen and his opponents would be happy to rephrase things in this way, since that's how they understood the debate in the first place. See Williamson (2003, p. 420).

will want to say that a debate over its truth is nonsubstantive, and thus cannot accept that all of its expressions carve at the joints. But it's hard to see how they could blame the nonsubstantivity on the truth-functional connectives or the identity sign (or the predicates needed to restrict the quantifiers to concreta).

9.5 Quantifier variance

Thus ontological deflationists cannot accept that quantifiers carve at the joints. In my view they should go further and uphold *quantifier variance*, to use Hirsch's term: the claim that there are multiple candidates to be meant by quantifiers, none of which carve perfectly at the joints, but none of which are exceeded in joint-carving by any other quantifier candidate. It's a bit unfair to commandeer this term, since Hirsch himself does not speak of joint-carving.[19] Still, the view I call "quantifier variance" is in the spirit of Hirsch's own view, a spirit he attributes to Hilary Putnam and describes as follows:

. . . the quantificational apparatus in our language and thought—such expressions as "thing", "object", "something", "(there) exists"—has a certain variability or plasticity. There is no necessity to use these expressions in one way rather than various other ways, for the world can be correctly described using a variety of concepts of "the existence of something". One of [Putnam's] favorite examples concerns a disagreement between mereologists and anti-mereologists as to how many objects there are in some domain. Suppose we are evaluating the truth of the sentence, "There exists something that is composed of Clinton's nose and the Eiffel Tower". Mereologists will accept this sentence, whereas anti-mereologists will reject it. Putnam's doctrine of quantifier variance implies that the expression "there exists something" can be interpreted in a way that makes the sentence true or in a way that makes the sentence false. Since both interpretations are available to us, we have a choice between operating with a concept of "the existence of something" that satisfies the mereologist or operating with a different concept that satisfies the anti-mereologist.

Quantifier variance, on my formulation, says that "there are" many candidates for being meant by quantifiers; but the quantifier variantist needn't take this quantification seriously. Granted, he *could* reify quantifier-meanings (under his current quantifier-meaning!), but he needn't. He could instead rephrase his claims (as Hirsch does) so as not to reify the candidates; he could say, for example, that we could choose to use the sentence "There exists something that is composed of Clinton's nose and the Eiffel Tower" so that it comes out true, or we could choose to use it so that it comes out false; and under neither choice would our words carve at the joints better than under the other. My discussion will quantify over candidates since otherwise it's hard to state the view in any generality, but I won't take such quantification as part of the view's metaphysical core.

How should we think about these quantifier candidates, these alternate meanings for 'all' and 'some'? At the very least, quantified sentences are supposed to have truth-values relative to them. Hirsch's sentence

[19] See Hirsch (2002*a*; *b*; 2005; 2007; 2008; 2009), and also Putnam (1987) and Eklund (2008).

(H) There exists something that is composed of Clinton's nose and the Eiffel
Tower

is supposed to be true relative to one of them and false relative to another. But
can anything more be said?

One approach associates quantifier meanings with alternate languages: languages whose sentences look just like English sentences—same grammar, same-
looking lexicon—but have different truth-conditions. The different quantifier-
meanings are the meanings that quantifiers have in these languages. For example,
following a suggestion of Cian Dorr (2005) on behalf of the quantifier variantist,
we could introduce a language L_U in which a sentence ϕ is true if and only if the
following sentence of ours is true:[20]

> If composition had been unrestricted (that is, if it had been the case that for
> any x and y there exists a mereological sum of x and y), then it would have
> been the case that ϕ.

If composition had been unrestricted then there would have existed something
composed of Clinton's nose and the Eiffel Tower; so Hirsch's sentence (H) is true
in L_U. But (H) is false in a second language, L_N, in which ϕ is true if and only if
the sentence that results from ϕ by restricting each quantifier with the predicate
'is a mereological atom' is true in English. (The idea isn't that speakers of these
languages think the content of ϕ *via* its "translation" into English. They think
natively.) [21]

It might be objected that these languages do not really correspond to different
meanings *for quantifiers*. The specification of truth-conditions for L_U, for example,
did not give any distinctive rule for interpreting quantifiers. It's hard to see how
to divide the difference between English and L_U into a difference exclusively
concerning quantifiers and other differences. But this may not bother quantifier
variantists. For what they really care about is vindicated simply by the claims that:
i) there are multiple possible languages of this sort; ii) quantificational claims
can have different truth-values in the different languages; and iii) none of the
languages are more joint-carving than the rest.

Quantifier variance might at first sound trivially correct. Language is conventional, after all, so who would deny that quantifiers could have meant different
things? Everyone agrees that we could have used the bare symbol 'there exists'
as a sign for negation, a predicate for faculty of Harvard University, a name for
Rudolf Carnap, or even as a punctuation mark.

But remember that quantified sentences (same grammar as ours, and same-
looking lexicon) are supposed to have truth-values relative to these meanings. So
the quantifier meanings can't correspond to taking 'there exists' to be a name,

---

[20]Dorr (plausibly) assumes that not all "counterpossible" conditionals are true.

[21]I specified the semantics of L_U and L_N by giving truth-conditions for their sentences using English
as a metalanguage; but the quantifier variantist might instead specify partial, implicit definitions
governing quantifiers within alternate languages, as in Båve (2010).

predicate, or punctuation mark. Moreover, the meanings are supposed to be *candidates*, in the sense of section 4.2. "Semantically alien" meanings (relative to the actual meanings of quantifiers) are thus disqualified. Section 4.2's characterization of 'candidate' was admittedly thin, but in the present case we can say a little more: the candidates here must be *inferentially adequate* in that the core inference rules of quantification theory must come out truth-preserving (for example, any candidate must count 'Something is a philosopher' as true if it counts 'John is a philosopher' as true).[22] And the fact that the candidates are said to be unsurpassed in joint-carving by any other quantifier-candidate renders the claim still less trivial. It's not hard to concoct arbitrary and bizarre assignments of truth-values to quantified sentences while preserving the inference rules of quantification theory (there exist assignments of this sort for each model for the language in question, for example). But such concocted meanings will, in general, fail horribly to carve at the joints.

9.5.1 *Quantifier variance and domain restriction*

There is a different way in which quantifier variance threatens to be trivial, however; which raises delicate issues and is not so easily answered. There is a sort of "quantifier variance" that is wholly mundane and accepted by everyone: quantifier domain restriction.[23] For example, the sentence "Everyone was at the party" can be used to say that everyone who works at the office was at the party, that all the Hollywood celebrities were at the party, or even (in admittedly extraordinary circumstances) that absolutely all human beings were at the party. The meanings of ordinary restricted quantifiers are reasonably joint-carving candidates, yet they are clearly not what quantifier variantists have in mind, since otherwise they would have no objection to substantive ontology conducted with unrestricted quantifiers.[24]

Quantifier variantists need to answer this threat of triviality. This section explores two ways of doing so, corresponding to two types of quantifier variance.

The quantifier variantist claims that some pairs of possible languages are otherwise similar except for what their quantifiers mean. In some such pairs, he will want to say, one quantifier is an *expansion* of the other. Let's use "q_1 expands q_2" and "q_2 contracts q_1" synonymously. The intuitive idea of expansion is that q_2's domain is a proper subset of q_1's; but there are obstacles to regarding this as a definition. For one thing, the definition would function as intended only when, intuitively, the domains of both q_1 and q_2 are properly contained in the domain of the quantifiers that are implicit in the definition—the quantifiers that would reveal themselves when 'the *domain* of q_2 is a *proper subset* of the *domain* of q_1'

---

[22]Compare Hirsch (2002*b*, p. 53).

[23]Whether this is conceived semantically or pragmatically is irrelevant here.

[24]Even a defender of "indefinite extensibility" should allow that we can disavow all restrictions except those concerning indefinitely extensible domains; this would allow for more substantive ontology than a quantifier variantist will want to admit.

is unpacked.[25] But set this aside for now; let's just give the quantifier variantist 'expands' and 'contracts'.

Question: does the quantifier variantist think of contraction as domain restriction? When q_2 contracts q_1, could a speaker using q_1 characterize the meanings of existentially q_2-quantified statements thus: "They mean what I would mean by 'there is a member of S that is . . .', for some restricting set (or class) S"? The two types of quantifier variance to be discussed differ over how they answer this question.

The first type says: yes. Contraction is restriction. But this faces an obstacle. The quantifier variantist might well recognize a *maximal* quantifier—a quantifier of which all other quantifiers are contractions. Cannot substantive ontology then be resuscitated—as concerning the maximal quantifier? For this maximal quantifier seems to enjoy a privilege: it alone ascribes unqualified being. For any other quantifier, to say that there is a ϕ in its sense is to say that there is, in the maximal sense, some ϕ that has some further, restricting, feature. Users of the nonmaximal languages are just *ignoring* some of what there unrestrictedly is. The nonmaximal quantifier meanings are nothing more than second-rate restrictions $r_1(q), r_2(q)\ldots$ of a single privileged unrestricted quantifier meaning, q:

$$q$$
$$r_1(q)$$
$$r_2(q)$$
$$r_3(q)$$
$$\vdots$$

The defender of the first type of quantifier variance replies that quantifier meanings are not "objectively" restricted or unrestricted. Restrictedness is relative to which quantifier one is using "as one's unrestricted quantifier". The picture above is from the perspective of someone who adopts q as her unrestricted quantifier; and from this perspective the meanings $r_i(q)$ are indeed restricted. But one can just as well adopt one of the other meanings as one's unrestricted quantifier; and from this perspective the adopted meaning is unrestricted. The notation "q" and "$r_i(q)$", and the boldfacing and enlargement of 'q' in the picture, misleadingly depict an asymmetry between q and the other meanings $r_i(q)$, whereas in fact the quantifier meanings are all on a par, and are better depicted thus:

$$q_1$$
$$q_2$$
$$q_3$$
$$q_4$$
$$\vdots$$

If one adopts a nonmaximal quantifier meaning, then some of the other meanings cannot be defined as restrictions of one's own. Does this generate an unwanted asymmetry amongst the meanings, since some cannot be used to define others? The defender of this type of quantifier variance will say no. Let q_e expand q_c. One can adopt q_e and define q_c by restriction; but alternatively, one can adopt q_c and define q_e in some other way. For example, one might, following Dorr again, define q_e in counterfactual terms: there exists$_{q_e}$ an F iff there would have existed$_{q_c}$ an F, had composition been unrestricted$_{q_c}$.[26] The fact that contracted meanings cannot define expanded meanings by restriction does not privilege the expanded ones because counterfactual expansion is just the converse of restriction. Just as quantifier meanings are not objectively restricted or unrestricted, they are also not objectively counterfactual or noncounterfactual. Indeed, it would be natural to pair this type of quantifier variance with a very coarse-grained conception of content.[27]

This first type, then, claims that contracted quantifier meanings are indeed restrictions of expanded ones, but denies that this privileges the maximal meaning in a way that would resuscitate substantive ontology since restrictedness and unrestrictedness are relative to one's adopted quantifier meaning.

Recall the crucial question for quantifier variantists: is contraction just domain restriction? The second type of quantifier variance answers: no. None of the quantifier meanings distinctive of quantifier variance are restrictions of any of the others. This type instead embraces an objective distinction between restricted and unrestricted quantifier meanings, and claims that there are multiple objectively unrestricted quantifier meanings $q_1, q_2 \ldots$. Each q_i can, of course, be restricted in various ways, but the results are objectively restricted quantifier meanings $r_1(q_i), r_2(q_i) \ldots$. So the quantifier meanings may be pictured as follows:

$$
\begin{array}{cccc}
q_1 & q_2 & q_3 & \cdots \\
r_1(q_1) & r_1(q_2) & r_1(q_3) & \\
r_2(q_1) & r_2(q_2) & r_2(q_3) & \\
r_3(q_1) & r_3(q_2) & r_3(q_3) & \\
\vdots & \vdots & \vdots &
\end{array}
$$

This type requires hyperintensionally individuated meanings. For some $r_i(q_j)$ might be "necessarily coextensive" with some q_k; they would nevertheless be distinct, since the former is objectively restricted and the latter is objectively unrestricted.

The defender of this type has an easy response to the worry motivating this section: his position differs from the recognition of mundane domain restriction

---

[26] One might do it plurally instead, taking 'There is$_{q_e}$ a table', for example, to mean that there are$_{q_c}$ some things that are arranged tablewise.

[27] For this reason, I believe this type to be closer to Hirsch's own position than the second.

because mundane domain restriction results in objectively restricted quantifiers whereas his q_is are objectively unrestricted.

But what does it mean to say that the q_is are objectively unrestricted? It can't mean that "each q_i includes absolutely everything in its domain". For "There is no more than one domain that includes absolute everything" would seem to be something like a logical truth (if domains are distinct then something is included in one but not the other, in which case they can't both include absolutely everything); combining this with the putative definition would imply that there is only one of the q_is. The defender of this type will, in fact, deny that his q_is should be understood as corresponding to domains. What, then, are the q_is? The defender might refuse to answer in reductive terms. They are entities with respect to which sentences have truth-values, but one cannot define any q_i using any distinct q_j.

Even granting this much—that the q_is do not correspond to domains and indeed cannot be reductively defined—we still need an account of objective unrestrictedness: what is it about each q_i that makes it objectively unrestricted and its restrictions $r_j(q_i)$ objectively restricted? The quantifier variantist might appeal to joint-carving: although no q_i carves perfectly at the joints, each carves *better* at the joints than do its restrictions.[28] Alternatively, he might appeal to facts about meaning identity: a quantifier meaning m is objectively restricted if in some possible language some explicitly restricted quantifier "Some member of S is . . ." (for some name S of some restricting set or class) means m; m is objectively unrestricted if no such explicitly restricted quantifier means m (even if some such explicitly restricted quantifier is "necessarily coextensive" with m). Yet another alternative would be to simply take the notion of objective restriction as primitive.

It is unclear whether either of the two types of quantifier variance can be adequately spelled out; and there are further questions about how to formulate quantifier variance.[29] But let us rest content with what is on the table so far, and move on to discuss objections to the doctrine.

9.6 Objections to quantifier variance

Ontological deflationism is probably the most popular form of metaphysical deflationism. This is ironic since it is particularly hard to sustain. A dispute involving a crucial term T is nonsubstantive only if there is "T-variance"—an array of multiple, equally joint-carving candidates to be meant by T; and as we will see, quantifier variance is a particularly problematic form of variance. (There are no general problems with claims of predicate-variance, for example).

---

[28]This might require a commitment to primitive comparative joint-carving. For otherwise, the claim would have to be that each q_i has a more direct basis in the perfectly joint-carving notions than its restrictions; but what conception of the perfectly joint-carving notions could the quantifier variantist adopt that would sustain this? (See also section 9.6.2.)

[29]See Sider (2007*a*; 2009).

9.6.1 *The semantic argument*

I begin, however, with an objection to quantifier variance that can, I believe, be answered. The objection is due to Matti Eklund (2007; 2009) and John Hawthorne (2006c). Consider two characters, Big and Small. Big speaks an "expansive" language, Biglish, in which speakers freely quantify over tables. Big introduces a name, '*a*', for a table, and thus accepts 'Table(*a*)'. Small speaks a "smaller" language, Smallish, in which speakers refuse to quantify over tables. But Small is a quantifier variantist, and thinks that he does not genuinely disagree with Big. So Small says to himself, speaking in Smallish: "Even though there are no tables, the sentence 'Table(*a*)' is true in Biglish." But this commits Small—and all quantifier variantists, who must accept the scenario as described—to rejecting familiar Tarskian ideas about semantics.[30] According to Tarskian semantics, for any language, *L*, a subject–predicate sentence is true-in-*L* iff its subject term has a denotation-in-*L* that is a member of the extension-in-*L* of its predicate. If this quantified biconditional is true in Smallish, then in order for ' "Table(*a*)" is true in Biglish' to be true in Smallish, 'There is something that "*a*" denotes-in-Biglish' must be true in Smallish. But what would this object—in the Smallish sense of "object"—be, if not a table? So runs the Eklund–Hawthorne argument.

The quantifier variantist should, I think, reply as follows. When we vary what the quantifiers mean, we thereby also vary the meanings of all other expressions that are tied up with the "idea of a thing": names, predicates, function symbols.[31] Indeed, the meanings of these *categories*, construed as semantic categories, must vary. For the notions of name, predicate, function symbol, and quantifier are interconnected. A name (in predicate logic, anyway) is an expression that refers to a single thing; a predicate is an expression that applies to one or more things; a function symbol is an expression that stands for a function mapping one or more things to a further thing. These connections to quantification are definitive of 'name', 'predicate', and 'function symbol', and are what underlie Tarskian ideas about semantics. It is natural to expect, therefore, that different conceptions of quantification would result in different conceptions of what it is to be a name, predicate, or function symbol.[32] In particular, Small should deny that Big's ex-

---

[30]Eklund and Hawthorne focus on atomic sentences, but Small must also reject the Tarskian clause for quantified sentences. Small thinks that '∃*x* Table(*x*)' is true in Biglish, but is unwilling to assert "There exists something that is in the extension-in-Biglish of 'Table'."

[31]Plausibility argument: pretend that giving meaning to a language is just a matter of describing its intended model. Models are described using quantifiers in the metalanguage. One uses metalanguage quantifiers to specify a domain, which fixes the meaning of the object-language's quantifiers; and one uses metalanguage quantifiers to give the meanings of object-language names, predicates, and function symbols (a constant means an object in the domain; a predicate means a set of tuples from the domain; a function symbol means a function on the domain). So if one changes the meanings of the metalanguage quantifiers, one would change the meanings of the object-language's quantifiers, names, predicates, and function symbols.

[32]This is so for a semantic conception of grammatical categories, anyway. On a purely syntactic conception, the Tarskian ideas lose force.

pression 'a' is a name (i.e., deny that it is a name$_{Small}$), since 'a' in Biglish doesn't have the semantic function of referring to a thing.[33] By denying that 'a' is a name, Small can deny that 'Table(a)' is a subject–predicate sentence, and so can deny that the Tarskian biconditional applies to 'Table(a)'.

The reply so far is, I think, *correct*, but it doesn't fully answer Eklund and Hawthorne. For even if Small is right to deny that Biglish contains names or subject–predicate sentences, it would be hard for Small to deny that Big's use of language is in *some* sense compositional. And so, shouldn't Small say something systematic about how Big's sentences get their truth-conditions?

Yes; but Small need not do so in Tarski's way. *Anyone* can agree that *some* extreme cases call for novel semantic ideas in order to make sense of alien but compositional linguistic behavior. From Small's point of view, the case of Big calls for a departure from the Tarskian paradigm. One strategy Small might pursue would be to say that Big's sentence $\ulcorner F\alpha \urcorner$ is true iff there are some referents (plural) of the "subject" term α that are in the "extension" (in a plural sense) of the "predicate" F. The resulting theory might be complex and ugly. But if a full semantics is difficult (or even impossible) to give using Small's language, that wouldn't undermine quantifier variance. Granted, it would be an asymmetry between Small and Big, for there is no corresponding disadvantage to speaking Biglish. But quantifier variantists can admit that bigger is better for certain purposes; all they are committed to saying is that neither language adheres better to nature's joints.

9.6.2 *No foundation*

A more promising objection presses the following questions on the quantifier variantist: what *is* fundamental, if quantification is not?[34] What is the world fundamentally like? How will you write the book of the world? As we'll see, these questions are difficult for the quantifier variantist to answer.

Whereas the previous section's argument was specific to quantifier variance, this argument—as well as the arguments of the next two sections—applies to all ontological deflationists, since all ontological deflationists must deny that quantifiers carve at the joints.

As we saw in section 7.1, it's natural to assume that the fundamental is "complete", which I spelled out as meaning that it must be possible to give a metaphysical semantics for each nonfundamental language, using a fundamental metalanguage. So in particular, it must be possible to give a metaphysical semantics for the language of physics, using a fundamental language.

Now, the ontological realist can do this in familiar ways. It's easiest if the ontological realist has a reasonably permissive ontology, for then he can take the physicist's language—including the mathematical bit—to *be* a fundamental

---

[33] Compare Hirsch (2002*b*, p. 57).

[34] Not much has been written on this, though see Hawthorne and Cortens (1995); Turner (2008).

language.[35] It will be harder if the ontological realist accepts a more restrictive ontology—say, one that contains no mathematical entities. Still, there are well-known programs for at least attempting to formulate physical theories in nominalistic terms.

But *no* serious work on the foundations of physics and mathematics has been done in a quantifier-free setting. So the quantifier variantist must begin from scratch. He must choose some alien quantifier-free language as his fundamental language, and then he must somehow give a metaphysical semantics for the quantificational language of physics in its terms.

Some attempts to do this evaporate under closer inspection. Suppose, for example, that the quantifier variantist says the following:

I have no need for objects in my fundamental description of the world. The world fundamentally consists of the distribution of properties over spacetime. One can then introduce the ordinary notion of an object in various ways atop this foundation.

This is just confusion. Far from renouncing quantifiers in his fundamental language, this variantist helps himself to quantification over points and regions of spacetime.[36] Quantification is deeply embedded in all physical theories as normally understood, as well as in the mathematical theories they employ. Imagine trying to state a physical theory without quantifying at all. You couldn't quantify over points or regions of space or time or spacetime. You couldn't quantify over points or regions of configuration space or phase space or any other higher-order space. You couldn't quantify over real numbers, or functions of real numbers, or vectors, or tensors, or any other mathematical entities. Your attempt wouldn't even get off the ground.

It is sometimes said that we need no *things* at the fundamental level, only *stuff*. To help in the present context, the suggestion must be that we can replace quantification in a fundamental language with stuff-theoretic lingo, and then use this to give a metaphysical semantics for physical theories. Now, the stuff gambit tends to be paired with the idea that stuff lingo is basically like natural language talk using mass nouns. Thus, the stuff language would include sentences of the form "Some α is ϕ", "All α is ϕ", "δ is the same α as γ"; "δ is part of γ", and so on, for mass nouns α and β and "mass singular terms" δ and γ. After all, in English one can say "Some water is polluted", "All water is wet", "The water on the floor is the same water as the water that was in the tub"; and "The water in Lake Erie is part of the water in the Great Lakes." Thus, the stuff language contains "stuff quantifiers", "stuff-predication", "stuff-identity" and "stuff-parthood". One then

---

[35] At least, after the physical theory has been appropriately formulated.

[36] This point is regularly missed, for example by those who claim that modern physics has no need for "objects". Perhaps modern physics has no use for *particles*, but this doesn't show that it has no use for quantifiers.

wonders whether this stuff language differs in any nonterminological way from the thing language it is supposed to supplant.[37]

Resolving whether two proposed fundamental languages differ genuinely or merely notationally can be very difficult. Indeed, it's often hard to know what's at stake. But here we can bypass the issue. For even if the stuff language differs genuinely from the thing language, it won't scratch the quantifier variantist's real itch. The variantist's reason for introducing the stuff language was that he regarded questions about the existence of things as being nonsubstantive, but conceded that questions in a fundamental language *are* substantive—the stuff language was to be a fundamental language in which questions about the existence of things cannot be raised. But analogous questions about the existence of stuff *can* be raised in the stuff language, such as the question of whether for any stuff and any distinct stuff, there exists some further stuff containing them as stuff-parts. The quantifier variantist should at this point retrace his steps, for he will be no happier admitting that this new question is substantive than he was admitting that the question of whether any two things are parts of some further thing is substantive.

Similar remarks apply to some other attempts to construct quantifier-free fundamental languages. The variantist might think to use the predicate-functor formulation of predicate logic popularized by Quine (1960b).[38] In this language, one replaces quantifiers and variables with predicate functors. Grammatically, predicate functors turn predicates into predicates (with perhaps different 'adicies). We can get the hang of the system by considering the predicate functor that takes the place of the existential quantifier: c. c turns a (perhaps complex) $n + 1$-place predicate F^{n+1} into an n-place predicate cF^{n+1}, which can be thought of, intuitively, as being true of $u_1 \ldots u_n$ iff for some u, F^{n+1} is true of $u, u_1 \ldots u_n$. Thus in predicate functorese one says cF instead of $\exists x F x$. (We just used the existential quantifier to explain the meaning of c in an intuitive way, but the proposal on the table is that c and the other predicate functors are metaphysically primitive.) Other predicate functors are needed to gain the full expressive power of predicate logic. $\sim$ is for negation: $\sim F^n$ is a predicate that is (can be thought of as being) true of $u_1 \ldots u_n$ iff F^n is not true of $u_1 \ldots u_n$. $\wedge$ is for conjunction: $F^n \wedge G^m$ is true of $u_1 \ldots u_{\max(n,m)}$ iff F^n is true of $u_1 \ldots u_n$ and G^m is true of $u_1 \ldots u_m$. σ "rotates argument places": σF^n is true of $u_1 \ldots u_n$ iff F^n is true of $u_n, u_1, \ldots u_{n-1}$. ι permutes

[37]Ned Markosian (2004a) distinguishes between stuff and things, accepts the existence of both, and assigns them different roles in a theory of material objects (for example, stuff obeys unrestricted composition and mereological essentialism, whereas things do not). My criticisms of the stuff defense of quantifier variance do not apply to Markosian, since he is not trying to replace thing language with stuff language, nor is he trying to avoid substantive questions about either things or stuff.

[38]Turner (2010a) discusses a related proposal critically. Dasgupta (2009b) appeals to the predicate-functor formulation, but in defense of the idea that a permutation of individuals across qualitative roles doesn't change the world, rather than in defense of quantifier variance, so my criticism does not apply to him. See also Burgess (2005).

the first two argument places: ιF^n is true of $u_1 \ldots u_n$ iff F^n is true of $u_2, u_1, u_3 \ldots u_n$. p "pads" a predicate by adding a vacuous argument place: $p F^n$ is true of $u_1 \ldots u_{n+1}$ iff F^n is true of $u_2 \ldots u_{n+1}$. It can be shown that predicate functorese has the expressive power of predicate logic (without individual constants); so the variantist might regard it as a suitable replacement for predicate logic in his fundamental language. But this would again be misguided, since it would saddle the variantist with substantive questions that are precisely analogous to the substantive questions he was trying to avoid. For example, the variantist was trying to avoid substantive questions like this: "Does there exist something containing an F and a G as parts?" But corresponding to this question's predicate logic symbolization:

$$\exists x \exists y \exists z (Fy \wedge Gz \wedge Pyx \wedge Pzx)$$

there is the following sentence of predicate functorese:

$$ccc(\iota o\, pP \wedge \sigma\sigma\, pP \wedge p(F \wedge pG))$$

(This is a "sentence" in the sense that it's a zero-place predicate; it "corresponds" in the sense that if one gives the obvious definition of truth in a model for the language of predicate functorese, the functorese sentence is true in exactly the same models as the predicate logic sentence. cF corresponds in this sense to $\exists x F x$.) The variantist we are discussing thinks that the second displayed sentence is couched in joint-carving terms, and so must admit that its truth-value is a substantive matter. But this will surely be no less objectionable to him than regarding the original, quantificational, question as being substantive.

Here's another thought the variantist might try. The fundamental language *does* contain quantifiers, but these are "particle quantifiers"—quantifiers over subatomic particles. The philosophical ontologist's quantifiers, on the other hand, are not fundamental; rather, they can be defined in terms of the particle quantifiers in multiple, equally good ways.

The putative particle quantifiers, $\exists_p$ and $\forall_p$, are conceded to range over particles. But we can now raise a philosophical question: do they range over more entities? For example, where $<$ is a predicate for parthood, we can now ask whether the following is true: $\forall_p x \forall_p y \exists_p z (x<z \wedge y<z)$. Since $\exists_p$ and $\forall_p$ are conceded to be fundamental, the quantifier variantist cannot invoke quantifier variance to dismiss this question as nonsubstantive. $\exists_p$ and $\forall_p$ were called "*particle* quantifiers"; but what does that mean? The claim that they range *only* over particles is simply a bit of doctrine, and can be coherently challenged. Given these quantifiers, there is nothing conceptually incoherent about the claim that they range over more than just particles.

There is one final nonquantificational proposal I'd like to consider. It's just a picture, really; but it's arguably the best intuitive fit with quantifier variance. The picture is that of a "fact-level" metaphysics. According to this picture, the fundamental facts are indivisible wholes, with no privileged decomposition into subfactual components. Joint-carving notions are somehow all at the level of the complete sentence, the entire fact. All descriptions of the world that refer to subfactual matters—objects, properties, and relations—are nonfundamental, and may be understood in multiple, equally good ways, in terms of the fundamental unstructured facts. I suspect that Hirsch has something like this in mind (minus the bits about joint-carving).[39] It may perhaps be thought of as the metaphysical correlate of Frege's (1884, Introduction) context principle, which says that sentence-meaning is in some sense prior to word-meaning. But it's no good stopping with just this intuitive picture. What *exactly* is the proposed array of fact-level fundamental notions, how can they be shown to underlie the quantificational languages of science, and do they really not re-introduce analogs of the very questions they were designed to avoid? As we have seen in this section, these questions need to be faced.

It's a pipe dream, this idea of a nonquantificational language that is adequate to science and ordinary life while not re-introducing substantive questions just like those of traditional ontology. The quantifier variantist could keep chasing the dream. But perhaps a better course would be to reject the assumption that the fundamental is complete, thus eliminating the need for the chase. He could then say: even though quantificational languages fail to carve at the joints, we can do no better. There are many quantificational languages (corresponding to the many candidate quantifier meanings); we can use some of them to give semantic accounts of others; none of them is a fundamental language; and there is no fundamental language in which one can give a semantics for all of them. What is reality fundamentally like, one wants to ask? This quantifier variantist denies the need for an answer. There is no way that reality is fundamentally like; there simply is no book of the world.

Is this a defensible position? Well, it is utterly at odds with the intuitive idea of fundamentality—of there being facts that underlie everything else. Further, it faces a dilemma. Do some predicates (or other object-theoretic expressions) carve at the joints?

Horn 1: no predicates carve at the joints. Here only two unattractive options seem open. One is Goodmania: all talk of objective joints in reality is simply mistaken. The other is reverting to the pipe dream—hoping that some nonquantificational fundamental language might one day be discovered which would allow one to recover some sort of inegalitarian distinction over predicates, even though the predicates don't themselves carve at the joints.

Horn 2 is a more likely resting place: some predicates *do* carve at the joints, even though the quantifiers don't. But this is hard to square with purity (section 7.2). If some predicate F carves at the joints, then surely some sentence S containing F is

---

[39] ". . . we can retain the notion of an unstructured fact. I think this is indeed our most basic notion of 'reality', 'the world', 'the way it is', and this notion can remain invariant through any changes in our concept of 'the things that exist'." (2002*b*, p. 59)

a fundamental truth. But *S* must surely also contain either a name or a quantifier. Given quantifier variance, quantifiers don't carve at the joints, and surely names don't either. So *S*, a fundamental truth, contains an expression that doesn't carve at the joints—a violation of purity.

We have seen substantive questions of ontology re-emerge, even from the barren soil of fundamental ideology constructed expressly to inhibit their growth. The pattern here is instructive, and not specific to ontology. The philosophical instinct is an almost perverse tendency to ask questions that push us out of our epistemic comfort zone. Just as a child asks her parents who made God, so the philosopher asks who or what makes torturing wrong, how we know we're not all dreaming, how we can be blamed when our actions are causally determined, and so on. Our normal epistemic practices easily answer many questions about right and wrong, knowledge and blame, but are perplexed by these philosophical questions. Just so for ontological questions: the philosopher takes the notion of there being something, a notion integral to ordinary and scientific practice, and asks an extraordinary question using it. There's nothing wrong with the notion itself; and so there's nothing wrong with extraordinary questions asked in terms of it. They're just hard to answer.

9.6.3 *No epistemic high ground*

A third argument attacks a certain putative reason for accepting quantifier variance (and other forms of ontological deflationism) rather than the view itself. Many are attracted to quantifier variance because they think it will give them the epistemic high ground. They see ontologists perennially searching for answers to the same old questions, sometimes with new methods, sometimes with old, but never with much success. Given ontological realism, ontological questions are "epistemically metaphysical": they resist direct empirical methods but are nevertheless not answerable by conceptual analysis. Epistemically metaphysical questions can seem unanswerable. But given quantifier variance, ontological questions are no longer epistemically problematic in this way: now they can be answered by conceptual analysis.

I argued in abstract terms in section 5.6 that such attempts to gain the epistemic high ground are misguided, and this particular case is no exception. For quantifier variance doesn't dispel the unanswerable questions—not even those in the vicinity. First, as we saw in section 9.6.2, once the quantifier variantist has banned quantifiers from her fundamental language, there is pressure to specify their replacements. And on many of the replacements discussed there, new epistemically metaphysical questions—analogous to the rejected questions of ontology—re-emerge. Moreover, quantifier variance itself—the assertion that quantifiers do *not* carve at the joints—seems to be epistemically metaphysical. So it's not as if the quantifier variantist can avoid such questions altogether. In fact, there is a sense in which even ontological questions remain epistemically metaphysical for the quantifier variantist. For since direct empirical methods and conceptual analysis don't tell us that quantifier variance itself is true, such methods don't tell us that ontological realism is false; nor do they, conditional on the hypothesis of ontological realism, rule out the truth of 'There are no tables' under the joint-carving meaning of the quantifiers. So for all direct empirical methods and conceptual analysis tell us, tables might fail to exist (at least in the fundamental sense).

Quantifier variance is just another metaphysical story about ontology, alongside views like mereological universalism and mereological nihilism that presuppose ontological realism. The appearance that it is an epistemic panacea is sustainable only if one forgets both i) the need for a replacement for quantifiers in one's fundamental ideology; and ii) the epistemic status of quantifier variance itself. Of course, quantifier variance might still represent a modicum of epistemic advance. Still, I expect that for some, once a decisive march to high ground is seen as unattainable, the position will lose its appeal.

9.6.4 *Indispensability*

The best argument against quantifier variance, and indeed against all forms of ontological deflationism, is really quite simple. As I argued in section 2.3, the way to tell which notions carve at the joints is broadly Quinean: believe in the fundamental ideology that is indispensable in our best theories. This method yields a clear verdict in the case of quantification. Every serious theory of anything that anyone has ever considered uses quantifiers, from physics to mathematics to the social sciences to folk theories. And as we saw in section 9.6.2, there is no feasible way to avoid their usage. Quantification is as indispensable as it gets. This is defeasible reason to think that we're onto something with our use of quantifiers, that quantificational structure is part of the objective structure of the world, just as the success of spacetime physics gives us reason to believe in objective spacetime structure.

Further, just as the success of particle physics suggests that 'charge', 'mass', and the like correspond to unitary structure, rather than fragmented structure as with 'jade', so the indispensability of quantification suggests that quantificational structure is unitary. It therefore argues against ontological pluralism, the view that there are multiple fundamental sorts of quantification.[40]

Questions framed in indispensable vocabulary are substantive; quantifiers are indispensable; ontology is framed using quantifiers; so ontology is substantive—that's the best argument for ontological realism.

---

[40]The argument is defeasible; ontological pluralists might argue that the balance of evidence favors their view. (Here it's important that the common belief in the incoherence of ontological pluralism is mistaken, as McDaniel (2009) and Turner (2010*b*) have effectively argued.) Note that ontological pluralism would not reinstate deflationism; rather, it would split hitherto univocal ontological questions into multiple questions, each as substantive as the original.

9.7 Easy ontology

There are forms of ontological deflationism other than quantifier variance. My last three arguments against quantifier variance were arguments that quantifiers carve at the joints, and hence are effective against any form of ontological deflationism. Still, let us consider some of these other forms in detail.

The main other form is what we might call "easy ontology". Its defenders say that questions of philosophical ontology are settled by analytic truths together with certain obvious facts. For example, the question of holes is settled by the analytic truth that *if a sock is perforated then there is a hole in that sock*, together with the obvious fact that some socks are perforated.

Ontology is "easy", according to this conception, because it is easy to know what is analytic—we simply need to reflect on how we use language. Given easy-to-know analytic truths, and given further information that's easy to know (such as the fact that some socks are perforated), it's easy to answer (in the affirmative) many ontological questions. This is not to say that the resulting entities owe their existence to our language use—that their existence is *caused by*, or *counterfactually dependent on*, our language use. It's a linguistic convention that 'There are electrons' means what it does, but this does not make electrons themselves dependent on us; similarly, though it's a linguistic convention to count 'There is a hole in that sock' true whenever the sock is perforated, this doesn't make the hole dependent on us. Indeed, the linguistic conventions governing 'hole' likewise secure the analyticity of sentences like these:

> Before there were people, when something was perforated (e.g., a certain mountain) there was a hole in that entity (e.g., a cave).
>
> If there had been no people and something had been perforated, there would have been a hole in that entity.

Easy ontology has many defenders, in different branches of philosophy. In the philosophy of language, Stephen Schiffer (2003) has argued that the existence of properties, propositions, events, and various other entities is easy, being secured by what he calls "something-from-nothing transformations"—analytic conditionals like the following:

> If Lassie is a dog then Lassie has the property of being a dog.

Schiffer imagines a linguistic community that does not speak of properties, asks what it would take for them to come to know that properties exist, and answers:

What it would take, and all that it would take, would be for them to engage in a certain manner of speaking, a certain language game—namely, our property-hypostatizing practices, in particular our property-yielding something-from-nothing transformations. . . How can merely engaging in a linguistic, or conceptual, practice give one knowledge of things that exist independently of that practice? Because to engage in the practice is to have the concept of a property, and to have the concept of a property is to know a priori the conceptual truths that devolve from that concept, such as the conceptual truth that every dog has the property of being a dog. (Schiffer, 2003, p. 62)

In the philosophy of mathematics, an instance of easy ontology is the neo-Fregeanism discussed by Crispin Wright and Bob Hale. According to neoFregeanism, Hume's Principle is analytic:

> If the Fs and the Gs are equinumerous, then the number of Fs equals the number of Gs.

Thus we have an easy route to the existence of numbers. Suppose there are two apples and two oranges in the bowl. Then the apples in the bowl are equinumerous with the oranges in the bowl, whence by Hume's Principle the number of apples in the bowl equals the number of oranges in the bowl. But then, there is such a thing as the number of apples in the bowl. So, there are such things as numbers.[41]

In the philosophy of art, Amie Thomasson has defended the view that conceptual truths assure us of the existence of works of art (2005; 2006) and fictional characters (2003). Unlike holes and numbers, works of art and fictional characters are quite generally brought into existence by human beings. But as above, this does not mean that the adoption of linguistic conventions brings these entities into existence. It rather means that the conceptually sufficient conditions for their existence make reference to certain human activities, and specify that the entities come into existence only when the activities are performed. Thomasson writes:

Our literary practices . . . definitively establish the existence conditions for fictional characters . . . According to those criteria, what does it take for an author to create a fictional character? This much is clearly sufficient: That she write a work of fiction involving names not referring back to extant people or characters of other stories, and apparently describing the exploits of individuals named . . . (2003, 148)

Thomasson also defends a similar view about the ontology of material objects.[42] On her view, statements giving the existence and persistence conditions

---

[41]And we can go much further: the entirety of second-order arithmetic can be derived in second-order logic from Hume's Principle. See Wright (1983); Hale (1987); Hale and Wright (2001).

[42]See Thomasson (2007; 2009). There is much else in this broad-ranging and careful work that deserves comment; I'll indulge in a few all-too-brief remarks. 1. Thomasson writes as if the "qua-problem" for the causal theory of reference argues for her view: in order for singular and sortal terms to have determinate reference, i) they must be governed by analytic descriptive conditions; and ii) these must have the form of what she calls "application" and "coapplication" conditions. But the opponent of easy ontology can grant i) while denying ii): the conditions might instead have the form of conditions that *select* which entities we are referring to. For example, the name 'Orky' could be governed by the condition *'Orky' refers to the animal in such-and-such a location (if there is no such animal then 'Orky' refers to nothing)*; and the sortal term 'animal' could be governed by the condition *'animal' refers to something iff it has such-and-such features and thus-and-so persistence conditions*. This is consistent with denying that analytic principles secure the existence of things with the specified features and persistence conditions. 2. Thomasson regards sortal-relative vs. bare quantification as a battle-line between her and her opponents. But a friend of easy ontology could regard the relevant analytic sentences as governing the bare quantifier. In some cases, the sentences would involve no sortal predicates at all; in others, they would. For example, the analogs of Thomasson's application and co-application conditions would be analytic sentences of the forms "$\exists x(Fx \wedge \phi(x,t))$" and "$\exists x(Fx \wedge \phi(x,t) \wedge \psi(x,t'))$", respectively, where F is a sortal predicate and t and t' name times. Conversely, a foe of easy ontology could argue that the bare quantifiers do not carve the joints; what does carve at the joints is a quantifier that has a "slot" for a sortal predicate. 3. Thomasson doubts that her opponents' quantifiers could have determinate

of ordinary objects such as tables, sticks, and baseballs are analytic. For example, it is analytic that if some particles are arranged baseball-wise, then there exists a baseball.

Easy ontology rests on the notion of analyticity. But what does it mean to say that a sentence is analytic?

9.8 Analyticity

While I reject the claims of Quine (1936; 1951*b*; 1960*a*) and his minions that analyticity is an incoherent notion, much of Quine's critique is, I believe, correct. There are several notions in the vicinity, some legitimate, some not; and often an illusion of progress comes from illicitly shifting between different notions.[43]

Two of these notions are truth by convention and definitional constraint. Truth by convention is a putatively metaphysical notion: a sentence is said to be true by convention when the conventions governing that sentence somehow suffice on their own to produce the sentence's truth. Definitional constraint is a semantic notion: a sentence S is a definitional constraint on expression E when S plays a certain distinctive role in helping to determine the meaning of E. The role, intuitively, is that there is "metasemantic pressure" towards interpretations of E under which S is true. A natural thought about the source of this metasemantic pressure is that it results from our intending (in a meaning-constituting way) E to mean something under which S is true. Examples: 'All bachelors are married' is a definitional constraint on 'bachelor'; a sentence expressing the transitivity of '=' is a definitional constraint on '='; 'Nothing is red and green all over' is a definitional constraint on 'red' and 'green' jointly. We may also speak of rules of inference as definitional constraints: the idea here is that there is metasemantic pressure towards interpretations under which the rule comes out truth-preserving. The rules of 'and'-introduction and 'and'-elimination, for example, are definitional constraints on (the logician's) 'and'.

As we saw in section 6.5, truth by convention was discredited long ago, in large part by Quine. This part of the Quinean critique is beyond reproach. But with many I reject the part that is directed at definitionality. Quine argued in "Two Dogmas of Empiricism" that confirmation holism implies meaning holism, which he then alleged to be inconsistent with the coherence of analyticity—here clearly

---

meanings; why? Because, I think, there is no consensus amongst her opponents over *cases* (over, e.g., whether 'There exist tables' is true) or *useable rules* (over, e.g., whether this rule holds: "'There exist tables' is true iff there exist things arranged tablewise"). (By a "usable" rule I mean—vaguely—one that a linguistic community as a whole, perhaps through a subcommunity of experts, could knowledgeably apply. Everyone can agree on the homophonic rule "'There exist tables' is true iff there exist tables"; but this isn't useable, since Thomasson's opponents disagree over whether the right-hand side holds.) However, realists quite generally say that terms can have determinate meanings despite disagreement over cases and useable rules of use (think of theoretical terms in areas of physics in which there is controversy). Why couldn't the same hold for the quantifiers? (Reference magnetism is one model of how quantifiers might nevertheless be semantically determinate.)

[43] See in this vein Boghossian (1997).

meaning definitionality; but this argument had a dubious verification theory of meaning as a premise.[44] A second argument from "Two Dogmas" was that it is difficult to reductively define 'analytic' (again, in the sense of definitionality) without appealing to related notions such as meaning or rule of language. But as Grice and Strawson (1956) quickly pointed out, inability to define a term should not make us doubt that term's sense. Definitionality depends, somehow, on dispositional, psychological, historical, and environmental facts about language users. Turning this bland observation into a philosophical definition is a monumental task. But so are all tasks of philosophical definition. Failure to define 'definitional' is no more cause for alarm than failure to define 'city', 'smile', or 'candy'.

Though I cannot define 'definitional', I can say a bit about it. Meaning is determined, somehow, by a complex array of facts about us—call these the facts about how we "use" language—as well as a complex array of facts about our relation to the world. Definitionality is primarily a function of the first array of facts, the facts of use.[45] Think of definitional constraints as messages we send to the semantic gods: "Insofar as you can, interpret our words so that these sentences come out true, and these inferences come out truth-preserving." Definitionality presumably comes in degrees: sentences or inferences can be more or less definitional (perhaps even: more or less definitional with respect to different terms). I think of definitional constraints as being in-principle available to competent speakers, or groups of competent speakers, though not infallibly or immediately so.

Definitional sentences need not be true; and definitional rules need not be truth-preserving.[46] For definitionality can be trumped. A definitional sentence or rule of inference governing certain terms might not be the only metasemantic pressure on those terms' interpretation. Countervailing metasemantic pressure from other sources might lead the semantic gods to assign those terms no meanings at all, or to assign them meanings that render definitional sentences or rules false or non-truth-preserving. The countervailing pressure might come from other facets of our usage of the terms (including, but not limited to, other definitional sentences or rules), or it might have a more metaphysical source.

Some examples. 1. Arguably, 'There is absolutely no space between two objects in contact' is false but definitional of 'contact'. The countervailing pressure comes primarily from use: other things we say using 'contact' lead the semantic gods to sacrifice this one definitional constraint. 2. Compatibilists reject the sentence 'No free action is determined by the past + laws'; but this sentence is arguably definitional of 'free'. Part of the countervailing pressure comes from the usage of 'free' in other contexts, but another part has a metaphysical source: the nonexis-

---

[44]See Boghossian (1997, section II).

[45]I do not say that the relevance of use to meaning is exhausted by its determination of the definitional sentences.

[46]See also Eklund (2002); Tappenden (1993).

tence (and even incoherence, on some views) of incompatibilist freedom. 3. The introduction and elimination rules for 'tonk' are definitional, but are not (both) truth-preserving. Here the countervailing source has nothing to do with use, but rather is purely metaphysical (or perhaps we should say logical): the semantic gods cannot acquiesce to the definitional constraints on pain of contradiction. 4. Pretend that physical theory includes a primitive theoretical predicate of times, 'earlier-than'. No physicist, let us suppose, questions the assumption that this relation is connected—that for any two distinct times, one of them is earlier than the other. Indeed, if asked to give "a definition" of 'earlier-than', physicists might cite connectedness as one of its defining characteristics. So a sentence expressing connectedness is at least somewhat definitional of 'earlier-than'. Nevertheless, we can imagine the sentence to be false. Suppose there is just one joint-carving rela-tion in the vicinity and that it is not a connected relation. Under this joint-carving relation, times are grouped into two separate time-lines, say. Surely this relation is what 'earlier-than' would denote. The definitional sentence about connectedness would be trumped by countervailing metasemantic pressure of a metaphysical source: the pressure to assign the joint-carving relation to 'earlier-than'. This pressure *could* be due to reference magnetism, but it needn't be. It could instead be based on the fact that 'earlier-than' is a theoretical term: it is intended to stand for whatever joint-carving notion is in the vicinity. 5. Consider an intuitionist of a rather metaphysical stripe,[47] who thinks that there is just one joint-carving notion in the vicinity of negation, which satisfies an intuitionistic logic. Such an intuitionist does not accept the rule of double-negation elimination, but might nevertheless concede that this rule is definitional, in ordinary English, of 'not'. On this view the definitional claim of that rule to be truth-preserving would again be trumped, as in example 4, by the presence of a rogue joint-carving notion that does not satisfy the definitional constraint.

Though definitional sentences *can* turn out false, often they turn out true. We need a word for true definitional sentences. I propose: 'analytic'. Analytic sentences thus understood are meaning-constraints that, as it happens, succeed. It might be thought inadvisable to re-use that old word here, since (as we will see) true definitional sentences do not play all of the traditional role of analyticity. But it plays some of that role; and as for the rest, nothing plays it. True + definitional is what we *ought* to mean by 'analytic'.

Analyticity, thus understood, carries no commitment to truth by convention. To count as analytic, a sentence must first be *true*—true on its own steam, so to speak. To say that a sentence is analytic is to say that it is a certain kind of truth; it is not to explain why it is true. As a result, analyticity does not have the epistemic significance it is often taken to have—we will return to this.

Analyticity is often accompanied by nonsubstantivity in the sense of chapter 4. For the point of a definitional constraint is often to (help) select one out of a

---

[47] In contrast to the more usual, semantically motivated, sort, such as Dummett (1973).

range of equally joint-carving candidates. We are aware, for example, that there are many, equally joint-carving, pairs of meanings we could assign to the words 'foot' and 'inch'. So we partially constrain the interpretation of this pair by laying down (F) as a definitional constraint:

(F) Something is a foot long iff it is twelve inches long.

Since some alternate constraints that we could have laid down, such as '11 inches make a foot', would not have been semantically alien, (F) is nonsubstantive (conventional, in fact, in the sense of section 4.3). Further, since there is no countervailing metasemantic pressure against interpreting 'foot' and 'inch' so that (F) is true, (F) is indeed true, and hence analytic.

However, analyticity and nonsubstantivity can come apart. One instance is when there is a fortuitous convergence of definitionality and joint-carving. Suppose (what I do not believe) that parthood is a fundamental relation, and that the sentence expressing the transitivity of 'part' is definitional of 'part'. If this sentence is true, then it is analytic; but it is substantive: any candidate meaning for 'part' on which the sentence is false would presumably fail to carve at the joints. An analogous point can be made for "analytic inferences": truth-preserving inferences that are definitional. The inferences that are distinctive of conjunction (from a conjunction to either of its conjuncts; and from the conjuncts together to the conjunction) are both truth-preserving and definitional, but are substantive, I would argue. Conjunction carves at the joints; and there are no equally joint-carving candidates for 'and' under which the rules fail to be truth-preserving.

Nothing can fully play the role traditionally associated with analyticity, for much of that traditional role presupposed the doctrine of truth by convention.[48] For instance, a sentence's analyticity was supposed to explain how we could know it to be true—we could know it to be true because the conventions we know ourselves to have adopted sufficed to make it true. That is why the positivists were so keen to demonstrate the analyticity of logic and mathematics. The downside of this favorable epistemic status was the apparent triviality of analytic truths.

Analyticity, on my conception, does not explain knowledge. Obviously, analytic sentences must be true, given my definition, but knowing that a given sentence is analytic is the rub. At best, we have unproblematic knowledge of definitionality (and even that is not really epistemically unproblematic). But no matter how definitional a sentence (or inference rule) is, it may still fail to be true (or truth-preserving), in the ways described earlier. Nor are analytic truths trivial. As we learned from Quine's critique of truth by convention, even the logical truths say something about the world. Analytic sentences do not comprise some weird representational species, somehow managing to be true without really saying anything. Like any other sentence, a definitional sentence must measure up; the world must be as it says in order for it to be true.

---

[48] See Harman (1999, chapters 5–7).

The failure of analyticity to generate knowledge is especially significant in logic, given the aspirations of the traditional conception. The case of 'tonk' shows that definitional inference rules in logic needn't be truth-preserving. How, then, a skeptic might ask, do we know that the standard rules, such as 'and'-introduction and elimination, are truth-preserving? Perhaps 'and' is tonk-like, in that its introduction and elimination rules somehow lead to contradiction. Or perhaps candidate meanings vindicating those rules are simply missing. Or perhaps joint-carving candidate meanings vindicating those rules are missing, and 'and' is a theoretical term intended to stand for a joint-carving meaning. Or perhaps 'and' is a theoretical term, and there is a single joint-carving candidate in the vicinity that fails to vindicate 'and'-introduction and elimination. We don't believe any of these odd possibilities to be actual, but how can we claim to know this, without presupposing the sort of logical knowledge that is at issue? This hard problem in the epistemology of logic cannot be solved by reflection on meaning.[49]

There is a kernel of truth in the traditional view. In contexts in which the existence of equally joint-carving candidate meanings is not in question, and in which it is known that there are no conflicting facets of use, definitional sentences have the traditional features "relative to the context". Consider a context in which everyone takes it as wholly obvious that there exist equally joint-carving properties *being an unmarried male, being an unmarried male eligible for marriage, being an adult unmarried male, being an adult unmarried male eligible for marriage*, and so on (and in which a suitable logic is being taken for granted). Someone then offers up a stipulative definition: 'bachelor' is to mean the same as 'unmarried male'. Everyone in the conversation would then regard 'Something is a bachelor iff it is an unmarried male' as epistemically secure, and they would regard assertions of this sentence as trivial, as contributing nothing to conversations. But that is only because the facts required to bridge the gap between definitionality and analyticity are not in question in the context.

9.9 Against easy ontology

Let's return to the easy ontologist's claim that we can tell, just by reflecting on language, that sentences like (T) are true:

(T) If some things are arranged tablewise then there exists a table.

[49] It is no answer to the skeptic to say, as Paul Boghossian (1997; 2003) does, that since skeptical doubts are phrased using logical concepts, if our logical constants lacked meanings then we could not even entertain those doubts—the sentences expressing the doubts would fail to express propositions. The fact—if it is a fact—that the doubts are unentertainable if true is peculiar but not probative. (Eliminativism about propositional attitudes or people (Churchland, 1981; Unger, 1979) also cannot be doubted if true, but so what?) We cannot, for example, combine the fact with the additional premise that we clearly *are* capable of entertaining the doubts, and thus conclude in Cartesian fashion that the skeptic is wrong; for the added premise is dialectically inappropriate. To "entertain" the doubts in the relevant sense requires bearing the propositional attitude of doubt towards skeptical propositions; and our ability to doubtingly wield skeptical sentences is no guarantee that the skeptical sentences express propositions.

As we saw in the previous section, linguistic reflection can deliver at best the conclusion that (T) is definitional. And being definitional is insufficient for truth: (T)'s definitional status might be trumped by some other factor.

In particular, suppose first that there is a joint-carving candidate to be meant by 'there exists' that satisfies enough of the other definitional constraints on 'there exists', but which does not satisfy (T). (This is, in fact, exactly what "mereological nihilists" believe.) And suppose, second, that the simple charity-based descriptivist metasemantics discussed in section 3.2 is true. In that case, this joint-carving candidate would be meant by 'there exists' (its superior eligibility having trumped its failure to satisfy (T)), and (T) would be false.

Or, make the first supposition again; but now, instead of assuming simple charity-based descriptivism, suppose instead that 'there exists' is a theoretical term—a term intended to stand, if possible, for a joint-carving meaning. 'There exists' might again mean the joint-carving candidate, rendering (T) false. Or—continuing to take 'there exists' to be a theoretical term—if the definitional claim of (T) is strong enough, 'there exists' might then be semantically defective (the conflicting metasemantic pressures being too strong to resolve), in which case (T) would be untrue because semantically defective.

In these ways, the presence of a joint-carving sort of quantification could render (T) untrue, even if (T) is definitional. Easy ontologists cannot, therefore, claim merely that (T) is definitional. They must also reject joint-carving quantification.[50] And so my arguments for ontological realism in sections 9.6.2–9.6.4 tell also against easy ontology.

In section 9.3 we saw that even an ontological realist might admit that *English* quantifiers do not carve at the joints. Something similar is true here: even an ontological realist might admit that *English* ontology is easy. Suppose, for example, that English quantifiers aren't theoretical terms; English speakers aren't "trying" to carve at the joints with such terms. Then, assuming the falsity of simple charity-based descriptivism, there would be comparatively little danger of the joint-carving sort of quantification trumping English usage. Alternatively, even given simple charity-based descriptivism, suppose that in the joint-carving sense, all that exists are subatomic particles. In that case, it might be argued, since so many ordinary statements about macro-entities would come out false under that austere candidate, this mismatch with usage outweighs its superior joint-carving. Either way, the ontological realist might then say that English quantifiers have a meaning that fits their ordinary usage, that (T) has an untrumped definitional status, and thus that (T) is analytically true in English. Thus, when applied to *English* quantification,

---

[50]I've been describing easy ontology as an alternative to quantifier variance; but the two can be combined. On this combination, the function of laying down (T) as a definitional constraint is to *select* one of many quantifier-candidates to be meant by 'there exist'. Sider (2007a) describes in more detail the combination of neoFregeanism about mathematical ontology with quantifier variance. Note also that even given quantifier variance, the easiness of ontological questions is only modulo knowledge of quantifier variance itself—see section 9.6.3.

the easy ontology picture might well be correct, even if ontological realism is true. But in that case, the appropriate language for conducting ontology would be Ontologese, in which the quantifiers are stipulated to carve at the joints, and in which sentences like (T) are not definitional. English is second-rate; the value of inquiry in joint-carving terms is superior (recall section 4.5). Ontology in Ontologese remains hard—and better.

9.10 Other forms of easy ontology

There are other approaches to ontology that one might classify as "easy". For example, Thomas Hofweber (2000; 2005; 2007) distinguishes between "internal" and "external" uses of quantifiers. External uses are "metaphysically loaded"; they are used to make statements about objects that are "'out there' as part of reality" (2007, p. 27). Internal uses, on the other hand, have an entirely different linguistic function—roughly, to form sentences that inferentially connect to their "instances" in the usual way, even if the "singular terms" in those instances do not in fact have the semantic function of referring to entities. For example, the existential quantifiers in (J) and (F) are internal:[51]

(J) There is a number which is the number of moons of Jupiter.

(F) There is someone who is admired by Fred and many other detectives.

(J) follows from 'The number of moons of Jupiter is four', and (F) follows from 'Sherlock Holmes is admired by Fred and many other detectives.' But in the latter sentences, 'the number of moons of Jupiter' and 'Sherlock Holmes' are not referential expressions. ('The number of moons of Jupiter is four' is, according to Hofweber, a syntactic variant of 'Jupiter has four moons', which contains no singular term purporting to refer to a number.)

Internal ontology is easy. You don't need to know that there are numbers "out there" in order to know that there are numbers in the internal sense; it is enough to know that Jupiter has four moons. Nevertheless, Hofweber's view does not conflict with ontological realism (not that he says it does), for the simple reason that even if he is right about natural language quantifiers, ontologists could always relocate to the metaphysics room, and conduct their dispute in Ontologese.[52]

---

[51] See Hofweber (2005, section 4.3) and (2007, section 6.4).

[52] Three further points here. (i) An ontological realist might take Hofweber's arguments to show that internal uses of the quantifiers do not carve at the joints. Such arguments based on Hofweber's linguistic analysis of the internal use of quantifiers must be distinguished from the metasemantic argument for non-joint-carving quantifiers considered in section 9.3. (ii) An ontological realist following Hofweber might say that external quantifiers in English carve at the joints. But she might say instead that, for metasemantic reasons, even these fail to carve at the joints. For even if external quantifiers don't carve at the joints, they might still relate to the world in a different way from how internal quantifiers do, a way that lets us justifiably say that they are about objects that are "out there". (Such an ontological realist would need to do ontology in Ontologese.) (iii) A quantifier variantist might accept Hofweber's arguments, and thus distinguish between two types of non-joint-carving quantifiers.

A similar point can be made about Stephen Yablo's (1998; 2000) view that some quantificational language is metaphorical, and indeed about any other view according to which some natural language quantifiers are "lightweight". Even if correct, such views do not challenge ontology as practiced in Ontologese. (Such views may, of course, help to support sparse positions in first-order ontology, by undermining arguments such as the following: "(i) John walked; so (ii) there is something John did; so (iii) nominalism about events is false." Nominalism about events says that there are no events in the heavyweight sense; so the quantifier in (ii) must be heavyweight; but, one might argue, the move from (i) to (ii) is valid only if the quantifier in (ii) is lightweight.)

D. M. Armstrong (1997, section 2.12) defends another form of easy ontology:

[A supervenient entity] is not something ontologically additional to the subvenient, or necessitating, entity or entities. What supervenes is no addition of being. Thus, internal relations are not ontologically additional to their terms. Mereological wholes are not ontologically additional to all their parts . . . One may call this view . . . the doctrine of the ontological free lunch.

Although Armstrong does not give a precise meaning to "no addition of being", the phrase has intuitive content.[53] It connects to the notion of the world being more or less "full": if accepting x makes the world no fuller, then x is no addition to being. It connects to commitment: the admonition to choose theories with fewer commitments (whether ontological or ideological) tells us to choose sparser, less full, worlds. The term remains vague; but even so, I think we can see that Armstrong is wrong that the supervenient is ipso facto no addition to being. For additions to being should be measured at the fundamental level. If you add to fundamental reality, you add to being, make the world a fuller place, commit yourself further—even if what you added is supervenient. Supervenience is just a kind of modal connection, and such a connection might hold between equally fundamental entities or facts.

Suppose, for example, that quantifiers carve at the joints, and that there is something (in the joint-carving sense), x, that is composed of $y_1 \ldots y_n$. The existence of x is an addition to being, even if it's necessarily true that a composed entity must exist whenever $y_1 \ldots y_n$ exist. For the composed entity's existence isn't "metaphysically reducible" to the existence of $y_1 \ldots y_n$; 'Something is composed of $y_1 \ldots y_n$' is a true sentence in a fundamental language, and has no metaphysical truth-condition (except perhaps a homophonic one). This can be put in Fine's terms as well: even if the existence of a composed object is necessitated by the existence of $y_1 \ldots y_n$ (and even if this necessitation holds in reality), if the proposition that something is composed of $y_1 \ldots y_n$ holds *in reality*—i.e., is a fundamental truth—then intuitively, the composed object is still an addition to being. But suppose, on the other hand, that it's not the case in reality that there is a com-

---

[53] Armstrong does say that if neither of two objects is an addition of being to the other, then the objects are identical.

posed object; rather, the proposition that something is composed of $y_1 \ldots y_n$ is grounded in the proposition that $y_1 \ldots y_n$ exist and stand in a certain relation. Or suppose, in my terms, that 'Something is composed of $y_1 \ldots y_n$' is not true under the fundamental sense of the quantifiers; rather, that sentence is true under a nonfundamental sense of the quantifiers, and is governed by the metaphysical truth-condition that $y_1 \ldots y_n$ exist (in the fundamental sense) and stand in a certain relation. Either way, we *can* then say that the composed object is no addition to being to $y_1 \ldots y_n$. For it is not a fundamental addition.

The supervenient lunch doesn't even *look* free in certain cases. Given a certain form of platonism, numbers are necessary existents and so are trivially supervenient (on anything), yet they clearly seem extra. Given a certain theology, there necessarily exists a god (though his states are presumably contingent); such a god would obviously be extra. In these cases, there is no tendency at all to say that supervenient entities are no additions to being. What went wrong? "Platonic" numbers and the god would exist fundamentally; and supervenience is a sign of a failure to be extra only when the supervenient is nonfundamental. The ontological free lunch is based on the thought that modality is the measure of all things metaphysical. We have yet another example of the inadequacy of that thought, of modality as a foundation for metaphysics.

9.11 Metaontology and conceptions of fundamentality

My discussion of ontological realism and ontological deflationism has mostly assumed my framework for talking about fundamentality. How might alternate frameworks affect the discussion?

Consider, first, Fine's framework, which appeals to the notions of grounding and reality. As noted in section 8.3.5, this ideology has a hard time distinguishing deflationary views from nihilistic views. For example, the causal deflationist holds that statements about causation are nonsubstantive, whereas the causal nihilist holds that statements about causation *are* substantive, and furthermore, that fundamentally, nothing causes anything. In *my* terms, the difference is that the causal nihilist thinks that there is a sense of 'cause' that carves at the joints, whereas the causal deflationist denies this; but in Fine's terms, the views are hard to distinguish.

This same problem emerges in the present context. How can a Finean distinguish an ontological deflationist from an ontological nihilist, who thinks that ontological questions are substantive but that nothing fundamentally exists? Each will presumably want to deny that existentially quantified propositions—propositions of the form $\exists x \phi$—are real. Might the difference be that the ontological nihilist will say that in reality, nothing exists? No. Since 'in reality' is surely factive, it would follow that nothing exists, which our ontological nihilist needn't accept.

Consider, next, Schaffer's framework, which appeals to a relation of grounding between objects. Schaffer takes his framework to support one sort of deflationism and another sort of anti-deflationism. The supported deflationism is about the Quinean question *do there exist Fs?*:

> ... while the Quinean will show great concern with questions such as whether numbers exist, [I] will answer such questions with a dismissive *yes, of course*. (2009a, p. 352)

The supported anti-deflationism is about the question *assuming that Fs exist, are they grounded in further objects, and if so, in which further objects?* Philosophical ontology, according to Schaffer, takes any given category of interest (numbers, for example), assumes that there are objects in that category, and tries to figure out whether and if so how those objects are grounded.

On the face of it, though, it's hard to see why dismissive affirmative answers to the Quinean question are justified. Suppose we believe in entities that would successfully ground Fs, if Fs exist. Even so, what would be wrong with denying that Fs exist? If such a denial would not be incoherent, then the Quinean ontological question of whether Fs exist at all would seem to remain open.

Quantifier variance, or some other form of easy ontology, would justify the dismissive affirmative answers. Given quantifier variance, it will be obvious (in many cases, anyway) that there are quantifier meanings on which 'There are Fs' comes out true, meanings that carve at the joints as well as any on which the sentence comes out false. Given that our usage of 'There are Fs' favors its truth, we can be confident that it is in fact true (modulo our knowledge of quantifier variance). But Schaffer does not base the dismissive affirmative answers on such thoughts (2009a, p. 360). His idea, rather, is that belief in numbers, composites, and so on, is just so much common sense. It's not that disbelieving in them is *incoherent*; it's rather that disbelieving in them would be maximally unjustified. But now the framework of grounding is playing no role in the deflation of the Quinean question; the question's answer is obvious purely because of the Mooreanism. An ontological realist of my sort who accepted this Mooreanism would agree, for precisely the same reason, that it's obvious that there are numbers, composites, and so on.

I must grant, though, that grounding *does* play this role: it preserves, for anyone who accepts Mooreanism, a domain for philosophical inquiry. For even if it's obvious that there are numbers, composites, and so on, given Schaffer's framework there remain questions of how numbers, composites, and the rest are grounded. But even an ontological realist can say something similar. The propositions that are certain, given Mooreanism, are surely those expressed by *ordinary* sentences. So even if it's quite certain that numbers, composites, and so on, exist in the ordinary sense, there would remain the question of what exists in the fundamental sense—of what is true in Ontologese.[54]

Consider next what Matti Eklund (2006) calls "maximalism", according to which reality is in a sense "full". Within certain limits,[55] all objects that can

---

[54] I argue against this sort of Mooreanism, however, in Sider (2011).

[55] There are real questions about how exactly to formulate maximalism; but set them aside.

coherently be supposed to exist, *do* exist. Thus there exist numbers, sets, properties, propositions, events, mereological composites, and so on. Maximalism, moreover, does not rest on quantifier variance. The maximalist's picture, rather, is that these objects exist under the one and only meaning for 'exist'.

Eklund thinks of maximalism as a form of ontological deflationism; but on the face of it, maximalism seems instead to be just another stand on substantive first-order ontology, and indeed, an extreme one. But perhaps a second look is warranted. Maximalism is a quite general hypothesis about reality, such that *given* the hypothesis, there can be no *further* doubt about the existence of *F*s (for appropriate choices of *F*). If you accept that existence is quite generally maximal, you should have no further doubt about whether composites, or numbers, or other "philosophical" entities exist. Of course, you can doubt maximalism itself. But compare the situation with quantifier variance. There too, it's only under the assumption that quantifier variance is true that there is any guarantee that there are tables. Even a quantifier variantist could entertain doubts about tables, since he could entertain doubts about quantifier variance. The most that *any* ontological deflationist can hope for, I think, is to show that doubts about ontological questions in *particular* domains are misguided, granted some quite *general* hypothesis about the nature of ontology.[56] So there is a sense, after all, in which maximalism is a kind of deflationism.[57]

But notice this. As a substantive metaphysical hypothesis, maximalism should be assessed by comparing its ontology and ideology to its rivals. Even setting aside the objection that its ontology is profligate, there is a more serious worry: its *ideology* is extremely profligate.[58] For the maximalist presumably recognizes distinctive fundamental ideology for each of the groups of entities he embraces: integers, sets, composites, events, propositions, and so on.[59] (Reducing successor to set-membership, for example, rather than taking it to be primitive, would seem to turn maximalism into a more standard sort of reductionism.)

9.12 Ontological commitment

The remainder of this chapter will be a bit of a digression: a discussion of a scattered set of ontological issues, in the light of ontological realism, beginning with ontological commitment.

[56] For more on this see Sider (2007*a*, sections 3 and 4).

[57] This way of thinking might, incidentally, be adopted by Schaffer in place of the Mooreanism.

[58] Compare this analogous argument: since Lewis's pluriverse contains myriad "alien" natural properties and relations, modal realism sins against Ockham's razor in a big way. Perhaps Lewis could respond that his pluriverse has a corresponding simplicity since it lacks arbitrariness—all possible natural properties and relations, so to speak, are present. (Compare Bennett (2004, section 4).) This raises interesting issues about how to evaluate simplicity.

[59] Phillip Bricker (1992) gives an interesting defense of maximalism both about entities and about natural properties and relations, within the realm of mathematics. An alternative is combining a sort of maximalism about mathematical entities with a much smaller, solely logical, albeit higher-order, ideology, as in Lewis's (1991) set-theoretic structuralism.

Contemporary use of the term 'ontological commitment' is perplexing in a few ways. To take a representative example, it is debated whether saying that there is a hole in one's sock "ontologically commits" one to holes. This is supposed to be an open philosophical question, alongside the other greats such as the question of whether we have free will and the question of whether we know anything. But 'ontological commitment' is a technical term, and has no semantic life outside of what we stipulate for it. Moreover, the most straightforward stipulation is that 'ontologically committed to Fs' just means 'committed to Fs', which, in addition to being a waste of screen real-estate, precludes what people seem to take to be an open position: believing in holes in one's sock without ontologically committing to holes.

Ontological realism clears all this up. Define 'ontologically committed to Fs' as meaning 'believing that there are Fs, in the fundamental sense of "there are"'. This allows someone to say in English that there are Fs without ontologically committing to Fs, if English quantifiers are nonfundamental. And it makes sense of the fact that ontological commitment is supposed to be a big deal.

Other talk of ontological commitment can be cleared up in similar fashion. We can speak of ontological commitment for quantifiers (or quantifier-interpretations), for example: a quantifier (interpretation) is ontologically committing iff it carves at the joints. Thus an ontological realist could claim that whereas some quantifiers are ontologically committing (those in Ontologese, and perhaps also some natural language quantifiers), other quantifiers (perhaps those in "There are many ways to win this chess match" and "Some detectives are fictional") are not. If each singular term is associated with a unique quantifier—a natural assumption—then we can also speak of ontological commitment for singular terms: a singular term is ontologically committing iff its associated quantifier is ontologically committing. For example, 'Sherlock Holmes' would fail to be ontologically committing if it is associated with the quantifier in "Some detectives are fictional" and that quantifier fails to be ontologically committing.

Another perplexing thing is the common focus on unwitting ontological commitments. There is supposed to be a question of whether a person who says that an apple is red has ontologically committed herself to a universal (or property) of redness, even if she claims not to believe in universals. Nominalists live in fear that they will be shown, by philosophical argument, to have unwittingly committed themselves all along to the position of their opponents!

We would be better off not talking this way, I think. If you think that apples can't be red without there being universals, then just say that. It muddies the waters to put this by claiming that anyone who says that the apple is red commits herself to universals.

It might be argued that one unwittingly commits to abstracta via the true metaphysical semantics.[60] If the true metaphysical semantics regards 'The ap-

---

[60]Analogous points could be made about commitment via the true linguistic semantics.

ple is red' as having the metaphysical truth-condition that the apple instantiates the universal of redness, then, we might say, one is "metaphysically committed" to universals simply by saying that an apple is red—the fundamental fact that one is getting at when one says 'The apple is red', after all, involves universals. Fine; but the only way to establish this metaphysical commitment—to establish that the metaphysical truth-conditions for natural-language predications involve universals—would be to argue that there are, fundamentally, universals. Thus it's just a distraction to bring up metaphysical commitment to universals in a debate over universals. Further, 'metaphysical commitment' is a misleading name. 'Commitment' suggests some sort of obligation to believe, whereas metaphysically committing to Fs means, in essence, making a statement whose underlying metaphysics involves Fs; and ignorance about underlying metaphysics is typically blameless. One might just as well say that anyone who says "There are tables" is "physically committed" to subatomic particles.

9.13 Quantifiers versus terms

I formulated ontological realism as concerning quantifiers. Thus quantified sentences express fundamental facts. But against this, a "Tractarian" form of ontological realism might be advanced: the fundamental facts are *individualistic*, not general; they are facts of the form Fa, Rbc, and so forth, not facts of the form $\exists x Fx$ or $\exists x \exists y Rxy$.

How we make sense of Tractarianism depends on how we think about fundamentality. Under my approach, we must locate some expression or expressions crucial to ontology as conceived by the Tractarian, and claim that those crucial expressions carve at the joints. If quantifiers are not the crucial expressions, then what are?

One answer would be that each name carves at the joints. Another answer would be that some names carve at the joints. A final answer, elusive and yet perhaps more satisfying, would be that *the grammatical category of the singular term* carves at the joints. Objecthood, so to speak, carves at the joints.[61]

Each of these may seem strained. The strain is caused by my "atomistic" approach to structure, which requires the ontological realist to locate a crucial joint-carving expression. The strain would be eased by adopting Fine's more holistic approach for talking about fundamentality (chapter 8). The Tractarian could then simply say that individualistic propositions are real, without needing to identify any particular expression to which this is due.

Tractarianism, in either form, faces an immediate problem. Consider, first, its formulation in my terms: quantifiers do not carve at the joints; names (or the category of the name) do. If quantifiers do not carve at the joints, quantified statements require a metaphysical semantics in fundamental terms. But what

---

[61] See section 11.8 on grammatical categories carving at the joints.

metaphysical truth-condition for the sentence $\exists x F x$ can be given in purely individualistic terms? Any disjunction $Fa_1 \vee Fa_2 \vee \ldots$ faces the modal objection that there *could* have been some further entity b, distinct from the a_is. $Fa_1 \vee Fa_2 \vee \ldots$ is therefore not modally equivalent to $\exists x F x$, and so, it might be alleged, cannot be a metaphysical truth-condition for it. For similar reasons, $\forall x F x$ seems to have no purely individualistic metaphysical truth-condition; in particular, it is not modally equivalent to any conjunction $Fa_1 \wedge Fa_2 \wedge \ldots$.

In Fine's terms, the modal argument could be put as follows. If Tractarianism includes the view that no quantified statements hold in reality, then all (factual) quantified statements must presumably be grounded in individualistic statements. But no collection of individualistic statements is modally sufficient for $\forall x F x$. Since grounding requires modal sufficiency, there is no individualistic ground for $\forall x F x$. (The fact that Finean fundamentality need not obey the combinatorial principle of section 8.3.2 opens up a weakened position according to which some but not all quantified claims hold in reality. Perhaps only one quantified claim holds in reality: $\forall x(x{=}a_1 \vee x{=}a_2 \vee \ldots)$; this, together with various individualistic claims—including negative individualistic claims—suffices to ground all quantified claims.[62] I wonder, though, what the attraction of this position is.)

The modal argument is inconclusive given "modal deflationism"—given, that is, that modal words are not particularly fundamental and have multiple candidates.[63] For then the Tractarian might deny that a sentence's metaphysical truth-condition must be necessarily equivalent to it, or that grounding requires necessitation. In principle these denials are open to anyone, but they are more defensible given modal deflationism. For defenders of fundamental modality surely regard modality as a "measure of the facts", in the following sense: if p can be true even though q is not, then p and q are "entirely separate facts"; and so, p cannot ground or be a metaphysical truth-condition for q. Modal deflationists, on the other hand, could regard modal distinctions as metaphysical epiphenomena. They might regard $\forall x F x$ and $Fa_1 \wedge Fa_2 \wedge \ldots$ as really being "the same fact", and so might embrace the view that the latter is the metaphysical truth-condition, or ground, of the former—even if our idiosyncratic concept of possibility counts "possibly $Fa_1 \wedge Fa_2 \wedge \ldots$ but not $\forall x F x$" as being true.[64] (This is not to say that knowing or asserting the generalization is the same as knowing or asserting the conjunction. The sense of sameness of fact here is metaphysical, not epistemic or semantic.)

Why might one be drawn to Tractarianism, or more generally, to fundamental individualistic facts? I will consider three arguments. First, there is an admittedly powerful intuition that, for example, the general fact that $\exists x F x$ holds *because* of

---

[62] If there are infinitely many things this would require an infinitary disjunction to hold in reality.

[63] The Humean theory of chapter 12 is a form of modal deflationism.

[64] If the latter is the metaphysical truth-condition of the former, then infinitary disjunction must be fundamental.

the individualistic fact that Fa. I wonder, though, whether this intuition should be trusted. It seems to concern a distinctively metaphysical sort of production or causation—the latter *makes-true* the former—and I reject such thoughts unless they can be rephrased in explanatory terms (chapter 8). And in this particular case, the thought does not survive the rephrasal.[65] The rephrased thought would be that a theory without the quantifiers is more explanatory. But this thought is not at all compelling, since quantificational explanations are usually better than purely individualistic explanations.

Second, there is an elusive but somewhat compelling argument in favor of recognizing something individualistic at the fundamental level in addition to, rather than instead of, fundamental quantification. Suppose your fundamental ideology includes existential and universal plural quantifiers in addition to the usual existential and universal singular quantifiers. Suppose, further, that you believe in some fundamental predicates. Now, these fundamental notions all seem *interconnected*, through a single notion of "objecthood". By this I don't mean a distinction between entities that are objects and those that are not. I mean something more basic (and hard to express): a notion of objecthood is "presupposed" by all quantifiers and predicates.[66] The singular quantifiers quantify over objects; the plural quantifiers also quantify over objects, albeit in a different way; and predicates, too, are distinctively object-theoretic. Intuitively: singular quantifiers, plural quantifiers, and predicates are intimately connected notions; and so, according to the argument, you ought to recognize, in your fundamental ideology, a notion of objecthood for their overlapping content.

The basis of the argument is the thought that something needs to be explained: namely, the connection between the various object-theoretic notions. Now, there would indeed be something in need of explanation if the various notions were all *varying in sync*. To illustrate, consider things from the quantifier variantist's point of view. He will agree that each object-theoretic notion can be (equi-structurally) varied. But variation of one requires correlated variation of the others. You can't change what you mean by the ordinary singular quantifiers, say, without also changing what you mean by the plural quantifiers and predicates. This *constrained* variation needs to be explained. And it would be natural to explain it by saying the following. First, there is an ur-notion of objecthood—of how to "carve the world up into objects". We have an arbitrary choice of how to understand this ur-notion. And this ur-notion acts as a parameter for all the object-theoretic notions. Once we select a value for the parameter (a way of carving the world up into objects), we thereby fix meanings for all the interconnected notions: the quantifiers, both singular and plural, and the predicates. Second, every predicate and quantifier has a "hole" in it, corresponding to the parameter. For example, ∃

---

[65] Contrast the rephrasal of the argument concerning the source of structure in section 8.3.1.

[66] Jason Turner's (2010a) notion of pegboard structure is a good metaphor here.

is really $\exists_X$, where X is filled in with a value for the parameter.[67] The explanation of the constrained variation is then this: an object-theoretic notion can be varied only by varying the parameter, which then induces a corresponding variation in all the other object-theoretic notions.

But for an ontological realist, there is no constrained variation to be explained. And so, there seems to be no reason to posit the "holes" in object-theoretic notions. Positing such holes would be positing a parameter-slot for which there's only one value. And if the holes aren't posited, then it isn't clear what explanatory gain is to be had by positing the parameter—by positing a joint-carving notion of objecthood.

Third, there is an argument for recognizing fundamental individualistic facts—again, in addition to fundamental quantification rather than instead of it—based on completeness (section 7.1). If fundamental languages have *only* quantified sentences, and no names, then how will we give a metaphysical semantics for individualistic statements of nonfundamental languages, such as 'Socrates is snub-nosed'?

But this argument, too, can be resisted. For we *can* give a purely general metaphysical semantics for a language with names: each named object could be associated with descriptive identifying conditions, and the metaphysical semantics could translate names as appropriate Russellian descriptions. This is not to lapse into early twentieth-century philosophy of language. For metaphysical semantics, recall, is distinct from the linguistic semantics pursued by linguists and philosophers of language. Descriptivist metaphysical semantics is compatible with antidescriptivist linguistic semantics. "Natural language proper names are never synonymous with definite descriptions" might well be true in the metalanguage of Kripkean linguists, even if that metalanguage has a descriptivist metaphysical semantics.[68]

9.14 NonQuinean first-order ontology

The ontological question, Quine (1948) says, is that of what there is. Quine belittles the fictitious Wyman (a proxy for Meinong), who thinks of the ontological question as being instead: which of the many things that there are have a further distinction of being *actual*? Other neoMeinongian terms for this or related further distinctions include 'exists' and 'subsists'.[69] According to a Quinean approach to ontology, what the opponent of holes denies is that there are holes; but according to neoMeinongians, the opponent of holes concedes that there are holes while denying that holes exist (are actual, subsist, etc.) According to this picture there

---

[67] An intriguing possibility would be for a quantifier variantist to say that these meanings with holes *do* carve at the joints. Does this allow a reply to the argument of section 9.6.2?

[68] Dasgupta (2009a) defends a "generalist" metaphysics in a different way against this sort of objection, and also gives an interesting positive argument in favor of generalism. See also Dasgupta (2010).

[69] Recent neoMeinongian work includes McGinn (2000, chapter 2); Parsons (1980); Routley (1980).

are holes, numbers, unicorns, fictional characters, and round squares; it's just that many (or perhaps all) of these objects do not exist.

Quine and many following him regard (neo)Meinongianism as being conceptually confused.[70] The distinction between what there is and what exists simply isn't there to be made. Now, I think that, as a matter of metaphysics, this criticism is correct: there are no joints in reality corresponding to the neoMeinongian ideology. But in what sense is the neoMeinongian conceptually confused? A neoMeinongian form of ontological realism could hold that quantifiers and the predicate 'exists' both carve at the joints. Reality includes both quantificational and existential structure. There are two sorts of fundamental ontological facts: facts about what objects there are, and facts about which objects exist. The division between existent and nonexistent objects is distinguished from other fundamental divisions (other joint-carving properties) by being more abstract. There are charged particles on either side of the division, spatial relations hold on either side of the division (though perhaps not across it, depending on what we want to say to Quine about fat men in the doorway), and so on. What is conceptually confused in this picture? It makes a clear choice of fundamental ideology, and says clear things in terms of that ideology. I do think the picture is *wrong*; Quine's ideology is metaphysically superior. But the thought that the neoMeinongian is *confused* seems to be a product of the magical-grasp picture of understanding rejected in chapter 2. One can fault the neoMeinongian for inadequately explaining the theoretical role that his ideology is supposed to play, or for giving bad arguments for his theory; but we shouldn't fault him simply for being *different*.

Other nonQuinean conceptions of ontology are possible. Rather than a quantifier + predicate fundamental ideology, one could instead have multiple quantifiers. Kris McDaniel (2009; 2011*a*; *b*) and Jason Turner (2010*b*) have explored the idea that there are different kinds or modes of being, which they understand as the idea that there are two or more joint-carving quantifiers.[71] Shamik Dasgupta (2009*a*) has explored the idea of an "objectless" fundamental ontology, according to which fundamental languages do not have quantifiers at all, but instead have versions of Quine's (1960*b*) predicate functors. Various people have flirted with rejecting the Fregean "bare" quantifier in favor of a quantifier with a slot for a sortal predicate—one cannot ask whether there is a ϕ; one must always ask whether some F is a ϕ, for sortal predicate F.

There is a lot going on behind the scenes, in orthodox Quinean ontology. Choices have been made, both about the ideology in which to pose the ontological question, and about the methodology used to answer the question. These choices

---

[70]Compare van Inwagen (1998).

[71]This needs to be distinguished from the idea that there is just one fundamental quantifier which may be restricted by multiple fundamental predicates. I will not take up this issue here (McDaniel and Turner have much to say about it), except to say that quantifiers grammatically are very different from predicates since they bind variables; thus, the fundamental facts, intuitively, have a very different shape if there are two fundamental quantifiers.

are not inevitable, and they embody a tacit, substantive metaphysical commitment concerning the fundamental structure of reality, to the view that the joint-carving ontological notions are the quantifiers of first-order logic. This is the unacknowledged foundation of contemporary ontology. It is a good foundation I think. But it would be better to acknowledge the commitment.

9.15 Higher-order quantification

Quantificational extensions of first-order logic include the addition of second-order quantifiers, plural quantifiers, and generalized quantifiers such as 'most' and 'there are infinitely many'. These additions add expressive power: given a fixed stock of predicates, one cannot define the new quantifiers in terms of the first-order quantifiers $\forall$ and $\exists$.

It is common to do model theory for these new quantifiers in a first-order set-theoretic metalanguage. In the model theory for second-order logic, for example, the second-order quantifiers range over sets of n-tuples of the domain, and the second-order predication $Xy_1 \ldots y_n$ is taken to be true (relative to a variable assignment) iff the n-tuple of the referents of $y_1 \ldots y_n$ is a member of the referent of X. But philosophers sometimes claim that the new quantifiers can be interpreted "innocently", as not meaning their first-order set-theoretic interpretations, but rather as expressing *sui generis* new contents.[72] Interpreted innocently, the second-order sentence $\exists X \forall y Xyy$ is not supposed to mean that there exists a set containing the ordered pair $\langle y, y \rangle$ for each object y. Nor is it supposed to mean that there exists a relation such that for every y, the relation is instantiated by y and y. Under the innocent interpretation, it does not make a claim about sets or relations or any other things at all. What *does* it mean? Well, it means $\exists X \forall y Xyy$!

Many questions about innocent second-order quantification (and innocent plural quantification, etc.) have been asked: whether it is legitimate, whether it really commits one to sets, whether we understand it, whether it is intelligible, and so on. But in addition to these methodological, normative, and psychological/semantic questions, there is also a squarely metaphysical question: do second-order quantifiers carve at the joints? Does reality contain second-order quantificational structure?

Anyone who thinks that reality *does* contain second-order quantificational structure is in a position to affirmatively answer the methodological, normative, and psychological/semantic questions. Imagine, for example, a nominalist who believes in second-order quantificational structure, and who introduces second-order quantifiers and variables by i) specifying the new symbols' grammar and envisaged inferential role; and ii) stipulating that they are not to be understood as quantifiers over sets or relations or anything of the kind. She can then reasonably claim, first, that nothing has gone wrong methodologically, since her introduction of the second-order quantifiers is on a par with the positing of electrons. Such

---

[72] See, for example, Boolos (1984); Rayo and Yablo (2001).

ontological posits are justified by their theoretical payoff; her ideological posit should be evaluated in the same way. And she can reasonably claim, second, that in the following sense she is not committed to sets: if her overall position is correct, then her second-order quantifiers are meaningful despite the nonexistence of sets. For her overall position includes the claim that reality contains irreducibly second-order quantificational structure; and given that claim, her stipulations surely succeed in giving a non-set-theoretic meaning to her second-order quantifiers. And she can reasonably claim, third, to grasp her second-order quantifiers in the way we grasp all theoretical terms: by understanding their inferential role. The thought that the second-order quantifiers would be psychologically/semantically suspect seems rooted in the misguided magical-grasp model of understanding (section 2.1).

The nominalist's introduction of the second-order quantifiers is methodologically, normatively, and psychologically/semantically faultless. Still, something may well have gone wrong. If reality lacks second-order quantificational structure (and also lacks an ontology of sets—see below), semantic disaster will strike the nominalist's attempt to stipulate a meaning for her second-order quantifiers. Those quantifiers may be semantically indeterminate, or even semantically defective. Perhaps "disaster" overstates it since some second-order sentences may have their truth-values settled by the stipulated inferential role. For example, if the nominalist stipulates that $\exists Y\, Ya$ is to be true whenever Fa is true, then if some sentence Fa is indeed true, perhaps $\exists Y\, Ya$ becomes true as well. But second-order sentences whose truth-values are not thus settled will presumably be semantically indeterminate.[73]

Suppose reality lacks second-order quantificational structure but includes an ontology of sets. Then the true metaphysical semantics might interpret the second-order quantifiers as first-order quantifiers over sets (that might be the only way for second-order sentences to be determinate). Thus interpreted, the second-order quantifiers would "metaphysically commit" their users to sets. But as we saw earlier, metaphysical commitment barely deserves the name. (We are also metaphysically committed to there being subatomic particles by saying "There are tables" if its metaphysical truth-condition quantifies over subatomic particles; but that doesn't make the denial of subatomic particles irrational.) What is important is that the nominalist holds a coherent overall position according to which second-order claims can be true, and determinate, despite the nonexistence of sets.

Coherent, yes; but reasonable? The addition of second-order quantifiers to fundamental ideology immensely increases the complexity of one's fundamental theory, and should be undertaken only to gain some great explanatory benefit—to *fundamental* theory. Here again the term 'ideology' is unfortunate, leading us

---

[73]Timothy Williamson (1994) says that there's a particular hair that makes a bald man bald, but this hair has no particular metaphysical significance. I wonder whether he would hold the analogous position in this case, e.g., that a second-order sentence corresponding to the continuum hypothesis has a truth-value, but this truth-value has no metaphysical significance.

to focus on questions of psychology and semantics. To posit the second-order quantifiers as fundamental ideology is to go out on a *metaphysical* limb, to posit that the world contains the requisite structure. Why think that the world contains that structure? Why not retain, at the fundamental level, a simpler quantificational ideology, that of good old first-order logic?

Many of the arguments in favor of innocent higher-order quantification do not look powerful when taken metaphysically, as arguments for the conclusion that second-order quantifiers carve at the joints. (This is not a criticism; the arguments typically aren't intended in this way.) For example, in their defense of innocent second-order quantification, Agustín Rayo and Stephen Yablo (2001) argue that ordinary English already contains such quantification, extending Arthur Prior's (1971, p. 37) example of "I hurt him somehow". Suppose they are right; and suppose further that, as they argue, English second-order quantifiers are innocent in the sense that using those quantifiers while denying that one is quantifying over sets does not compromise one's semantic competence. It's hard to view this putative datum as supporting the idea that second-order quantifiers carve at the joints.[74] English second-order quantification might be—like much natural-language talk—metaphysically second-rate. It might have a complex or disjunctive metaphysical semantics, and it might be semantically indeterminate. Alternatively—and I suspect this is indeed true—English second-order quantifiers might have a first-order set-theoretic metaphysical semantics. The fact that a competent speaker can coherently think "I hurt him somehow, but there do not exist sets" does not rule out a set-theoretic metaphysical semantics, any more than the fact that a competent speaker can coherently think "There is a chair but there do not exist electrons" rules out a metaphysical semantics based on modern particle physics. The way we, or our brains, conceptualize 'There are tables' and 'I hurt him somehow' is one thing, and the underlying metaphysics of these matters is quite another; there's no reason to take the former as a guide to the latter.

A famous argument due to George Boolos (1984) for irreducibly plural quantification is similarly unconvincing if taken as concerning metaphysically fundamental ideology. (Again, this is not a criticism; Boolos didn't intend his argument in this way.) Ordinary English speakers say many things that cannot be regimented in first-order logic without using set-theoretic predicates. There is the Geach-Kaplan sentence, for example: 'Some critics admire only one another'. Moreover, ordinary English speakers say other things that are *best* represented in non-first-order terms, even though their truth-conditions *can* be given in first-order terms; for example: "There are some monuments in Italy of which no one tourist has seen all."[75] Boolos concludes that i) the best formal regimentation of such sentences is

---

[74]Moreover, it would be hard to view the falsity of the putative datum as evidence *against* the idea; why think that English is maximally metaphysically expressive?

[75]The most natural regimentation is $\exists X(\exists x Xx \wedge \forall x(Xx \rightarrow Mx) \wedge \sim \exists y(Ty \wedge \forall x(Xx \rightarrow Syx)))$, which is equivalent to the first-order sentence $\exists x Mx \wedge \sim \exists y(Ty \wedge \forall x(Mx \rightarrow Syx))$.

into the language of monadic second-order logic; ii) the sentences of monadic second-order logic may be interpreted by translating them into a (somewhat augmented) fragment of ordinary English containing plural quantifiers; and iii) the use of the existential plural quantifier "There are some things such that . . ." in this fragment of English does not commit (his word) one to sets. For example, we may regiment the Geach-Kaplan sentence in second-order terms as follows:

$$\exists X (\exists x X x \wedge \forall x (X x \rightarrow C x) \wedge \forall x \forall y ((X x \wedge A x y) \rightarrow (X y \wedge x \neq y)))$$

We may then translate this into plural English as follows:

> There are some things such that i) there is at least one of them; ii) each of them is a critic; and iii) anything that one of them admires is distinct from that one of them, and is itself one of them.

Finally, according to Boolos, this final sentence, and other sentences in which we quantify plurally over critics, monuments, and other nonsets, do not commit one to sets. As he memorably puts it (1984, p. 448), "It is haywire to think that when you have some Cheerios, you are eating a *set*—what you're doing is: eating THE CHEERIOS."[76]

The questions Boolos was addressing were i) how should we "represent"— "symbolize", "regiment"—certain sentences in English; and ii) do English plurally quantified sentences "commit" one to sets? I suspect that his answers are correct, given a natural way of taking his questions. There is indeed a certain level of logico-linguistic representation of English (connected with capturing natural-language logical relations) at which the Geach-Kaplan and other sentences should be given second-order representations; and I also agree that there's a good sense in which English speakers don't commit themselves to sets when they utter plural sentences. But none of this tends to show that plural quantification carves at the joints. First, none of it conflicts with the idea that the metaphysical semantics for English plural quantifiers is second-rate in one or more ways: it could be complex and/or disjunctive and/or semantically indeterminate. Second—and again, this is where my own money is—the underlying metaphysical semantics for English plural quantification might be set-theoretic. This wouldn't conflict with Boolos's claim that English plurally quantified sentences don't "commit" their users to sets. Compare: even if the right metaphysical semantics for "There is a table" refers to subatomic particles, there's a perfectly straightforward sense in which normal English speakers aren't *saying* that there are subatomic particles when they utter that sentence, and a perfectly straightforward sense in which they don't *commit* themselves to subatomic particles when they utter it. Similarly, even if the right metaphysical semantics for the Geach-Kaplan sentence is set-theoretic, ordinary speakers aren't *saying* that there are sets when they are uttering it. Nor

---

[76] Boolos's confidence about what we're eating is unjustified; perhaps the underlying metaphysics of eating Cheerios *is* set-theoretic. What's haywire is to think that we are *saying* that we're eating sets when we say that there are some Cheerios that we're eating.

are they committing themselves (in the only sense that matters) to sets: uttering the sentence while disbelieving in sets is neither irrational nor a sign of linguistic incompetence.

A different argument for irreducibly plural quantification, given by Boolos and others, fares a bit better—but only a little bit—if taken as concerning metaphysically fundamental plural quantification. Ordinary English speakers who believe that there exists at least one F are generally disposed to accept: "There are some things such that they are all the Fs." So, ordinary English speakers who believe in sets are disposed to accept:

(AS) There are some things such that they are all the sets.

But given standard ZF set theory, there is no set of all the sets; thus we cannot interpret the plural quantifier in (AS) set-theoretically if we want (AS) to be true.

There is no significant pressure here to admit metaphysically fundamental plural quantification. First, plural sentences might have non-set-theoretic but metaphysically second-rate metaphysical truth-conditions. Second, the metaphysical semantics of English plural quantification might be nonuniform: some plurally quantified sentences might have set-theoretic truth-conditions while the metaphysical truth-condition of (AS) might be simply that there exists at least one set. (The metaphysical truth-condition of any sentence of the form "There are some things such that they are all the Fs" could be that there exists at least one F.) Compare the truth-conditions for ordinary English *first-order* sentences. Many of them may have quite "straight" metaphysical truth-conditions. For example, the ordinary English "There is an electron" may well have the metaphysical truth-condition that there exists, in the fundamental sense, an electron. But it's unlikely that all first-order English sentences have such truth-conditions; think of 'A man, a plan, a canal; Panama!", 'There are five ways to win this chess match', 'My sock contains a hole', 'Every smirk disappeared from every face at the return of the exams', and so on. It seems likely that the metaphysical truth-conditions will be nonuniform across the range of first-order English sentences. (Remember, these are metaphysical truth-conditions; the idea isn't that competent speakers know about all this.) Third, (AS) might be false, ordinary belief in its truth be damned.

It may be objected that each of these alternatives is unpalatable, and hence that we would be better off positing irreducibly plural quantification. But it takes more than a casual observation about what we ordinarily say and believe to justify a truly dramatic complication of our fundamental theory of the world. The argument from (AS) to fundamental plural quantification doesn't look much better than the old argument from the apparent truth of "John and Ted share many vices" to the fundamental existence of universals as abstract entities. Note also that the objection depends on two attitudes that are hard to sustain simultaneously: squeamishness about error-theories and squeamishness about nonuniform metaphysics. Squeamishness about error theories is most compelling when the terms in question are everyday rather than theoretical, so that we're entitled to confidence that paradigmatic uses of sentences containing them are true. (No one contemplates an error theory about our belief that Newton didn't lie when he said that space and time are absolute; 'lie' is an everyday term.) But there's nothing wrong with a nonuniform metaphysical semantics for such terms (which is largely why the confidence is justified). It's only for theoretical terms ('charge', 'gold') that we think a good metaphysical semantics must be uniform; but then we're more open to error theories.

A far more convincing strategy for defending fundamental plural quantification would be to argue that it is required for some important theoretical purpose. And a further argument of Boolos's may seem to do this: the argument that we need plural (or second-order) quantification to give an adequate axiomatization of ZF set theory. The standard first-order axiomatization of ZF set theory contains as axioms all of the infinitely many instances of the first-order replacement schema. A strictly stronger, second-order, formulation dispenses with the infinitely many first-order axioms in favor of a single second-order sentence. Boolos shows that the second-order quantifiers in this second-order sentence cannot be regarded as short for first-order quantifiers over sets. Our choice is therefore between a first-order axiomatization of ZF and a second-order axiomatization in which the second-order quantifiers are either taken as primitive or—Boolos's preferred alternative—interpreted plurally. Boolos then goes on to argue that the first-order axiomatization is insufficient.

. . . to rest content with a set theory formulated in the first-order predicate calculus with identity . . . must be regarded as a compromise, as falling short of saying all that we might hope to say. We accept [the first-order formulation of ZF] because we accept a stronger theory consisting of a *finite* number of principles, among them some for whose complete expression second-order formulas are required. We ought to be able to formulate a theory that reflects our beliefs. (1984, p. 441)

At first glance the argument looks very weak (again, if taken as concerning metaphysical fundamentality—which is not what Boolos intended by this argument). "We ought to be able to formulate a theory that reflects our beliefs": in the present context this would have to mean that the beliefs in question have *fundamental* plural content, that they be stated in terms of fundamental plural quantifiers. But why suppose this? The fundamental contents of our beliefs are not in general transparent to us. On my view, neither causation nor modality is fundamental; on Hirsch's view, quantification is not fundamental; neither I nor Hirsch can be refuted simply by pointing to the fact that people have causal, modal, and quantificational beliefs.

However, the argument can be formulated so as not to concern our beliefs at all; it can be formulated as the claim that second-order ZF is a *better theory*. We generally prefer unified theories, theories that explain diverse phenomena using a small number of posits. First-order ZF posites a disunified infinite array of facts, the infinitely many instances of the replacement schema. By replacing this infinite array with a single principle, it may be thought, second-order ZF is more explanatory. First-order ZF doesn't have the right kind of "laws"; second-order

ZF does. But is our *overall* theory made simpler by introducing the higher-order quantifiers?[77] Our laws of set theory no longer include the replacement schema, but our laws of logic now must include the plural comprehension schema:

$$\exists x \phi(x) \rightarrow \exists X \forall x (X x \leftrightarrow \phi(x))$$

And we must make use of instances of this schema to draw consequences from our second-order set theory. So the argument seems inconclusive.

The final argument I'll consider—the best I know—for fundamental higher-order quantification derives from Timothy Williamson's (2003) argument that we need second-order quantification to state semantic theories for languages with absolutely unrestricted quantifiers. Standard semantic theories introduce entities known as interpretations, and then use those interpretations to define various familiar semantic and logical concepts. (For example, a set of sentences Γ is said to logically imply a sentence S iff S is true in each interpretation in which every member of Γ is true.) But, as Williamson shows, one can derive an analog of Russell's paradox for interpretations. Williamson's solution is to adopt a different approach to semantics that isn't subject to the paradox. On this approach one does not introduce interpretations as entities at all. Rather, one uses primitive second-order quantification (with dyadic predicate variables) to formulate a second-order notion of an interpretation, with which one can formulate second-order analogs of familiar definitions of logical consequence and other semantic and logical notions. Thus, Williamson argues, we need second-order quantification in order to do semantics without falling into paradox. And finally, one might add that the second-order quantifiers must be fundamental if the logical and semantic notions we define using them are to be fully determinate.

The argument here is formidable (though one worries it will demand still higher-order ideology for defining interpretations of the second-order language). But note that the demand for extra ideology is coming from linguistic theory and metalogic. Elsewhere we resist demands from high-level sciences to add significant complexity to our fundamental account of the world. Such resistance is exactly what drives familiar projects to naturalize mental and semantic content. As Fodor (1987, p. 97) puts it:

I suppose that sooner or later the physicists will complete the catalogue they've been compiling of the ultimate and irreducible properties of things. When they do, the likes of spin, charm, and charge will perhaps appear upon their list. But aboutness surely won't; intentionality simply doesn't go that deep.

Williamson might reply that we need the extra ideology to do *logic*, not semantics. But notice that the ideology is needed, at most, for metalogic, for giving fully general theories of such metalogical notions as logical consequence. It is not needed for the *use* of logical notions (such as conjunction, quantification, and so

---

[77]Thanks to Cian Dorr here.

on), within science and mathematics. It is hard to give up on beautiful metaphysics for the sake of metalogic.

10 Logic

If one can query expressions from all grammatical categories for joint-carving, then one can query logical expressions. This leads to interesting questions about the metaphysics of logic, which bear on substantivity, objectivity, determinacy, and so forth in logic, and also on the nature of joint-carving itself.

Questions about joint-carving can be asked about both logical and metalogical concepts. Logical concepts are those concepts expressed by logical constants, concepts such as conjunction, disjunction, negation, and quantification; metalogical concepts are theoretical concepts such as logical consequence, logical truth, provability, semantic consequence, and the concept of a logical constant. Questions about joint-carving for logical and metalogical concepts should be presumed independent unless shown otherwise.

It may seem odd to ask metaphysical questions about logic. But recall Russell's conception of the subject, as differing from other inquiries only by being more "abstract and general". This (vague) picture of the continuity between logic and other disciplines is a crucial presupposition of this chapter (and book). If a hangover from logical conventionalism leads you to distrust the questions: pop a couple of aspirins, re-read your Quine (1936) (and section 6.5), and report back.

10.1 Fundamental logic

First question: do any logical concepts carve at the joints? There is a powerful argument that at least some of them do. The best guide to joint-carving is a Quinean criterion of ideological commitment: it is (defeasibly) reasonable to regard indispensable ideology as carving at the joints. But we cannot get by without logical notions in our fundamental theories. In particular, since Frege (1879) it has become clear that the notions of first-order predicate logic are indispensable in serious foundational theorizing. Section 9.6.4 pressed this argument for the first-order quantifiers. But a parallel argument suggests that the identity sign and the sentential connectives of propositional logic also carve at the joints: these are as indispensable as the quantifiers.

The case for joint-carving is much weaker for certain other "logical" notions. Modal operators and nontruthfunctional conditionals, for example, seem dispensable in fundamental theorizing, even though they are deeply embedded in our ordinary conceptual scheme. The material "conditional" of first-order logic suffices for conditionality in mathematics and the fundamental sciences, and neither discipline seems to need modality. Our best theories are extensional, and talk simply about what *is*. This is not to say that there are no modal or conditional facts; it is simply to call for metaphysical reductions of those facts. And reductions seem possible—chapter 12 defends a reduction of modality, for example.

10.2 Hard choices

Next question: *which* logical concepts carve at the joints? I said a moment ago that the sentential connectives of propositional logic carve at the joints. But which ones? Just ∧ and ∼? Just ∨ and ∼? Or perhaps the only joint-carving connective is the Sheffer stroke |? Similarly, which quantifier carves at the joints, ∀ or ∃?

You don't have to be a logical positivist to feel that something is wrong with these questions. Yet my approach to fundamentality seems to force them upon us. Structure is structural, and applicable to notions of arbitrary sort; so we can ask of any logical notion whether it carves at the joints and expect a substantive, objective answer.[1]

What's particularly hard to swallow is the need to *choose* amongst the propositional-logic connectives. It's comparatively easy to swallow the idea that propositional logic as a whole is metaphysically on-track. But one wants to treat the choice of which connectives to take as primitive and which to take as defined as a conventional one (assuming classical logic anyway), whereas my account elevates this choice to one of high metaphysics.

One might try to avoid the choice by saying that, although it's determinately the case that some connectives carve at the joints, it's indeterminate which ones do. But section 7.12 argued against indeterminacy at the fundamental level.

Sometimes one can move to a different, more fundamental, theory to make hard choices like these go away. Which is fundamental: earlier-than or later-than? The following theory gets us off the hook: neither is fundamental; the fundamental temporal relation is temporal betweenness; time is fundamentally symmetric; the past–future asymmetries derive from certain de facto asymmetries about how matter is distributed in the universe.[2] Or again, which distance function is the fundamental one? Which function from pairs of points of space to real numbers is fundamental: the distance-in-meters function, or the distance-in-feet function, or a function corresponding to some other unit? We get off the hook by saying: none of them is; the fundamental metrical facts are facts of spatial congruence.[3]

---

[1] If a logical notion such as ∨ does *not* carve at the joints, then the question of whether it carves at the joints is not phrased in purely joint-carving terms. But this does not make the question nonsubstantive. For every candidate metaphysical semantics for the sentence '∨ carves at the joints', i.e., '$\mathcal{S}(∨)$' will count it false. A metaphysical semantics that assigns a true truth-condition, such as '$\mathcal{S}(∈)$' or '$\mathcal{S}(∧)$' (assuming that both '∧' and '∈' carve at the joints) won't fit the use of '$\mathcal{S}(∨)$' well enough to count as a candidate. The candidates will take the form $\mathcal{S}(\alpha)$ where α is logically complex—'$\mathcal{S}\!\sim\!(\sim\!P\wedge\sim\!Q)$', perhaps, in one of the notations introduced in section 6.3—and such sentences are false (a metaphysical semantics is given in purely joint-carving terms, so if α is logically complex then it does not carve at the joints).

[2] Those who reify relations might instead get off the hook by identifying earlier-than with later-than; see Fine (2000); Williamson (1985); but see also Dorr (2004).

[3] See, for example, Field (1980, chapters 3, 5).

Unfortunately, escape of this sort seems unlikely in the case of logic: what more fundamental theory could we shift to?

I don't see how to escape the hard questions, provided we're willing to speak of joint-carving at all, since I see no principled way to shield logic from such questions. And anyway, we face similar hard questions outside of logic: believers in mereology face the question of whether it is parthood or overlap that carves at the joints; believers in an intrinsic direction of time face the question of whether it is earlier-than or later-than that carves; and so on. So I am led by argument, against inclination, to accept the questions. There *is* a real question about which of propositional logic's connectives carve at the joints, and similarly for ∀ and ∃.

Here are two points to make this go down easier. First, egalitarian answers can be given to the questions. For example, one might hold that both ∃ and ∀ carve at the joints, or that all the truth-functional connectives do,[4] and thus avoid drawing invidious metaphysical distinctions.

You might think that a "nonredundancy" constraint is constitutive of the notion of joint-carving, and that this rules out egalitarianism. Lewis (1986b, 60), for example, says of his perfectly natural properties that "there are only just enough of them to characterise things completely and without redundancy". But the nonredundancy constraint should be rejected.

Suppose first that the nonredundancy constraint is taken modally: no joint-carving notions can supervene on others. This would prohibit all mathematical joint-carving notions, given the usual dogma about the necessity of mathematics, since those notions supervene trivially on any notions whatsoever. It would also prohibit certain kinds of higher-order structure. For example, it's an attractive position for a platonist about properties to say that higher-order relations generate the determinate–determinable structure of families of properties, and underlie the use of numbers to represent quantities (Mundy, 1987). One such higher-order relation would be a relation of *greater-than*, which holds between two determinate mass properties m_1 and m_2 iff objects that instantiate m_1 are more massive than objects that instantiate m_2.[5] It would be natural for such a platonist to say that i) the holding of these relations is a matter of necessity (and so they supervene trivially on any basis whatsoever); and ii) these relations carve at the joints.[6]

These problems could be avoided by taking the nonredundancy constraint in a logical rather than modal sense, so as to prohibit joint-carving expressions E where every sentence containing E (and perhaps other joint-carving expressions) is logically equivalent to a sentence not containing E. But this sort of special pleading is suspect. The examples of mathematical and higher-order structure show that the redundancy constraint is based on a misguided idea—the idea that there cannot

---

[4]I have in mind pairing this view with an acceptance of classical logic (at the fundamental level, that is; see section 10.6). And I have in mind only the one- and two-place connectives.

[5]This is not a definition. If anything is to be defined, it should be 'more massive than': x is more massive than y iff x has some mass property that is greater than some mass property of y.

[6]See Eddon (2012).

be "necessary connections" between distinct joint-carving expressions. Even if facts about numbers bear the modal relation of necessitation to all other facts (and thus trivially supervene), they are genuine facts, and involve joint-carving notions; missing out on such facts would mean missing out on some of reality's structure. When ϕ modally entails ψ, the fact that ψ may nevertheless be a distinctive fact, with a distinctive structure, and so we may wish to say that expressions in ψ, as well as those in ϕ, carve at the joints. And all of this remains the case even if the "necessary connection" is a purely logical one. That ψ is a logical consequence of ϕ does not mean that there isn't a fact that ψ, or that the fact that ψ has no structure distinct from the structure of the fact that ϕ. It means merely that a certain connection holds between the facts: one logically entails the other. So there is no reason to treat logical redundancy differently from modal redundancy. And so, since we shouldn't prohibit modally redundant joint-carving notions, we shouldn't prohibit logically redundant joint-carving notions either.

Rejecting the idea that nonredundancy is constitutive of joint-carving is consistent with accepting some sort of nonredundancy constraint on *reasonable belief* about joint-carving. (This should have been the status of nonredundancy all along.) In general, we shouldn't multiply ideology beyond necessity; and redundant ideology is often unnecessary ideology. Redundant in what sense? Not a modal or logical sense: the principle shouldn't summarily rule against the rationality of adopting fundamental mathematical or logical ideology. Rather, an explanatory sense: we shouldn't posit ideology that is not needed for reaching our explanatory goals. For example, in a language containing (sentential) disjunction, primitive predicates F and G, and a further primitive predicate for the disjunctive property of *being either F or G*, the latter predicate can simply be deleted without explanatory loss. This ideological Ockham's razor is consistent with modally or logically redundant ideology because the razor, like most constraints on reasonable belief, can be defeated by opposing considerations. One potential opposing consideration comes from symmetries: other things being equal, one shouldn't draw distinctions between symmetrical hypotheses without good reason; to do so would be arbitrary. For example, one might regard the symmetry between 'earlier' and 'later' (or that between 'part' and 'overlap') as a reason to ignore the razor and regard both as carving at the joints. A second opposing consideration comes from explanatory work done by the candidates for deletion. Deleting a given bit of ideology from one's theory might incur theoretical loss, despite modal or logical redundancy. Simply deleting mathematical or determinate/determinable-theoretic vocabulary would (arguably) result in a worse theory, because explanations couched in the deleted vocabulary would be forfeited. While it is unclear whether the second opposing consideration is significant in the case of the propositional connectives (are explanations stated in terms of the Sheffer stroke worse than those stated in terms of negation, conjunction, and disjunction?), the first does seem significant, and is the intuitive source of egalitarianism.

So: the availability of egalitarianism is the first point to make the hard questions go down easier. The second point is that we should not dismiss the questions simply because of the interdefinability of propositional connectives, for there is a parallel sort of interdefinability in cases where there are clearly legitimate questions about joint-carving. Given temporal and observational vocabulary, 'grue' and 'bleen' are interdefinable with 'green' and 'blue'; but if talk of joint-carving is ever legitimate, it is surely legitimate here. Indeed, despite the interdefinability, *in*egalitarianism is surely right here: 'green' and 'blue' carve at the joints, whereas 'grue' and 'bleen' do not.[7] (Inegalitarianism is hard in the case of the truth functions, but perhaps not impossible. Perhaps parallels with Boolean algebras in mathematics, together with a preference for commutativity/symmetry at the fundamental level, privileges conjunction, disjunction, and negation over the other truth functions.)

It might be argued that the question of which truth functions are joint-carving arises only as an artifact of my approach to joint-carving, and would disappear under other approaches. On my subpropositional approach (chapter 8), the locus of joint-carving is (to put it linguistically) the word; it is words that do or don't carve at the joints. One can, as a result, raise meaningful questions about whether 'and', or 'or', or both, or neither, carves at the joints. But suppose instead that the locus is the *sentence*, or rather, the proposition (to put it, now, nonlinguistically): it is entire propositions that do, or don't, carve at the joints. Then one could not directly raise the question of whether logical words carve at the joints. One might try to indirectly raise the question by asking whether propositions expressed using 'and', or propositions expressed using 'or', or both, or neither, carve at the joints. But suppose further that propositions are "coarse-grained", so that "*a* is F and *b* is G" expresses the same proposition as its Sheffer stroke equivalent: "(*a* is F | *b* is G) | (*a* is F | *b* is G)". This would block raising the question, even indirectly, of whether 'and' or 'or' carves at the joints.

But as argued in chapter 8, structure should not be located at the sentence level. Intuitively put, if "*a* is F and *b* is G" carves at the joints, that is because of something about F-ness, G-ness, and conjunction. Better: "*c* is F and *d* is G", "*e* is F and *f* is G", and so on, also carve at the joints; this pattern is surely explained by the recurrence of the joint-carving words 'F', 'G', and 'and'.

Further, the motivation for adopting this picture—propositional joint-carving plus coarse-grained propositions—should be questioned. Is it to avoid having to answer a hard question about propositional connectives? But there would remain analogous hard questions in other cases, perhaps with 'earlier' and 'later', or with 'part' and 'overlap', depending on how coarse-grained propositions are taken to be. And there would also remain the hard question of whether the propositional picture itself is correct, and if so, of how coarse the grain is. (Propositions must be coarse-grained enough to avoid the choices we don't want, but not so coarse-

---

[7] Replacing 'green' and 'blue' with predicates of fundamental physics would result in an example with the vice of unfamiliarity but the virtue of correctness.

grained to avoid those we *do* want, such as the choice between green + blue and grue + bleen.)

There remains a nagging doubt. If questions about joint-carving can be asked even about logic, then where does it all end? Can we also ask whether writing in Spanish, or in red ink, or in boldface, carves at the joints better than the alternatives?[8] Surely *some* differences are just notational!

There are a few different worries one might have here. Consider:

(B) **Charge** carves at the joints whereas charge does not.

The simplest worry is that I would be forced to admit that (B), or something like it, is *true*. But there is just no reason to admit this. '**Charge**' has no more explanatory value than 'charge' in fundamental physics, for example.

The worrier will regroup: "I see that you needn't admit that (B) is in fact true, but you do need to admit that (B) is an epistemically open possibility (just as you admit as open the possibility that conjunction but not disjunction carves at the joints)." But do I need to admit this? It would be natural to say that (B) is the same sentence as the logically contradictory sentence 'Charge carves at the joints whereas charge does not', and therefore is not an open possibility.

The worry may be put in a slightly different way. The epistemology proposed in section 2.3 instructs us to search for the most explanatory pair $\langle I, T_I \rangle$ of ideology I, and theory T_I in terms of I. A natural concern is that there will be no unique most explanatory pair. My response to the concern is that when pairs are tied, we should be agnostic which pair is correct (i.e., which is the pair of the joint-carving ideology and true theory in that ideology). But—so the worry goes—this will lead to misplaced agnosticism if a new ideology-theory pair can be produced by changing to Spanish, red ink, or boldface. The answer to the worry is that these changes needn't produce new pairs. In a properly developed version of this epistemology, the ideology-theory pairs must be formulated in some language, and the sentences of this language will not be individuated so finely as by language family, font, or ink color.

"Your response to the worry appeals to sentential identity; but that is not a fundamental notion." Agreed; but what is the problem? The worry I am facing is that I must admit that (B) is an open possibility. The crucial notions in this worry are epistemic, and epistemic notions are not fundamental. And it is quite natural to think that the nonfundamental matter of how we ought to form beliefs is intimately tied up with the nonfundamental matter of sentential identity (or propositional identity, if one wanted to put it less linguistically).

"What constrains the individuation of sentences?" There is no once-and-for-all answer. We introduce different notions of sentence—with different associated identity conditions—for different theoretical purposes. For the purpose of formulating an epistemology, the sentences must be fine-grained enough to draw

---

[8]Fine also faces the worry; can we ask whether: in reality, some things are charged, but it's not the case that in reality, some things are **charged**?

the epistemically relevant distinctions, but no finer. Distinctions based on language family, font, or ink color are epistemically irrelevant; thus the language for epistemology will identify sentences differing solely in those respects.

"Why are these differences epistemically irrelevant?" A precise answer would require a general theory that I do not have about the nature of epistemic facts; but I can say that the reason is externalist. There are in fact no joints in nature corresponding to language family, font, or ink color. More generally, language family, font, and ink color belong to a larger, reasonably unified class of features, *none* of which correspond to joints in nature. There are no joints of nature corresponding to font size, font shape, font weight, writing versus speaking, volume, timbre, pace, accent, . . . Given the lack of such joints in nature (and given the not unrelated fact that none of these features affects truth-conditional content), there is no point to a conception of epistemic value that makes distinctions based on factors like these. If boldface marked a joint in nature, then we would need to individuate sentences on the basis of font weight; but it doesn't.

"You appeal to facts about sentence-identity to dismiss questions of joint-carving for language family, font, and ink color; but couldn't one do the same for the hard questions about logic?" I don't *dismiss* questions about joint-carving for language family, font, and ink color. The identification of (B) with a logically contradictory sentence was based on a substantive metaphysical claim (albeit an obvious one): that there are no joints corresponding to "representationally inert" features like font weight. (Given this substantive claim, I said, a sensible conception of sentence-identity for epistemology abstracts away from differences in such features.) In the case of logic, by contrast, it's plausible to think that there *are* joints in nature.

10.3 Nonfundamental metalogic

Let us turn from logical to metalogical concepts. Consider first the concept of a logical constant. The question of what counts as a logical constant is tied up with the question of the scope of logic. Both the inference from $P \wedge Q$ to P, and the inference from 'a is a bachelor' to 'a is male', are truth-preserving, and necessarily so (in any reasonable sense of 'necessary'). But we typically count only the first inference as being logical. The first inference holds in virtue of distinctive features of $\wedge$, the second in virtue of distinctive features of 'bachelor', and we typically think of $\wedge$, not 'bachelor', as a logical constant.

This distinction between logical constants and other expressions: is it fundamental? Is there a corresponding joint in nature? If so, then questions about which expressions are logical constants—or, alternatively, questions about the scope of logic—are substantive; and in cases where our concept of a logical constant—or of inferences that are logical—yields no determinate verdict, there might still be a fact of the matter. But surely there is no such joint in nature; the concept of a logical constant is not required in our most fundamental theories. Some say that logical constants are those expressions that are defined by their proof-theoretic roles, others that they are the expressions whose semantic values are permutation-invariant, and still others that they are the topic-neutral expressions.[9] Given that 'logical constant' does not carve at the joints, these proposals should be regarded as conceptual analyses (or perhaps Carnapian explications) of our conception of the scope of logic.[10] If our conception is determinate enough so that one proposal uniquely fits it, then there will be a fact of the matter that that proposal is correct (though the fact might not be substantive). But if our conception is indeterminate, there may be no fact of the matter which proposal is correct.

Consider, next, the notion of logical consequence. Here, too, there is a question of whether we have a joint in nature, and there are closely related questions about substantivity, objectivity, and determinacy.

How are claims of objectivity (substantivity, determinacy) regarding logical consequence related to claims of objectivity regarding the scope of logic? One might uphold a kind of objectivity for the former but not the latter: one might think that 'logical constant' does not carve at the joints, but that the relational predicate 'is a consequence in virtue of the meanings of expressions $e_1 \ldots$', for variable $e_1 \ldots$, *does* carve at the joints. According to this view, even if there is no objective fact as to whether '=' is a logical constant, there is nevertheless an objective fact as to whether '$x = y$' and '$y = z$' imply, in virtue of the meaning of '=', '$x = z$'. But in the other direction, if 'is a logical consequence of' (simpliciter) carves at the joints, so that questions about logical consequence are objective, then one could define a logical constant as an expression that figures essentially in some logical implications, in which case questions about the scope of logic would be objective (even if 'logical constant' didn't carve at the joints).

As with the concept of a logical constant, there is reason to doubt that logical truth or logical consequence carve at the joints. Surely these notions do not improve our *fundamental* understanding of the world.[11]

If logical truth and logical consequence are not metaphysically basic, then they must be metaphysically reduced in some way. I don't have any distinctive view to advocate here, but I would like, in a speculative spirit, to think a bit about whether my extended version of the Ramsey/Lewis "best-system" account from section 3.1 could be taken as a theory of logical truth.

According to that account, laws are members[12] of the system that best balances simplicity and strength, where "balancing" can be taken in different ways

---

[9] See MacFarlane (2005) for a survey.

[10] This seems to be how the proposals are generally viewed; see Etchemendy (1990, introduction).

[11] Field's (1980; 1989) nominalist account of fundamental physics makes use of a primitive notion of logical consequence. But this notion plays no role in Field's official nominalist versions of fundamental physical theories. It comes into play only in his account of why it's legitimate to use mathematics within physics.

[12] Lewis restricts 'law' to the members that are regularities—universal generalizations. I don't quite see the point; but anyway it's inappropriate in the case of logic: logical truths like 'If snow is white then

depending on how much complexity is taken to "cost". The more it costs, the more restrictive our account of laws becomes. If complexity is cheap, then special-science generalizations count as laws; if it has middling cost then they do not but generalizations of physics still do; and if complexity is made expensive then even the laws of physics drop away, and all that remain are "laws of logic".[13]

For Lewis, a "system" is a set of true sentences that is closed under some relation of implication. That relation can't here be logical consequence, on pain of circularity. Nor can I take it to be modally strict implication, again on pain of circularity, since I will define necessity in terms of logical consequence in chapter 12. Instead, let it be deducibility in an axiomatic system whose logical axioms and rules of inference are part of what we're choosing when we're choosing the best system. That is: let a system now be understood as a set of true sentences, any set of true sentences. (As for Lewis, the language must be constrained; it must contain only joint-carving expressions, only now this is construed more expansively; all expressions—including quantifiers and sentential connectives—must carve at the joints, not just the predicates.) One system is simpler than another depending on how simply it may be axiomatized. (Like Lewis, I won't try to say what makes an axiomatization simple.) An axiomatization of a set, S, is a pair $\langle A, R \rangle$, where i) A, the set of "axioms", is any subset of S; ii) R, the set of "rules", is a set of 2 or more place relations on S; and iii) S is the closure of A under R; i.e., S is the smallest superset of A such that for any $n + 1$-place $r \in R$ and any $s_1 \ldots s_n \in S$ and any sentence s, if $r(s_1 \ldots s_n, s)$ then $s \in S$. Given these definitions, the best-system account doesn't rely on an antecedently understood notion of implication.

Nor does it rely on an antecedent division of terms into logical and nonlogical. When evaluating a given set for simplicity, we simply look for the simplest axioms and rules that generate the set. The thought is that in a competition for the simplest axiomatizations, logical terms will be bound to figure in the axioms, because of their pervasiveness and topic neutrality. Indeed, we might define the logical terms as those terms that figure in the axioms.[14]

The question, then, is whether the laws of logic, thus understood, could be thought of as the logical truths. How close is this notion of a law of logic to the ordinary notion of logical truth? If the language in question is first-order, the notions might well coincide. For, one could argue, standard axioms and rules for first-order logic are bound to emerge in the competition as the axioms and rules in one of the simplest axiomatizations of the winning system. This system must be exceedingly simple, remember; increasing strength by adding extra-logical

---

snow is white' aren't regularities. (Though if the language in question has propositional quantification, then it can state regularities like 'For all p, if p then p.')

[13] Objection: a system that includes only laws of logic has *zero* strength. Reply: logical truths do have content; they concern the world's most general and abstract aspects.

[14] Given the vagueness in the account (e.g., in terms like 'balance'), there might be vagueness in which terms count as logical. If mereological terms carve at the joints, for example, it might be vague whether they count as logical.

information will require too much complexity. Since these axioms and rules are sound and complete, the laws of logic will be exactly the logical truths.

(A potential problem for this argument is that some axiomatizations of the first-order logical truths have infinitely many axioms. But how can systems that require infinitely many axioms be simple? Relatedly, suppose one of the axiom schemas is "If ϕ then ϕ." Then for each sentence ϕ in the language, there will be a corresponding axiom. 'If grass is green then grass is green', 'If something is grue then something is grue', and so on, will all be axioms. Thus each notion that can be expressed in the language—grass, green, grue, and so on—will be involved in some axiom. How then can the axiomatization be simple? An answer might be that even if the axioms are infinite in number, and involve many different notions (many of which fail to carve at the joints), each axiom falls under one of a small number of simple axiom schemas; and the schemas involve only logical notions. But notice that this turns the simplicity of the axiomatization into a fact that's "external" to the language in question; it depends on facts that cannot be in general articulated from within the language.)

Logical lawhood will not coincide with logical truth, as usually understood, if the language includes more expressive resources, such as second-order variables and quantifiers. For since there are no sound and complete axiom systems for second-order logic, the best systems will not include all the semantically valid second-order sentences. This is a clash with typical usage, since such sentences are usually taken to be logical truths. (I doubt, however, that the second-order quantifiers carve at the joints; so I doubt that this mismatch is a problem when it comes to fundamental languages.)

Also, it's telling that the best-system account of the metaphysics of logical truth doesn't seem be what inspires formal work on metalogic, in particular on model theory. The model-theoretic definition of logical truth in formal languages as truth-in-all-models seems to be inspired, rather, by the vague conception of logical truth as truth "in virtue of" the meanings of logical constants.[15] Further, this vague conception seems to be our ordinary conception of logical truth. It's doubtful, then, that the best-systems account captures our ordinary concept, or the logician's concept, of logical truth.

10.4 Logical pluralism

JC Beall and Greg Restall (2006) defend "logical pluralism", the claim that there is no single correct notion of logical consequence. Classical consequence, intuitionistic consequence, relevant consequence, and other such competitors are all on a par. According to Beall and Restall, there is no sensible question as to whether the argument "P; $\sim P$; therefore, Q" is *really* valid. It's classically and intuitionistically

---

[15] We can think of truth in virtue of the meanings of the logical constants as truth that remains no matter how everything else is varied, and truth-in-all-models as a way of formalizing the intuitive notion of truth-no-matter-how-everything-else-is-varied. Thanks to Agustín Rayo.

valid, but not relevantly valid, and that's all that can be said. This meshes with the previous section's claim that metalogical notions do not carve at the joints. But various theses in the vicinity should be distinguished.

First, one might be a pluralist about logical consequence simply because one is a pluralist about the notion of a logical constant. Suppose i) logical consequences are defined as consequences in virtue of the meanings of the logical constants; ii) pluralism about the notion of a logical constant is true; but iii) *antipluralism* about the notion of a "consequence in virtue of the meanings of expressions $e_1 \ldots$" is true. This would result in a sort of pluralism about logical consequence. But it would not be Beall and Restall's pluralism, since they would continue to uphold pluralism even after the logical constants have been fixed (by convention, say).

Second, one might be a pluralist only at the level of the family of logical consequence, so to speak, rather than at the level of its genera. One might, for example, be an antipluralist about both provability and semantic consequence, but hold that provability and semantic consequence are equally good notions of logical consequence. Again, this isn't Beall and Restall's pluralism. The pluralism they are most concerned to defend is at the genus level: that there is no uniquely correct notion of semantic consequence.[16]

Third, and most importantly, the denial of a single "correct" notion of logical consequence might be taken either in a metaphysical sense, as the denial that any one of various candidates is metaphysically privileged (none carves at the joints better than the others), or in a conceptual sense, as the denial that any one of the candidates is conceptually privileged (none is uniquely *our* concept). Beall and Restall primarily defend the conceptual thesis. Classical, intuitionistic, and relevant consequence, they in effect argue, are all legitimate notions—perhaps useful for different purposes—and no one of them uniquely captures our concept of logical consequence. But they had better defend the metaphysical claim too, since the conceptual claim does not on its own rule out the existence of further facts about logical consequence that outstrip our conception. In a case where classical and relevant consequence (say) come apart, and our conception is silent, there may yet be an objective fact of the matter as to whether logical consequence really holds. Compare: an ethical pluralist will not stop with the claim that utilitarian and deontological conceptions both satisfy, well enough, the way we think about morality. She will also want to reject the idea that in cases where utilitarian and deontological conceptions come apart, there is a further fact of the matter as to what is really morally right to do.

Beall and Restall's pluralism, then, should be augmented with a metaphysical claim: none of the candidate notions of logical consequence carves at the joints

---

[16] At the level of family they write as antipluralists, assuming that semantic consequence is the core concept of logical consequence. But this may be just for the sake of definiteness.

better than the others.[17] Thus augmented it implies that questions about logical consequence are nonsubstantive in the sense of chapter 4—a result that seems to mesh with their picture. I suspect that this view is correct.

Even thus augmented, though, notice that their pluralism is a claim about the *metalogical* notion of logical consequence, not about logical notions like disjunction and negation. (Thus it might better be called metalogical pluralism.) It is therefore compatible with the claim that logical notions carve at the joints. But if logical notions carve at the joints, then questions stated in terms of those notions—for instance, questions of the form "ϕ or not-ϕ?"—are substantive.[18] As a result, their pluralism is not as deflationary as it might first seem—not even in the realm of metalogic, in fact.[19] For many questions about logical consequence have ramifications for purely logical questions.

Consider, for example, the law of the excluded middle, "ϕ or not-ϕ", whose instances are logical truths (i.e., logical consequences of the empty set of sentences) in classical but not intuitionistic propositional logic. If the dispute over excluded middle were *only* about whether those instances are logical truths—if, that is, all disputants accepted the instances but merely disagreed over whether they are logical truths—then Beall and Restall's pluralism would imply that the dispute is nonsubstantive. But the dispute is also about those instances themselves. Mathematical intuitionists reject classical logic in favor of intuitionistic propositional logic precisely because they do not accept certain instances of excluded middle in which neither disjunct has been proven, such as:

(*) The string "666" either does or doesn't occur at least 666 times in the decimal expansion of π.

---

[17] Side issue: Beall and Restall seem to be antipluralists about metaphysical modality. But the case against joint-carving metaphysical necessity seems at least as strong as the case against joint-carving logical consequence: metaphysical necessity seems at least as theoretically dispensable, "spooky", and epistemically intractable as logical consequence.

[18] Beall and Restall are at pains to show that their pluralism is consistent with realist metaphysics, and in this vein point out that it doesn't imply relativism about truth. The present point goes much further: their pluralism is compatible with the substantivity of logic.

[19] In another respect it is more deflationary: it generates pluralism about epistemic notions that are constitutively connected to logical consequence. Beall and Restall address this, and say two things (2006, 94–97). First, they say that everyone already admits a sort of epistemic pluralism: pluralism about what threshold of epistemic value is required for positive appraisal—for "justification", say. But consider: from an intuitionist's point of view, belief in (*) (see text) is epistemically *terrible*, no better than a guess; whereas from the point of view of a classical logician it is epistemically superlative. Beall and Restall will want to say that neither point of view is objectively mistaken, which requires pluralism about the underlying scale on which the threshold is defined, and not just pluralism about the threshold. Second, they say that epistemic value is not determined solely by logical consequence. But in cases where the only source of epistemic value would be a belief's status as a logical truth—a belief in (*), for example—their pluralism would indeed imply pluralism about epistemic value.

Since (*) contains no metalogical notions, (meta)logical pluralism allows a dispute over it to be substantive.[20] Thus (meta)logical pluralism allows this aspect of the dispute over classical logic to be substantive. Further, intuitionists who refuse to accept (*) cannot even recognize classical logical truth as *a* legitimate notion of logical truth. For under any legitimate notion of logical truth, surely one can infer ϕ from "ϕ is a logical truth".

Relatedly, certain dialetheists respond to the semantic paradoxes by asserting contradictions, sentences of the form "ϕ and not-ϕ" (Priest, 1987). Again, the dispute isn't just over the metalogical status of contradictions; it's also over the contradictions themselves. Here again we have an aspect of the dispute over classical logic that (meta)logical pluralism allows to be substantive, since the relevant notions are logical, not metalogical. Further, dialetheists who accept contradictions cannot even recognize classical consequence as *a* legitimate notion of logical consequence. For under any legitimate notion of logical consequence, surely one can infer ψ from "ψ is a logical consequence of ϕ" and ϕ; but in classical logic, all sentences are logical consequences of contradictions, which would commit the dialetheist to accepting all sentences.

10.5 Objectivity in model theory

Beall and Restall are pluralists about the genus semantic consequence, but do not question the objectivity of its species—classical semantic consequence, intuitionistic semantic consequence, and so on. Objectivity might fail even here, for a quite different reason: the vocabulary used to make statements about models might admit multiple equally good interpretations—even holding fixed what sorts of models are at issue (classical, intuitionist . . .).

For example, suppose statements about models are to be taken at face value, as quantifying over abstract entities; suppose that the quantifiers fail to carve at the joints; and suppose in particular that various equally joint-carving quantifier-meanings differ in what truth-values they assign to statements about infinite totalities of abstracta. Then there would correspond various equally joint-carving meanings for statements about what is true in all models of a given type.

Or suppose again that statements about models are to be taken at face value; but now suppose that although quantifiers carve at the joints, the set-theoretic predicate $\in$ does not. Failure of objectivity in statements about models might then result from multiple candidate meanings for $\in$.

Or suppose that there are no abstract entities, and that statements quantifying over abstracta must be reinterpreted in some nominalistic way. Objectivity might again fail, if the ideology used in the reinterpretation fails to carve at the joints. For

---

[20]In a "dispute" over a sentence, one side normally accepts the sentence while the other side accepts its negation; but not here: intuitionists do not accept the negation of (*) since the negation of the negation of (*) is a logical truth in intuitionistic logic. (Intuitionists reject double-negation-elimination in addition to excluded middle.) What the intuitionists want is to resist classical logic's demand to assert (*), not to accept its negation.

example, if the nominalist claimed that Γ semantically implies ϕ iff it's impossible for there to exist a model of Γ in which ϕ is false, then if the modal notion of possibility fails to carve at the joints, statements about semantic consequence could fail to be objective.[21] Alternatively, instead of using modal ideology in the reinterpretation, the nominalist might use higher-order quantifiers claimed to be "innocent"—not to be understood as first-order quantifiers over sets (nor for that matter as plural quantifiers over the same domain as the first-order quantifiers).[22] If the higher-order quantifiers fail to carve at the joints, then statements about models understood in the higher-order terms might fail to be objective.

Another nominalist possibility: Stephen Yablo (2000) defends the practice of quantifying over abstract entities such as models without thereby committing to the literal existence of abstracta, since one can regard such quantification as taking place within a pretense. An advocate of this approach might go further than merely defending the propriety of this practice, and offer a pretense theory of the metaphysical nature of semantic consequence: for Γ to semantically imply ϕ is for the metaphor of set theory to render pretense-worthy the following statement: "ϕ is true in every model (of some specified sort) in which every member of Γ is true." But if—as is surely the case—the relation of rendering pretense-worthy doesn't carve at the joints, facts about semantic consequence would be in danger of being nonobjective.

I say "in danger of" because the failure of 'renders pretense-worthy' to carve at the joints wouldn't, on its own, undermine objectivity. What is pretense-worthy depends on how the world really is, and the facts about how the world really is might include facts about *other* joint-carving notions that secure objectivity.[23] Suppose, for example, that an appropriate modal notion carves at the joints, so that facts about which models might have existed are objective. Facts about which models exist according to pretenses might then be objective, even if 'renders pretense-worthy' doesn't itself carve at the joints. Compare: some children are pretending that a certain phone is a bomb, and the ringing of the phone represents the explosion of the bomb. In fact, unbeknownst to the children, the phone is about to ring. It's then objectively true that "The bomb is about to go off" is true in the pretense. What's doing the heavy lifting here is the objectivity of statements about the future, not the relation of rendering-pretense-worthy. (If the future were "open", then there would be no determinate fact of the matter of whether

[21] As Stephen Yablo pointed out, similar remarks apply to related proposals that replace metaphysical with epistemic possibility.

[22] The approach I have in mind uses formal strategies from Rayo and Yablo (2001), Rayo and Uzquiano (1999), and Williamson (2003). In outline: first think of the domain of a model as containing properties, of predicate-extensions as higher-level properties and relations, and of the model itself as a still higher-level relation between linguistic items and their extensions; then reconstrue all this talk of properties and relations in terms of "innocent" higher-order quantification. The required ideology is obviously very powerful; it's hard to see why such ideological commitment would be preferable to ontological commitment to sets.

[23] Compare the related points in Yablo (2001, sections 4 and 5).

this is true in the pretense.) Similarly, if higher-order quantifiers carved at the joints, then objective higher-order facts could ground facts about truth under the pretense of set-theory, thus resulting in objective facts about consequence, even if rendering-pretense-worthy does not itself carve at the joints. So Yablo's account is consistent with objectivity in facts about consequence. But assuming, as we surely should, that 'renders pretense-worthy' does not carve at the joints, the objectivity would derive from modal or higher-order facts that are external to the pretense-theoretic account—the world would contain real facts that are nearly isomorphic to the facts that are being pretended to exist. So why not appeal directly to those real facts, and defend a modal or higher-order theory? (This is not a criticism of Yablo, since his aim is not, I think, to provide a metaphysics of logical consequence.)

Incidentally, we can now see a weakness in a popular argument against platonist conceptions of logical consequence. Yablo (2000, §IX) argues against the model-theoretic account thus:[24]

An argument's validity-status would seem to be a conceptually necessary fact about it. Surely we don't want the validity of arguments to be held hostage to a brute logical contingency like what model-like entities happen to exist!

The charge is that the model-theoretic account gives away a hostage to fortune: it makes the facts about consequence hostage to the existence of abstracta. If the world doesn't cooperate, facts about logical consequence will fail to be objective. But nominalistic metaphysical accounts also give hostages. If the world doesn't cooperate—if truth-in-pretense, modality, higher-order quantification, and so on fail to carve at the joints—then facts about consequence will fail to be objective. Even the primitivist about logical consequence is hostage to the unhappy possibility that the primitive expression 'logically implies' (or, 'it is logically necessary that') doesn't, after all, carve at the joints. The nonplatonist's hostages are ideological, not ontological, but they are hostages all the same. If we want to believe in objective facts about consequence, we must make a commitment, ideological or ontological. And the attraction of making this commitment in the platonistic, ontological, way is that it keeps our ideology simple.[25]

The fact that nominalist approaches to metalogic also give hostages is often missed. I wonder whether this is yet another wage of Quine's sin of terminology. "Ideological" commitments, far from being merely psychological, are as much commitments to metaphysics as are ontological commitments.

---

[24] See also Etchemendy (1990).

[25] There is a quite different way of taking Yablo's anti-platonist argument (perhaps hinted at by his mention of "conceptual necessity"). He might be insisting that the facts of logical consequence are somehow intrinsic to the sentences (or propositions) involved, whereas for the platonist, facts of logical consequence inherently involve further entities: models. (Compare Field's (1980, chapter 5) objection to Platonist accounts of measurement.)

10.6 Classical logic and fundamentality

Despite its brilliant success in mathematics and fundamental science, classical logic applies uneasily to natural language. The mismatch between natural language conditionals and the material conditional is well known. Ordinary language philosophers challenged even classical logic's account of 'and', 'or', and 'not'[26] (though Grice's (1975) powerful reply won the classical logician a respite). Free logicians argue that natural language names—which may be empty, like 'Sherlock Holmes'—and quantifiers are not related as they are in classical logic. More significantly, linguists have identified numerous ways in which the syntax and semantics of natural language logical words is richer than in classical logic. 'And' and 'or' have a richer function than expressing sentential conjunction and disjunction (they connect nonsentences, for example); 'not' does more than express sentential negation (Horn, 1989); natural language quantifiers are syntactically unlike classical logic's (Montague, 1973), and can bind anaphora beyond sentence boundaries (see King (2005) for an overview); and so on.

It is overwhelmingly tempting to respond to this combination of success and failure by saying that, although classical logic is an inadequate model of all the complexities of natural language, it is adequate for the simpler languages of mathematics and fundamental science. And it is also tempting to privilege the latter languages in some way. Logic is *ultimately* classical; it's just that natural languages hook up to reality in complex and indirect ways.

A great advantage of realism about structure is that it lets us succumb to this temptation. Classical logic, we can say, holds in fundamental languages. That is, in fundamental languages: i) the logical ideology includes that of classical first-order logic; and ii) the consequence relation (over the first-order fragment anyway) is classical.[27] This view is unthreatened by the mismatch between natural language and classical logic, it preserves the role of classical logic in more fundamental endeavors, and it privileges classical logic: languages whose logic is nonclassical are metaphysically second-rate.

The semantic paradoxes and the paradoxes of vagueness also challenge classical logic. Some have argued that the right response is to renounce classical logic; suppose for the sake of argument that they are right. Should we continue to uphold the tempting view, and say that the renouncement is only for nonfundamental languages? Or should we give up classical logic at the last, and adopt a nonclassical logic at the fundamental level (perhaps a logic that reduces to classical logic in special cases like mathematics and fundamental science)? I will argue for the first choice, and draw some morals about the relationship between fundamental and nonfundamental languages.

---

[26] See in particular Strawson (1952, chapter 3, section 2).

[27] Requirement ii) is not meant to imply that 'consequence' is a predicate of the fundamental language; that predicate is one of *my* language.

Suppose our language is powerful enough to speak of elementary arithmetic. Then we can speak of linguistic items by Gödel-numbering. For any sentence, A, let $\langle A \rangle$ be a name of A (i.e., of A's Gödel number; I'll suppress this from now on). Suppose further that our language includes a truth predicate, 'True', which obeys the following inference rules:[28]

Truth-introduction $S \vdash \text{True}(\langle S \rangle)$

Truth-elimination $\text{True}(\langle S \rangle) \vdash S$

Provided we accept a minimal amount of arithmetic, we can use techniques from Gödel to construct, for any formula $B(y)$, a sentence G that "says" *I am B*, in the sense that $G \vdash B(\langle G \rangle)$ and $B(\langle G \rangle) \vdash G$. Applied to the formula $\sim\text{True}(y)$, these techniques yield a sentence L such that:

(1a) $L \vdash \sim\text{True}(\langle L \rangle)$

(1b) $\sim\text{True}(\langle L \rangle) \vdash L$

L says, in effect, *I am not true*. We can now derive a contradiction using classical logic:

1. $\text{True}(\langle L \rangle)$ assume for reductio

2. L 1, Truth-elimination

3. $\sim\text{True}(\langle L \rangle)$ 2, (1a)

4. $\sim\text{True}(\langle L \rangle)$ reductio, 1-3

5. L 4, (1b)

6. $\text{True}(\langle L \rangle)$ 5, Truth-introduction. This contradicts 4.

Something has to give. There are many choices for what gives, some of which involve retaining classical logic. But there are attractive ways to block the paradox by revising classical logic.[29] These nonclassical approaches to the paradox are attractive in part because they (or some of them, at any rate) let us retain truth-introduction and truth-elimination, thus preserving the inferential role that we naïvely take the truth predicate to have. Indeed, the core inference rule underwriting our naïve use of the truth predicate is stronger:

Truth-transparency $S \vdash S'$ whenever S and S' differ only in that one of them contains one or more occurrences of some sentence A where the other contains $\text{True}(\langle A \rangle)$.

One of the main purposes of having a truth predicate in natural language is to give access to the content of what someone said, when one cannot reproduce her words (whether because one has forgotten exactly what she said, or because one

---

[28] I'll be a bit loose in my use of the $\vdash$ symbol. $A_1 \ldots A_n \vdash B$ means that sentences $A_1 \ldots A_n$, perhaps with a background mathematical theory we accept, logically imply sentence B. The "logic" may include the logic of the truth-predicate, and the underlying propositional logic in question will vary from context to context. Here at the outset the assumed propositional logic is classical; later it won't be. I'll sometimes explicitly indicate the underlying propositional logic with a subscript on $\vdash$.

[29] See Field (2008) for a survey.

is making a general statement that is supposed to hold good regardless of what she said).[30] We need truth-transparency to move from the premise "Everything Jones said is true" to such conclusions as "If Jones said 'snow is white' then snow is white", "If Jones said 'grass is green' then grass is green", and so on. So securing truth-transparency is a high priority.

One very simple nonclassical account of the liar runs as follows. We claim that the correct propositional logic is the nonclassical logic K_3—the logic generated by Kleene's (strong) three-valued tables:

$\sim$	
1	0
0	1
#	#

$\wedge$	1	0	#
1	1	0	#
0	0	0	0
#	#	0	#

$\vee$	1	0	#
1	1	1	1
0	1	0	#
#	1	#	#

An argument is K_3-valid iff its conclusion gets value 1 whenever its premises get value 1, as evaluated under the Kleene tables, for every assignment of values drawn from $\{1,0,\#\}$ to its atomic sentences. The adoption of K_3 blocks the argument given above from (1a) and (1b) to contradiction, since it invalidates[31] *reductio ad absurdum* ("if $A \vdash B \wedge \sim B$ then $\vdash \sim A$"), which was used in that argument. More generally: suppose we begin with a first-order theory, T, which includes enough arithmetic to do syntax, but which does not include a truth predicate. Kripke's (1975) paper on truth shows how to construct, for any initial classical (two-valued) model, M_0, of T, a three-valued model M for the language of T plus a one-place predicate 'True', in which:

- propositional connectives are valuated using the Kleene tables; quantifiers are valuated in the obvious analogous way;[32]

- nonlogical expressions in the original language have the same denotations (extensions, etc.) in M as in M_0;

- sentences not containing 'True' get the same values in M and M_0;

- each sentence S gets the same value in M as does $True(\langle S \rangle)$. Thus, Truth-transparency—and so Truth-introduction and Truth-elimination as well—are validated in M (each preserves value 1).

So if we begin with a consistent theory (in the classical model-theoretic sense), there is a way to add a truth predicate obeying Truth-transparency to obtain a consistent (in the K_3 model-theoretic sense) extension of that theory.

The K_3 solution to the liar paradox is imperfect. Most notably, K_3 contains no reasonable conditional: one cannot define a conditional $\rightarrow$ using $\wedge, \vee, \sim$ such

---

[30]See Horwich (1990).

[31]For example, $p \wedge \sim p \vdash_{K_3} p \wedge \sim p$, but $\nvdash_{K_3} \sim(p \wedge \sim p)$ since $\sim(p \wedge \sim p)$ is # when p is #.

[32]e.g. $\exists v A$ gets value 1 if A gets value 1 under some assignment to v, value 0 if A gets value 0 under all assignments to v, and gets value # otherwise.

that $\vdash_{K_3} A{\to}A$.[33] There are ways to add a reasonable conditional to K_3, but they add complexity that isn't relevant here.[34] So let's stick to the K_3 solution as our working example of a nonclassical solution to the liar paradox.

Classical logic is also threatened by vagueness. The sentence:

(J) Jones is bald $\vee \sim$ Jones is bald

is a classical logical truth, but seems inappropriate to accept if Jones is a "borderline case" of baldness. Anyone who accepted that Jones is either bald or not bald could reasonably, it would seem, wonder which it is—is Jones bald, or is he not bald? Since such wondering seems *in*appropriate, acceptance of (J) seems illegitimate.[35]

There are various proposals for how to modify classical logic to deal with vagueness. One of them is simply to move to K_3. Since the law of the excluded middle does not hold in K_3, the defender of K_3 need not accept (J). As mentioned earlier, the K_3 solution has warts (most notably the absence of a decent conditional), but again, it will do as an example of a nonclassical solution.

Whether or not the K_3 solution to the paradoxes is really correct, we can ask what it would show about fundamental reality if it were correct. What do nonclassical approaches to paradox teach us about reality's fundamental logical structure?

Nothing, one wants to answer. In our most secure and successful domains of inquiry, fundamental science and mathematics, classical logic works like a charm. "Works" understates it: classical logic is an integral part of our theories in those domains. So the view that reality's *fundamental* logical structure is classical, and that classical logic breaks down only in nonfundamental languages, is initially compelling.

The opposing view would be that logical reality is fundamentally nonclassical, but that the classical laws hold within certain restricted domains, for example within fundamental science and mathematics. The restricted success of classical logic might be compared to the approximate success of classical physics in macroscopic domains.

But the comparison is imperfect. It's attractive generally to keep fundamental theories simple. That's why it's attractive to keep logic classical, at the most fundamental level. But keeping fundamental *physics* simple, by retaining (say) Newtonian physics, is simply not an option. The asymmetry between the two cases is this: in physics, the simple theory breaks down at the fundamental level, though it holds (at least approximately) for certain less fundamental domains, whereas in logic, the simple theory looks good at the fundamental level, and only apparently breaks down in nonfundamental domains.

---

[33] It's easy to see that for *no* sentence B is $\vdash B$, since whenever every atomic sentence is #, so is every complex sentence.

[34] Field (2003; 2008) adds a conditional to K_3 and uses the resulting logic to give a solution to the semantic and vagueness paradoxes.

[35] See Field (2008, pp. 152–3). The sorites paradox also challenges classical logic.

So it would be nice to keep logic fundamentally classical, to say that classical logic holds in fundamental languages. And we can say this even while embracing the K_3 solution to the paradoxes if we say that the paradoxes arises only in non-fundamental languages. Fundamental languages lack the features that threaten paradox: there is no vagueness at the fundamental level (section 7.12), and truth-theoretic ideology is not fundamental.[36] These are substantive claims of metaphysics: vagueness and truth are nonfundamental.

Adopting this strategy, however, requires saying some striking things about the relationship between fundamental and nonfundamental languages. In the terminology of section 7.4, it requires a distinctive form of metaphysical semantics. The remainder of this section will explore this issue.

Let $\mathscr{L}$ be a nonfundamental language in which we wish to make the K_3 response to the liar and vagueness paradoxes. Assume that the form of metaphysical semantics for $\mathscr{L}$ is truth-conditional (rather than expressivist, say). Let $\mathscr{F}$ be a fundamental language in which metaphysical truth-conditions for $\mathscr{L}$ are given. Assume that $\mathscr{F}$ contains the notions of classical first-order predicate logic; and assume further that we can identify in $\mathscr{L}$ analogs of $\mathscr{F}$'s logical constants—connectives whose inferential roles in $\mathscr{L}$ are analogous to the roles of their fundamental counterparts in $\mathscr{F}$. (When necessary, we will write $\mathscr{F}$'s logical constants in boldface to distinguish them.) Let μ be the function that maps sentences of $\mathscr{L}$ to their metaphysical truth-conditions in $\mathscr{F}$. Assume that we have a truth predicate for $\mathscr{F}$: 'true in $\mathscr{F}$'. ($\mathscr{F}$ does not itself contain a truth predicate, but *we* can introduce a truth predicate for it.) Assume that this truth predicate behaves normally with respect to the connectives—that, for example, a disjunction is true in $\mathscr{F}$ iff one of its disjuncts is true in $\mathscr{F}$. (Given the lack of vagueness or semantic vocabulary in $\mathscr{F}$, there is no reason to doubt this.) And assume, finally, the following connection between metaphysical truth-conditions and acceptance: if $\mu(A)$ is true in $\mathscr{F}$, then A is to be accepted in $\mathscr{L}$. I intend "to be accepted" in an objective sense; whether a sentence is to be accepted does not depend on what evidence one has.

Question: what form must the metaphysical truth-conditions for $\mathscr{L}$ take? In particular, how will those truth-conditions treat the logical constants of $\mathscr{L}$?

The first thing to note is that those metaphysical truth-conditions cannot be "logical form preserving", in that for any formulas A, B, and variable x of $\mathscr{L}$, $\mu(\sim A) = \sim \mu(A)$, $\mu(A \vee B) = \mu(A) \vee \mu(B)$, $\mu(\exists x A) = \exists x \mu(A)$, and so on. Given logical form preservation, the metaphysical truth-condition of sentence (J) would have the form $A \vee \sim A$. Given classical logic in $\mathscr{F}$, the latter is true in $\mathscr{F}$. Thus (J)

---

[36]There are other paradox-threatening features, such as property- and set-theoretic quantification and ideology. The friend of fundamental classical logic can either reject a given feature at the fundamental level, or else accept it but adopt some classical resolution of the corresponding paradoxes. (My own choice is rejection for property-theory and a classical approach—ZF, say—to fundamental set theory.)

is to be accepted in $\mathscr{L}$. But the defender of the K_3 approach to vagueness instructs speakers of $\mathscr{L}$ not to accept (J).

Logical form-preserving metaphysical truth-conditions were in jeopardy anyway. For as we saw in section 7.7, given a very minimal fundamental ontology, the metaphysical truth-conditions for existential sentences might not be existential in form. But in fact, the K_3 approach to the paradoxes rules out even negation-preserving metaphysical truth-conditions—truth-conditions under which $\mu(\sim A) = \sim \mu(A)$, for all A. The reason is that for certain sentences, the approach requires us to *reject* both those sentences and their negations.

Return to the K_3 account of vagueness. According to that account, we must not accept (J). But nor may we accept (J)'s negation:

($\sim$J) $\sim$(Jones is bald $\vee \sim$ Jones is bald)

If we did accept ($\sim$J), we would have to accept B, for every sentence B. For $\sim(A \vee B) \vdash \sim A$ and $\sim(A \vee B) \vdash \sim B$ are both K_3 valid, as is *ex falso*: $A, \sim A \vdash B$. The situation with the liar is similar: we must accept neither L nor $\sim L$. For if we accepted L we could reason to arbitrary B thus:[37]

1. L by hypothesis
2. $\sim$True($\langle L \rangle$)   1, (1a)
3. True($\langle L \rangle$)   1, Truth-introduction
4. B 2, 3, *ex falso*

and likewise from $\sim L$:

1. $\sim L$ by hypothesis
2. $\sim$True($\langle L \rangle$)   1, Truth transparency
3. L 2, (1b)
4. B 1, 3, *ex falso*

So the K_3 solution to the paradoxes requires that for certain sentences we accept neither them nor their negations. But it calls for something more. When we are ignorant of a sentence's truth-value, we also accept neither that sentence nor its negation. I do not accept 'There are an even number of trees in North America', nor do I accept its negation. But I in no sense *repudiate* this sentence, whereas some sort of repudiation of $L, \sim L$, (J), and its negation seems to be called for. For as we saw, acceptance of $L, \sim L$, or (J)'s negation would require accepting every sentence; and accepting (J) would require being in a state of ignorance that seems inappropriate. The requisite sort of repudiation, stronger than mere failure of acceptance but weaker than accepting the negation, is often called *rejection*. Rejecting A is not merely failing to accept A, but does not require accepting $\sim A$.

---

[37] The arguments for the inferences (1a) and (1b) go through provided classical logic may be assumed for the purely mathematical part of the language.

The K_3 resolution of the paradoxes, then, instructs speakers of $\mathcal{L}$ to reject both B and $\sim B$, for various B. But given negation preservation, the metaphysical truth-conditions of B and $\sim B$ are $\mu(B)$ and $\sim\mu(B)$, respectively. Given classical logic in $\mathcal{F}$, $\mu(B) \vee \sim\mu(B)$ is true in $\mathcal{F}$, and so either $\mu(B)$ or $\sim\mu(B)$ is true in $\mathcal{F}$, and so either B or $\sim B$ is to be accepted in $\mathcal{L}$. Since no sentence is to be both accepted and rejected, the K_3 resolution is incompatible with negation preservation.

So the K_3 solution to the paradoxes rules out negation-preserving metaphysical truth-conditions. But what then will metaphysical truth-conditions for negations look like? Here is a natural picture. Suppose some three-valued model M, as described in the discussion of Kripke above, can be regarded as an intended model for the language $\mathcal{L}$. Suppose further that $\mathcal{F}$ can speak of model theory. A metaphysical semantics might then assign to each sentence, A, of $\mathcal{L}$ the metaphysical truth-condition "Sentence A has value 1 in model M." Notice that the metaphysical truth-condition for $\sim A$, namely "Sentence $\sim A$ has value 1 in model M", is not the negation of the metaphysical truth-condition for A. Indeed, both truth-conditions can fail to be true in $\mathcal{F}$, since M is three-valued. Both the liar sentence L and its negation, for example, will have value # in M, and so neither has a true-in-$\mathcal{F}$ metaphysical truth-condition. It is natural to pair this metaphysical semantics with the principle that a sentence whose metaphysical truth-condition is not true in $\mathcal{F}$ is to be rejected. Thus both the liar sentence and its negation are to be rejected.

(It is crucial to distinguish "has a true metaphysical truth-condition" from $\mathcal{L}$'s truth predicate 'True'. L does not have a true metaphysical truth-condition since it has value # in M; but we must not accept $\sim\text{True}(\langle L \rangle)$ because doing so would lead to contradiction—to L by (1b), and so to $\text{True}(\langle L \rangle)$ by Truth-introduction.[38])

So: one can combine classical logic at the fundamental level with nonclassical resolutions of the paradoxes, but at a price. In the nonfundamental languages in which the paradoxes are nonclassically resolved, negation doesn't mean fundamental negation.

One final point. I have been speaking of metaphysical truth-conditions, but have not specified in which language this occurs. If it occurs in $\mathcal{L}$ itself—as well it might; $\mathcal{L}$ is supposed to model our own language, after all—then a problem arises, as Hartry Field pointed out to me. (The problem would also arise on approaches to the liar other than the K_3 approach.) A liar argument may be formulated in $\mathcal{L}$ using the predicate 'has a true metaphysical truth-condition'.

Let Cxy mean in $\mathcal{L}$ that x is a metaphysical truth-condition for y, and make the following assumptions. 1: $\mathcal{L}$ has no nonfactual sentences, so that completeness (section 7.5) implies that every sentence of $\mathcal{L}$ has a metaphysical truth-condition. 2: The vocabulary of $\mathcal{F}$ is contained in $\mathcal{L}$; thus metaphysical truth-conditions can

---

[38]In essence, having-a-true-metaphysical-truth-condition is the non-disquotational, "external", notion of having value 1 in Kripke's minimal fixed point, whereas the K_3 solution to the liar identifies truth with what is expressed by 'True'—the "internal", disquotational notion. See Field (2008, section 3.4).

actually be expressed in $\mathscr{L}$. Thus for any sentence A in $\mathscr{L}$, there is a sentence A_0 in $\mathscr{L}$ such that $C\langle A_0\rangle\langle A\rangle$ is true in $\mathscr{L}$. 3: Metaphysical truth-conditions are unique; for simplicity, construe this as allowing the following inference: $Czy,\sim\phi(z)\vdash \sim\exists x(Cxy\wedge\phi(x))$. 4: $C\langle A_0\rangle\langle A\rangle, A_0\vdash A$ (recall the claim above that a sentence in $\mathscr{L}$ with a true metaphysical truth-condition is to be accepted). Let $\tau(y)$ abbreviate $\exists x(Cxy\wedge\mathrm{True}(x))$. Gödel's techniques applied to the formula $\sim\tau(y)$ yield a "metaphysical liar sentence" M, which says that its metaphysical truth-condition is not true; that is: i) $M\vdash\sim\tau(\langle M\rangle)$; and ii) $\sim\tau(\langle M\rangle)\vdash M$. By assumption 2, M has a metaphysical truth-condition M_0; thus $C\langle M_0\rangle\langle M\rangle$. M_0 is a sentence of $\mathscr{F}$, so presumably this instance of excluded middle holds: $M_0\vee\sim M_0$. We can then reason by cases to M: from the left by assumption 4, and from the right as follows: suppose $\sim M_0$; then $\sim\mathrm{True}(\langle M_0\rangle)$ by Truth-transparency; so $\sim\tau(\langle M\rangle)$ by uniqueness; so M by ii). Then from M we can conclude $\sim\tau(\langle M\rangle)$ by i); and so $\sim\mathrm{True}(M_0)$ by K_3-predicate-logic,[39] and so $\sim M_0$ by Truth-transparency. So for the sentence M, we can prove both it and the negation of its metaphysical truth-condition!

My tentative reply: the notion of a metaphysical truth-condition is a theoretical one, introduced for a certain theoretical purpose. Thus certain approaches to the paradoxes are more attractive when applied to the paradoxes of metaphysical truth-conditions than to the paradoxes of truth itself, construed as an ordinary, intuitive notion.[40] For example, the situation with M and M_0 might simply be accepted. A metaphysical semantics is supposed to be an explanatory theory of a certain sort; and for languages like $\mathscr{L}$, perhaps the most explanatory theory involves a notion of metaphysical truth-condition that has certain anomalous cases. The fact that "having a true metaphysical truth-condition" does not behave exactly like the ordinary notion of *truth* would not, according to this perspective, count against the explanatory worth of the theory. Alternatively, a Tarskian hierarchical approach to metaphysical truth-conditions could be taken. On this approach, no language can speak of metaphysical truth-conditions for its own sentences (and so we cannot accept an unrestricted thesis of completeness). The usual objection to the Tarskian approach stresses how we apply the ordinary notion of truth without regard to Tarskian level, and thus is no objection to a Tarskian approach to the theoretical concept of metaphysical truth-conditions.

---

[39]See Field (2008, chapter 3, Appendix) for the inference rules.
[40]Compare those who distinguish between correspondence and disquotational truth.

11   Time

A cloud of suspicion hangs over the philosophy of time. Although the pictures are vivid—the static manifold, the growing block, the policeman's bullseye—many doubt that coherent positions and genuine contrasts lie behind them.

I think, however, that the traditional questions about time are good ones. Let us view them through the prism of realism about structure.

11.1   Presentism

Our focus will be "A-theories" of time, theories according to which "time passes". Let us begin with (Priorian[1]) presentism.

What defenders of time's passage share is opposition to the spatializing philosophy of time familiar from Quine, Russell, Smart, and many others.[2] The central question in the philosophy of time is: How alike are time and space? Russell, Quine, and Smart answer: Very alike indeed. Reality consists of a four-dimensional "block universe"; time is "just another dimension"; past, present, and future all have the same "status"; change is dissimilarity between earlier and later parts of the block universe; and so on.

A-theorists complain that this grants no special status to the present, and that it does not admit genuine change since reality as a whole, on this picture—the block universe—does not change. And presentists—a subgroup of the A-theorists—complain in addition that it grants too much reality to the past and future.

The presentist's rival conception is that *only the present is real*: the truth is from the perspective of the present moment. Part of this conception is ontic: if an object does not exist now, then it does not exist simpliciter. For the presentist, there simply are no such things as dinosaurs or human colonies on Mars (though there were and perhaps will be such things). In contrast, dinosaurs, computers, and perhaps colonies on Mars are all equally real in the spatializer's block universe. The pastness of dinosaurs and futurity of colonies on Mars is locational, not ontic: the dinosaurs are located before us—before the portion of the block universe that *we* occupy—and the human colonies are located after us; in this way dinosaurs and colonies on Mars are analogous to spatially distant objects. The presentist's conception also has a qualitative part: if an object does not have a feature now, then it does not have the feature simpliciter. Since I am not in pain now, I am not in pain simpliciter (though I was once in pain and will again be in pain). In

---

[1]Arthur Prior's (1967; 1968a; 1970; 1976; 1996) tense-logical approach to presentism justly dominates the market.

[2]See Quine (1960c, §36); Russell (1915); Sider (2001b, chapter 2); Smart (1963, chapter 7).

contrast, for the spatializer, my being in pain is equally real whether it's located in the past, present, or future.

Thus the presentist privileges the present, and claims to admit genuine change since presentist reality as a whole is current reality, which changes.

This all is pretty impressionistic. To get a firmer grip on what presentism amounts to, let's take a closer look at the presentist's fundamental ideology.

11.2 Presentist ideology: quantified tense logic

Tense logic is for me, if I may use the phrase, metaphysically fundamental, and not just an artificially torn-off fragment of the first-order theory of the earlier-later relation. —Arthur Prior[3]

The presentist's fundamental ideology is that of quantified tense logic, a logic that results from adding *tense operators* to predicate logic. The usual tense operators are one-place sentence operators that are to time what modal operators are to modality:[4]

operator	meaning
P	it was the case in the *past* that
F	it will be the case in the *future* that
G	it is always *going* to be the case that
H	it always *has* been the case that
S	it is *sometimes* the case that
A	it is *always* the case that
N	it is *now* the case that

(Some can be defined in terms of others: $S\phi \leftrightarrow (P\phi \vee \phi \vee F\phi)$, $F\phi \leftrightarrow {\sim}G{\sim}\phi$, etc.)

The presentist's fundamental sentences describe reality from the current perspective, so to speak, rather than from an atemporal perspective on the whole of

---

[3] Prior and Fine (1977, p. 32).

[4] The usual tense operators are insufficient; presentists also need a way to talk about temporal distances. This is often accomplished by "metrical tense operators", such as P^x: "it was the case x minutes in the past that". But taking such an operator as metaphysically primitive would involve real numbers in the ultimate metaphysics of time, and would apparently require a distinguished unit of temporal measure. The presentist might instead adapt Mundy's (1987) approach to quantities: i) replace P^x with infinitely many properties of propositions, which are properties of having been true at some particular fixed distance in the past; ii) introduce primitive relations between these properties (e.g. the relation of p_1 being *twice* p_2, meaning in effect that the temporal distance associated with p_1 is twice that of p_2); and iii) lay down assumptions about these primitive relations from which one can prove a representation theorem guaranteeing a function f (unique up to an arbitrary choice of unit) that assigns one of these properties to each real number; and finally iv) define $P^x \phi$ as meaning that the proposition that ϕ has the property $f(x)$. But this involves propositions in the ultimate metaphysics of time. A better strategy, I think, is less platonistic: replace P^x with primitive polyadic tense operators such as $C(\phi, \psi, \alpha, \beta)$ (C for *congruence*), meaning intuitively that *some* pair of cases of ϕ and ψ are separated in time by the same amount, and in the same direction, as *some* pair of cases of α and β. (Unlike the usual presentist operators, C is time-reversal symmetric.) Project: figure out how tightly the sentences containing such operators constrain their Kripke models. (The issues in Hawthorne and Sider (2002) are relevant.)

temporal reality. Thus the presentist accepts $\phi \leftrightarrow N\phi$, for all ϕ. "Jones sits", Sj, is true iff Jones now sits; "Everything is sitting", $\forall x Sx$, is true iff all current entities are currently sitting. When the presentist wishes to speak of the past, she prefixes her sentences with tense operators, as in: "It was the case that there are dinosaurs", $P\exists x Dx$. This can still be regarded as being from the current perspective since from that perspective, dinosaurs are in the past. But this is not to say that the presentist regards their pastness as a relative matter. Their pastness is absolute, since the current perspective is the only perspective. It is true simpliciter—not relative to a "perspective"—that $P\exists x Dx$.

Contrast this present-centric picture with the atemporal picture of the spatializer. The spatializer does not regard his sentence ϕ as meaning that ϕ is now the case. He regards it, rather, as a description of reality from the atemporal perspective, so to speak. Thus he accepts "There are dinosaurs", $\exists x Dx$.[5] If he wants to make a statement that is specific to the present, he will restrict quantifiers or relativize predicates. Where t_0 is the moment at which he is speaking, he might say "Nothing located at t_0 is a dinosaur", $\sim \exists x (Lxt_0 \wedge Dx)$, or "Jones sits at t_0", Sjt_0. (Notice the symmetry between Sjt_0 and Sjt_1, where t_1 is some past or future time—neither is privileged.) For the spatializer, the presentist's statement "Jones sits", Sj, without a parameter for the time, makes no sense, because from the atemporal perspective, sitting isn't something you just *do*; it's something you do *at* times. (This is what those who reject temporal parts say, anyway.[6]) For him, the pastness of dinosaurs is a relative matter: although they are located before his own perspective in time, they are simultaneous with their own perspective and are located after perspectives in the Paleozoic era; and no perspective is privileged.

Spatializers do not admit tense operators into their fundamental ideology, since they can describe temporal reality without them—by quantifying over past and future entities and predicating features of them relative to times. Spatializers may use tense operators in their *non*fundamental languages, since they can give a metaphysical semantics for the language of quantified tense logic in their tense-operator-free fundamental language. Such a semantics will, for example, count an utterance of $P\exists x Dx$ that takes place at t_0 as being true iff some dinosaur is located before t_0. Since the presentist rejects the existence of dinosaurs, she rejects this semantics. She instead regards the tense operators as metaphysically ultimate, as carving at the joints, and so as not needing a metaphysical semantics. If asked what makes $P\exists x Dx$ true, she will either refuse to answer, or shrug and say: Well, it's true because *there once existed a dinosaur*! We all think something like this about negation, after all. We do not believe in a realm or point or index, **u** (for "unreal"),

---

[5] I write the predicate D without a parameter for a time because I think of an entity's species as being permanent. Spatializers who deny this would regiment the atemporal "There are dinosaurs" as $\exists x \exists t Dxt$—"Something is at some time a dinosaur".

[6] See Lewis (1986*b*, 202–4); Hinchliff (1996); Merricks (1994).

such that $\sim\phi$ iff ϕ in $\mathbf{u}$.[7] We think that there is *not* an F iff, well, there is not an F. 'Not' is primitive ideology (a primitive part of the best fundamental ideology, in my view). Same for the tense operators, according to the presentist.

Presentists need their primitive tense operators. Without them, their denial of the existence of dinosaurs would land them in the looney bin along with the young-earth creationists. With them, they can stand tall and say that there were dinosaurs: $\mathsf{P}\exists x D x$.

11.3 Is the dispute over presentism substantive?

Part of the dispute between presentists and spatializers is purely ontological. Spatializers say, for example, that there are dinosaurs, $\exists x D x$, whereas presentists reject this claim.[8] Now, some suspect that there is less to this dispute than meets the eye.[9] After all, they say, everyone believes that there are dinosaurs in the sense that there *were* dinosaurs; and everyone denies that there are dinosaurs in the sense of dinosaurs located in the present; so what proposition is under dispute?

This suspicion is an instance of the sort of metaphysical deflationism considered in section 5.1. A sentence under dispute ("There are dinosaurs") is given an obviously true interpretation ("There were dinosaurs") and an obviously false interpretation ("There are dinosaurs located in the present"); these are claimed to be on a par with other interpretations; and so it is concluded that, in one way or another, the dispute is nonsubstantive. But such deflationist challenges are mistaken if the crucial terms in the dispute carve at the joints. The crucial term in the dispute over whether $\exists x D x$ is $\exists$, the existential quantifier; and I argued in chapter 9 for the thesis of ontological realism: quantifiers do indeed carve at the joints. Given this thesis, presentists and spatializers can stamp their feet and say: Our dispute is not over whether there were dinosaurs, or whether there are dinosaurs located in the present, but rather over whether *there are dinosaurs*! Since the existential quantifier carves at the joints, this latter question is a substantive one, a question about reality's fundamental structure.

[7]Just for fun: how might it go? Take $\wedge$, $\vee$, $\exists$, and $\forall$ primitive; and suppose that there are two points, r and u (real and unreal), relative to which objects have features. For instance, I am human relative to r and a dragon relative to u—that is: philosopher(Ted,r) and dragon(Ted,u). Let's recursively define the expression "$(\phi)^x$" (read: "the translation of sentence ϕ with respect to point x"), where x may be either r or u, as follows: $(\sim\phi)^r = (\phi)^u$; $(\sim\phi)^u = (\phi)^r$; $(\phi\wedge\psi)^r = (\phi)^r\wedge(\psi)^r$; $(\phi\wedge\psi)^u = (\phi)^u\vee(\psi)^u$; $(\phi\vee\psi)^r = (\phi)^r\vee(\psi)^r$; $(\phi\vee\psi)^u = (\phi)^u\wedge(\psi)^u$; $(\exists v\phi)^r = \exists v(\phi)^r$; $(\exists v\phi)^u = \forall v(\phi)^u$; $(\forall v\phi)^r = \forall v(\phi)^r$; $(\forall v\phi)^u = \exists v(\phi)^u$; $(R\alpha_1\ldots\alpha_n)^x = R\alpha_1\ldots\alpha_n x$. The theory, then, analyzes any sentence, ϕ, where ϕ may contain $\sim$ in addition to $\wedge$, $\vee$, $\exists$, and $\forall$, as $(\phi)^r$. Notice that the theory requires both $\wedge$ and $\vee$, and both $\forall$ and $\exists$, to be primitive.

[8]Is there a more general ontological claim that is the canonical locus of the dispute? One might propose "Everything is present", but a dispute over this is apt to be nonsubstantive since neither presentists nor spatializers should accept a fundamental feature of "presentness" (compare Williamson (1988)). In fact, it's unclear whether the dispute over dinosaurs is even diagnostic, since it's unclear whether Williamsonian passage (see below) is a kind of presentism.

[9]See, for example, Lombard (1999); Savitt (2004).

Someone determined to debunk the dispute over presentism could simply reject ontological realism. But might the debunker instead accept ontological realism, in some form anyway, and nevertheless maintain that the dispute over presentism is nonsubstantive?

The debunker might accept ontological realism in the sense of accepting *some* sort of fundamental quantifier, but deny that the "absolute" quantifiers assumed by the disputants carve at the joints. The dispute is allegedly over whether there are dinosaurs. But, the debunker might say, the absolute quantified claim "There are dinosaurs" makes no sense. The only intelligible claims in the vicinity are temporally relativized quantified claims, claims of the form "At time t, there are dinosaurs". But no claim of this form (it might be thought) is in serious doubt. Everyone agrees, for example, that in 2011 A.D. there are no dinosaurs, and that at certain earlier times, there are dinosaurs.

The crucial claim here is that "It makes no sense to say 'There are dinosaurs'", that all quantified statements require temporal qualifiers. What does this mean and why think that it is true?

One might argue that in natural language, one cannot make absolute claims about what there is; one must always relativize to a time. At some deep level of syntactic analysis, a temporal parameter is always required.

This claim about natural language may be true, but it is irrelevant. The question is whether quantification is metaphysically absolute (whether quantified claims in fundamental languages are absolute), not whether it is linguistically absolute (whether quantified claims in natural language are absolute). Given metaphysical absoluteness, the dispute over presentism is substantive, even given linguistic relativity, since the presentist and her opponent may simply enter the philosophy room and resume their debate using quantified claims that are stipulated to be absolute. And if quantified claims are metaphysically relative to time, then the debate will be nonsubstantive, even if such claims are linguistically absolute. For natural language quantificational claims would then be analogous to actual natural language claims about simultaneity, if spacetime is Minkowskian. The deep syntax of such claims requires no parameter for a frame of reference, but Minkowski spacetime demands such a parameter. As a result, natural language disputes over simultaneity can be nonsubstantive if the answer turns on which frame of reference one adopts. Similarly, natural language disputes over whether there are dinosaurs would be nonsubstantive when the answer turns on which temporal parameter is adopted.

So the attack on the substantivity of the dispute over presentism must be metaphysical; it must claim that in fundamental languages, quantificational claims are always relative to time.[10] Leaving out the time in a claim like 'There are dinosaurs' would be like leaving out the orientation when telling someone to turn left. Just as there is no such thing as just plain *left*, there is no such thing as

---

[10]Jackson (2010) defends such a view.

there just plain being a dinosaur. Any attempt to stipulate unrelativized fundamental quantification in the metaphysics room would fail because no joint in nature answers to the attempted stipulation. Given this metaphysics, there simply is no fundamental question of whether there are dinosaurs. The only fundamental questions are whether there are dinosaurs relative to 2011 A.D., whether there are dinosaurs relative to times in the Triassic era, and so on; and over such questions (it may be thought) there is no disagreement.

There are different ways to develop this idea, since the demand for a temporal parameter could be pinned on different sources. One idea would be that every assertive utterance somehow requires completion by a time, in order to result in a truth-evaluable content. Another idea—the one I will focus on—is that fundamental quantifiers have "slots" for times: $\exists_t$, $\forall_t$. Using a quantifier without filling in the time slot would be like saying that a certain direction is left simpliciter.

The mere fact that what there is varies *in some sense* over time does not on its own favor the relativizer, since spatializers and presentists both accept absolute quantifiers and can nevertheless account for variation. Spatializers can say that dinosaurs are located at some times but not others, and presentists can say that there were dinosaurs but now there are none: $\mathsf{P}\exists xDx \wedge \sim\!\exists xDx$. The need for temporal supplementation is not forced on us by the "data"; it must be a substantial metaphysical hypothesis.

And it's an unattractive hypothesis. The simple logical ideology of standard predicate logic—with its absolute quantifiers—systematizes discourse in diverse domains across the sciences and mathematics. Incorporating time into the quantifiers seems inappropriate in mathematics, so the relativizer needs a bare quantifier in mathematics, $\exists$, in addition to the temporally relativized $\exists_t$. His overall ideology is thus fractured. Overall ideology is further fractured by the need to quantify into the time-slot of the quantifiers. One might need to say, for example, that for some time, t, $\exists_t xDx$; but how should the outer quantifier, 'for some time', be understood? It seems forced (though barely consistent, I suppose) to regard it as the temporally relativized quantifier (relativized, say, to any chosen time t_0): $\exists_{t_0} t\,\exists_t xDx$. It likewise seems forced to regard it as the bare quantifier from mathematics: $\exists t\,\exists_t xDx$. Least forced would be to further complicate ideology by introducing a third sui generis quantifier, whose sole purpose is to quantify over times; but then the ideology's ugliness is manifest.[11]

These considerations of ideological simplicity, incidentally, favor the spatializer against the presentist. The presentist adds the tense operators to fundamental ideology in order to account for temporal variation, whereas the spatializer needs no special logical addition. (Spatializers do need temporal, or spatiotemporal, predicates over points of spacetime, but these are of a piece with the spatial predicates over space that presentists need.) Presentists will reply that the extra

---

[11]Matters would be even worse if relationalism about time is true; compare Sider (2001*b*, chapter 4, section 8).

required ontology of past and future objects, and the failure to privilege the present, are too high a price to pay for the simplification in ideology. Whether the price is worth it is a question about, in Mark Johnston's phrase, the endgame.[12]

I have argued against the relativizing ideology, but now set this aside. Even if it is correct, so that the *ontological* aspect of the dispute between presentists and their foes is nonsubstantive, another aspect remains substantive: the dispute over the correct temporal *ideology*. And the relativizer has given no reason to doubt that this dispute is substantive.

Indeed, he has himself entered into this dispute. A metaphysical theory is a theory about reality at the most fundamental level; and the very first choice-point in putting forward such a theory is that of what ideology to use. This choice determines the "shape of the facts" according to that theory. The relativizer, the presentist, and the spatializer each put forward a distinctive position on the shape of the fundamental facts since each puts forward a distinctive fundamental ideology: temporally relativized quantifiers for the relativizer; absolute quantifiers and tense operators for the presentist; absolute quantifiers and no tense operators for the spatializer.

Granted, if the relativizer is right then the *further* dispute over whether there are dinosaurs is nonsubstantive. But that's not to say that presentists and spatializers are being *irrational* or *methodologically confused* in pursuing that further dispute—they reject the relativizer's ideology, after all. Nor can they be faulted for pursuing this further "doctrinal" dispute before first settling the ideological dispute. The disputes must be addressed simultaneously since a metaphysical theory is a "package deal" of ideology plus doctrine; ideological and doctrinal choices interact.

Note also that the relativizer does not occupy the epistemic high ground, for he presumably supports his relativizing ideology by the same sort of metaphysical argumentation that presentists and spatializers use to support their theories. Granted, he can say that if his ideology is correct, then we do not face *another* hard question, that of whether presentism is correct; indeed, we avoid a choice between two alternatives, presentism and spatializing, which may *each* be regarded as unpalatable.[13] These claims may or may not prevail in the endgame. But at any rate, the fact remains that the availability of the relativizing ideology does not provide a detour around the first-order debate over presentism, for the road to this ideology leads straight through the first-order debate.

Our discussion of relativization has reprised a now-familiar theme: meta-metaphysical critiques tend to substitute one substantive dispute for another. The relativizer rejects a substantive dispute over whether there are dinosaurs; but in doing so he takes a substantive stand on fundamental temporal ideology. Moreover, doesn't his own ideology still allow substantive ontological questions

---

[12]Attributed in Armstrong (1986).
[13]See Jackson (2010).

about dinosaurs? He denies, I have been assuming, that $\exists_{2011AD}xDx$; but couldn't a rogue relativizer coherently think that for all t, $\exists_t xDx$? There are dinosaurs at all times; it's just that for all t, no$_t$ dinosaurs are located in 2011 A.D. Given the relativizer's stand on fundamental ideology, the dispute with the rogue is a substantive one.

11.4 Passage

Consider next that most infamous of doctrines, "time's passage". Presentism is one version of this doctrine, but let us now focus on its combination with the denial of presentism. Defenders of this combination accept (in some sense) the spatializer's ontology of past, present, and future objects. But the spatializer's block universe, they say, is missing a crucial element: time's "passage", "genuine change". Change, they say, isn't just variation across the spatiotemporal manifold. There is also time's "flow". The block universe is "static".[14]

At first glance anyway, this view richly deserves the ridicule heaped on it by Donald Williams—"prophets of passage" and the like—and so many others. What does it mean to say that time "flows"? Absurdity threatens on one hand, triviality on the other. The suggestion seems to be that time itself moves. Does that mean that time moves with respect to some "hyper-time"? Or merely that in one second, a time one second from now will be present?[15]

When time passes and things change, reality is temporally heterogeneous. The prophet of passage insists that this is different from heterogeneity across space. (The alleged problem with spatializing is that it collapses the two.) But what exactly is the difference? Beware of the temptation to use temporal vocabulary to get at the difference: "Space is *static*, whereas things *move* through time; things genuinely *change*." 'Static', 'move' and 'change' usually have purely temporal significance, but also have spatial senses. A stationary sine wave spatially "moves" up and down; unlike a "static" straight line, its height "changes" as one progresses from left to right. The italics bespeak conviction that the temporal senses of these words are special; but in what way?

So on the face of it, there are questions about whether time's passage is a coherent, distinctive, position. We can begin to answer them by focusing on fundamental ideology. A prophet could formulate a coherent, distinctive philosophy of time by advocating a distinctive fundamental ideology. For example, whereas the spatializer's ideology is that of standard predicate logic (including spatiotemporal predicates), the prophet might advocate the ideology of predicate tense logic. If

---

[14] I am not sure how my discussion relates to the view that Tim Maudlin (2007c) calls time's passage. Part of Maudlin's view is that time has an intrinsic direction, and directionality is not the issue here (directionality is accepted by many philosophers who self-identify as spatializers; it can be thought of as the view that there is a fundamental asymmetric temporal relation). Moreover, he disavows the rhetoric of "flow". But he says that there's more to his position than directionality, and he seems to tie time's passage to the traditional conception of genuine change.

[15] See Smart (1963, chapter 7); Williams (1951).

"time passes" just means that the tense operators carve at the joints, then the view is coherent, nontrivial, does not imply the existence of hyper-time, and sharply distinguishes temporal from spatial change: the former involves irreducibly tensed claims, whereas the latter involves the instantiation of properties in distinct parts of a spatial manifold.[16]

Thus understood, the dispute over time's passage is simply the ideological half of the dispute over presentism. Recent philosophy of time has been kinder to the dispute over presentism than to the dispute over time's passage, probably because the former has an ontological aspect as well, and ontological disputes are regarded with less suspicion than purely ideological disputes. But this attitude is misguided. Many of the most important metaphysical disputes—over, for example, whether reality is ultimately modal, causal, nomic . . .—are ideological, not ontological. So there is no reason to distrust the dispute over time's passage if it, too, is ideological.

Nevertheless, questions remain. For one thing, *why* does the prophet regard the tense operators as fundamental? Since the prophet does not follow the presentist in rejecting past and future objects, he agrees—one might think—that "It was the case that ϕ" is true *if and only if* ϕ is true before the utterance. So why not regard such biconditionals as providing a metaphysical reduction of tense operators?[17]

Moreover, there is a question of how primitivism about tense operators fits the intuitive picture of time's passage. Why does this primitivism supply a better account of "genuine change"? And how does it fit the traditional rhetoric of the prophets? Think, for example, of McTaggart's (1908) criticism of Russell's (1903, section 442) spatializing conception of change. For Russell, a poker changes from hot to cold by being hot *at* one time and cold *at* another. But, McTaggart complains, on Russell's view the *facts* don't change, since it's always the case that the poker is hot at the first time and cold at the second. How is this complaint underwritten by tense-operator-primitivism? The complaint, moreover, is extremely perplexing. If the poker is hot at one time but not at another, doesn't it follow that "the facts change"? If not, what is this notion of fact on which McTaggart rests so much weight?

To answer these questions we must delve more deeply into the mindset of the prophet of passage, and into further questions about fundamental ideology. Doing so will reveal the existence of a number of different versions of the doctrine of time's passage.

11.5 Williamson on saturation and contingency

Let's begin by shifting focus to a related topic: modality. Consider this argument by Timothy Williamson (2002) against David Lewis's (1986*b*) modal realism:

There is genuine contingency in how things are only if, once values have been assigned to all variables, the resulting proposition could still have differed in truth-value. It is not

---

[16] See Markosian (1993).

[17] See Zimmerman (2005).

contingent that Blair was Prime Minister in 2000 in @ and that he was not Prime Minister in 2000 in w. What is contingent is simply that Blair was Prime Minister in 2000. Its contingency requires it not to have a variable waiting to be assigned a world. The reply 'But contingency just is variation in truth-value with variation in the value of the world variable' betrays a failure to grasp what contingency is.

According to David Lewis's modal realism, contingency consists in differences between possible worlds, which are conceived as equally real, mutually disconnected spatiotemporal systems. Consider the common sense claim 'It is contingent that there are no talking donkeys' $(\sim\exists x(Tx\land Dx)\land\Diamond\exists x(Tx\land Dx)$.) If one interprets the quantifier as unrestricted, modal realism makes the claim false by making its first conjunct false: the modal realist holds that there really are talking donkeys, in spatiotemporal systems other than ours. For modal realism to make the claim true as uttered in the actual world, one must interpret the quantifier as implicitly restricted to the objects in a world . . . The restricted quantifier is given an implicit argument place for a world. . . Even if there are mutually disconnected spatiotemporal systems such as Lewis postulates, they are not the distinctive subject matter of modal discourse. They are simply more of what there is, about which we can ask genuinely modal questions: for instance, whether there could have been more or fewer spatiotemporal systems than there actually are.

As I read him, Williamson isn't just offering the familiar complaint that if Lewis's worlds existed, they'd be part of actuality. (Or maybe he's offering a deeper version of that complaint.) The argument's engine is a notion that I'll call *saturation*— the notion of "all variables and parameters being filled in". Williamson's idea is that the possible-worlds theory of modality is incompatible with the evident fact that saturated statements are capable of contingency. According to Williamson, the possible-worlds theory delivers contingency only for something like an open formula: 'In w, ϕ', where w is a free variable. This is said to be contingent because it is satisfied by some worlds and not others. But this formula is unsaturated. What are saturated, for the possible-worlds theorist, are statements like 'In world a, ϕ', where a is a name of a particular world. But such statements are not contingent. More fully, the argument may be interpreted thus:[18]

1. For some ϕ concerning the nonexistence of talking donkeys, ⌜It is contingent that ϕ⌝ is true.

2. ⌜It is contingent that ϕ⌝ is true only if: ϕ is true and saturated and ⌜possibly, not: ϕ⌝ is true.

3. If modal realism is true, then 'There are no talking donkeys' (unrestricted quantifier) is not true.

---

[18] A counterpart theorist (Lewis, 1968) might object to premise 4 by extending counterpart theory to claims of the form "possibly, ψ", where ψ contains a name of a possible world. Thus "Possibly, not: there are no talking donkeys in @" would be true iff some counterpart of @—some other possible world, presumably—contains talking donkeys. In reply to such a move, Williamson might shift his focus from saturation to restriction: counterpart theory cannot provide for the intuitively correct claim that it is contingent whether there *unrestrictedly* are talking donkeys (and not just whether @ contains talking donkeys). Thanks to Williamson for discussion. See Dorr (2010) for a discussion of a number of issues in this vicinity.

4. If modal realism is true, then 'Possibly, not: there are no talking donkeys in @' is not true.

5. 'There are no talking donkeys in w' (where w is a variable) is not saturated.

6. If modal realism is true, then no other ϕ concerning the nonexistence of talking donkeys is true, saturated, and such that $\ulcorner$possibly, not: $\phi\urcorner$ is true.

7. Therefore, modal realism is not true.

If modal realism doesn't deliver genuine contingency, then what would? A natural answer for Williamson would be the conjunction of "actualism" and "modalism". According to actualism, the facts are all from the perspective of the actual world. Below I will cash "facts" out as saturated statements; thus the claim is that actual-world-perspective statements like "There are no talking donkeys" are saturated. According to modalism, the modal operators carve at the joints. These operators can be used to characterize the contingency of the nonexistence of talking donkeys: "There are no talking donkeys and ◇(there are talking donkeys)."

Williamson has hit on a deep clash between modal realism and our ordinary notion of contingency. Intuitively, genuine contingency requires contingency in the *facts*, not just contingency in unsaturated fact-parts. As we'll see next, one can construe the complaint that the block universe is "static" in an analogous way.

11.6 Change and saturation

According to the spatializer, the "atemporal perspective" is fundamental. The statements from this perspective are, intuitively, changeless: 'Ted is sitting at 12:00 AM EST on 1/1/10', 'World War 2 is occurring in 1943', 'Humans learned sea travel before they learned space travel', and so on. The prophets of passage then complain that this makes reality static. I propose to understand this complaint as being analogous to Williamson's complaint about modal realism. The complaint, thus understood, is that the spatializer cannot allow for genuine change in the sense of change in saturated statements. The spatializer's saturated statements are those with "filled in temporal parameters", such as 'Ted is sitting at 12:00 AM EST on 1/1/10', and these statements do not change. Only statements that omit temporal parameters, such as 'Ted is sitting', change; but they're not saturated. So there is no genuine change in the block universe.

As a spatializer, I reject this argument. *My* metaphysical crystal ball doesn't reveal this sort of genuine change. (Nor does it reveal Williamson's genuine contingency, I have to say.) But my purpose here isn't to take sides; it's rather to dig more deeply into this notion of genuine change, and into the mindset of the prophets of passage.

If spatializing doesn't provide genuine change, then what would? The defenders of the Williamsonian argument should say: the doctrine of passage. So far I've been construing this doctrine as the claim that the tense operators are fundamental. This is analogous to modalism in the previous section. But securing genuine contingency also involved actualism, the claim that the facts are those from the perspective of the actual world—that statements lacking a parameter for a possible world, such as 'There are no talking donkeys', are nevertheless saturated and hence capable of genuine contingency. This suggests that in addition to holding that the tense operators are fundamental, the defenders of passage should embrace "temporalism", the temporal analog of actualism, according to which the facts are those from the perspective of the present moment—that statements lacking a parameter for a time, such as 'Ted is sitting' and 'World War 2 is occurring', are nevertheless saturated and hence capable of genuine change. Genuine change, on this view, amounts to the truth of tensed claims of the form $P\phi\wedge\sim\phi$, $\phi\wedge F\sim\phi$, and so on.

If we think of saturated statements as McTaggart's "facts", then this view vindicates his claim that the facts themselves change—we have our connection to the traditional rhetoric.

As we will see below, there is more than one view along these lines. But notice how much weight is being put on the notion of saturation, and related notions like that of a "perspective". Before going further we must satisfy ourselves that talk of saturation is legitimate, and that there are genuine issues about which statements are saturated.

11.7 Talk of saturation is legitimate

The spatializer and the defender of passage disagree, I have said, over which statements are saturated. Consider, for example:

(T) Ted is sitting

(T-rel) Ted is sitting at 12:00 AM EST on 1/1/10.

The defender of passage thinks that (T) is saturated (and can nevertheless change), whereas the spatializer thinks that only (T-rel) is saturated (and he supplies no notion of change for such statements). But in what sense must a spatializer think that (T) is "unsaturated", "missing a parameter"?

Is it because (T) doesn't correspond to a *fact*? Earlier I associated one sense of 'fact' with saturation in order to formulate actualism and temporalism. But my intent was to use saturation to explain that sense of 'fact'; it's doubtful that there is any notion of facthood that can be used to explain saturation. The ordinary notion of facthood cannot do the job. It does little violence to ordinary usage if we define a 'fact' as a property of times; but under this definition, (T) does correspond to a fact, namely the property of *being a time at which Ted is sitting*. Under this definition, facts obtain relative to times; fact F obtains relative to t iff t instantiates F. Of course, one could introduce a different sense of 'fact' on which obtaining is nonrelative; but the question of whether (T) is saturated had better not turn on the merely terminological question of what we mean by 'fact'. One might reply that the question isn't terminological if we take 'fact' in a joint-carving sense, but it is doubtful that there is any such sense; and anyway, the debate over passage surely doesn't require its acceptance. (I would reply similarly to the claim that (T) is unsaturated because it doesn't express a *proposition*: we could define up propositions that obtain relative to times; the existence of a joint-carving sense of 'proposition' is doubtful; and anyway the debate over passage surely doesn't turn on its existence. See also section 6.3.)

One might say instead that (T) is unsaturated because it isn't true—true simpliciter that is. Only saturated statements like (T-rel) are true. But now we have defined saturation in terms of the notion of a sentence being true simpliciter, and the latter notion seems to be in the same boat as the notion of saturation. Furthermore, deflationists about truth cannot take this line. For even spatializers must admit that one can assert sentences like (T) without specifying a time (the time is somehow "supplied by context"); and given deflationism, this requires asserting that (T) is true.

Assume that spatializers will indeed admit that (T) is true (perhaps because they accept deflationism about truth). This introduces a further problem with the notion of saturation: how do we single out an appropriately metaphysical sense of saturation? The fact that (T) is true means that it is *semantically* complete, so to speak. A spatializer might also allow that (T) is *grammatically* and *psychologically* complete: (T) is a grammatical sentence given our best syntactic theory (unlike 'loves Sally') despite the absence of a syntactic element for a temporal parameter, and one can think (T) without thinking a temporal parameter (again unlike 'loves Sally'). It's only in a *metaphysical* sense that the spatializer thinks (T) is incomplete: it is the spatializer's metaphysics of time—not psychology or syntax or semantics— that demands a temporal parameter. But what is this distinctively metaphysical notion of saturation?[19]

There are, therefore, questions about what saturation might amount to. Nevertheless, reflection on some further examples will make it intuitively clear that there is indeed a distinctively metaphysical notion of saturation. As we will see in the next section, there are difficult questions about the underlying metaphysics of saturation, but that should not lead us to doubt that some such notion is intelligible and important.

Suppose you're facing the Empire State Building from the south. To the left of the ESB is the Hudson River. Now, the fact in question is *really* that the Hudson is to the left of the ESB *relative to your orientation*. It's not to the left of the ESB *full stop*; there's no such thing as being to the left, full stop. That's not to deny that the Hudson is to the left of the ESB; it's just to say that "The Hudson is to the left of the ESB" isn't "complete" until an orientation is filled in.

According to me, God does not exist. According to Dean Zimmerman, God does exist. But that doesn't exhaust the facts in this case. There's another fact: that God doesn't exist. (Were Dean writing this paragraph, of course, the previous sentence would read differently.) When I say this, I'm not merely reporting the

---

[19]Tim Williamson pointed out that similar questions confront other attempts to formulate logical principles and schemas—such as the indiscernibility of identicals—in natural language.

claim with which this paragraph began, keeping the relativization to my beliefs implicit. The claim that God doesn't exist needs no completion concerning my beliefs. God doesn't exist, full stop.

Contrast this with the case of the Empire State Building. We don't want to say that, in addition to the relativized facts: *the Hudson is to the left of the ESB relative to this orientation*, and *the Hudson is to the right of the ESB relative to that orientation*, there is an unrelativized fact: *The Hudson is to the left of the ESB, **full stop***. There simply is no such fact. Whereas, in addition to the relativized facts *God exists according to Dean* and *God does not exist according to Ted*, there is an unrelativized fact about whether God exists, full stop.

Few would accept unrelativized facts of directions or reject an unrelativized fact about God's existence; but in other cases there is room for disagreement. In addition to facts about what is morally wrong according to various cultures, are there further facts about what is wrong, full stop? Moral realists will answer *yes*; moral relativists *no* (though they might grant that nonrelativized utterances of the form '*X* is wrong' can be true, since they attribute wrongness-in-the-speaker's culture.)

It seems clear from these examples that the notion of saturation makes sense. There is no need for a further parameter to get a truth-value out of 'God exists'; there *is* need for a further parameter with 'The Hudson is to the left of the ESB'; '*X* is wrong' may or may not need a further parameter.

Also, the need for a parameter is metaphysical, not psychological or linguistic. I don't know whether there's a syntactic or semantic or psychological demand for a parameter of orientation in 'the Hudson is to the left of the ESB'. But at any rate, think of other cases. A moral relativist needn't think that there's a linguistic or psychological need for a parameter specifying a culture in '*X* is wrong'. Given the special theory of relativity, we need to fill in a frame of reference to get a truth-value out of 'e_1 and e_2 are simultaneous', but neither the mind nor the language organ demands it.

There's something metaphysically distinctive, then, about all parameters being filled. When all parameters are filled, we can call the result a fact. And this is a metaphysical—not linguistic or psychological—notion of fact.

We can think of all this in terms of "perspective". Among all the belief-perspectives, one is distinguished (the one corresponding to someone whose beliefs are all true).[20] Concerning left–right, there is no distinguished perspective. The Hudson is to the left of the ESB with respect to one orientation, to the right of the ESB with respect to another; neither orientation (perspective) is privileged.

11.8 The metaphysics of saturation

The examples of the previous section make a compelling case that there's *some* metaphysically distinctive notion of saturation—and relatedly, *some* metaphysically

---

[20]I have in mind only beliefs about objective matters, not beliefs about, e.g., left and right.

distinctive notion of fact, and *some* metaphysically distinctive notion of the correct perspective. But the underlying metaphysics of these notions is far from clear.

Begin with a three-place relation like *between*, and start filling in its slots:

— is between — and —
a is between — and —
a is between *b* and —
a is between *b* and *c*.

The idea of saturation is that the final case differs importantly from the first three. There's something metaphysically distinctive about all of the argument places of a relation being filled in. In my terms, the distinction between the final case and all the previous cases is some sort of joint in nature. Or again, where F is a one-place predicate, R is a two-place predicate, and a and b are particulars, there is something in common between a case where something is F and a case where a bears R to b; and this something in common is *not* shared by the property F, the relation R, the property of bearing R to b, and so on. Some kind of joint in nature separates (saturated) facts, on the one hand, from (unsaturated) properties and relations on the other. But what kind of joint?

We might appeal to the existence of facts or propositions to make the distinction, but the existence of facts or propositions at the fundamental level is doubtful. And anyway, the intuitive idea requires no such reification: it is that utterances of "New York is between Washington and Boston", "The Phillies play in the National League", and "Ted is a philosopher" are to be grouped together (at a very high level of abstraction!), and are to be distinguished from "New York is between", "in the National League", "Ted", and so forth; and that this grouping is no arbitrary choice on our part, but rather reflects the world's nature.

It's initially tempting to invoke a joint-carving notion of "argument place". The idea would be that a distinguished description of the world will include a specification, for each relation, of all of its argument places. Then we could define a saturated sentence as one that specifies a value for each argument place of each relation that it concerns.[21] But this approach requires reifying relations. Worse, it apparently requires reifying *argument places*.[22] Also the approach recognizes only one potential source of unsaturation: a relation with an unfilled argument place. But there are other potential sources. For example, some claim that quantifiers have argument places (places for times as with the relativizer of section 11.3, or for sortal properties).

We are searching for a joint in nature that unifies "complete" sentences like "$\exists x F x$" and "$R a b$", as against fragments like "F" and "$R a$". The problem is that there seems to be no particular linguistic expression to which this joint corresponds.

---

[21]This is still vague; "specifying a value" needs to include doing so by quantification, as in "$\exists x \exists y \exists z\ x$ is between y and z".

[22]Not that this is incoherent; see Fine's (2000) discussion of "positionism" (a view he ultimately rejects).

My solution is to think of the joint as not corresponding to any particular linguistic expression at all, but rather to a linguistic *category*: that of the complete sentence in a fundamental language. In a fundamental language, a language in which the category of sentence carves at the joints, sentences are always "metaphysically complete"—saturated. In languages like English, which includes metaphysically incomplete as well as metaphysically complete sentences ('Ted is sitting' as well as 'Ted is sitting at noon on May 17, 2010'), the category of sentence does not carve at the joints.

Think of it this way. Sentences play a distinctive and central role in our cognitive and linguistic lives, a role that Frege explored in "Thought". It is with sentences that we make assertions, express our beliefs, desires, conjectures, and so forth. (We do these things with complete sentences, not fragments like "between", "*a* is between", and so on.) It is natural to think that there is an aspect of the world's structure that we are getting at with this role. We would get at this aspect perfectly only if we eschewed all implicit parameters; and we do not do this in English (sentences like 'Ted is sitting' include an implicit temporal parameter). Nevertheless, we get at this aspect reasonably well in English. Parameters in English must normally be explicit; we cannot—without ellipsis—assert 'between', '*a* is between', and so forth. Such exceptions as there are, are in the minority, and they are rule-governed.

Asking whether the category of sentence carves at the joints is less familiar than asking whether a given predicate carves at the joints, but the underlying idea is the same. When we ask whether quantifiers, modal operators, or causal predicates carve at the joints, we are asking whether certain facets of our conceptual scheme latch onto reality's distinguished structure. Whether our discourse using the facet is objective, semantically determinate, worthy of attention, and so on, turns on this matter of joint-carving. These questions do not go away when we turn to more ubiquitous, abstract, and pervasive facets of our conceptual scheme. Just as we can ask how well we are getting at the nature of things when we quantify, modalize, or speak of causation, we can ask how well we are getting at the nature of things when we accord a cognitively central role to the category of sentence.

Might there be no joint in nature in the neighborhood of our use of sentences? Metaphysicians must always live with the possibility of a bad mismatch between how we think and how the world really is. But in this case the realization of this possibility would be dire. Our cognitive lives revolve around sentences. To claim that all of our asserting, believing, desiring, and so forth is just badly on the wrong track—not just the small imperfection that results from our use of implicit parameters, but a massive mismatch with reality resulting from there simply being no joint in the vicinity—would be far more of a skeptical position than claiming that we are on the wrong track with quantification (say), or with some particular predicate, or even with predication itself. I can't even imagine what it would be like to reorient my cognitive life so as not to revolve around sentences.

Hitherto I have defined a "fundamental language" as one in which all the primitive expressions carve at the joints. Let us now expand this formulation, to require that the category of sentence also carves at the joints.[23] We may then introduce a distinction between saturated and unsaturated sentences in nonfundamental languages—at least when those languages have an appropriate sort of metaphysical semantics. Suppose, for example, that the sentences of some nonfundamental language divide into two sorts, depending on the relationship between the sentence S and its metaphysical truth-condition $\mu(S)$. If S is of the first sort, then S and $\mu(S)$ share logical form. But if S is of the second sort then $\mu(S)$ is logically richer than S; in particular, $\mu(S)$ contains a part that is syntactically like S, but also a further part that systematically depends on some feature of the context in which S is uttered. (This further part of $\mu(S)$ has no syntactic counterpart in S.) We may then call the first sort of sentences saturated and the second sort unsaturated.[24]

For example, suppose that the spatializing metaphysics of time is true, and suppose the metaphysical truth-condition for 'Ted is sitting at noon on May 17, 2010' has the form ⌜Ted is ϕ at α⌝ (ϕ and α are translations into a fundamental language of 'is sitting' and 'May 17, 2010', respectively). This metaphysical truth-condition is syntactically parallel to 'Ted is sitting at noon on May 17, 2010', and so that sentence is saturated. Suppose further that the metaphysical semantics for an utterance u of 'Ted is sitting' has the form ⌜Ted is ϕ at β_u⌝, where β_u names the time of u. Then 'Ted is sitting' is unsaturated: its metaphysical truth-condition consists of a portion that is syntactically like it, but contains in addition a further systematic enrichment: ⌜at β_u⌝.[25]

The failure of the category of sentence in English to carve at the joints is due, intuitively, to the fact that this category is metaphysically heterogeneous. The category includes both dated sentences, which match their metaphysical truth-conditions in syntactic structure, as well as present-tense sentences which do not. (Other kinds of context-sensitivity also contribute to the heterogeneity.) This metaphysical imperfection of English is of an unfamiliar sort. More familiar sorts result from the English lexicon containing particular words that fail to carve

[23] Must the marks of punctuation, or indeed, the typeface and color also carve at the joints? No, only representational facets must carve. Saying this does not require any sort of metaphysically fundamental distinction between representational and nonrepresentational facets of a language, since the notion of a fundamental language itself—a partly linguistic notion—need not be fundamental. Recall section 10.2.

[24] The distinction between saturated and unsaturated sentences could be extended to cases where sentences are not so syntactically similar to their metaphysical truth-conditions. We would need to identify some natural correspondence between parts of sentences and parts of their metaphysical truth-conditions, under which S is saturated if its parts correspond to all the parts of $\mu(S)$, whereas it is unsaturated if $\mu(S)$ has some extra parts under the correspondence.

[25] Throughout I am taking the natural language sentence 'Ted is sitting' at face value, as containing no syntactic constituent that represents a time. But perhaps this is false at some deep level of syntactic analysis. See Stanley (2000) for a discussion of the general issues here.

at the joints, whereas this less familiar sort results from a structural feature of the metaphysical semantics of English.

Applying the notion of joint-carving to linguistic categories like the category of sentence requires us to revisit the question of how to regiment structure-talk. Section 6.3 distinguished two regimentations. On one, the primitive operator $\mathscr{S}$ attaches to individual expressions we are querying for joint-carving: $\mathscr{S}(\exists)$, $\mathscr{S}$(is negatively charged), and so on. This regimentation apparently cannot formulate the claim that the category of sentence carves at the joints, since there is no particular expression to be queried. On a second regimentation, $\mathscr{S}$ attaches to full sentences, but the sentences contain dummy variables taking the place of sentence-parts we are not querying. Thus "$\mathscr{S}(\exists xP)$" is how we regiment the claim that existential quantification carves at the joints. Given this regimentation we may formulate the idea that the category of sentence carves at the joints by attaching $\mathscr{S}$ to a dummy sentence-variable: $\mathscr{S}(P)$. The intuitive idea is that we are querying the category of the dummy variable P—the category of the sentence.

Since this approach to regimentation seems a bit artificial, it's worth mentioning an alternative, "quietist" approach to introducing the idea of a fundamental language. On the quietist approach, we no longer speak of the category of sentences carving at the joints. Instead, we say that a fundamental language is one that results from *raising the standards*—in a distinctively metaphysical way—for making assertions and doing other things with complete sentences. When we raise the standards in this way, we disavow various typical mechanisms for tacitly supplying parameters, such as the current time for tensed sentences, quantifier domain restriction, comparison classes for gradable adjectives, and so on. Whereas normally we are willing to say things like "It is now raining", "everyone is at the meeting", "Allen Iverson is short", and so forth, we refuse to say such things when attempting to speak a fundamental language. We say only fully articulated things like "It is raining in New York City at noon on May 17, 2010", "Every member of the NYU Philosophy Department was at the philosophy faculty meeting on May 6, 2010", "Allen Iverson is short for a basketball player" and so on. This raising of standards is parallel to other sorts of standard-raising in metaphysics room. Ordinary talk of properties and similarity, for example, is flexible and context-dependent: we are apt to speak of things as sharing some property in common when they share nearly any salient feature, never mind whether that feature carves at the joints. In the metaphysics room, on the other hand, one speaks of shared properties only when the shared feature carves at the joints. Relatedly, ordinary quantification might plausibly be regarded as not being joint-carving; outside of the philosophy room we'll say that there is a way to win this chess match or that we have more in common with our college friends than with our high school friends, whereas in the metaphysics room we will say these things only if we think that there *really are*—in the joint-carving sense—such entities as ways or things-in-common.

So: instead of introducing the fundamental language by means of an explicit stipulation ("The category of sentence is to carve at the joints"), on the quietist approach we instead introduce it implicitly, by exhibiting the raised standard. The hope is that by doing so, the semantics of the resultant language will disallow all unarticulated parameters. If we do this, then assuming that reality does indeed contain structure in the vicinity of saturation (however that might be understood), it would take a perverse interpreter indeed to interpret our sentences using implicit parameters. It must be admitted, though, that the quietist approach would be a major departure from the approach to joint-carving that I have been developing in this book, since it gives up on the idea that one can characterize joint-carving by means of a distinctive addition to ideology.

The reader may have a sense that we have gone off the rails. To be honest, I share that sense. The claim that the category of sentence carves at the joints, for example—and that it may be regimented as $\mathscr{S}(\mathsf{P})$—strains to the breaking-point my intuitive grip on the notion of joint-carving. But on the other hand, it's evident from examples that there *just is* a metaphysically significant notion of saturation. I invite the skeptical reader not to simply dismiss the issue, but rather to join my struggle to make sense of this notion, and perhaps come up with something better.

11.9 Varieties of passage

However exactly it is understood, the idea of saturation can be used to distinguish amongst various varieties of the doctrine that time passes. All varieties agree that the tense operators are metaphysically basic, but they disagree over what objects exist, and in what sense the "current perspective" is fundamental.

The first variety is just presentism. We have already discussed presentism, but now we can clarify what it means to say that "The presentist's fundamental sentences describe reality from the current perspective." Not only does this mean that $\ulcorner \phi \leftrightarrow N\phi \urcorner$ is true, for any sentence ϕ; it also means—we can now say—that present-tense sentences like 'Ted is sitting' and 'Someone is sitting' are saturated. Intuitively: the *facts* are from the current perspective.

The second variety I call *Williamsonian passage* because it is inspired by (albeit independent of) Williamson's views on modality.[26] This view is like presentism except that it claims that objects exist permanently. More exactly, to the presentist's i) primitivism about tense operators; and ii) claim that the current perspective is fundamental, it adds iii) the claim that all instances of the temporal Barcan and converse Barcan schemas are true:

---

[26] See Williamson (1998; 2002). Although these works are primarily concerned with modality, p. 245 of the latter article contains remarks that are consistent with Williamsonian passage.

$$P\exists x\,\phi\rightarrow\exists x\,P\phi$$
$$F\exists x\,\phi\rightarrow\exists x\,F\phi$$
$$\exists x\,P\phi\rightarrow P\exists x\,\phi$$
$$\exists x\,F\phi\rightarrow F\exists x\,\phi$$

Williamson himself accepts the modal Barcan schema, $\Diamond\exists x\,\phi\rightarrow\exists x\,\Diamond\phi$, and its converse, $\exists x\,\Diamond\phi\rightarrow\Diamond\exists x\,\phi$. These lead to surprising ontological conclusions. To use Williamson's example, Wittgenstein might have fathered something, so, by the Barcan schema, there is something that Wittgenstein might have fathered. Given plausible essentialist assumptions, this something couldn't be any ordinary object. (No person could have been fathered by Wittgenstein since Wittgenstein in fact fathered no one, and no one could have had a father different from his or her actual father; and no electron or mountain or . . . could have been fathered by Wittgenstein since no electron or mountain or . . . could have been fathered by anything.) According to Williamson this possible Wittgensteinian offspring is a "merely modal" entity: its only positive properties are modal properties, such as the property of possibly being fathered by Wittgenstein.[27] It doesn't have a mass, or a charge, or a smell, or a color. It isn't even in space, and thus is "nonconcrete" in one sense.

Analogously, the defender of Williamsonian passage accepts the (current) existence of extraordinary objects. Since there once existed dinosaurs ($P\exists x\,Dx$), by the past Barcan schema there (now) exist things that *were* dinosaurs ($\exists x\,PDx$). These "past dinosaurs" are not dinosaurs (the current perspective is fundamental for the Williamsonian, remember; and nothing is *now* a dinosaur); they are rather things that *were* dinosaurs. Since no ordinary current object was once a dinosaur, these past dinosaurs are extra entities, in addition to the ordinary objects that the presentist accepts. Their only positive properties are temporal properties like previously being a dinosaur.[28] Like Williamson's possible objects, they are nonconcrete in the sense of (currently) not being located in space.

In a sense, the Williamsonian accepts the spatializer's ontology. But since the Williamsonian takes the current perspective to be fundamental, he disagrees with the spatializer's descriptions of those objects; he rejects, for example, the spatializer's claim that there are dinosaurs ($\exists x\,Dx$). Thus the Williamsonian has a ready answer to the question: given that you accept the spatializer's ontology, why do you take the tense operators as basic? Since the Williamsonian does not take the atemporal perspective to be the fundamental one, he does not take his objects to have the features attributable from that perspective (such as the feature of being a dinosaur); but it is precisely these features that are needed to provide metaphysical truth-conditions for tensed sentences. For example, the spatializer's

---

[27] And perhaps also mathematical/logical properties like being self-identical and being a member of its unit set.

[28] And perhaps modal and logical and mathematical properties.

reductive truth-condition for an utterance at t_0 of 'There were dinosaurs' is 'There are dinosaurs that are located before t_0'; but the Williamsonian rejects this truth-condition since he denies that there are dinosaurs. The only existential claims in the neighborhood that he accepts are claims like $\exists x PDx$ which, of course, cannot be used in a reduction of tense.[29]

(Notice that the difference between Williamsonians and spatializers over which perspective is fundamental emerges even in connection with the present. I am currently sitting, so the defender of Williamsonian passage will say that 'Ted is sitting' is saturated. But the spatializer will deny this—continuing to assume no temporal parts—since it is missing a temporal parameter.)

The third variety is the "moving spotlight" view. It may be introduced by contrast to Williamsonian passage. The Williamsonian admits the existence of "past and future objects" but says that their only features are temporal. Past dinosaurs aren't dinosaurs (though they were), past noises make no sound (though they did), and so on. The defender of the spotlight theory also embraces past and future objects, but she accepts a "fuller" conception of these objects than the Williamsonian. According to her, these objects have all the features that the spatializer thinks they have. We can put this by saying that the spotlight theorist joins the spatializer in accepting the block universe. But the spotlight theorist accepts something in addition: a joint-carving monadic property of presentness (or instead a joint-carving one-place predicate 'is present'), which is possessed by just one moment of time, and which "moves", to be possessed by later and later times, as time passes. This motion, on my construal, amounts to tensed facts about which moment of time possesses the property.

For the moving spotlight theorist, it is an external yet temporal perspective on the block universe that is fundamental. More carefully: sentences such as 'Ted is sitting at 12:00 AM EST on 1/1/10' and 'World War 2 is occurring in 1943' are saturated. Sentences like 'Ted is sitting' and 'World War 2 is occurring' are not saturated.[30] In addition, statements of the form 'Time t has presentness' are saturated. Presentness is possessed absolutely; exactly one time has presentness simpliciter; all other times lack presentness simpliciter. Finally, the spotlight theorist accepts primitive tense operators, which generate saturated sentences when prefixed to saturated sentences. Using the tense operators, the spotlight theorist can describe the change in which moment has the property of presentness, by means of sentences like: 'There is a time, t, such that t does not have presentness but $P(t$ has presentness).' (Note that the change described here is "genuine" change—change in the truth of a saturated statement.) Describing this change—

---

[29]The Williamsonian could accept claims of the form "Something is a dinosaur at time t" if analyzed in terms of tensed claims; but then they could not be used in a reduction of tense.

[30]If the spotlight theorist believed in temporal parts, she could say instead: sentences like 'Temporal part t is sitting', 'Temporal part t is part of Ted', 'Event e occurred in 1943', and 'Event e is part of World War 2' are saturated. Sentences like 'Ted is sitting' are saturated but false since 'Ted' denotes a space-time worm that is not sitting simpliciter (though see Wasserman (2005, chapter 3)).

the "motion of the spotlight"—is, in fact, the only purpose of the tense operators in the spotlight theory: tense operators, according to the spotlight theory, have no effect when prefixed to statements that do not concern presentness. For any such sentence ϕ, ϕ is true iff $\ulcorner O\phi \urcorner$ is true, where O is any of the tense operators we have discussed.

So intuitively, the facts are those that one would see if looking at the block universe from an external perspective. From this perspective, one would see everything that the spatializer believes in, but one would also see a single time "lit up". That is the time that possesses presentness. Further, if one continued to look from this atemporal perspective—"continued" in the sense of the tense operators—everything would continue to look exactly the same except that the lit time would move from past to future.

Nonpresentist defenders of passage face the question of why they accept primitive tense operators, given that they accept past and future objects. As we saw, the Williamsonian had a quick answer: since he rejects the atemporal perspective, he must reject the spatializer's reduction of the tense operators. The situation is very different with the spotlight theorist. For example, she accepts that there exist dinosaurs located before 2011; but this is the spatializer's proposed truth-condition for an utterance in 2011 of 'There were dinosaurs.' More generally, the spotlight theorist can accept the spatializer's reduction of tense for all tensed statements except those concerning presentness. For the latter, there can be no reduction. "1776 once had presentness" cannot be analyzed as saying that 1776 has the property of presentess relative to itself, since presentness is a monadic property, and is not had relative to anything. 2011 has presentness *simpliciter*; nothing else has presentness; there are no other nontensed facts about presentness; hence we cannot analyze the tensed claim that "1776 once had presentness" in nontensed terms.

So the spotlight theorist can say *something* to justify her primitivism about the tense operators. But one might wonder whether it's convincing. The tense operators play no role in her theory other than characterizing change in the possession of the monadic property of presentness. And the only reason for invoking this property at all is to be able to say that there is genuine change in which moment is present. But notice that the spotlight theorist does not admit genuine change for anything else! For her there is no genuine change in whether I am sitting, or in whether there are dinosaurs, or in whether a war is occurring, since her account of these matters is identical to the spatializer's. All that genuinely changes is which moment has presentness. Is securing this smidgen of genuine change worth the postulation of primitive tense?

A spotlight theorist could admit more genuine change by adopting a hybrid theory according to which more statements are treated in the presentist rather than spatializing way. The spotlight theorist might, for example, treat *pain* the way a presentist would. On this view, statements of the form "α is in pain" are saturated despite lacking a temporal parameter; indeed, no fundamental statements about pain include a temporal parameter. Moreover, the tense operators are not inert when prefixed to statements about pain; "$P(\alpha$ is in pain)" is not equivalent to "α is in pain". Sentences of the form "α is in pain" can be saturated and true and temporary in the sense that "$P(\alpha$ is not in pain)" is also true; hence there is genuine change in the matter of pain, not just the matter of which moment is present.[31] (Depending on how many other properties are treated in this way, the spotlight theorist might do away with the property of presentness altogether.) But notice that following this course to an extreme would turn the position into Williamsonian passage.

There is a powerful epistemic objection to the moving spotlight theory (and to related theories such as the "growing block" theory, to be discussed below).[32] We believe that we exist in the present; indeed, we take ourselves to know this. But given the spotlight theory, there are ever so many people, with similar evidence to our own, who also think they are in the present but are wrong—they're wrong because the times at which they are located do not have the monadic property of presentness. George Washington, for example, thinks in 1776 that 1776 is present; we think, here in 2011, that 2011 is present. We cannot both be right, since the property of presentness is monadic and possessed by only one moment. And our evidence is no better than Washington's (we see flowers brightly blooming in 2011; he sees flowers brightly blooming in 1776, and so on), so it's hard to believe that we're more likely to be right than Washington. Indeed, it seems likely that we're both wrong, since 1776 and 2011 are merely two of the infinitely many times, only one of which has presentness. The spotlight theory leads to skepticism about whether we're in the present.

Notice that Williamsonian passage is immune to this objection. The objection turns on the fact that the spotlight theorist thinks that many people such as Washington i) think they're in the present; and ii) are wrong because the times at which they're located don't have presentness. But the Williamsonian rejects both i) and ii). He rejects i) because Washington, for example, is a noncrete object, and can't think anything at all. (What's true is that he *was* a concrete object, and *did* think that he was in the present.) And the Williamsonian rejects ii) because he rejects the spotlight theorist's property of presentness.[33] The epistemic objection doesn't work against Williamsonian passage (not that it was intended to) because

---

[31] See Zimmerman (1998) on related matters. Forrest (2004) defends a related view (although Forrest (2006) strikes me as backtracking).

[32] See Bourne (2002); Braddon-Mitchell (2004); Merricks (2006); and compare Lewis (1970*a*, section 9) on actuality.

[33] There are two ways a Williamsonian could construe the thought "I am in the present"; in neither way could anyone mistakenly think this thought. He could construe it as meaning "This very thought, t, is *now* occurring"; thus t is true iff $N(t$ is occurring). But then no one thinking t could be mistaken: if they're thinking t then t is occurring; so t is *now* occurring (the Williamsonian accepts $\phi \leftrightarrow N\phi$, recall); so t is true. Alternatively, he could construe it as meaning "I am concrete." But only concrete things think; so again, no one thinking the thought could be mistaken.

it's designed to refute views that accept the spatializer's atemporal perspective, but then add to it some notion of the objective present. Williamsonian passage doesn't do this; rather, it rejects the atemporal perspective. In this respect it's more like presentism (indeed, it survives the argument for the same reason that presentism does).

The fourth variety of time's passage is a little weird. It says that there are *two* perspectives on reality that are equally fundamental: the current perspective and the atemporal perspective. From the current perspective one says what the presentist says, but one can make a "gestalt switch" to the atemporal perspective and say what the spatializer says.

The root problem for nonpresentists who accept primitive tense operators is that of how to combine the atemporal perspective that is apparently demanded by quantification over past and future entities with the current perspective that is apparently demanded by the tense operators. The Williamsonian solves the problem by rejecting the atemporal perspective but accepting the Barcan and converse Barcan schemas. The spotlight theorist solves the problem by rejecting the current perspective but applying the tense operators to certain statements from the external perspective on the block universe (statements about presentness). The gestalt-switcher solves the problem by embracing both perspectives.[34]

I have been cashing out talk of "perspectives" in terms of saturation, and saturation in terms of truth in a language in which the category of sentence carves at the joints. I cash out this second spotlight view, therefore, as the claim that there are *two* joint-carving categories of sentence; nature has two joints in the vicinity of a metaphysically complete statement, not one. (Compare jadeite and nephrite.) There are, therefore, two equally good languages one could speak in the metaphysics room. And so there are two different sorts of saturation: call them atemporal saturation and tensed saturation.[35]

Thus there are two fundamental descriptions of the world. One is an atemporal description of reality from the atemporal perspective; the other is a tensed description of reality from the current perspective. Neither description is incomplete; rather, the notion of giving the entirety of the fundamental facts is just bifurcated.

What exactly can be said from these two perspectives? What statements are atemporally saturated, and what statements are tense-saturated? And how do the tense operators interact with these statements? The answer depends on temporal parts.

Suppose, first, that temporal parts are accepted. In that case, from the atemporal perspective the gestalt-switcher speaks exactly like a spatializer who accepts

---

[34]Views that embrace the atemporal perspective are in the best position to solve the problem of relations (Sider, 2001*b*, chapter 2, section 2). The Williamsonian, for example, has as much trouble with cross-time relations as does the presentist.

[35]Compare Fine's (2005) idea of reality relative to a time. Fine speaks of what is real at *t* for arbitrary times *t*. Perhaps in my terms the idea is that there is a different joint-carving category of sentence for each time.

temporal parts. Statements like 'Ted$_0$ is the (instantaneous) temporal part of Ted at time t_0', 'Ted$_0$ is sitting', 'Ted is sitting at t_0', and so on, are atemporally saturated. Moreover, in this context, the tense operators are inert. From the tensed perspective, on the other hand, the spotlight theorist speaks like a presentist who accepts temporal parts. If t_0 is the current time, then 'Ted is sitting' and 'Ted$_0$ is sitting' are both tense-saturated and true. If nothing is currently standing, 'Nothing is standing' is tense-saturated and true. Further, the tense operators are no longer inert, so one can truly utter: 'Nothing is standing, but P(something is standing).'

Suppose, on the other hand, that temporal parts are rejected. There are then various possibilities.

1. Atemporal perspective: indexing—things talk, sit, etc., with respect to times. Statements missing their temporal indices, such as 'Ted is sitting' are atemporally unsaturated. Quantification is over the entire block universe: there are dinosaurs. Tensed perspective: like presentism. 'Ted is sitting' is tense-saturated and true. There are no dinosaurs (and no things that were dinosaurs), though there were dinosaurs.

2. Atemporal perspective: as with 1. Tensed perspective: one can ascribe a sui generis monadic property of presentness—and one cannot ascribe any other properties.

3. Atemporal perspective: extreme version: one can say nothing. Less extreme version: one can quantify over and name objects and ascribe identity and distinctness to them. Still less extreme version: one can additionally apply sortal predicates. Tensed perspective: like presentism.

View 1 has an odd feature: each (temporary) predicate has a monadic version usable from the present perspective and a distinct indexed version usable from the atemporal perspective. For example, from the present perspective we say that Ted is sitting; from the atemporal perspective we say that Ted is sitting *at* various times. How does sitting relate to sitting-at? Views 2 and 3 avoid this by "thinning" one of the two perspectives. (There are also intermediate views, according to which one or both perspectives are more or less thinned.)

The fifth and final variety is the doctrine of the growing block universe. According to C. D. Broad (1923), the past and present are real, but the future is not. Reality consists of the present and past portions of the spatializer's block universe, which grows by the addition of new "layers of being" to its future edge. We can clarify the content of these metaphors by using our framework.

Like the defender of the moving spotlight, the growing blocker believes in a changing external perspective on the block universe—changing in the sense of the tense operators. But unlike the moving spotlight view, it's not just a smidgen of the facts about the block that change; and the changing facts have nothing to do with a primitive property of presentness. The changing facts involve the constant addition to the block.

Like the spatializer, the growing block theorist thinks that the saturated statements are those that are from an external perspective on the block. Thus each of the following is saturated:

There is a second World War.

There are human colonies on Mars.

Ted sits at time t.

But unlike the spatializer, the growing blocker thinks that 'There are human colonies on Mars' is false. It's false because the block ends at the present, and humans haven't yet colonized Mars.

Also, the growing block theorist—given my construal, anyway—accepts primitive tense operators.[36] These are not inert when prefixed to saturated sentences about the contents of the block universe. Using these tense operators we can describe the growth of the block:

There is a second World War but P (There is no second World War).

There are no human colonies on Mars but F (There are human colonies on Mars).

Thus the facts about the block universe change, according to the growing block view. But there is a constraint on this change.[37] Once "positive" statements (examples include 'Ted is sitting at t' and 'There exists a dinosaur', but I won't try to make the notion precise) become true they remain true forever after (e.g., $A(\exists x Dx \rightarrow G\exists x Dx)$). For the *only* change from the atemporal perspective is that of the addition of new layers of being.

Many defenders of the growing block view are motived primarily by the thought that the future is "open" whereas the past is not. (They're less motivated by a desire for genuine change; thus the view perhaps doesn't belong in this section.) One sort of openness is secured simply by denying the truth of statements that assert the existence of future individuals and facts, such as 'There are human colonies on Mars' and 'Ted lives in Ithaca in 2012.' A stronger sort of openness would be secured by denying the truth or (nonepistemic) determinacy of future-tensed statements such as 'F (There are human colonies on Mars)' and 'F(Ted lives in Ithaca in 2012).'[38]

---

[36]There's an interesting question of whether the defender of the block universe who thinks that the future is "open" could do away with the primitive tense operators.

[37]Compare van Inwagen (2010, pp. 11–12).

[38]Such denials are often restricted to statements that are not settled by the past plus laws of nature. But if it were me, I wouldn't restrict the denial—provided we're talking about what is fundamental. The intuitive idea here is that there simply aren't any facts about what is going to happen, and the fact that the laws and past sometimes yield determinate predictions doesn't put any pressure on this intuitive idea. These are only predictions, after all; why regard them as *constituting* facts about what will happen?

The denials are also open to presentists and Williamsonians. A related but distinct option for the Williamsonian is to deny the future Barcan formula and its converse. And, in the spirit of multiplying views beyond necessity, note this Williamsonian variant on the growing block view: there exist

To conclude. I myself am a spatializer. I reject all the A-theories of time that I have considered, since I deny that tense operators are metaphysically fundamental. The A-theorists' fundamental languages are therefore deeply defective, by my lights. Nevertheless, my disagreement with the A-theorists is substantive, since it concerns the nature of the correct fundamental ideology.

nonconcrete, spatiotemporally unlocated entities with future-tense properties; these individuals will eventually join the block universe by gaining concreteness and a spatiotemporal location, which they will then retain forever after.

12   Modality

At bottom, the world is an amodal place. Necessity and possibility do not carve at the joints; ultimate reality is not "full of threats and promises".[1] The book of the world says how things are, not how they must or might be.

This is not to say that there is no modality. The book of the world does not mention cities, smiles, or candy either; yet there are cities, smiles, and candy.

Previous chapters have discussed logical and nomic necessity—logical truth and laws of nature—and have argued that neither is fundamental. The kind of necessity here in question is so-called "metaphysical necessity", a kind supposedly intermediate in strictness between logical and nomic necessity. This chapter argues that metaphysical necessity is not fundamental, and shows how to fit it into a fundamentally amodal world.

12.1 No fundamental modality

Why hold that metaphysical necessity is nonfundamental? Let us first disavow a bad reason. You may have noticed that the philosopher's conception of metaphysical necessity is frustratingly thin. We are told that logic and mathematics is metaphysically necessary. We are usually told that laws of nature are not. We are told that it is metaphysically necessary that "nothing can be in two places at once", and so on. This conception falls far short of a full criterion. But a thin conception is not in itself problematic. For when a notion is taken to be fundamental, one often assumes that the facts involving the notion will outrun one's conception. (Why take to be fundamental what you can define?) We cannot define the primitive predicates of physics, but no one supposes our conceptions of those predicates to settle all cases. We rather introduce such predicates, more or less, by a theoretical analog of *pointing*. "What do I mean by 'charge'? Here are some examples; here is a partial theory of charge; charge is what is common to (enough of) the examples and makes (enough of) the theory come out true." Defenders of metaphysical necessity will say similar things. "What do I mean by 'metaphysical necessity'? Here are some examples (logic and mathematics are necessary, laws of nature aren't necessary, and so on); here is a partial theory of necessity (this might include principles of modal logic). Metaphysical necessity is whatever is common to (enough of) the examples and makes (enough of) the theory come out true." Now, such speeches are often phrased as introductions to a *concept* or *meaning*. Thus Alvin Plantinga:

But what exactly do these words—'necessary' and 'contingent'—*mean*? What distinction do they mark? Just what is supposed to be the difference between necessary and contingent

[1]Goodman (1955, p. 40)

truths? We can hardly explain that p is necessary if and only if its denial is impossible; this is true but insufficiently enlightening. *It would be a peculiar philosopher who had the relevant concept of impossibility well in hand but lacked that of necessity.* Instead, we must give examples and hope for the best. (1974, p. 1, my emphasis)

Taken as introductions to a concept, such speeches will invariably disappoint. I don't know how to begin with the necessity of logic, mathematics, not being in two places at once, and answer new questions about metaphysical necessity (such as the question of whether the dimensionality of spacetime is metaphysically necessary or contingent). But the speeches are, or should be, nothing of the kind. What they do is supply enough of a semantic constraint so that, if reality contains the requisite structure, the term 'metaphysically necessary' will be semantically determinate.

The good reason for opposing modal primitivism is simply: ideological economy.[2] Modal talk is certainly common in ordinary and special-science discourse. But we do not generally take notions from these high-level domains as good candidates for being metaphysically basic, as "proper annex[es] to austere scientific language" (Quine, 1976b, p. 863), since they are unneeded for the most fundamental inquiries of mathematics and physics. We tend to think of psychological, economic, political, and other special-science notions as being nonfundamental. Many of us think the same about various philosophical notions: semantic, moral, epistemic, causal. Since modality is unneeded for the most fundamental inquiries, it too is metaphysically nonfundamental, however conceptually fundamental it may be.

(There is similar reason to oppose primitivism about essence, construed nonmodally. Kit Fine convincingly argues against the standard modal definition of essence: a is essentially F iff it is necessary that a is F (provided a exists). Even though it is necessary that Socrates is a member of his unit set if he exists, Fine points out, we do not think it part of the essence of Socrates—part of "what it is to be Socrates"— that he be a member of his unit set (though we do think it part of the essence of his unit set that it contain Socrates). Essence, for Fine, is not to be understood modally at all.[3] This is an attractive view; but we should not regard nonmodal essence as being metaphysically basic (not that Fine does): fundamental theories need essence no more than they need modality. Perhaps a reductive account of essence along the lines of the reduction of modality to be given below could be developed.)

---

[2] Contrast the less direct approach of Sider (2001b, chapter 2, section 3), which disparaged primitive modality as a gateway drug to stronger stuff: primitive counterfactuals, dispositions, and tense.

[3] Indeed, Fine defines modality in terms of essence: to be metaphysically necessary is to be true in virtue of the essences of all objects, including abstract objects (1994a, p. 9; see also 1994b). One reservation: assume Platonism about set theory, and that there is a fact of the matter about the continuum hypothesis. We would then expect the continuum hypothesis to be either necessarily true or necessarily false. But it's hard to see how its truth or falsity could flow from the essences of the relevant entities: existence, sethood, and membership.

12.2 A Humean strategy for reduction

If modality is not fundamental, then it must be nonfundamental. (The alternative would be to say that there is no modality at all, not even in a nonfundamental sense, which is about as reasonable as saying the same about cities, smiles, and candy.) We need a reduction of modality—in my terms, a metaphysical semantics for modal language.

A familiar strategy for reduction is to define necessity as truth in all possible worlds. But this constitutes a *reduction* of modality only if possible worlds both exist and can be nonmodally defined. David Lewis's (1986*b*) concrete possible worlds are nonmodally defined,[4] but it is very difficult to believe that they exist. The usual nonLewisian alternative is to construct possible worlds out of pre-existing "abstract" materials: sentences, propositions, and so on.[5] But the usual constructions are defined modally (viz., "a possible world is a maximal *consistent* set of propositions").[6]

A very different strategy locates modality in linguistic convention. According to the old "linguistic" or "conventionalist" theory of necessity, analyticity in the sense of truth by convention was held to explain necessity. If analytic truths "do not make any assertion about the empirical world, but simply record our determination to use symbols in a certain fashion", as Ayer put it (1936, p. 31), then, it was thought, we can understand how they are guaranteed to be true no matter how the world turns out to be. In its crudest form, conventionalism claimed that a statement of necessity, such as 'It is necessary that all bachelors are male', *says that* the component sentence ('All bachelors are male') is true by convention.

Today this theory has few adherents, for the most part with good reason. If $\Box\phi$ says that ϕ is true by convention, then $\Box\phi$ would apparently turn out contingent, since statements about what conventions we adopt are not themselves true by convention. Thus the characteristic axioms of modal systems S4 ($\Box\phi\rightarrow\Box\Box\phi$) and S5 ($\sim\Box\phi\rightarrow\Box\sim\Box\phi$) would be in all cases false. Further, conventionalism is apparently inapplicable to Kripke and Putnam's examples of the necessary a posteriori (and, relatedly, to *de re* modality). But most importantly, as we saw in section 6.5, the notion of truth by convention is thoroughly confused. Linguistic conventions can put semantic relations in place (since facts about semantic relations are partially constituted by linguistic conventions). Thus by adopting the convention that 'bachelor' means the same as 'unmarried man', we can bring it about that 'An object is a bachelor iff it is an unmarried man' means the same as 'An object is an unmarried man iff it is an unmarried man'. But there convention's power runs out; it plays no role in explaining why the latter sentence is true, or necessary. Nor

---

[4]Although see Divers and Melia (2002); Shalkowski (1994); I reply in my (2003).

[5] See Adams (1974); Plantinga (1976); Stalnaker (1976).

[6]Other nonLewisian stories about possible-worlds talk are combinatorialist, fictionalist, or both (Armstrong (1989; 1997); Rosen (1990)), but I have argued elsewhere (2002; 2005) that these projects fail to reduce modality.

does convention play any role in explaining the truth or necessity of mathematics, or of any other domain. As Quine says, ". . . definitions are available only for transforming truths, not for founding them" (Quine, 1936, p. 81).

I prefer a third strategy for reducing modality, which I'll call Humean, for lack of a better word.[7] To say that a proposition is necessary, according to the Humean, is to say that the proposition is i) true; and ii) of a certain sort. A crude Humean view, for example, would say that a proposition is necessary iff it is either a logical or mathematical truth. What determines the "certain sort" of propositions? Nothing "metaphysically deep". For the Humean, necessity does not carve at the joints. There are many candidate meanings for 'necessary', corresponding to different "certain sorts" our linguistic community might choose. Since none of these candidates carves at the joints, our linguistic community is free to choose whichever of these it likes. Perhaps the choice is arbitrary, in which case the facts about necessity are "conventional" in the sense of section 4.3. Perhaps the choice reflects something important about the role 'necessary' plays in our conceptual lives, in which case the facts are "subjective" (or "projective"). More likely, the truth is somewhere in between. But at any rate, the conceptual choice is not forced on us by the facts.

Contrast Humeanism with conventionalism. Conventionalists claim that statements that are necessary (such as logical and mathematical truths) are made true by linguistic convention, and they deny that such statements are fundamentally true (if they speak of fundamentality at all). Further, at least the cruder ones claim that a statement of necessity, $\Box\phi$, *says* that ϕ is true by convention. The Humean denies each of these claims. Neither logical nor mathematical truths owe their truth to convention (except in the banal sense in which every true sentence partly owes its truth to the conventions that secure its meaning). If mathematical and logical notions carve at the joints, then mathematical and logical truths are fundamental truths.[8] Statements of necessity say nothing about conventions. What 'It is necessary that $2 + 2 = 4$' says is that $2 + 2 = 4$ is either a logical or mathematical truth (given the crude Humean view, anyway).

For the Humean, convention plays no role in truthmaking. Insofar as the Humean wants to speak of truthmaking at all, she will say the following. The proposition that $2+2 = 4$ is made true by whatever makes mathematical truths true generally (facts about mathematical entities, perhaps). Its status as a *mathematical* truth is secured by whatever generally makes mathematical truths mathematical (perhaps the fact that its subject matter is solely mathematical). And the further proposition that the proposition that $2 + 2 = 4$ is either a logical truth or a

---

[7] I choose the term because of my denial of modal "further facts", but the term is imperfect since universality plays no role in my account. I'm not sure whom else to count as Humeans, but to varying degrees the following philosophers share the spirit: Heller (1996; 1998); Mortensen (1989); Nolan (2011); Peacocke (1997; 1999); Sidelle (2009).

[8] Statements of necessity are not fundamental truths, since they contain the non-joint-carving term 'necessary'.

mathematical truth—that is, the proposition that it is necessary that $2 + 2 = 4$—is made true by all of the above, plus a general (logical) fact about disjunction: a disjunction is true whenever one of its disjuncts is.

Nevertheless, convention, or something like it, does play a role for the Humean. The Humean shares the conventionalist's goal of accounting for modality in a fundamentally amodal world. To that end, it's important that the "certain sorts" of propositions invoked by the Humean are not objectively distinguished, that no joint in reality encircles the class of logical and mathematical truths. So what *does* select this class? Something about *us*, says the Humean. Perhaps the choice of the "certain sorts" is conventional. Convention can do this without purporting to make true the statements of logic or mathematics (or, for that matter, statements to the effect that these truths are necessary), for the choice of the certain sorts is just a choice about what to mean by 'necessary'. Or perhaps the choice is partly subjective/projective rather than purely conventional. Either way, necessity is accounted for without metaphysically privileging the class of necessary truths.

Truth by convention was an essential part of conventionalist epistemology: it was to explain how we know logical and mathematical truths. The Humean account of necessity, in contrast, is metaphysically, rather than epistemologically, driven. It tries to fit modality into a demanding metaphysics, not into a demanding epistemology. Thus the Humean is free to simply ditch the idea of truth by convention. The price is that no headway is made on epistemology: nothing in the Humean account of necessity sheds any light on the epistemology of logic or mathematics.

Truth by convention was also perceived as an essential part of conventionalist metaphysics, insofar as there was such a thing. As Paul Boghossian (1997, p. 336) puts it:

Guided by the fear that objective, language-independent, necessary connections would be metaphysically odd, [conventionalists] attempted to show that all necessities could be understood to consist in linguistic necessities . . . Linguistic meaning, by itself, was supposed to generate necessary truth; *a fortiori*, linguistic meaning, by itself, was supposed to generate truth.

But the Humean account shows that we do not need truth by convention to avoid the "metaphysically odd" in our account of modality.[9]

Distinguish between *governance* and *classification* conceptions of necessity. According to the governance conception, necessity is a source of truth. When $\Box \phi$ is true, ϕ is true *because* $\Box \phi$ is true.[10] (Compare the governance conception of laws of nature, on which laws "guide" the evolution of the world.[11]) On the classification conception, on the other hand, the truth of ϕ comes first. Necessity plays no role in truthmaking. To say that a true proposition is necessary is to classify

---

[9] Truth by convention would not have demystified modality on its own. Even if linguistic meaning somehow generated truth, it would not follow immediately that it also generated *necessary* truth.

[10] Michael Jubien (2007) and Marc Lange (2005) seem to defend governance theories.

[11] See Beebee (2000); Loewer (1996).

that proposition as being of a certain sort, but the proposition is true on its own merits.[12]

The Humean theory is on the classification side of this divide. (As is combinatorialism, and Lewis's modal realism. What is most fundamental for Lewis is truth from the perspective of the pluriverse; necessities are just certain kinds of truths about the pluriverse.[13] For the combinatorialist, a necessary truth is just a truth that remains true in all combinations.) Everyday modal thought may fit the governance conception better than the classification conception (much as everyday thinking about laws of nature arguably fits the governance conception). But according to the Humean, nothing answers to the governance conception; modality isn't what we ordinarily take it to be.

The core idea of the Humean account, then, is that necessary truths are truths of certain more or less arbitrarily selected kinds. More carefully: begin with a set of *modal axioms* and a set of *modal rules*. Modal axioms are simply certain chosen true sentences; modal rules are certain chosen truth-preserving relations between sets of sentences and sentences. To any chosen modal axioms and rules there corresponds a set of *modal theorems*: the closure of the set of modal axioms under the rules.[14] Any choice of modal axioms and modal rules, and thus of modal theorems, results in a version of Humeanism: to be necessary is to be a modal theorem thus understood.[15] ("Modal" axioms, rules, and theorems are so-called because of their role in the Humean theory of modality, but the goal is to characterize them nonmodally; otherwise the theory would fail to be reductive. Also, the set of modal "axioms" need not be recursive.)

A simple version of Humeanism to begin with: the sole modal rule is first-order logical consequence, and the modal axioms are the mathematical truths. (Logical truths are logical consequences of any propositions whatsoever, and so

---

[12]There is an intermediate conception, which like the governance conception holds that necessity is a "further status" that is intimately connected with truth, but unlike the governance conception does not hold that the further status "produces" truth. But what exactly is the nature of the intimate connection, if not production? Could it be understood in terms of necessity itself: it's necessary that any proposition with the further status is true? Thanks to Ryan Robinson and Kit Fine.

[13]This is what drives Jubien's (2007, section 1) objection to Lewis:

Suppose it's necessary that all A's are B's. This is supposed [by the possible worlds theorist] to mean that in every possible world, all A's are B's. So the necessity arises from what goes on in all the worlds taken together. There's nothing about any world individually, even in all of its maximal glory, that forces all of *its* A's to be B's. It's as if it just *happens* in each world that all of its A's are B's, that from the strictly internal point of view of any world, it's *contingent*, a mere coincidence. But then shouldn't we expect that this internal contingency will not be repeated in every world, that there will be worlds where some A's "happen" not to be B's? After all, nothing within any given world prevents it, and these are supposed to be *all* the possible worlds.

[14]That is, the intersection of all sets A such that: i) each modal axiom is in A; and ii) for any $B \subseteq A$, if B bears some modal rule to some sentence ϕ then $\phi \in A$.

[15]It's best to proceed in terms of rules and axioms because, e.g., logical consequences of propositions of different types may not fall under any type, but are nevertheless necessary.

do not need to be included as modal axioms.) The following sections develop the Humean account by considering a series of worries, and responding with a combination of refinement and argument. The resulting account will be partial[16] in various ways; but it will be enough, I think, to justify the claim that Humean metaphysical truth-conditions for modal statements can in principle be given.

12.3 Logical consequence and mathematical truth

"How can the notions of logical consequence and mathematical truth be characterized?"

Humeanism is incompatible with some theories of logical consequence. Any modal account would obviously render the theory circular. The simplest modal account is that logical consequence is just necessary consequence; another modal account says that logical consequences are modal consequences that involve only logical words essentially, in Quine's sense (see below).[17] The Humean must reject each.

Humeanism could consistently be combined with primitivism about logical consequence. But the reasons for rejecting primitive modality lead also to rejecting primitive logical consequence: there seems to be no need for the metalogical notion of logical consequence in our most fundamental inquiries. Humeanism plus primitivism about logical consequence would, I think, be an advance over primitivism about metaphysical necessity. But the true lover of desert landscapes will want to reject each form of primitivism.

Quine once defined logical truths as those truths which involve only logical words essentially:[18]

First we suppose indicated, by enumeration if not otherwise, what words are to be called logical words; typical ones are 'or', 'not', 'if', 'then', 'and', 'all', 'every', 'only', 'some'. The logical truths, then, are those true sentences which involve only logical words *essentially*. What this means is that any other words, though they may also occur in a logical truth (as witness 'Brutus', 'kill', and 'Caesar' in 'Brutus killed or did not kill Caesar') can be varied at will without engendering falsity.

Extended to a theory of logical consequence, this account could be combined noncircularly with Humeanism. But it would generate implausible results. If '=' is counted as a logical word, certain true sentences specifying information about the number of things, for example '$\sim\exists x \forall y\; x=y$' ("it is not the case that there exists exactly one thing") count as logical truths. Since the Humean account implies that all logical truths are necessary, this would rule out the possibility of there existing only one thing. And even if '=' is not counted as a logical word, if there

---

[16]For example, the account defines a property of propositions that do not themselves concern modality, and thus is insufficient to interpret iterable modal operators.

[17]Compare Hanson (1997).

[18]Quine (1960a); p. 103 in Quine (1966).

are in fact a finite number, n, of entities, then any sentence of the following form turns out to be necessarily true:[19]

$$\forall x_1 \ldots \forall x_n \forall y(([Fx_1 \wedge G_1 x_1] \wedge [Fx_2 \wedge G_2 x_2 \wedge \sim G_1 x_2] \wedge [Fx_3 \wedge G_3 x_3 \wedge \\ \sim G_1 x_3 \wedge \sim G_2 x_3] \wedge \cdots \wedge [Fx_n \wedge \sim G_1 x_n \wedge \cdots \wedge \sim G_{n-1} x_n]) \rightarrow Fy)$$

Any sentence of this form is true whenever there are n or fewer entities (the only way to make the antecedent true is to assign n distinct entities to $x_1 \ldots x_n$, each of which satisfies F; but if there are no more than n entities, then y must be assigned one of these things as well, in which case the consequent comes out true.) So no matter what substitutions we make for the predicates, the sentence remains true; thus it counts as logically true given Quine's criterion, and so counts as necessarily true given Humeanism. But some sentences of this form seem only contingently true: they could have been falsified if there had existed n things satisfying the antecedent, and some additional entity that failed to satisfy the consequent. It might be responded that these consequences are unproblematic: since abstract entities are infinite in number and exist necessarily, it is impossible for there to exist just one thing, or just finitely many things.[20] But a Humean might deny the existence of abstracta. Moreover, the contextualist (see below) might want to allow contexts in which 'abstract entities exist necessarily' is false. Whatever its other merits, Quine's theory of logical truth does not mesh with the Humean account of modality.

The "best-system" account of logical truth mentioned in section 10.3, on the other hand, if extended to a theory of logical consequence, would mesh just fine with Humeanism. So would a model-theoretic conception of logical consequence. The model-theoretic conception (and Quine's as well) faces the question of how to characterize the notion of a logical constant. Only logical constants receive constant interpretations in all models, so the characterization affects the resultant notion of logical consequence.[21] But an element of conventionality or subjectivity or projection or semantic indeterminacy in the notion of a logical constant, resulting in such an element in the notion of necessity, will be acceptable to the Humean.

The Humean theory is mostly neutral on the characterization of mathematical truth, provided the characterization is non-modal and plausibly yields necessary truths. One vague conception: a mathematical truth is a proposition that concerns just mathematics and is true. There is a question parallel to that of how to characterize the logical constants: what is to count as a part of mathematics? But again, an element of conventionality, subjectivity, or the like will be tolerable to the Humean. If there are sharp lines to be drawn around logic and mathematics, then

---

[19] See Etchemendy (1990).

[20] A similar response could be based on the views of Williamson (1998; 2002).

[21] The set of logical words should not include modal words. That would threaten circularity; also, some modal languages arguably contain logical truths, such as ⌜If ϕ then Actually ϕ⌝, that are not necessary.

necessity here is sharp; if not, not. The spirit of Humeanism is that necessity is not a realm to be discovered. *We* draw the lines around what is necessary. It should be no surprise that we sometimes do this incompletely, arbitrarily, or projectively.

Note that the Humean need not assume that mathematical statements are true. If they are not, then there are no mathematical truths, and hence no mathematical necessities, which would seem to be the right consequence given this philosophy of mathematics.

12.4 Analyticity

"Analytic truths should turn out necessary."

Granted. We should include each analytic truth—in the sense of section 9.8—as a modal axiom. Analytic sentences were there characterized, recall, as sentences that are both true and definitional (where a definitional sentence is a sentence intended to constrain the meanings of its terms). This does not require truth by convention, since part of the characterization of an analytic sentence is that that sentence be ("already") true.[22]

12.5 Laws of metaphysics

"Statements of fundamental metaphysics should turn out noncontingent."

It seems to be part of the concept of metaphysical necessity that certain statements of fundamental metaphysics are noncontingent. Consider for example:[23]

Parthood is transitive.

There are no (merely) past or future objects.

Objects have temporal parts.

Any objects have a mereological sum.

In particular, consider these sentences as they occur in discussions of fundamental metaphysics, where the terms in question are intended to carve at the joints, and where the truth of the sentences is a matter of controversy. In such contexts, the sentences seem to be noncontingent: necessarily true if true; necessarily false if false.[24] But in such contexts the sentences do not seem analytic. They are the subject of controversy, and so are not construed as definitional of the terms they contain. It might be argued that certain *ordinary* sentences containing the disputed vocabulary ('part', quantification, temporal vocabulary) are definitional; but philosophers who think that this vocabulary carves at the joints and engage in dispute over the nature of these joints suspend any such definitional constraints. If the sentences (in this context) are not analytic, how shall the Humean account for their noncontingency?

---

[22]Like the Humean account of necessity, this is a classification rather than governance account.

[23]For simplicity, I write as if mereological vocabulary is fundamental, but see chapter 13.

[24]Although see Cameron (2007).

By adding a new group of modal axioms: the true propositions about such fundamental and abstract matters. What justifies their status as modal axioms? This is just how the concept of necessity works. Such propositions have no further feature that explains their inclusion as modal axioms.

Exactly what sorts of truths about "fundamental and abstract matters" get included as modal axioms? I'm not sure how much sharpening of this vague formulation is possible (or necessary), but we might wheel in the generalized Lewisian account of lawhood from section 3.1. If complexity is expensive, only the laws of logic count as laws (recall section 10.3). If it is cheap, then physical and special-science generalizations also count as laws. If its cost is middling, the special-science laws drop away but the laws of physics remain. Now, consider a cost of complexity intermediate between the first ("expensive") and the last ("middling"). Here we drop the laws of physics but still retain more than the laws of logic: we also retain what one might call laws of metaphysics. (Despite the grand name, no heavy-duty metaphysics is intended; the underlying account of lawhood is reductive.) The sacrifice in simplicity needed for their inclusion is greater than that required for the laws of logic, since the relevant terms (such as mereological and temporal vocabulary) are not quite so topic-neutral and pervasive as those of logic. But the laws of metaphysics are simpler because more abstract, pervasive, and topic-neutral than the laws of fundamental science, and because less "specific".

The Humean view about necessity requires no commitment to any particular laws of metaphysics. It says merely that the laws of metaphysics, whatever they happen to be, are to be included as modal axioms. The Humean could, for example, be neutral about whether objects have temporal parts; she would say simply that whichever of 'Things have temporal parts' and 'Things do not have temporal parts' is true is a modal axiom. The roster of modal axioms is a function of whatever the nonmodal facts concerning fundamental and abstract matters turn out to be.

The laws of metaphysics provide examples of synthetic necessary truths. Supposing it to be true that past and future objects do not exist, it is impossible that they exist, despite the fact that there is no conceptual incoherence in supposing that they do. Some metaphysicians find synthetic necessities deeply disturbing, and go to great lengths to avoid them. Ross Cameron (2007), for example, argues that i) mereological sums exist; but ii) existential claims are never analytic; and so, desiring to avoid synthetic necessities, concludes that iii) it is contingent that mereological sums exist. Thus, for example, although the subatomic particles in my body compose something—namely, me—there is a possible world exactly like ours at the subatomic level in which those particles compose nothing. A second example: Cian Dorr's (2004) hostility to synthetic necessities plays an important role in his argument against non-symmetric relations. And Cameron and Dorr are just two recent examples of a centuries-old tradition that finds synthetic necessities metaphysically mysterious. As Dorr (2004, section 3) puts it, "Metaphysical necessity is never 'brute': when a logically contingent sentence is metaphysically necessary, there is always some explanation for this fact."

I wonder whether the aversion to synthetic necessities survives the full repudiation of truth by convention. Dorr requires necessities to be "explained". He explains the necessity of the logically contingent "All water is H_2O", for example, by the fact that metaphysical analysis reveals it to express the same proposition as the logical truth "All H_2O is H_2O." But why doesn't the necessity of this logical truth then need to be explained? Assuming that truth by convention is off the table, the question must be faced.

A certain sort of picture-thinking is initially compelling. It couldn't be necessary that mereological sums exist, for what would *force* the existence of a further whole, in addition to the existence of a given set of parts? The fact of the parts' existence is one fact, the existence of the whole another fact; how could the first necessitate the second? But the picture does not withstand scrutiny. Why not reason also as follows: the fact that it is raining is one fact; the fact that it is either raining or snowing is a distinct fact; how could the first necessitate the second? One is tempted to respond that the cases are different: the fact that it's either raining or snowing isn't a separate fact from the fact that it's raining. But the temptation dissipates once truth by convention has been repudiated. Once we recognize that logical content is as "wordly" as nonlogical content, we see that there is no interesting construal of fact-identity on which the first pattern of reasoning is sustained but the second is not. The picture-thinking loses its grip. For the picture was that we perceive in allegedly unproblematic cases of logical necessitation a certain kind of connection, a connection which explains the necessitation; and we see that this connection is missing in the case of mereological sums. But now we see that the perceived connection was never there in the first place.

From a Humean perspective, synthetic necessities are no more puzzling than analytic or logical necessities. As it happens, we use the word 'necessary' to encompass certain synthetic truths in addition to analytic and logical truths. But there's no deep fact here: we could have used 'necessary' for just the analytic and logical truths—or for a more inclusive set of truths. The fact that certain synthetic truths are necessary is no more surprising than the fact (if it is a fact) that cups are glasses.

The aversion to synthetic necessities makes a bit more sense from a non-Humean perspective, but even then its status is hardly that of metaphysical bedrock. Suppose, for example, that necessity is a primitive feature of the world, an irreducible "glow" in some true propositions. What then would be wrong with saying that certain synthetic propositions glow, in addition to logical and analytic propositions? There can be no "constitutive" explanation of why the logical truths glow, for example, in the sense of an explanation which says: to glow is to be such-and-such; logical truths are examples of such-and-suches; so logical truths glow. For the glow is primitive. And if the modal primitivist lacks a constitutive explanation of why the logical truths glow, what's so bad about lacking a constitutive explanation of why certain further propositions glow? The modal primitivist might respond that a leaner, more attractive view about primitive modality would restrict its application as much as possible. The more restriction of the glow the better; best-case scenario: restriction solely to the logical truths. Fair enough, but the resulting doctrine is then one speculative metaphysical hypothesis among many, not a bedrock truth whose denial would be "unintelligible" (as Lewis (1983b, p. 366) describes a related denial).

The Humean treatment of the necessity of laws of metaphysics undermines "arguments from possibility" for conclusions in fundamental metaphysics. Such arguments begin by claiming that a certain proposition is possible—perhaps on the grounds that "modal intuition" informs us that it is possible, perhaps because of some general presumption in favor of possibility. Next, the possibility is argued to be incompatible with a certain fundamental proposition of metaphysics. So the fundamental proposition is possibly false. Finally, it is concluded that the fundamental proposition is actually false, since fundamental propositions of metaphysics are noncontingent. For example, I once argued that mereological nihilism (the view that only mereologically simple entities exist) is actually false on the grounds that gunk is possible (Sider, 1993b). And even arguments about weightier matters, such as David Chalmers's (1996) argument against materialism, fall in this category.

Such arguments are undermined by Humeanism. This is not because Humeanism undermines the premise that fundamental propositions of metaphysics are noncontingent. On the contrary, Humeanism vindicates this premise, since fundamental propositions of metaphysics count as modal axioms when true.[25] It is rather because Humeanism undermines our reason for accepting the possibility in question. Intuitively, this is because for propositions of fundamental metaphysics, possibility boils down to the actual falsity of rivals.

A proposition p of fundamental metaphysics typically has *rivals*: other propositions of fundamental metaphysics that are incompatible with p. (I have in mind competing accounts of the same subject matter. For example, rivals to materialism include dualism and idealism.) Now, the set of modal axioms is defined as containing, among other things, the propositions of fundamental metaphysics that are true, whatever those happen to be. And to say that a proposition is possible, on the Humean view, is to say that that proposition's negation is *not* a logical consequence of the modal axioms. Thus, to say that the fundamental metaphysical proposition p is possible is to say that its negation is not a logical consequence of a set that is defined as containing its true rivals. Given this, there is next to

---

[25] Qualification: Humeanism doesn't quite imply that fundamental propositions of metaphysics are necessarily false when false; what it implies is that this holds whenever the fundamental proposition has a true "rival" in the sense to be explained.

no epistemic difference between asserting that *p* is possible and asserting that its rivals are false.[26]

Assuming the Humean theory, then, neither modal intuition nor a putative presumption in favor of possibility can be regarded as probative in matters of fundamental metaphysics—unless intuition or the presumption are somehow probative concerning the *actual* falsity of rivals; but then there would be no need to bring in possibility; one could argue directly against the rivals.

Arguments from possibility in effect assume that modality is separate, in a certain sense, from actuality. They assume that the status of possibility is one we can assess independently of questions about actuality, and so, in the case of noncontingent propositions, make genuine epistemic advances on questions of actuality by reasoning through this separate status. But for the Humean, modal notions are not separate from actuality in this way. To be necessary *just is* to be true and of a certain sort.

I have been disparaging arguments from possibility; but it may be objected that surely *some* such arguments are good. Imagine a physical theory that predicts bizarre results if there are exactly seventeen particles, but makes sensible predictions otherwise. Can we not object that the theory makes the wrong predictions with respect to those physically possible scenarios involving exactly seventeen particles? We could; but we could also object without bringing in modality. Since the theory makes an exception for the case of seventeen particles, it is surely needlessly complex, and is therefore less explanatory than an otherwise similar theory without the exception. I suspect that something similar is true generally: when there is good in an argument from possibility, it can be recast in other terms—explanation, for instance.

12.6 Determinates and determinables

"Why are distinct determinates of a given determinable incompatible? Why is it impossible for something to be both 5g mass and 6g mass, for example?"

It's tempting to respond that it's analytic that nothing has two distinct masses. 'Nothing has two masses' is both true and a definitional constraint on the interpretation of the term 'mass'. But suppose we come across a new property which we name 'schmass'.[27] Since schmass has only just been discovered, it is not definitional of 'schmass' that different values of schmass are incompatible. Indeed, let us stipulate that we are not yet sure whether schmass comes in degrees. But in fact, suppose, schmass does come in degrees—indeed, the determinate schmass properties have the structure of the positive real numbers, just like the masses. Further, nothing has two of these determinate properties. In such a case, it's surely necessary, but not analytic, that nothing has two distinct schmasses.

---

[26] See Sider (2011, section 9) for a fuller presentation of this point.
[27] Thanks to Ernie Sosa here.

The explanation of necessity here lies not in analyticity, but rather in the fact that it's a law of metaphysics that nothing has two schmasses. (Likewise, it's a law of metaphysics that nothing has two masses.) In general, facts about determinate/determinable structure are "fundamental and abstract" features of reality of the sort discussed in the previous section.

For the sake of concreteness, let's go into the metaphysics of quantities a bit. Consider first Brent Mundy's (1987) view of quantities.[28] According to Mundy, numerical representation of quantities is justified by the first-order and higher-order structure of the quantities in question. The infinitely many determinate mass properties, for example, are structured by higher-order relations, for instance a binary relation, R, signifying "is a larger mass", or a ternary relation S of summation ($m_1 m_2 S m_3$ iff masses m_1 and m_2 "sum to" mass m_3). Assuming that certain constraints hold, one can prove representation theorems to the effect that there exists a unique (up to an appropriate transformation) function from the first-order mass properties into the real numbers that "meshes" with the higher-order relations. Mesh requires, for example, that the number assigned to one mass property be greater than the number assigned to another iff the first bears the relation R to the second, and that whenever three masses stand in S, the sum of the numbers assigned to the first two masses must equal the number assigned to the third. The constraints assumed by the representation theorem include constraints on the higher-order structuring relations (for example, R must be transitive) as well as constraints on the distribution of the first-order determinate mass properties (for example, no particular can have two of them). Notice that similar constraints are obeyed by other quantities as well. Some quantities are structured *somewhat* differently; for example, temperature has a zero point. Still, there is a pattern of constraints that are mostly obeyed by multiple quantities. The pattern is widespread and fundamental enough to count as a law of metaphysics. The first-order portion of the pattern—nothing instantiates two of the determinates—is what accounts for the incompatibility between distinct determinates.

A rival account of quantities is the first-order account of Krantz et al. (1971), according to which the numerical representation of quantities is justified by the holding of first-order relations over particulars. In the case of mass, in place of Mundy's relations R and S over the determinate mass properties we have corresponding structuring relations more-massive-than and summation over massive objects. As with Mundy, representation theorems can be proved on the assumption that the structuring relations hold in certain patterns; and as with Mundy, similar (though not identical) patterns recur with other determinables. We can again include these patterns as modal axioms under the rubric of laws of metaphysics.

Some confirmation that this account is on the right track can be gained by reflecting on some examples. First example: suppose some quantity is discrete,

---

[28]Similar remarks apply to Funkhouser (2006).

and has a small number of values—say, eight. The structuring relations (whether higher-order or first order) hold in a rather different pattern from the pattern for other, continuous, quantities. Does the pattern for the discrete quantity count as a law of metaphysics? There seems to be no fact of the matter. The concept of a law of metaphysics does not decide the case one way or the other, and that concept is certainly not a fundamental one. The present account thus predicts that there is no fact of the matter whether it's possible for a thing to have two "determinates" of the discrete "determinable". This prediction seems intuitively correct.

Second example: imagine discovering that one particular determinable property—mass, say—lacks most of the structure it is generally presumed to have. In Mundy's terms, suppose there are no second-order relations over the determinate masses (no joint-carving second-order relations, I would say); in the first-orderist's terms, suppose there are no (joint-carving) relations of the sort described above over massive objects. What we call mass is in fact heterogeneous. (Perhaps the class of masses has various structured subgroups, perhaps not.) Now, even if no object in fact has two masses in this example, having two masses seems less impossible, intuitively, than having two determinates of one of the other determinables where the structure is not missing. And this is what the present account predicts: 'No object has two masses' less clearly fits into the fundamental and abstract pattern exhibited by the other determinables, and hence is less clearly a law of metaphysics.

12.7 Contextualism

It's a familiar point that natural language modal words are contextually variable. "Johnny can't watch TV next door", I might say, indicating that going next door is forbidden to Johnny. But I might later say, with no change in the facts being described: "Johnny can watch TV next door (since our neighbors leave their doors unlocked), but he can't watch across the street (since the doors there are locked)." Still later I might say: "Johnny can go across the street (since that's close by), but he cannot go across town (since he doesn't yet know how to drive)." More extremely, I might say: "Johnny can go to the moon (since the technology exists), but not to Mars", whereas later I might say "Johnny can travel to Mars but not to star systems 10,000 light years away (since supraluminal travel violates the laws of nature and humans don't live to be 10,000 years old)."

This contextual variation might be regarded as happening only with *restricted* modalities. There is some one "outer" modality, according to this view, of which each contextual modality is a restriction.[29] The outer modality might be claimed to be "metaphysical necessity", for example. On this view, a restricted necessity "necessarily, ϕ" is analyzed as $\Box(R{\rightarrow}\phi)$, and a restricted possibility "possibly, ϕ" is analyzed as $\Diamond(R{\wedge}\phi)$, where $\Box$ and $\Diamond$ express the outer notions of metaphysical necessity and possibility and R is a restricting sentence. In the case of 'Johnny can't watch TV next door', for example, the restrictor R might be the sentence

---

[29] Perhaps epistemic and deontic modalities are included in this picture, perhaps not.

'Johnny satisfies his obligations'; in the case of 'Johnny can go to the moon', R might specify the current state of space travel (but not the fact that Johnny has no money for a ticket). On this picture, though R can vary contextually, talk of outer possibility and necessity is contextually constant.

A more attractive picture, I think, is that there is no such contextually constant outer modality. Even the outer $\Box$ and $\Diamond$ vary contextually. In Humean terms, there can be contextual variation both in the modal axioms and in the modal rules, resulting in variation in the modal theorems and hence in what is necessary and possible.

This contextual variation may be motivated both from within the perspective of Humeanism and directly from ordinary use of modal words. From within a Humean perspective, contextual variation is natural to admit, since nothing deep holds the modal axioms and rules together in the first place. If there were a primitive glow associated with all necessary truths, then it would be natural to have a contextually invariant word for that glow; but in the absence of such a glow, why not allow contextual variation? And such contextual variation seems called for by ordinary usage. Just as the following speeches seem admissible:

> "Johnny can't go to the moon. Well, he could if he had enough money to buy a ticket from NASA." [shift from a kind of personal possibility to technological possibility]
> "Things can't just disappear. Well, they could if the law of conservation of matter were false." [shift from nomic possibility to metaphysical possibility]

so do the following:

> "Nothing can be at two places at once. Well, something could if the occupation relation held in a one–many pattern." [metaphysical possibility to logical possibility?]
> "Contradictions can't be true. Well, they could if dialetheism were true." [logical possibility to ??]

It might be objected that we can follow up each of the second two speeches with disavowals: "but the occupation relation just couldn't hold in a one–many pattern", "but dialetheism just couldn't have been true". But these seem to be no better conversational moves than the analogous moves in the first speeches: "but he just couldn't have obtained enough money for a ticket", "but the law of conservation of matter just couldn't have been false". English modals are context-dependent through and through; there is no stable "outer modality".

This instability can also be seen in talk of the necessity of laws of metaphysics. First, although philosophers—especially metaphysicians—tend to speak of the laws of metaphysics as being noncontingent, in ordinary contexts it isn't unnatural to speak of the laws of metaphysics as being contingent. And second, there seems to be some contextual variation, or at least indeterminacy, in what counts as a law of metaphysics. Think, for example, of the boundary between metaphysics and fundamental physics. Supposing spacetime to in fact have four dimensions: is this a "mere physical necessity", or is it a "metaphysical necessity"? There's no contextually constant answer. Likewise for "Points of spacetime exist."

What I have been characterizing in this chapter has been an outer modality, a modality that is usually restricted in context. But what has emerged in this section is that even this outer modality varies contextually. In context, various modal axioms or rules may be contextually dropped, resulting in a more restrictive notion of necessity and hence a broader sort of possibility. Some modal axioms or rules may be harder to suspend than others, as may be some patterns of suspension; but any pattern is in-principle possible.[30] Thus, there is no sharp line between restricted and unrestricted metaphysical necessity.

12.8 The necessary a posteriori

"What about the necessary a posteriori?"

Hilary Putnam (1975*b*) argues by thought experiment that a substance on another planet with all the superficial features of water would nevertheless not count as water if it were not made up of H_2O, but were instead made up of some alien molecule XYZ. He concludes that it is necessary that all water is made up of H_2O. Since it was not knowable a priori what the chemical composition of water was, we have an example of a necessary truth that is knowable only a posteriori.

As Alan Sidelle (1989) argues, the necessary a posteriori provides a prima facie challenge for "conventionalist" theories of modality. A very simple conventionalism that identified necessity with analyticity, construed as truth by convention, would face the challenge most directly, for conventionalists regarded analytic truths as being a priori. More vaguely, conventionalists reject the picture that there is an independent modal realm "out there waiting to be discovered", holding instead that necessity, somehow, has its source in us; it is then tempting to think that all modal truths would be knowable a priori. Since Humeans also reject the picture of modality being "out there", they too face the vague challenge.

Sidelle defends conventionalism from this objection. His strategy is to "factor" a necessary a posteriori truth into an analytic component and a nonmodal component. All the "modal force" (p. 37) of the necessary truth is to come from the analytic component, whereas the a posteriority is to come from the nonmodal component.[31] In the case of 'All water is made up of H_2O', the analytic truth is:

(W) Whatever water's deep explanatory feature, F, happens to be, it is necessary that all water has F.

And the nonmodal component is that the deep explanatory feature of water is in fact: being made of H_2O.

---

[30]We may want to allow addition as well as suspension. For example, in a context where we are considering the possibility of dialetheism, but in which we don't want to count everything as possible, we must suspend classical rules of inference, but we must then put some weaker rules in their place.

[31]See also Chalmers (1996); Coppock (1984); Hirsch (1986); Jackson (1998).

There is a question of how the analyticity of (W) is supposed to help the conventionalist. As Stephen Yablo (1992) points out, it wouldn't do to think of (W) as a definitional constraint on 'water', in the sense of a stipulation that *nothing is to count as water unless it possesses its deepest explanatory feature necessarily*. For that would seem to presuppose the existence of modal features (and select the reference of 'water' on their basis), rather than show modal features to be conventional. Sidelle has a different view of the role of (W); but rather than discussing it, I will put forward my own view—in the service of the Humean theory rather than conventionalism.[32]

The crucial thing is to regard (W) as a definitional constraint on 'necessary', not on 'water'. Thus we stipulate that *no property is to count as the property of being a necessary proposition unless it is had by the proposition that water has F, where F is water's deep explanatory feature*. Unlike the stipulation considered by Yablo, this stipulation is nonmodal, and thus does not presuppose modal features in its selection of reference.

Concretely: Humean necessity satisfies this stipulation provided we introduce a new class of modal axioms, the *natural kind axioms*:

Natural kind axiom: a proposition expressed by a sentence of the form ⌜All Fs are Gs⌝, where F is a natural-kind term (such as 'water') and G expresses the deep explanatory feature of the property expressed by F

Once these new axioms are included, the Humean theory implies that 'Necessarily, water is made of H_2O', as well as Putnam's other examples of the necessary a posteriori, are indeed true.

12.9 Micro-reduction

"What about Lewis's example of the talking donkey?"

One of the chief advantages Lewis claimed for his modal realism against rival theories of possible worlds was that only modal realism can reduce modality. Consider for example "linguistic ersatzism", according to which possible worlds are maximal consistent sets of sentences in some suitable world-making language. This rival apparently cannot reduce modality, since the relevant notion of a *consistent* set of sentences must apparently be modal. Mere logical consistency will not rule out possible worlds with married bachelors, for instance. Lewis considered the move of defining consistency as logical consistency with a set of

---

[32]Sidelle himself regards (W) as a definitional constraint on how to use 'water' in counterfactual situations, where those counterfactual situations are given in "identity-neutral" terms (in terms of "pre-objectual stuff"). I prefer the account in the text for two reasons. First, my account does not require a metaphysics of stuff (about which I am skeptical—recall section 9.6.2). Second, Sidelle's account presupposes talk of counterfactual situations and thus is not fully reductive (though I grant that since he does not presuppose talk of identities of natural kinds and ordinary objects between distinct counterfactual situations, his account is in an important sense conventionalist about *de re* modality).

"meaning postulates", but rejected it with an argument along the following lines (1986b, pp. 150–7).[33]

Let C_0 completely describe New York City in every microphysical detail (relationally as well as intrinsically). It is surely necessary that any C_0 is a city. The ersatzer must therefore include a sentence of the form:

(C) Any C_0 is a city

among the meaning postulates. But no one knows what different arrangements at the micro-level would suffice for the existence of a city, and so no one knows what meaning postulates of the form (C) to add. (Lewis's example making this point involved 'talking donkey' rather than 'city'.)

Even if the ersatzer does not know which *particular* sentences to add, she might still produce some defining condition that would delineate the class of meaning postulates so as to include the appropriate instances of (C). But this must be done nonmodally; the ersatzer cannot, for instance, stipulate that all necessary truths of form (C) are to count as meaning postulates.

Mark Heller has argued that the ersatzer need not solve this problem. In Heller's (1998) version of linguistic ersatzism, possible worlds are sets of sentences in a language that can describe only the distribution of fundamental properties over spacetime. Since the language contains no macro-predicates, it lacks the predicate 'is a city'. Consistency can then be just logical consistency.[34] The problem of micro-reduction then becomes one of how to *interpret* these worlds, how to say when it is true in one of them that there exists a city. But, Heller claims (1996), interpretation need not be regarded as part of the theory of possible worlds. It is part of a project of the analysis of ordinary concepts, and is optional for a philosopher of modality.

If all we wanted were a theory of possible worlds, then we could indeed postpone solving the problem of micro-reduction in this way. But we want a reduction of modality as well as a theory of worlds. The two are generally connected thus:

It is necessary that ϕ iff for every possible world, w, it is true that ϕ in w.

This biconditional contains the locution ⌜it is true that ϕ in [possible world] w⌝. If the locution remains undefined then no analysis of modality has been given. But to define it requires solving the problem of micro-reduction, for the locution must be defined in the case where w is a world with subatomic particles arranged in way C_0 and ϕ is 'There exists a city'.

---

[33] A second argument was that no one knows whether it is metaphysically impossible or merely nomically impossible for a particle to be both positively charged and negatively charged, and so the ersatzer does not know whether to include a meaning postulate prohibiting this combination (1986b, pp. 154–5). The Humean can respond that if 'nothing is both negatively and positively charged' is a law of metaphysics (like analogous sentences concerning distinct determinates of a given determinable), then it is a modal axiom and hence is necessary. (Perhaps it is indeterminate whether it is a law of metaphysics, in which case it is indeterminate whether it is necessary.)

[34] A question I will not pursue: why should fundamental properties necessarily apply to points rather than regions?

This problem threatens the Humean as well, since sentences like (C) do not seem to be mathematical truths, analytic truths, laws of metaphysics, natural kind axioms, or logical consequences of such sentences.

The Humean should introduce another group of modal axioms, derived from a theory of metaphysical truth-conditions (section 7.4) for the language in question. There are, I assume, metaphysical truth-conditions for statements about cities, smiles, and candy. The metaphysical semantics generating these metaphysical truth-conditions, let's assume, contains axioms of the form "Predicate F applies to object x iff $\phi(x)$", where F may be 'city', 'smile', 'candy', and so on, and where $\phi(x)$ is phrased in purely fundamental terms.[35] For each such axiom of the metaphysical semantics, we should add a corresponding modal axiom:

$$\forall x(Fx \leftrightarrow \phi(x))$$

It is surely indeterminate exactly what the axioms of the true metaphysical semantics are. Correspondingly, it is indeterminate which sentences of the form (C) count as modal axioms. Note, though, that if C_0 exactly describes the *actual* microstate of New York City (as stipulated above), then surely (C) will count as necessary on any reasonable way of resolving this indeterminacy. For surely, on any reasonable way of resolving the indeterminacy of what the theory of metaphysical truth-conditions looks like, the actual microstate of New York City will be subsumed under ϕ in the relevant axiom:[36]

$$\forall x(\text{city}(x) \leftrightarrow \phi(x))$$

I will not, because I cannot, give metaphysical truth-conditions for 'city', 'smile', or 'candy'. I have not, therefore, fully specified metaphysical truth-conditions for 'necessarily', since my specification of those truth-conditions makes reference to the general theory of metaphysical truth-conditions for the rest of the language. Nevertheless, we have all we should want in a reduction of modality. For we never succeed in giving anything more than "toy" metaphysical truth-conditions anyway, for notions of interest; recall section 7.6. The purpose of sketching toy truth-conditions is to show that words like 'cause', 'necessary', and so on, are as capable of resting upon the fundamental as more mundane words

---

[35] Given a restrictive fundamental ontology, existential quantification over Fs in natural language might have nonexistential truth-conditions, in which case the relevant axioms would have a different form (see section 7.4).

[36] 'Subsumed' here is deliberately vague. Two ways of making it precise. One: the language of the metaphysical truth-conditions is infinitary; the axiom has the form $\forall x(\text{city}(x) \leftrightarrow (\phi_1(x) \lor \ldots))$; C_0 is one of the ϕ_is (on each resolution of the indeterminacy of 'metaphysical truth-conditions'); the modal rule of inference in the Humean theory is infinitary logical consequence; thus (C) is a modal theorem. Two: the language of the metaphysical truth-conditions can represent quantification over properties; the axiom has the form $\forall x(\text{city}(x) \leftrightarrow \exists p(x \text{ instantiates } p \land \phi(p))$; 'the property of being C_0 is ϕ' is a modal axiom (including this sort of axiom would be natural given this higher-order setting; such sentences are analogous to mathematical truths) as are suitable sentences of the form $\forall x(\psi(x) \leftrightarrow x \text{ instantiates the property of being } \psi)$; therefore (C) is again a modal theorem.

like 'city', 'smile', and 'candy'. We do this by showing what form the unfathomably complex theory of metaphysical truth-conditions might take to deal with them. The present theory accomplishes this: if the theory of metaphysical truth-conditions can deal with 'city', 'smile', and 'candy', then it can deal with 'necessary' as well—the parts dealing with 'city', 'smile', and 'candy' get incorporated into the part dealing with 'necessary'.

It must be admitted that Lewis's account of the necessity of statements like (C) has an advantage. Lewis and I are both modal reductionists; thus we both want to show that the necessitations of sentences like (C) can be given nonmodal metaphysical truth-conditions (if I may transpose Lewis's talk of "analysis" into this key), thus showing that they fit into amodal fundamental reality. My Humean approach assumes that the theory of metaphysical truth-conditions contains biconditionals of the sort described above. Lewis, on the other hand, requires no such assumption. For Lewis, the metaphysical truth-condition of "Necessarily, every C_0 is a city" is basically [37] just "Absolutely every C_0 is a city"—a mundane quantified statement containing 'city'. So to show that the necessity of (C) fits into amodal fundamental reality, all Lewis needs to assume is that mundane quantified sentences containing 'city' have some nonmodal metaphysical truth-conditions or other.

Notice, by the way, that even a modalist, who takes necessity to carve at the joints, must concede an advantage here to Lewis. Unlike Lewis and me, the modalist is not trying to fit the necessitation of (C) into amodal reality. But given purity (section 7.2), even a modalist cannot say that (C) is a fundamental fact, for (C) contains the nonfundamental term 'city'. So even the modalist must supply metaphysical truth-conditions for (C) and other micro-reduction sentences. Unlike me, the modalist can appeal to primitive modal notions in doing so, but given purity, the sentences containing those primitive modal notions cannot involve any nonfundamental notions, and so don't seem to be of any particular help here. Modalists, it would seem, can do no better than I in giving metaphysical truth-conditions for microreduction sentences; they must apparently appeal to the same biconditionals in the theory of metaphysical truth-conditions to which I appeal.

12.10 De re modality

"What about de re modality?"

De dicto modal claims, it is often said, concern the modal features of propositions, whereas de re modal claims concern the modal features of objects. "Necessarily: the number of the planets is odd" is said to be de dicto because it attributes necessity to a proposition, the proposition that the number of the planets is odd; whereas "The number of the planets is such that: it is necessarily odd" is de re since

---

[37] Not quite: it's only the C_0s that are parts of maximal spatiotemporally interrelated entities—the entities that Lewis calls possible worlds—that must be cities.

it attributes a modal feature, being necessarily odd, to an object, namely the object that in fact numbers the planets—8, as we're now told. This characterization is imperfect, but all I need here is a rough-and-ready sense of the distinction.

The modal axioms and rules laid out so far need to be augmented to deliver the full range of de re modal truths. For example, 'Necessarily, Ted is human' is commonly supposed to be true: any entity of a nonhuman species, no matter how like me in other respects, simply would not be *me*. But 'Ted is human' is not a modal theorem, given the current definition.

One approach would parallel section 12.8's treatment of the necessary a posteriori. 'Ted is human' names a biological organism and specifies its species; and it's plausible that any such sentence is necessarily true if true at all. So we could simply add to our list of modal axioms, all such sentences that are true. More generally, Saul Kripke (1972) taught us of a wider class of sentences containing proper names that are necessarily true if true at all.[38] These include sentences of the following forms: i) "α is F", where α is a proper name and F is a "sortal" predicate (species predicates are a special case); ii) "α is F", where F specifies material origins; and iii) "$\alpha = \beta$", where α and β are proper names. All true sentences of these forms could be added as modal axioms. (A familiar theme: nothing deep need underlie the selection of these new modal axioms; the selection reflects how our concept of necessity happens to work.)

A second kind of de re modal claim involves "quantifying into modal contexts": a variable inside the scope of a modal operator is bound to a quantifier outside, as in '$\exists x \square \, \text{human}(x)$' ("Something is such that it is necessarily human"). The Humean theory so far supplies truth-conditions for $\square \phi$ only when ϕ lacks free variables; but to account for quantifying-in, truth-conditions must also be given in the case where ϕ may contain free variables ('$\square \, \text{human}(x)$'). The usual Tarskian strategy for assigning truth-conditions to formulas with free variables is to relativize those truth-conditions to variable assignments—functions from free variables to entities. Following this strategy, the Humean could allow modal axioms and theorems to contain free variables, and could relativize modal axiomhood, rulehood, and theoremhood to variable assignments. In categories i)–iii) of modal axioms mentioned in the previous paragraph, α and β can now be variables as well as proper names. So, for example, 'human(x)' would count as a modal axiom relative to a variable assignment g that assigned me to x (category i) above), and thus would count as a modal theorem relative to g; thus '$\square \, \text{human}(x)$' would be true relative to g; thus '$\exists x \square \, \text{human}(x)$' would be true simpliciter.

That, then, is one approach the Humean could take to *de re* modality. An alternate approach is counterpart-theoretic. David Lewis (1968; 1971; 1986b) defined modality in terms of possible worlds, but famously denied that individuals

---

[38] Accommodating the analogous sentences containing indexicals and demonstratives (Kaplan, 1989) would require relativizing modal axiomhood to context, and would also require other adjustments if, for example, the contingent sentence 'I am here now' is regarded as a logical truth.

are located in more than one possible world. As a result, he could not agree with the usual possible-worlds definition of *de re* modality, according to which an object is necessarily F iff that very object is F in every possible world. Rather, he said, an object is necessarily F iff in every possible world, that object's *counterpart* is F, where a counterpart of an object in a world is something that is similar enough to that object, and is more similar to that object than anything else in its world. A Humean could base her theory of *de re* modality on these ideas, as follows. First, take the Humean account offered in the preceding sections as an account of de dicto necessity. Second, use de dicto necessity to construct abstract possible worlds and individuals, in any of the standard ways. For example, possible individuals could be defined as certain sets of formulas, or certain sorts of properties.[39] Third, introduce a counterpart relation over the abstract possible individuals. Fourth, give counterpart-theoretic truth-conditions for de re modal sentences. Thus, 'Necessarily, Ted is human' will turn out true iff all of my abstract counterparts represent me as being human.[40]

Even Humeans who reject the counterpart-theoretic approach to *de re* modality may pursue the general strategy of the previous paragraph to enrich their account of modality in other directions. The general approach is to take the Humean account as an account of some initial notion of necessity; use that initial notion to introduce abstract possible worlds and individuals; and then use those abstract possible worlds and individuals to define a further, enriched, sort of necessity. For example, to introduce an actuality operator, @, the Humean might build up abstract worlds using a @-free language, and then give truth-conditions for @ in terms of those worlds. A similar strategy could be used to give truth-conditions for statements about counterfactuals, dispositions, supervenience, and other modal notions.

12.11 Family resemblances

Why are logical (or mathematical, or analytic, or . . .) truths necessary? The Humean's answer is that this is just how our concept of necessity works. One can give no deeper answer to this question than to the question of why a water glass counts as a cup (assuming that it does). There are many possible meanings we could have chosen for 'cup'; some include glasses, some don't; none carve nature at the joints better than any others; the meaning we have in fact chosen includes glasses; and that's all there is to it. Likewise for 'necessary'.

This is the most flatfooted Humean answer, at any rate. But a Humean need not be *quite* so flat-footed. Consider the various sorts of modal axioms. She resists the idea that there is a single necessary and sufficient condition for being a modal axiom. Nevertheless, she is free to exhibit similarities between various modal axioms, just as one might exhibit similarities between things that fall under our

---

[39] See Lewis (1986*b*, section 3.2).
[40] See Sider (2002; 2006) for more discussion.

concept of a game, to use Wittgenstein's example. Doing this would help to show that the Humean concept of necessity is not utterly arbitrary or heterogeneous.

In fact, many of the modal axioms I have listed do seem to have something in common: a prioricity. The sort of evidence relevant to logical and mathematical truths, to laws of metaphysics, and to most analytic truths, is what is traditionally called a priori. This is not to say that they are *known* a priori (for they may not be known at all), nor that they are even *knowable* a priori (perhaps we have no way of knowing certain mathematical or mereological truths), nor even to insist on a deep or sharp or absolute distinction between the a priori and the a posteriori. Still, such access as we do have to their truth does seem different from the kinds of access we have to empirical truths of everyday life or science.[41]

Many of the axioms also seem to share the feature of being difficult to conceive as being false; this, too, partially unifies the set of modal axioms.

There are notorious difficulties with attempts to define necessity in terms of a priority or conceivability. These would be explained if necessity is given by a list that is not unified by any single feature, but which is partly unified by a priority and conceivability. Compare the notorious difficulties with attempts to define 'game' in terms of its unifying concepts (fun, competition, and so on).

So some unification of the class of modal axioms is possible. But a Humean will live with some disunification. She will be willing to admit that there is no one feature that all the modal axioms have in common. The spirit of Humeanism, after all, is that the line between the necessary and contingent is not discovered, but rather drawn by us—perhaps somewhat arbitrarily.

12.12 Spreading arbitrariness

Humeanism's implications might seem disturbing given how central modality is to our cognitive lives. Historians speculate about what could have or would have happened; bankers make decisions based on what must happen; Humphrey regretted what might have been. If modal concepts are so disunified, up to us, metaphysically second rate, then isn't all this reasoning radically defective? Have we centered our cognitive lives on a notion so arbitrary as the notion of a bachelor, or cup, or martini?

Suppose someone viciously attacks a homeless person and steals his possessions. We want to blame the attacker. Now, blame is often thought to require the possibility of doing otherwise.[42] But, one might worry, Humeanism allows multiple, equally non-joint-carving, candidate meanings of 'could', some counting the following sentence true, others counting it false:

(AP) The attacker could have done otherwise.

---

[41]Those sympathetic with the two-dimensional approach to semantics might try to extend this similarity further, even to the necessary a posteriori.

[42]Let's not enter into the subtleties to which this formula has been subjected.

Therefore, the worry continues, the sentence 'The attacker is blameworthy' also comes out true on some candidates and false on others. So this and other attributions of blame are nonsubstantive in the sense of section 4.2.

In fact, Humeanism has no such consequence. First, although Humeanism allows multiple candidates for modal words, there are limits to these candidates. In particular, there surely are no candidates under which 'it is metaphysically impossible for the attacker to have done otherwise' comes out true. Any population using this sentence to express a truth would be semantically alien to us. (Not that they would be failing to carve at the joints. They would be like people who use 'hut' to refer to skyscrapers.)

This first observation is insufficient to rescue the substantivity of (AP), since the 'could' in (AP) does not express metaphysical possibility. The context of utterance of (AP) under consideration is an ordinary one, in which moral responsibility is at issue; and in such a context, 'could' does not express the broad notion of metaphysical possibility (the notion analyzed by the Humean), but rather expresses some much more restricted sort, which we might call "personal possibility". Thus (AP) means something like this:

(AP′) It's metaphysically possible that: R and the attacker do otherwise

where R is some "restrictor" sentence that specifies certain features of the agent. (The nature of R is part of what gets disputed in debates over free will. Compatibilists will include only a small set of features about the agent's nature and environment in R, whereas incompatibilists will include all facts about the past and laws of nature.) So despite the previous paragraph, if the restrictor sentence R has an appropriate range of candidate meanings, then (AP′) may itself have a range of (equally joint-carving) candidate meanings, some of which count it true, others of which count it false.

Thus if *restricted* notions of possibility have certain candidates, there would indeed be a disturbing sort of nonsubstantivity of attributions of blame.[43] But this is not forced on us by Humeanism. For it was candidates for R, not candidates for 'metaphysically possible', that generated the nonsubstantivity. It is open to a Humean to claim that the relevant restrictor R does *not* have candidates that count (AP′) as being false.

Furthermore, even if statements of blame do come out nonsubstantive, it is important to recall the distinction between conceptual and metaphysical substantivity from section 4.2. The existence of a range of equally joint-carving candidates generating a mix of truth-values establishes metaphysical nonsubstantivity, but is consistent with conceptual substantivity. It may be that *our* choice of a candidate for 'personally possible' is deeply embedded in our conceptual lives, and reflects our conception of moral responsibility. Alternate ways of speaking about possibility and blame may be *morally* alien, even if they aren't semantically alien. And so,

---

[43] See Hawthorne (2001) for a discussion of this issue.

it may be argued, the metaphysical nonsubstantivity of statements of blame isn't particularly disturbing, since such statements are conceptually substantive.

Another example: counterfactual reasoning is obviously integral to our cognitive lives in countless ways. Suppose, as is common, that counterfactuals are understood in the Lewis/Stalnaker way, as being variably strict conditionals defined over a space of possible worlds;[44] and suppose we reduce possible worlds to necessity in one of the usual ways. Given Humeanism, there will be multiple candidates for the space of worlds corresponding to the candidates of 'necessary'. But the differences between the candidates will affect only which "distant" possible worlds—distant in the sense of the nearness metric introduced by Lewis and Stalnaker—are included in the space, and thus will not affect the truth-values of ordinary counterfactuals, which depend only on nearby worlds. For example, perhaps some candidates for 'necessary' include the laws of metaphysics whereas others do not, so that some candidate spaces of worlds include metaphysically odd worlds (containing multi-located objects, singing numbers, and the like) whereas others exclude such worlds. This multiplicity of candidates would not cause an ordinary counterfactual like "If I had struck the match, it would have lit" to be nonsubstantive, since this counterfactual is true iff the match lights in the nearest world in which I strike it, and that nearest world is not going to be a metaphysically odd one, even if metaphysically odd worlds are present. It is the nearness metric, not the space of possible worlds, that is responsible for whatever objectivity or nonarbitrariness counterfactuals have.

[44] See Lewis (1973b); Stalnaker (1968). Similar remarks would apply to more recent contextualist accounts of counterfactuals as strict conditionals; see Lycan (2001); von Fintel (2001).

13   A Worldview

Let us end on a concrete note. What might a comprehensive "worldview" look like, given realism about structure?

Think of a worldview as consisting of i) an ideology; ii) a fundamental theory phrased in terms of the ideology, specifying laws of metaphysics and perhaps other principles; and iii) a sketch of a metaphysical semantics for nonfundamental discourse in terms of the ideology. I will put forward a worldview according to which fundamental reality contains nothing but physics, logic, and set theory. While I believe that this worldview may well be true, I won't say much in its defense; the point is to illustrate.

First, ideology. My primitive notions are those of first-order quantification theory (with identity), plus a predicate $\in$ for set-membership, plus predicates adequate for fundamental physics, plus the notion of structure.

Next, the fundamental theory. Since my ideology includes the first-order quantifiers, one part of giving the laws of metaphysics will be the statement of an ontology—a statement, in general terms, of what there is. My worldview's ontology contains only points of spacetime[1] and sets, both pure and impure. Thus it contains no composite objects. This is not to say, however, that 'There are no composite objects' or even 'Everything is a set or a point of spacetime' is a law of metaphysics. For 'composite', 'set', and 'point' are not in my fundamental ideology. What might an official statement of a law of metaphysics giving my ontology look like? Suppose one of the physical predicates is the topological predicate 'x is open' (meaning: *open set*). In that case the law could be:

> There is exactly one thing that has no members but is not a member of any open thing [this is the null set]; everything else either has a member [and so is a set], or is a member of some open thing [and so is a point of spacetime].

Since there are no composite entities in its ontology, my worldview is a version of mereological nihilism.[2] Since its ontology contains spacetime but no further entities occupying spacetime, it is a version of supersubstantivalism. Since there are no tense operators in its ideology, it is a version of the spatializing, "B-" theory of time. (Temporal discourse rests on the attributions of geometric predicates—which I assume to be required for physics—to spacetime points.) Since there

---

[1] Or perhaps points of some higher-order space, if the foundations of quantum mechanics lead in this direction.

[2] Ideological (rather than ontological) parsimony leads me to this view: nihilism lets us eliminate parthood from fundamental ideology; set-membership can take up the slack. See Sider (2011).

are no aesthetic, moral, or supernatural notions in its ideology, it is a version of naturalism. Since there are no causal, nomic, or modal notions in its ideology, it is a version of Humeanism.

Next we have laws of metaphysics concerning the behavior of $\in$. These can be taken to be the axioms of impure first-order ZFC set theory.[3] (Perhaps these should not be called laws of metaphysics, since they are also laws of mathematics.)

Next we have laws of metaphysics concerning the behavior of the physical predicates. These are given to us by physics. (Perhaps these should not be called laws of metaphysics, since they are also laws of physics.)

Next there are pseudo-laws of metaphysics concerning the behavior of the logical constants. These are the logical truths of first-order quantification theory (such as '$\exists x\ x{\in}x \rightarrow \exists x\ x{\in}x$'), which I take to be classical. They are perhaps not genuine laws because they are not generalizations (not all of them, anyway), but I call them pseudo-laws because they fall under generalizations such as "$\forall P\ (P{\rightarrow}P)$" or "For every sentence, ϕ, $\ulcorner\phi{\rightarrow}\phi\urcorner$ is true." (Since my fundamental ideology contains neither sentential quantification nor the notion of a sentence nor the corner-quotes nor a truth predicate, the generalizations themselves are not laws, and can only be stated in a nonfundamental language.)

Finally, there are principles asserting that my primitive notions carve at the joints: $\mathscr{S}(\sim)$, $\mathscr{S}(\exists)$, $\mathscr{S}(\mathscr{S})$, and so on.

What remains is to sketch a metaphysical semantics for ordinary and scientific language. This is a formidable task, since the worldview is so austere.

Let's begin with talk about ordinary physical objects. Although my ontology contains no physical objects per se, it does contain entities with which they may naturally be identified: the sets of spacetime points that they occupy.[4] I, for example, can be identified with a set whose earliest points are around 1967, whose temporal cross-sections are person-shaped, and which continues on into the future for an unknown duration.[5]

A metaphysical semantics based on this identification would construe talk of ordinary physical objects as being about sets of spacetime points. It would interpret names of physical objects as referring to the sets with which the objects are identified, predicates as applying to 'tuples of sets of spacetime points, and quantifiers as ranging over sets of spacetime points.

Despite the fact that my ontology is in a sense mereological nihilist, the proposed metaphysical semantics is not like the one at the end of section 7.7. It assigns to existential sentences about physical objects:

> There is an x such that: $\psi(x)$

metaphysical truth-conditions that are themselves existential in form:

---

[3] Define an urelement to be any member of anything that is open.
[4] Compare Quine (1976b).
[5] An alternate approach would be that of Sider (1996a).

There is an x such that: $\psi^*(x)$.

Even though my fundamental ideology lacks physical-object-theoretic notions, my fundamental ontology is rich enough to include entities—sets—that may be identified with physical objects. There is no need for an ontological reduction of physical objects, so to speak, only a predicate reduction of ordinary physical predicates ψ to fundamental predicates ψ^*.

What will this predicate reduction look like? Some predicates are straightforward. For example, the metaphysical truth-condition for 'Physical object x is located at spacetime point p' could be that x (i.e., the set identified with x) contains p as a member. The truth-condition for 'Physical object x is atemporally part of physical object y' could be '$x \subseteq y$.' The truth-condition for 'Physical object x is part of physical object y relative to time (hypersurface) t' could be '$x \cap t \subseteq y \cap t$.' Thus our metaphysical semantics encompasses talk of the location and mereology of ordinary physical objects.[6]

But what of predicates like 'x is a table' or 'y is a person'? How can we say, in the language of physics, logic, and set theory, which sets of points of spacetime are tables and persons?

Of course I have no clue. I don't even have much of a clue about how to construct a "toy" metaphysical semantics (section 7.4) for such predicates. Nevertheless, I am confident that a metaphysical semantics could in principle be given.

The reason is that the array of definable relations is extremely rich, given the iterative resources of set theory.[7] Let's identify relations with their extensions. (This is a harmless simplifying assumption, since we could instead substitute "structured relations" constructed set-theoretically from the extensions of fundamental predicates.[8]) Suppose we have defined some initial predicates of relations, $\phi(r)$ and $\psi(r,s)$, say. We can then define "higher-order" predicates of individuals using quantification over relations that satisfy the initial predicates, for example:

$$R_1(x,y) \text{ iff: } \forall r \forall z((\phi(r) \wedge z \text{ is more massive than } y) \rightarrow \langle x,z \rangle \in r)$$
$$R_2(x,y) \text{ iff: } \exists r \exists s(\psi(r,s) \wedge \langle x,y \rangle \in r \wedge \langle y,x \rangle \in s)$$

($R_1(x,y)$ holds iff x bears each ϕ relation to everything that is more massive than y; $R_2(x,y)$ holds iff some pair of relations standing in ψ hold between x and y in opposite directions.) Moreover, we can define higher-order predicates of relations, again by quantifying over relations that satisfy the initial predicates.

---

[6] My initial description of this worldview as a version of mereological nihilism must therefore be qualified. Although the worldview denies that there are fundamental ascriptions of parthood, it allows that sentences of nonfundamental languages can truly ascribe parthood. Moreover, since both composites and their parts are identified with sets, it even allows that there exist, in the fundamental sense of 'there exist', entities that are asserted by nonfundamental sentences to have parts.

[7] See also the discussion of infinite definitions in section 7.11.1.

[8] Compare Lewis (1986b, section 1.5).

This procedure can then be iterated. After defining higher-order predicates of relations using quantification over relations that satisfy ϕ and ψ, we can quantify over relations that satisfy those predicates to define still higher-order predicates of individuals and relations; and so on.

These iterative constructions can at each stage make use of any notions that can be defined in fundamental terms. For example, suppose we define a notion of metaphysical necessity as described in chapter 12; then modal notions may be employed in the iterations. Given a notion of necessity, we might define corresponding possible worlds—maximal consistent sets of sentences, perhaps. We might then use these worlds in a reduction of causation, counterfactuals, chance, and other notions, as Lewis envisaged.[9] All such reductionist programs may be brought into the iterative construction of further relations. Given these possibilities for definition, I see no in-principle barrier to the possibility of giving a metaphysical semantics for predicates of ordinary physical objects, as well as for the distinctive vocabularies of chemistry, biology, psychology, economics, semantics, and other disciplines.

We needn't always identify objects with sets of spacetime points; sometimes more complex set-theoretic constructions are called for. Consider, for example, metalinguistic talk—talk about language. My worldview includes no linguistic ideology, no notions of predicate, sentence, conjunct, satisfies, true, means, pragmatically implicates. So if we want to speak of languages (whether formal or natural), we need a metaphysical semantics. Now, it is perhaps natural to identify a "linguistic atom" (symbol, for a formal language; word, morpheme, phoneme, or whatever, for a spoken language) with a set of spacetime points: the set of points located inside some production (inscription or utterance) of that symbol. But we cannot construe all linguistic entities this way, since many complex linguistic entities will never be produced (the conjunction of the longest two sentences ever produced, for example). So it's natural instead to take complex linguistic entities to be set-theoretic constructions (perhaps sequences, perhaps tree-structures) of linguistic atoms, and thus as set-theoretic constructions of sets of points, rather than as mere sets of points.

This metaphysical semantics associates existential truth-conditions with sentences that quantify existentially over linguistic entities—set-theoretic constructions out of sets of spacetime points really exist. The hard work, as with physical-object talk, comes with the predicates. Syntactic predicates are comparatively easy. For example, if c is the set of spacetime points identified with the sign for conjunction, then the metaphysical truth-condition for the syntactic predicate 's is the conjunction of s_1 and s_2' might be something like this: 's is a tree with top node c containing two child nodes, one of which is s_1, the other of which is s_2.' Semantic, pragmatic, and other linguistic notions will be more difficult, but the project here is continuous with the general project of giving a metaphysical

[9]See Lewis (1973a; b; 1994).

semantics for talk about macro-entities, and the iterative techniques described above may again be used.

The identifications I have proposed—of physical objects with sets of occupied points, linguistic atoms with sets of production points, linguistic complexes with set-theoretic constructions from linguistic atoms—are somewhat arbitrary. They're not *wholly* arbitrary; it's not as if I've simply observed that the pure set-theoretic hierarchy has enough entities with which to identify everything, and left it at that. But there's no denying that there are multiple alternates to my sketch of a metaphysical semantics. Fortunately, this multiplicity is harmless. What we want out of a metaphysical semantics for L is a good explanation of the linguistic behavior of speakers of L, and there is often an element of arbitrariness when explaining higher-level phenomena. What we're after in linguistics (and psychology, and economics, and . . .) is a good model, not a unique model.[10]

I have imagined one way the book of the world might be. It is not a tale of common sense. But we can, I think, recognize it as our own.

---

[10]The arbitrariness would not be harmless if we applied notions from our fundamental ideology to the arbitrarily constructed entities—qua arbitrarily constructed entities, so to speak. It would not be harmless, for example, to construe sentences (qua sentences) as being fundamentally located in spacetime, in the sense of being subsets of open sets. On the one hand, we are surely free to choose any reasonable method for identifying sentences with sets; but on the other hand, what if the chosen method identifies sentences with sets that are *not* subsets of open sets? (See Forrest and Armstrong (1984); Sider (1996c).)

Recall the claim in section 6.3 that since semantics isn't fundamental, we can't take the facts about structure to fundamentally involve semantic entities. I wrote as if the problem was that semantic entities don't fundamentally exist. But that isn't quite right, since our metaphysical semantics might identify semantic entities with certain set-theoretic constructions, which do fundamentally exist. The problem is rather this: since *which* sets are identified with semantic entities is arbitrary, and since the notion of structure, $\mathscr{S}$, is part of our fundamental ideology, we can't apply it to semantic entities (qua semantic entities).

NEED FIRST-ORDER
SORT THUS TRUTHS
METAPHYSICALLY
ACCOUNT EVEN GROUND SET
DIFFERENT
SEE ALSO SEMANTIC TAKE
EXPRESSIONS QUANTIFIER VIEW
WAY MEANING SEMANTICS
MUCH PHYSICAL NOTHING
USING
LEWIS TRUE MIGHT
OBJECTS RELATION
STATEMENTS EXAMPLE FORM SIMPLY
SINCE ROLE MODALITY THOUGHT
NECESSITY QUANTIFIERS PREDICATE
ORDINARY MODAL
POSSIBLE NECESSARY IFF INTERPRETATION
METAPHYSICS QUESTION EXISTENCE
CONDITIONS FIRST
CARVE ONE SENTENCES WELL
BEST SEEMS
MANY SECOND PROPOSITION ARGUMENT
GENERAL
SOMETHING LOGICAL QUESTIONS
MEAN FACT FOLLOWING
PROBLEM ONTOLOGICAL THEORY SENSE GIVEN
NONFUNDAMENTAL
MAKE NOTIONS PRESS CERTAIN CASE MUST EXIST
USE NOW
THINGS STRUCTURE WHETHER
THINK LINGUISTIC CONSEQUENCE PHYSICS NATURAL PRIMITIVE
CORRECT
ENGLISH METAPHYSICAL MAY EXISTS
CONCEPTION
NATURE JUST
LOGIC IDEOLOGY TRUTH SUBSTANTIVE DISPUTE
JOINT-CARVING SPACE PROPERTY TIME PROPERTIES THEORIES
LANGUAGE TERMS ENTITIES
RATHER
FUNDAMENTAL
ONE
MEANINGS IDEA JOINTS SENTENCE
LAWS LIKE
THOUGH NOTION SECTION
PART FACTS ONTOLOGY
POINT ANSWER PREDICATES
RELATIONS WORLD PROPOSITIONS
LANGUAGES APPROACH
BETTER CLAIM CLAIMS REALITY CONCEPTUAL
PERHAPS TWO CHAPTER CARVES
OXFORD THUS QUANTIFICATION

References

Adams, Robert Merrihew (1974). Theories of actuality. *Noûs*, 8, 211–31.

Albert, David Z. (1996). Elementary quantum metaphysics. In *Bohmian Mechanics and Quantum Theory: An Appraisal* (eds. J. T. Cushing, A. Fine, and S. Goldstein), pp. 277–84. Kluwer Academic Publishers, Dordrecht.

Armstrong, David M. (1978a). *Nominalism and Realism*, volume 1 of *Universals and Scientific Realism*. Cambridge University Press, Cambridge.

— (1978b). *A Theory of Universals*, volume 2 of *Universals and Scientific Realism*. Cambridge University Press, Cambridge.

— (1983). *What Is A Law Of Nature?* Cambridge University Press, Cambridge.

— (1986). In defence of structural universals. *Australasian Journal of Philosophy*, 64, 85–8.

— (1989). *A Combinatorial Theory of Possibility*. Cambridge University Press, New York.

— (1997). *A World of States of Affairs*. Cambridge University Press, Cambridge.

— (2004). *Truths and Truthmakers*. Cambridge University Press, Cambridge.

Arntzenius, Frank (2008). Gunk, topology, and measure. In *Oxford Studies in Metaphysics* (ed. Dean W. Zimmerman), volume 4, pp. 225–47. Oxford University Press, Oxford.

Arntzenius, Frank and Hawthorne, John (2005). Gunk and continuous variation. *The Monist*, 88, 441–65.

Ayer, Alfred Jules (1936). *Language, Truth and Logic*. Victor Gollancz Ltd, London. 2nd edition.

Bach, Kent (1994). Conversational implicature. *Mind and Language*, 9, 124–62.

Bealer, George (1982). *Quality and Concept*. Clarendon Press, Oxford.

Beall, J. C. and Restall, Greg (2006). *Logical Pluralism*. Clarendon Press, Oxford.

Beebee, Helen (2000). The non-governing conception of laws of nature. *Philosophy and Phenomenological Research*, 61, 571–94.

Bennett, Karen (2004). Spatio-temporal coincidence and the grounding problem. *Philosophical Studies*, 118, 339–71.

— (2006). Zombies everywhere! MS. Available at http://courses.cit.cornell.edu/kb383/zombies.pdf.

— (2009). Composition, colocation, and metaontology. In Chalmers et al. (2009), pp. 38–76.

Bigelow, John (1988). *The Reality of Numbers: A Physicalist's Philosophy of Mathematics*. Clarendon Press, Oxford.

Blackburn, Simon (1993). *Essays in Quasi-Realism*. Oxford University Press, Oxford.

Boghossian, Paul (1997). Analyticity. In *A Companion to the Philosophy of Language* (eds. Bob Hale and Crispin Wright), pp. 331–68. Blackwell, Oxford.

— (2003). Blind reasoning. *Aristotelian Society, Supplementary Volume*, 77, 225–48.

Boolos, George (1984). To be is to be the value of a variable (or to be some values of some variables). *Journal of Philosophy*, 81, 430–49.

Bourne, Craig (2002). When am I? A tense time for some tense theorists? *Australasian Journal of Philosophy*, 80, 359–71.

Boyd, Richard (1988). How to be a moral realist. In *Essays on Moral Realism* (ed. Geoffrey Sayre-McCord), pp. 181–228. Cornell University Press, Ithaca, NY.

Braddon-Mitchell, David (2004). How do we know it is now now? *Analysis*, 64, 199–203.

Båve, Arvid (2010). How to precisify quantifiers. *Journal of Philosophical Logic*, 40, 103–11.

Bricker, Phillip (1992). Realism without parochialism. Read to the Pacific Division of the APA. Available at http://www.umass.edu/philosophy/PDF/Bricker/realism_without_parochialism.pdf.

— (1993). The fabric of space: Intrinsic vs. extrinsic distance relations. In *Midwest Studies in Philosophy XVIII: Philosophy of Science* (eds. Peter French, Theodore E. Uehling, Jr, and Howard K. Wettstein), pp. 271–94. University of Notre Dame Press, South Bend, IN.

Britton, Karl (1947). Are necessary truths true by convention? *Aristotelian Society, Supplementary Volume*, 21, 78–103.

Broad, C. D. (1923). *Scientific Thought*. Harcourt, Brace and Company, New York.

— (1936). Are there synthetic a priori truths? *Aristotelian Society, Supplementary Volume*, 15, 102–17.

Burgess, John (2005). Being explained away. *Harvard Review of Philosophy*, 13, 41–56.

Cameron, Ross P. (2007). The contingency of composition. *Philosophical Studies*, 136, 99–121.

— (2008). Turtles all the way down: Regress, priority and fundamentality in metaphysics. *Philosophical Quarterly*, 58, 1–14.

— (2010). From humean truthmaker theory to priority monism. *Noûs*, 44, 178–98.

— (2011). Truthmakers. In *Oxford Handbook of Truth* (ed. Michael Glanzberg). Oxford University Press, Oxford. Forthcoming.

Carnap, Rudolf (1937). *The Logical Syntax of Language*. Routledge & Kegan Paul, London.

— (1950). Empiricism, semantics and ontology. *Revue International de Philosophie*, 4, 20–40. Reprinted in *Meaning and Necessity: A Study in Semantics and Modal Logic*, 2nd edn. University of Chicago Press, Chicago.

Chalmers, David (1996). *The Conscious Mind*. Oxford University Press, Oxford.

— (2005). The Matrix as metaphysics. In *Philosophers Explore the Matrix* (ed. Christopher Grau), pp. 132–76. Oxford University Press, New York.

— (2009). Ontological indeterminacy. In Chalmers et al. (2009), pp. 77–129.

— (2011). Verbal disputes. *Philosophical Review*. Forthcoming.

Chalmers, David, Manley, David, and Wasserman, Ryan (eds.) (2009). *Metametaphysics*. Oxford University Press, Oxford.

Chisholm, Roderick (1976). *Person and Object: A Metaphysical Study*. Open Court Publishing Co., La Salle, Illinois.

Chomsky, Noam (2000). *New Horizons in the Study of Language and Mind*. Cambridge University Press, New York.

Churchland, Paul M. (1981). Eliminative materialism and the propositional attitudes. *Journal of Philosophy*, 78, 67–90.

Coppock, Paul (1984). Review of Nathan U. Salmon, *Reference and Essence*. *Journal of Philosophy*, 81, 261–70.

Correia, Fabrice and Schnieder, Benjamin (eds.) (2012). *Grounding*. Cambridge University Press, Cambridge. Forthcoming.

Dasgupta, Shamik (2009a). Individuals: An essay in revisionary metaphysics. *Philosophical Studies*, 145, 35–67.

— (2009b). Symmetry in reality. Ph.D. thesis, New York University, New York.

— (2010). On the plurality of grounds. MS. Available at http://www.shamik.net/Research_files/dasgupta%20on%20the%20plurality%20of%20grounds.pdf.

Davidson, Donald (1967a). The logical form of action sentences. In *The Logic of Decision and Action* (ed. Nicholas Rescher), pp. 81–95. University of Pittsburgh Press, Pittsburgh, PA.

— (1967b). Truth and meaning. *Synthese*, 17, 304–23.

— (1970). Mental events. In *Experience and Theory* (eds. L. Foster and J. Swanson), pp. 79–101. Duckworth, London.

— (1977). The method of truth in metaphysics. In *Midwest Studies in Philosophy II: Studies in the Philosophy of Language* (eds. Peter French, Theodore E. Uehling, Jr, and Howard K. Wettstein), pp. 244–54. University of Minnesota Press, Minneapolis, MN.

deRosset, Louis (2010). Getting priority straight. *Philosophical Studies*, 149, 73–97.

Devitt, Michael and Sterelny, Kim (1999). *Language and Reality: An Introduction to the Philosophy of Language*. MIT Press, Cambridge, MA, 2nd edition.

Divers, John (2002). *Possible Worlds*. Routledge, London.

Divers, John and Melia, Joseph (2002). The analytic limit of genuine modal realism. *Mind*, 111, 15–36.

Dorr, Cian (2002). The simplicity of everything. Ph.D. thesis, Princeton University.

Dorr, Cian (2004). Non-symmetric relations. In *Oxford Studies in Metaphysics* (ed. Dean W. Zimmerman), volume 1, pp. 155–92. Oxford University Press, Oxford.

— (2005). What we disagree about when we disagree about ontology. In *Fictionalism in Metaphysics* (ed. Mark Kalderon), pp. 234–86. Oxford University Press, Oxford.

— (2007). There are no abstract objects. In Sider et al. (2007), pp. 32–63.

— (2010). How to be a modal realist. `http://users.ox.ac.uk/~sfop0257/papers/ModalRealism.pdf`.

Dowty, David R., Wall, Robert E., and Peters, Stanley (1981). *Introduction to Montague Semantics.* Kluwer, Dordrecht.

Dreier, James (2004). Meta-ethics and the problem of creeping minimalism. *Philosophical Perspectives*, 18, 23–44.

Dretske, Fred (1977). Laws of nature. *Philosophy of Science*, 44, 248–68.

Dummett, Michael (1973). The philosophical basis of intuitionist logic. In *Proceedings of the Logic Colloquium, Bristol, July 1973* (eds. H. E. Rose and J. C. Shepherdson), pp. 5–49. North-Holland, Amsterdam.

Eddon, Maya (2012). Fundamental properties of fundamental properties. In *Oxford Studies in Metaphysics* (eds. Karen Bennett and Dean W. Zimmerman), volume 8. Oxford University Press, Oxford.

Eklund, Matti (2002). Inconsistent languages. *Philosophy and Phenomenological Research*, 64, 251–75.

— (2006). Neo-fregean ontology. *Philosophical Perspectives*, 20, 95–121.

— (2007). The picture of reality as an amorphous lump. In Sider et al. (2007), pp. 382–96.

— (2008). Putnam on ontology. In *Following Putnam's Trail: On Realism and Other Issues* (eds. Maria Uxia Rivas Monroy, Concepcion Martinez Vidal, and Celeste Cancela), pp. 203–22. Rodopi, Amsterdam.

— (2009). Carnap and ontological pluralism. In Chalmers et al. (2009), pp. 130–56.

Etchemendy, John (1990). *The Concept of Logical Consequence.* Harvard University Press, Cambridge, MA.

Everett, Anthony and Hofweber, Thomas (eds.) (2000). *Empty Names, Fiction and the Puzzles of Non-Existence.* CSLI Press, Stanford.

Field, Hartry (1980). *Science Without Numbers.* Blackwell, Oxford.

— (1989). *Realism, Mathematics and Modality.* Blackwell, Oxford.

— (2003). The semantic paradoxes and the paradoxes of vagueness. In *Liars and Heaps* (ed. J. C. Beall), pp. 262–311. Oxford University Press, Oxford.

— (2008). *Saving Truth from Paradox.* Oxford University Press, Oxford.

Fine, Kit (1994a). Essence and modality. In *Philosophical Perspectives 8: Logic and Language* (ed. James Tomberlin), pp. 1–16. Ridgeview, Atascadero, CA.

— (1994b). Senses of essence. In *Modality, Morality, and Belief* (ed. Walter

Sinnott-Armstrong), pp. 53–73. Cambridge University Press, New York.

— (2000). Neutral relations. *Philosophical Review*, 109, 1–33.

— (2001). The question of realism. *Philosopher's Imprint*, 1, 1–30.

— (2003). The problem of possibilia. In Loux and Zimmerman (2003), pp. 161–79.

— (2005). Tense and reality. In *Modality and Tense*, pp. 261–320. Oxford University Press, New York.

— (2009). The question of ontology. In Chalmers et al. (2009), pp. 157–77.

— (2010). Some puzzles of ground. *Notre Dame Journal of Formal Logic*, 51, 97–118.

— (2011). The pure logic of ground. MS.

— (2012). Guide to ground. In Correia and Schnieder (2012). Forthcoming.

Fitelson, Branden (2006). The paradox of confirmation. *Philosophy Compass*, 1, 95–113.

Fodor, Jerry A. (1974). Special sciences (or: The disunity of science as a working hypothesis). *Synthese*, 28, 97–115.

— (1987). *Psychosemantics*. MIT Press, Cambridge, MA.

Forrest, Peter (2004). The real but dead past: A reply to Braddon-Mitchell. *Analysis*, 64, 358–62.

— (2006). Uniform grounding of truth and the growing block theory: A reply to Heathwood. *Analysis*, 66, 161–3.

Forrest, Peter and Armstrong, David M. (1984). An argument against David Lewis' theory of possible worlds. *Australasian Journal of Philosophy*, 62, 164–8.

Frege, Gottlob (1879). *Begriffsschrift, ein der arithmetischen nachgebildete Formelsprache des reinen Denkens*. Verlag L. Nebert, Halle/Saale. Translated as *Concept Script, A Formal Language of Pure Thought Modelled Upon That of Arithmetic*, by S. Bauer-Mengelberg in *From Frege to Gödel: A Source Book in Mathematical Logic, 1879–1931* (ed. J. van Heijenoort, 1967), pp. 1–82. Harvard University Press, Cambridge, MA.

— (1884). *The Foundations of Arithmetic*. Blackwell, Oxford, 2nd edition.

— (1952/1892). On sense and reference. In *Translations of the Philosophical Writings of Gottlob Frege* (eds. Peter Geach and Max Black). Blackwell, Oxford.

— (1997/1918). Thought. In *The Frege Reader* (ed. Michael Beany), pp. 323–45. Blackwell, Oxford.

Frost, Robert (1936). *A Further Range*. H. Holt, New York.

Funkhouser, Eric (2006). The determinable–determinate relation. *Noûs*, 40, 548–69.

Gamut, L. T. F. (1991). *Logic, Language, and Meaning, Volume 2: Intensional Logic and Logical Grammar*. University of Chicago Press, Chicago, IL.

Gettier, Edmund L. (1963). Is justified true belief knowledge? *Analysis*, 23, 121–3.

Goodman, Nelson (1955). *Fact, Fiction, and Forecast*. Harvard University Press,

Cambridge, MA.

Goodman, Nelson (1978). *Ways of Worldmaking*. Hackett, Indianapolis.

Grice, Paul (1975). Logic and conversation. In *Syntax and Semantics, Volume 3: Speech Acts* (eds. Peter Cole and Jerry Morgan), pp. 41–58. Academic Press, New York.

Grice, Paul and Strawson, Peter F. (1956). In defense of a dogma. *Philosophical Review*, 65, 141–58.

Grünbaum, Adolf (1973). *Philosophical Problems of Space and Time*. D. Reidel, Dordrecht, 2nd edition.

Gunderson, Keith (ed.) (1975). *Language, Mind and Knowledge*, volume 7 of *Minnesota Studies in the Philosophy of Science*. University of Minnesota Press, Minneapolis.

Hale, Bob (1987). *Abstract Objects*. Blackwell, Oxford.

Hale, Bob and Wright, Crispin (2001). *The Reason's Proper Study*. Oxford University Press, Oxford.

Hall, Ned (2006). Philosophy of causation: Blind alleys exposed; promising directions highlighted. *Philosophy Compass*, 1, 86–94.

Hamilton, Andrew (2007). Laws of biology, laws of nature: Problems and (dis)solutions. *Philosophy Compass*, 2/3, 592–610.

Hanson, William H. (1997). The concept of logical consequence. *Philosophical Review*, 106, 365–409.

Harman, Gilbert (1999). *Reasoning, Meaning and Mind*. Oxford University Press, Oxford.

Haslanger, Sally (1995). Ontology and social construction. *Philosophical Topics*, 23, 95–125.

Hawthorne, John (2001). Freedom in context. *Philosophical Studies*, 104, 63–79.

— (2006a). Epistemicism and semantic plasticity. In Zimmerman (2006), pp. 289–322.

— (2006b). *Metaphysical Essays*. Oxford University Press, Oxford.

— (2006c). Plenitude, convention, and ontology. In Hawthorne (2006b), pp. 53–70.

— (2007). Craziness and metasemantics. *Philosophical Review*, 116, 427–40.

— (2009). Superficialism in ontology. In Chalmers et al. (2009), pp. 213–30.

Hawthorne, John and Sider, Theodore (2002). Locations. *Philosophical Topics*, 30, 53–76.

Hawthorne, John (O'Leary-) and Cortens, Andrew (1995). Towards ontological nihilism. *Philosophical Studies*, 79, 143–65.

Heller, Mark (1996). Ersatz worlds and ontological disagreement. *Acta Analytica*, 15, 35–44.

— (1998). Property counterparts in ersatz worlds. *Journal of Philosophy*, 95, 293–316.

Hempel, Carl (1945). Studies in the logic of confirmation I & II. *Mind*, 54, 1–26

& 97–121.

Hinchliff, Mark (1996). The puzzle of change. In *Philosophical Perspectives* (ed. James Tomberlin), volume 10, pp. 119–36. Blackwell, Cambridge, MA.

Hirsch, Eli (1986). Metaphysical necessity and conceptual truth. In *Midwest Studies in Philosophy XI: Studies in Essentialism* (eds. Peter French, Theodore E. Uehling, Jr, and Howard K. Wettstein), pp. 243–56. University of Minnesota Press, Minneapolis, MN.

— (1993). *Dividing Reality*. Oxford University Press, New York.

— (2002*a*). Against revisionary ontology. *Philosophical Topics*, 30, 103–27.

— (2002*b*). Quantifier variance and realism. *Philosophical Issues*, 12, 51–73.

— (2005). Physical-object ontology, verbal disputes, and common sense. *Philosophy and Phenomenological Research*, 70, 67–97.

— (2007). Ontological arguments: Interpretive charity and quantifier variance. In Sider et al. (2007), pp. 367–81.

— (2008). Language, ontology, and structure. *Noûs*, 42, 509–28.

— (2009). Ontology and alternative languages. In Chalmers et al. (2009), pp. 231–59.

Hodes, Harold (1984). Logicism and the ontological commitments of arithmetic. *Journal of Philosophy*, 81, 123–49.

Hofweber, Thomas (2000). Quantification and non-existent objects. In Everett and Hofweber (2000), pp. 249–73.

— (2005). A puzzle about ontology. *Noûs*, 39, 256–83.

— (2007). Innocent statements and their metaphysically loaded counterparts. *Philosopher's Imprint*, 7, 1–33.

— (2009). Ambitious, yet modest, metaphysics. In Chalmers et al. (2009), pp. 260–89.

Horgan, Terence and Potrč, Matjaž (2000). Blobjectivism and indirect correspondence. *Facta Philosophica*, 2, 249–70.

— (2002). Addressing questions for blobjectivism. *Facta Philosophica*, 4, 311–22.

Horn, Laurence R. (1989). *A Natural History of Negation*. University of Chicago Press, Chicago.

Horwich, Paul (1990). *Truth*. MIT Press, Cambridge, MA.

Hudson, Hud (2006). *The Metaphysics of Hyperspace*. Oxford University Press, Oxford.

Jackson, Alex (2010). Time and logic. MS.

Jackson, Frank (1998). *From Metaphysics to Ethics: A Defence of Conceptual Analysis*. Oxford University Press, Oxford.

Jubien, Michael (2007). Analyzing modality. In Zimmerman (2007), pp. 99–139.

Kaplan, David (1989). Demonstratives. In *Themes from Kaplan* (eds. Joseph Almog, John Perry, and Howard Wettstein). Oxford University Press, New York.

Kim, Jaegwon (1982). Psychophysical supervenience. *Philosophical Studies*, 41,

51–70.

Kim, Jaegwon (1989). The myth of nonreductive materialism. *Proceedings of the American Philosophical Association*, 63, 31–47.

— (1992). Multiple realization and the metaphysics of reduction. *Philosophy and Phenomenological Research*, 52, 1–26.

King, Jeffrey C. (2005). Anaphora. Available at `http://plato.stanford.edu/entries/anaphora/`.

Krantz, David H., Luce, R. Duncan, Suppes, Patrick, and Tversky, Amos (1971). *Foundations of Measurement*. Academic Press, New York.

Kripke, Saul (1972). Naming and necessity. In *Semantics of Natural Language* (eds. Donald Davidson and Gilbert Harman), pp. 253–355, 763–9. D. Reidel, Dordrecht. Revised edition published in 1980 as *Naming and Necessity* (Harvard University Press, Cambridge, MA).

— (1975). Outline of a theory of truth. *Journal of Philosophy*, 72, 690–716.

— (1982). *Wittgenstein on Rules and Private Language*. Harvard University Press, Cambridge, MA.

Lange, Marc (2005). A counterfactual analysis of the concepts of logical truth and necessity. *Philosophical Studies*, 125, 277–303.

Lewis, David (1968). Counterpart theory and quantified modal logic. *Journal of Philosophy*, 65, 113–26.

— (1969). *Convention: A Philosophical Study*. Blackwell, Oxford.

— (1970*a*). Anselm and actuality. *Noûs*, 4, 178–88.

— (1970*b*). How to define theoretical terms. *Journal of Philosophy*, 67, 427–46.

— (1971). Counterparts of persons and their bodies. *Journal of Philosophy*, 68, 203–11.

— (1973*a*). Causation. *Journal of Philosophy*, 70, 556–67.

— (1973*b*). *Counterfactuals*. Blackwell, Oxford.

— (1975). Languages and language. In Gunderson (1975), pp. 3–35.

— (1979). Counterfactual dependence and time's arrow. *Noûs*, 13, 455–76.

— (1983*a*). Extrinsic properties. *Philosophical Studies*, 44, 197–200.

— (1983*b*). New work for a theory of universals. *Australasian Journal of Philosophy*, 61, 343–77.

— (1984). Putnam's paradox. *Australasian Journal of Philosophy*, 62, 221–36.

— (1986*a*). Events. In Lewis (1986*c*), pp. 241–69.

— (1986*b*). *On the Plurality of Worlds*. Blackwell, Oxford.

— (1986*c*). *Philosophical Papers, Volume 2*. Oxford University Press, Oxford.

— (1991). *Parts of Classes*. Blackwell, Oxford.

— (1992). Armstrong on combinatorial possibility. *Australasian Journal of Philosophy*, 70, 211–24.

— (1994). Humean supervenience debugged. *Mind*, 103, 473–90.

— (2004). Void and object. In *Causation and Counterfactuals* (eds. John Collins, Ned Hall, and L. A. Paul), pp. 277–90. MIT Press, Cambridge, MA.

Lewy, Casimir (1976). *Meaning and Modality*. Cambridge University Press,

Cambridge.

Loewer, Barry (1996). Humean supervenience. *Philosophical Topics*, 24, 101–27.

Lombard, Lawrence Brian (1999). On the alleged incompatibility of presentism and temporal parts. *Philosophia*, 27, 253–60.

Loux, Michael J. and Zimmerman, Dean W. (eds.) (2003). *Oxford Handbook of Metaphysics*. Oxford University Press, Oxford.

Lycan, William (2001). *Real Conditionals*. Oxford University Press, Oxford.

MacFarlane, John (2005). Logical constants. Available at http://plato.stanford.edu/entries/logical-constants/.

Mackie, J. L. (1977). *Ethics: Inventing Right and Wrong*. Penguin, London.

Malcolm, Norman (1940). Are necessary propositions really verbal? *Mind*, 49, 189–203.

Markosian, Ned (1993). How fast does time pass? *Philosophy and Phenomenological Research*, 53, 829–44.

— (1998). Simples. *Australasian Journal of Philosophy*, 76, 213–26.

— (2004a). Simples, stuff, and simple people. *The Monist*, 87, 405–28.

— (2004b). Soc it to me? Reply to McDaniel on maxcon simples. *Australasian Journal of Philosophy*, 82, 332–40.

Marshall, Dan (2009). Can 'intrinsic' be defined using only broadly logical notions? *Philosophy and Phenomenological Research*, 78, 646–72.

Maudlin, Tim (1993). Buckets of water and waves of space: Why spacetime is probably a substance. *Philosophy of Science*, 60, 183–203.

— (1996). On the unification of physics. *Journal of Philosophy*, 93, 129–44.

— (2007a). *The Metaphysics Within Physics*. Oxford University Press, New York.

— (2007b). A modest proposal concerning laws, counterfactuals, and explanations. In Maudlin (2007a), pp. 5–49.

— (2007c). On the passing of time. In Maudlin (2007a), pp. 104–42.

McDaniel, Kris (2003). Against maxcon simples. *Australasian Journal of Philosophy*, 81, 265–75.

— (2007a). Brutal simples. In Zimmerman (2007), pp. 233–66.

— (2007b). Extended simples. *Philosophical Studies*, 133, 131–41.

— (2009). Ways of being. In Chalmers et al. (2009), pp. 290–319.

— (2011a). Being and almost nothingness. *Noûs*, Forthcoming.

— (2011b). A return to the analogy of being. *Philosophy and Phenomenological Research*, Forthcoming.

McGee, Vann (2005). Two conceptions of truth? *Philosophical Studies*, 124, 71–104.

McGinn, Colin (1981). Modal reality. In *Reduction, Time and Reality* (ed. Richard Healey), pp. 143–88. Cambridge University Press, Cambridge.

— (2000). *Logical Properties*. Oxford University Press, Oxford.

McLaughlin, Brian and Bennett, Karen (2005). Supervenience. Available at http://plato.stanford.edu/entries/supervenience/.

McTaggart, J. M. E. (1908). The unreality of time. *Mind*, 17, 457–74.

Melia, Joseph (1995). On what there's not. *Analysis*, 55, 223–9.

— (2000). Weaseling away the indispensability argument. *Mind*, 109, 455–79.

Merricks, Trenton (1994). Endurance and indiscernibility. *Journal of Philosophy*, 91, 165–84.

— (2006). Good-bye growing block. In Zimmerman (2006), pp. 103–10.

— (2007). *Truth and Ontology*. Oxford University Press, Oxford.

Millikan, Ruth Garrett (1989). Biosemantics. *Journal of Philosophy*, 86, 281–97.

Montague, Richard (1973). The proper treatment of quantification in ordinary English. In *Approaches to Natural Language* (eds. Jaakko Hintikka, J. M. E. Moravcsik, and Patrick Suppes), pp. 221–42. Reidel, Dordrecht, Boston.

Mortensen, Chris (1989). Anything is possible. *Erkenntnis*, 30, 319–37.

Mundy, Brent (1987). The metaphysics of quantity. *Philosophical Studies*, 51, 29–54.

Nerlich, Graham (1976). *The Shape of Space*. Cambridge University Press, Cambridge.

— (1982). The present state of realism. *Philosophical Quarterly*, 32, 272–9. Review of Richard Healey (ed.), *Reduction, Time and Reality: Studies in the Philosophy of the Natural Sciences*.

Nolan, Daniel (2011). The extent of metaphysical necessity. MS.

North, Jill (2009). The 'structure' of physics: A case study. *Journal of Philosophy*, 106, 57–88.

— (2010). Structure in classical mechanics. Available at http://courses.cit.cornell.edu/north/Structure_CM_Rev_newer.pdf.

Oliver, Alex (1996). The metaphysics of properties. *Mind*, 105, 1–80.

Pap, Arthur (1958). *Semantics and Necessary Truth*. Yale University Press, New Haven.

Parsons, Josh (2003). Entension, or how it could happen that an object is wholly located in each of many places. MS. Available at http://www.otago.ac.nz/philosophy/Staff/JoshParsons/papers/entension2.pdf.

Parsons, Terence (1980). *Nonexistent Objects*. Yale University Press, New Haven.

Paul, L. A. (2009). Counterfactual theories of causation. In *Oxford Handbook of Causation* (eds. Helen Beebee, Christopher Hitchock, and Peter Menzies), pp. 158–84. Oxford University Press, Oxford.

— (2010). A new role for experimental work in metaphysics. *Review of Philosophy and Psychology*, 1, 461–76.

Peacocke, Christopher (1997). Metaphysical necessity: Understanding, truth and epistemology. *Mind*, pp. 521–74.

— (1999). *Being Known*. Clarendon Press, Oxford.

Penrose, Roger (2005). *The Road to Reality*. Alfred A. Knopf, New York.

Pietroski, Paul (2003). The character of natural language semantics. In *Episte-*

mology of Language (ed. Alex Barber), pp. 217–56. Oxford University Press, Oxford.

Plantinga, Alvin (1974). *The Nature of Necessity*. Oxford University Press, Oxford.

— (1976). Actualism and possible worlds. *Theoria*, 42, 139–60.

Poincaré, Henri (1952). *Science and Hypothesis*. Dover, New York. Republication of the first English translation, published by Walter Scott Publishing, London, 1905.

Priest, Graham (1987). *In Contradiction: A Study of the Transconsistent*. Martinus Nijhoff, Dordrecht.

Prior, A. N. (1960). The runabout inference ticket. *Analysis*, 21, 38–9.

— (1967). *Past, Present, and Future*. Oxford University Press, Oxford.

— (1968a). *Papers on Time and Tense*. Oxford University Press, Oxford.

— (1968b). Quasi-propositions and quasi-individuals. In Prior (1968a), pp. 135–44.

— (1970). The notion of the present. *Studium Generale*, 23, 245–8.

— (1971). *Objects of Thought*. Oxford University Press, Oxford.

— (1976). Thank goodness that's over. In *Papers in Logic and Ethics*, pp. 78–84. Duckworth, London.

— (1996). Some free thinking about time. In *Logic and Reality: Essays on the Legacy of Arthur Prior* (ed. Jack Copeland), pp. 47–51. Clarendon Press, Oxford.

Prior, A. N. and Fine, Kit (1977). *Worlds, Times, and Selves*. Duckworth, London.

Putnam, Hilary (1975a). *Mathematics, Matter and Method*. Cambridge University Press, Cambridge.

— (1975b). The meaning of meaning. In Gunderson (1975), pp. 131–93.

— (1975c). On properties. In Putnam (1975a), pp. 305–22.

— (1975d). What is mathematical truth? In Putnam (1975a), pp. 60–78.

— (1978). *Meaning and the Moral Sciences*. Routledge and Kegan Paul, Boston.

— (1980). Models and reality. *Journal of Symbolic Logic*, 45, 464–82.

— (1981). *Reason, Truth and History*. Cambridge University Press, Cambridge.

— (1987). Truth and convention: On Davidson's refutation of conceptual relativism. *Dialectica*, 41, 41–67.

Quine, W. V. O. (1936). Truth by convention. In *Philosophical Essays for A. N. Whitehead* (ed. O. H. Lee), pp. 90–124. Longmans, New York.

— (1948). On what there is. *Review of Metaphysics*, 2, 21–38.

— (1951a). Ontology and ideology. *Philosophical Studies*, 2, 11–15.

— (1951b). Two dogmas of empiricism. *Philosophical Review*, 60, 20–43.

— (1953). Notes on the theory of reference. In *From a Logical Point of View*, pp. 130–8. Harvard University Press, Cambridge, MA.

— (1960a). Carnap and logical truth. *Synthese*, 12, 350–74.

— (1960b). Variables explained away. *Proceedings of the American Philosophy Society*, 104, 343–7.

— (1960c). *Word and Object*. MIT Press, Cambridge, MA.

Quine, W. V. O. (1966). *The Ways of Paradox*. Random House, New York.

— (1969). Natural kinds. In *Ontological Relativity and other Essays*, pp. 114–38. Columbia University Press, New York.

— (1976a). On multiplying entities. In *The Ways of Paradox*, pp. 259–64. Random House, New York. Revised and enlarged edition.

— (1976b). Worlds away. *Journal of Philosophy*, 73, 859–63.

Quinton, Anthony (1958). Properties and classes. *Proceedings of the Aristotelian Society*, 58, 33–58.

Railton, Peter (1986). Moral realism. *Philosophical Review*, 95, 163–207.

Rayo, Agustín and Uzquiano, Gabriel (1999). Toward a theory of second-order consequence. *Notre Dame Journal of Formal Logic*, 40, 315–25.

Rayo, Agustín and Yablo, Stephen (2001). Nominalism through de-nominalization. *Noûs*, 35, 74–92.

Reichenbach, Hans (1958). *The Philosophy of Space and Time*. Dover, New York.

Restall, Greg (1996). Truthmakers, entailment and necessity. *Australasian Journal of Philosophy*, 74, 331–40.

Rosen, Gideon (1990). Modal fictionalism. *Mind*, 99, 327–54.

— (1994). Objectivity and modern idealism: What is the question? In *Philosophy In Mind: The Place of Philosophy in the Study of Mind* (eds. Michaelis Michael and John O'Leary-Hawthorne), pp. 277–319. Kluwer, Dordrecht.

— (2010). Metaphysical dependence: Grounding and reduction. In *Modality: Metaphysics, Logic, and Epistemology* (eds. Bob Hale and Aviv Hoffmann), pp. 109–36. Oxford University Press, Oxford.

Routley, Richard (1980). *Exploring Meinong's Jungle and Beyond. An Investigation of Noneism and the Theory of Items*. Philosophy Department Monographs, Research School of Social Sciences, Australian National University, Canberra.

Russell, Bertrand (1903). *The Principles of Mathematics*. Routledge, London.

— (1915). On the experience of time. *The Monist*, 25, 212–33.

— (1919). *Introduction to Mathematical Philosophy*. Routledge, London.

Russell, Jeffrey Sanford (2010). The structure of gunk: Adventures in the ontology of space. In Zimmerman (2010), pp. 248–74.

Sagan, Carl (1980). *Cosmos*. Random House, New York.

Savitt, Steven (2004). Presentism and eternalism in perspective. Available at http://philsci-archive.pitt.edu/archive/00001788/01/PEP.pdf.

Schaffer, Jonathan (2007). From nihilism to monism. *Australasian Journal of Philosophy*, 85, 175–91.

— (2009a). On what grounds what. In Chalmers et al. (2009), pp. 347–83.

— (2009b). Spacetime the one substance. *Philosophical Studies*, 145, 131–48.

— (2010a). The internal relatedness of all things. *Mind*, 119, 341–76.

— (2010b). The least discerning and most promiscuous truthmaker. *Philosophical Quarterly*, 60, 307–24.

— (2010c). Monism: The priority of the whole. *Philosophical Review*, 119, 31–76.

Schiffer, Stephen (2003). *The Things We Mean*. Clarendon Press, Oxford.

Schnieder, Benjamin (2011). A logic for 'because'. *Review of Symbolic Logic*. Forthcoming.

Shalkowski, Scott (1994). The ontological ground of the alethic modality. *Philosophical Review*, 103, 669–88.

Sidelle, Alan (1989). *Necessity, Essence and Individuation*. Cornell University Press, Ithaca, NY.

— (2002). Is there a true metaphysics of material objects? *Philosophical Issues*, 12, 118–45.

— (2007). The method of verbal dispute. *Philosophical Topics*, 35, 83–114.

— (2009). Conventionalism and the contingency of conventions. *Noûs*, 43, 224–41.

— (2010). Modality and objects. *Philosophical Quarterly*, 60, 109–25.

Sider, Theodore (1993a). Naturalness, intrinsicality and duplication. Ph.D. thesis, University of Massachusetts.

— (1993b). Van Inwagen and the possibility of gunk. *Analysis*, 53, 285–9.

— (1995). Sparseness, immanence and naturalness. *Noûs*, 29, 360–77.

— (1996a). All the world's a stage. *Australasian Journal of Philosophy*, 74, 433–53.

— (1996b). Intrinsic properties. *Philosophical Studies*, 83, 1–27.

— (1996c). Naturalness and arbitrariness. *Philosophical Studies*, 81, 283–301.

— (2001a). Criteria of personal identity and the limits of conceptual analysis. *Philosophical Perspectives*, 15, 189–209.

— (2001b). *Four-Dimensionalism*. Clarendon Press, Oxford.

— (2002). The ersatz pluriverse. *Journal of Philosophy*, 99, 279–315.

— (2003). Reductive theories of modality. In Loux and Zimmerman (2003), pp. 180–208.

— (2004). Précis of *Four-Dimensionalism*, and replies to critics. *Philosophy and Phenomenological Research*, 68, 642–7, 674–87.

— (2005). Another look at Armstrong's combinatorialism. *Noûs*, 39, 679–95.

— (2006). Beyond the Humphrey objection. Available at `http://tedsider.org/papers/counterpart_theory.pdf`.

— (2007a). Neo-Fregeanism and quantifier variance. *Aristotelian Society, Supplementary Volume*, 81, 201–32.

— (2007b). Parthood. *Philosophical Review*, 116, 51–91.

— (2008a). Monism and statespace structure. In *Being: Developments in Contemporary Metaphysics* (ed. Robin Le Poidevin), pp. 129–50. Cambridge University Press, Cambridge.

— (2008b). Yet another paper on the supervenience argument against coincident entities. *Philosophy and Phenomenological Research*, 77, 613–24.

— (2009). Ontological realism. In Chalmers et al. (2009), pp. 384–423.

— (2011). Against parthood. MS.

Sider, Theodore, Hawthorne, John, and Zimmerman, Dean W. (eds.) (2007). *Contemporary Debates in Metaphysics*. Blackwell, Oxford.

Siegel, Susanna (2006). Which properties are represented in perception? In *Perceptual Experience* (eds. Tamar Szabó Gendler and John Hawthorne), pp. 481–503. Oxford University Press, Oxford.

Skow, Bradford (2010). Extrinsic temporal metrics. *Oxford Studies in Metaphysics*, 5, 179–202.

Smart, J. J. C. (1963). *Philosophy and Scientific Realism*. Routledge & Kegan Paul, London.

Soames, Scott (1992). Truth, meaning, and understanding. *Philosophical Studies*, 65, 17–35.

Sober, Elliot (1994). A Bayesian primer on the grue problem. In *Grue! The New Riddle of Induction* (ed. Douglas Stalker), pp. 225–40. Open Court, Chicago.

Sorensen, Roy (2001). *Vagueness and Contradiction*. Clarendon Press, Oxford.

Sosa, Ernest (1999). Existential relativity. In *Midwest Studies in Philosophy XXIII: New Directions in Philosophy* (eds. Peter French and Howard K. Wettstein), pp. 132–43. Blackwell, Oxford.

Sperber, Dan and Wilson, Deirdre (1986). Loose talk. *Proceedings of the Aristotelian Society*, 86, 153–71.

Stalnaker, Robert (1968). A theory of conditionals. In *Studies in Logical Theory: American Philosophical Quarterly Monograph Series, No. 2*. Blackwell, Oxford.

— (1976). Possible worlds. *Noûs*, 10, 65–75.

— (1977). Complex predicates. *The Monist*, 60, 327–39.

Stanley, Jason (2000). Context and logical form. *Linguistics and Philosophy*, 23, 391–434.

Strawson, Peter F. (1952). *Introduction to Logical Theory*. Methuen, London.

— (1959). *Individuals: An Essay in Descriptive Metaphysics*. Routledge, London.

Street, Sharon (2006). A Darwinian dilemma for realist theories of value. *Philosophical Studies*, 127, 109–66.

Strevens, Michael (2006). Scientific explanation. In *Encyclopedia of Philosophy*. Macmillan Reference USA.

Tappenden, Jamie (1993). Analytic truth—it's worse (or perhaps better) than you thought. *Philosophical Topics*, 21, 233–61.

Tarski, Alfred (1959). What is elementary geometry? In *The Axiomatic Method, with Special Reference to Geometry and Physics* (eds. Leon Henkin, Patrick Suppes, and Alfred Tarski), pp. 16–29. North-Holland, Amsterdam.

Tarski, Alfred and Givant, Steven (1999). Tarski's system of geometry. *Bulletin of Symbolic Logic*, 5, 175–214.

Thomasson, Amie L. (2003). Fictional characters and literary practices. *British Journal of Aesthetics*, 43, 138–57.

— (2005). The ontology of art and knowledge in aesthetics. *The Journal of Aesthetics and Art Criticism*, 63, 221–9.

— (2006). Debates about the ontology of art: What are we doing here? *Philosophy Compass*, 1, 245–55.

— (2007). *Ordinary Objects*. Oxford University Press, New York.

— (2009). Answerable and unanswerable questions. In Chalmers et al. (2009), pp. 444–71.

Tooley, Michael (1987). *Causation: A Realist Approach*. Clarendon Press, Oxford.

Turner, Jason (2008). Ontology, quantification, and fundamentality. Ph.D. thesis, Rutgers University.

— (2010*a*). Ontological nihilism. In *Oxford Studies in Metaphysics* (eds. Karen Bennett and Dean W. Zimmerman), volume 6, pp. 3–54. Oxford University Press, Oxford.

— (2010*b*). Ontological pluralism. *Journal of Philosophy*, 107, 5–34.

Unger, Peter (1979). I do not exist. In *Perception and Identity: Essays Presented to A. J. Ayer with His Replies to Them* (ed. G. F. Macdonald), pp. 235–51. Macmillan, New York.

van Fraassen, Bas (1989). *Laws and Symmetry*. Clarendon Press, Oxford.

van Inwagen, Peter (1990). *Material Beings*. Cornell University Press, Ithaca, NY.

— (1998). Modal epistemology. *Philosophical Studies*, 92, 67–84.

— (2010). Changing the past. In Zimmerman (2010), pp. 3–28.

von Fintel, Kai (2001). Counterfactuals in a dynamic context. In *Ken Hale: A Life in Language*, pp. 123–52. MIT Press, Cambridge, MA.

Wasserman, Ryan (2005). The problem of change. Ph.D. thesis, Rutgers University.

Weatherson, Brian (2003). What good are counterexamples? *Philosophical Studies*, 115, 1–31.

Williams, Donald C. (1951). The myth of passage. *Journal of Philosophy*, 48, 457–72.

Williams, J. Robert G. (2005). The inscrutability of reference. Ph.D. thesis, University of St Andrews.

— (2007). Eligibility and inscrutability. *Philosophical Review*, 116, 361–99.

Williamson, Timothy (1985). Converse relations. *Philosophical Review*, 94, 249–62.

— (1988). Equivocation and existence. *Proceedings of the Aristotelian Society*, 88, 109–27.

— (1994). *Vagueness*. Routledge, London.

— (1998). Bare possibilia. *Erkenntnis*, 48, 257–73.

— (2002). Necessary existents. In *Logic, Thought and Language* (ed. A. O'Hear), pp. 233–51. Cambridge University Press, Cambridge.

— (2003). Everything. *Philosophical Perspectives*, 17, 415–65.

— (2007). *The Philosophy of Philosophy*. Blackwell, Malden, MA.

Wilson, Deirdre and Sperber, Dan (2004). Relevance theory. In *Handbook of Prag-*

matics (eds. Laurence R. Horn and Gregory Ward), pp. 607–32. Blackwell, Malden, MA.

Wittgenstein, Ludwig (1958). *Philosophical Investigations*. Blackwell & Mott, Oxford, 3rd edition. Translated by G. E. M. Anscombe.

Wright, Crispin (1983). *Frege's Conception of Numbers as Objects*. Aberdeen University Press, Aberdeen.

— (1992). *Truth and Objectivity*. Harvard University Press, Cambridge, MA.

Yablo, Stephen (1992). Review of Alan Sidelle, *Necessity, Essence and Individuation*. *Philosophical Review*, 101, 878–81.

— (1998). Does ontology rest on a mistake? *Aristotelian Society, Supplementary Volume*, 72, 229–61.

— (2000). A paradox of existence. In Everett and Hofweber (2000), pp. 275–312.

— (2001). Go figure: A path through fictionalism. In *Midwest Studies in Philosophy XXV: Figurative Language* (eds. Peter French and Howard K. Wettstein), pp. 72–102. Blackwell, Oxford.

Zimmerman, Dean W. (1998). Temporary intrinsics and presentism. In *Metaphysics: The Big Questions* (eds. Dean W. Zimmerman and Peter van Inwagen), pp. 206–19. Blackwell, Cambridge, MA.

— (2005). The A-theory of time, the B-theory of time, and 'taking tense seriously'. *Dialectica*, 59, 401–57.

Zimmerman, Dean W. (ed.) (2006). *Oxford Studies in Metaphysics*. Oxford University Press, Oxford.

— (2007). *Oxford Studies in Metaphysics*, volume 3. Oxford University Press, Oxford.

— (2010). *Oxford Studies in Metaphysics*, volume 5. Oxford University Press, Oxford.

Index